D1083350

Triumph in Defeat

Triumph in Defeat

Infallibility, Vatican I, and the French Minority Bishops

Margaret O'Gara

The Catholic University of America Press
Washington, D.C.

Copyright © 1988
Margaret O'Gara

Printed in the United States of America

LIBRARY OF CONGRESS CATALOGING-IN-PUBLICATION DATA
O'Gara, Margaret, 1947–
  Triumph in defeat.
  Bibliography: p.
  Includes index.
  1. Catholic Church—France—Bishops—History—19th
century. 2. Popes—Infallibility—History of doctrines
—19th century. 3. Vatican Council (1st : 1869–1870)
I. Title.
BX1530.O37 1988   262'.131   87-17889
ISBN 0-8132-0641-3

For my parents,
James and Joan O'Gara

Contents

Foreword

The Second Vatican Council was not only an occasion for profound liturgical, pastoral, structural and doctrinal reformation within the Roman Catholic Church. It was also an extraordinary expression, however imperfect, of living Christian communion among leaders and other members of a church which has roots in virtually every part of the world. Unlike other very impressive international gatherings of Christians, such as those sponsored by the World Council of Churches or by world conferences, federations or alliances of particular churches, Vatican II was a council of a single church communion, a council or synod which understood itself, to use the canonical language of that time, to have "supreme power in the universal church."

With such a self-consciousness, the stakes were high at Vatican II: both the possibilities for renewal according "to no other truth but the words of the Lord, our one master" (Paul VI's address at the opening of the second session, September 30, 1963) and the potential dangers, particularly that of division between representatives of more "modern" and more "classical" ways of thought. Indeed, had the leadership of the church decided in advance to limit the council to what has become known as the First Session, October 12 to December 8, 1962—even though that is more than *twice* the time allotted to the assemblies of the World Council of Churches—it is more than possible that the Catholic Church would have suffered a dreadful schism, so great were the differences of vision in the one community of faith at the outset of the council.

Despite Pope John XXIII's optimism that a longer second session would enable the council to wrap up its business by December 1963, a third and fourth session proved necessary. It was not the heavy agenda alone that consumed all this time, but, at least equally, the requirements of Christian *koinonia* or communion. Unlike our revered democratic institutions which are governed by majority vote or even by a plurality, the Christian community, committed to a far deeper and more universal unity than any political society, has from its origins sought to achieve "oneness of mind," moral unanimity or consensus when matters pertaining to Christian faith or "precepts of the Lord" were at stake. This is so because the Christian community strives to be not simply a just society, which is the noble objective of all political societies worthy of the name, but a "Church of charity," to cite the same conciliar address by Pope Paul VI. The Second Vatican Council in its own life and processes came very close at times to exemplifying such a communion of love. Despite occasional breaches of love, attempts at unfair power plays, and the unhappy fact of lack of full communion with other Christians, the overall experience of the council, according to the virtually unanimous testimony of those who were present, was that of a peak moment of Christian communion in faith, hope, love and reconciliation. Moreover, as a result of much prayer, candid discussion, re-education, *and taking minority concerns seriously* (the nineteen suggested changes to the text of *The Constitution on the Church* by Paul VI are a prime example of this), all of the conciliar documents received the morally unanimous consensus and approbation of bishops and pope.

I have drawn attention to the Second Vatican Council as both a teaching event and as a living expression of the church as a communion of love, not only because of the intrinsic importance of both realities, but also in order to introduce this major work by Margaret O'Gara of the contrasting expression of the church that is evidenced in the way the First Vatican Council dealt with the French minority bishops in the debate concerning papal infallibility. The author is a Roman Catholic professor of theology who teaches with high distinction a wide range of theological topics. The present study indicates her ongoing interest in ecclesiology in general and the question of authority and infallibility in particular. Her competence in these areas has enabled her to make important contributions as a member of the Anglican–Roman Catholic Dialogue of Canada and of the Disciples of Christ–Roman Catholic International Commission.

Professor O'Gara's book significantly advances our understanding of Vatican I. It complements earlier studies of the performance at the council of bishops from various nations, as well as the more recent book by William Portier, *Isaac Hecker and the First Vatican Council.* Without losing its own critical perspective of the often shabby treatment of the Vatican I minority that was made possible by the inappropriate adoption of "majority rule," the study nevertheless

serves as a corrective to the learned but one-sided work of the late
August Hasler. The influential and still valuable older work of Cuthbert Butler is, on the other hand, demonstrated by O'Gara to be
flawed by its minimizing of the scandalous tactics of the leaders of
the majority and by its corresponding insensitivity to the legitimate
concerns of the minority.

Through meticulous research, including fresh archival work in
France, into the thought of the entire French minority, before, during and after the council, O'Gara is able to strengthen some opinions
in the scholarly literature while firmly but gently overcoming many
other views about the personal character and thought of the dissenting minority. In a recent book on the subject of infallibility, a Catholic theologian stated that organized dissent in the church is ultimate-
ly grounded in pride and arrogance. Similar judgments purporting
to read the motives of the heart were made about the organized
dissenting bishops at the First Vatican Council. Readers of Dr.
O'Gara's study will see how unjust *and* uncharitable such judgments
are, and they will be edified by the manifest Christian character and
Catholic mentality of the bishops she investigates.

Not only is history well served by this volume, but theology as
well, which is the author's primary intent. O'Gara demonstrates in
the very execution of her work that the theologian seeking understanding of the faith has to deal with the past if she is to serve the
present. When historians have done the relevant research, this saves
time for the theologian; when that is not the case, the historical task
must be undertaken by the theologian, unless she is willing to move
to a more historically researched question. Rahner, Lonergan,
Schmaus, Schillebeeckx, Dulles, Küng, Barth, Tillich and Macquar-
rie, to mention only some familiar names, have all exemplified this
view of theology. O'Gara stands in and contributes impressively to
that tradition.

O'Gara makes it clear that she is not undertaking a full-scale presentation of the doctrine of infallibility here. Rather, she contributes
to the present ecumenical reception of that doctrine by uncovering
for us the reasons for the serious opposition to the Vatican I definition by the French minority and the—widely varying—reasons for
their subsequent acceptance of it. She is negatively critical of some of
the aspects of their "case" which today seem inadequate; she is posi-
tively critical about insights of the minority that not only can be but

are being retrieved in the ongoing process of ecumenical reception of a doctrine which, not too long ago, seemed to many to be the final slamming of the door by Rome in the faces of Anglicans, Protestants and the Eastern Orthodox.

Aware that I have been invited to write a Foreword, not a review nor—a more delicious prospect!—the first round of a dialogue with the author on the implications of her study for future ecumenical statements on infallibility, I close simply by expressing my joy that, having worked with Margaret O'Gara during her preparation of this study, I continue to be associated with her as a cherished theological colleague and partner in dialogue. May her service to the church as a gifted theologian long continue.

HARRY McSORLEY, *Professor of Theology*
Faculty of Theology
University of St. Michael's College
Toronto School of Theology

Preface

If the history of theology is a history of forgetting as well as remembering,[1] of neglecting as well as assimilating, then perhaps no group is so thoroughly forgotten, so thoroughly neglected, as the minority at a great council of the church. Theology usually refers to the minority at a council to show how they were mistaken, one-sided, or even heretical in their views. Rarely is their thought studied for its own sake.

Into such oblivion fell the thought of the minority bishops of the First Vatican Council. I see at least two reasons for this oblivion. First, the minority—the bishops who opposed the definition of papal infallibility at the council—were criticized or discounted for their opposition. Their dissent was not seen to have positive value in itself. Second, their thought was misunderstood and thus misrepresented. Consequently, its inner coherence and positive contributions to the question of infallibility were ignored.

The purpose of this study is to bring one group from among the minority bishops, the French minority, out of their oblivion. It is necessary to study the thought of the French minority bishops on infallibility in the period before, during, and after the council in order to understand their opposition to the council's proposed definition, their acceptance of *Pastor aeternus*, and their grasp of the doctrine of infallibility.

The French minority has special importance within the entire minority for several reasons. First, with twenty-two members, the French bishops constituted the single largest group from one country within the seventy-three members of the council's minority. Second, these bishops worked as a group, holding regular meetings and discussions and thereby developing a coherent unified view on the question of infallibility. Not all members of this group held exactly the same views on all topics. Not every member was equally outspoken. But taken as a whole, their thought forms a coherent pat-

---

1. Karl Rahner, "Current Problems in Christology," in *Theological Investigations*, 20 vols. (Baltimore: Helicon Press, 1961), 1:151.

tern of ideas. It thus yields a somewhat fuller and more unified picture of minority arguments than has been obtained by studying the
thought of individual minority bishops. Third, the French minority
bishops' thought was shaped by their national tradition of gallicanism. In the Declaration of 1682, the French clergy had stated that in
matters of faith the pope enjoyed the principal role but that his judgments were not irreformable without the consent of the church.[2] The
French minority inherited a moderate version of these views, and the
troublesome phrase "and not from the consent of the Church [*non
autem ex consensu Ecclesiae*]" was inserted into *Pastor aeternus* to
counter the gallicanism suspected of some minority members. Thus
the decree seemed to contradict the very theological tradition in
which the French minority bishops had been formed.[3] To understand *Pastor aeternus*, therefore, it is important to understand the
thought of those it wished to criticize.

Evaluations of the French Minority

The French minority suffered the same fate as other minority
bishops at the First Vatican Council. During the council, they were
denounced and misunderstood. Jean-Baptiste Berteaud, bishop of
Tulle, calls the minority "scum," and Augustus Martin, bishop of
Natchitoches in Louisiana, writes home: "Two-thirds and more of
the council have but one heart and one soul: but we have to wrestle
with a turbulent and agitated opposition which considers all means
good. . . . Some are real revolutionaries, others servile creatures of
power, others more or less avowed enemies of the Holy See, others
those who from their youth have sucked the poison of heresy. They
form a phalanx which grows tighter each day. . . . I am ashamed of
the French episcopate, ashamed also of our own." Later, Martin
would denounce the minority again as men without fixed principles,
rallied together by the chiefs of "the old Gallicanism, modern
rationalism and a wicked spirit of independence."[4]
    Some of the bishops of the majority took a less negative view of

2. The text of the Four Articles of 1682 is in *Dictionnaire de théologie catholique*, s.v.
"Déclaration de 1682," by C. Constantin.
    3. Aimé Georges Martimort, *Le Gallicanisme* (Paris: Presses Universitaires de
France, 1973), p. 121.
    4. Roger Aubert, *Vatican I* (Paris: Editions de l'Orante, 1964), p. 113; Augustus
Martin, bishop of Natchitoches, Louisiana, to Napoleon Perché, administrator of the

the minority. One group formed a center party, which was sympathetic to the concerns of the minority and in fact channeled some minority thought into the revisions of the schema.[5] Some shared the views of Vincent Jandel, Dominican master general, who writes: "I await the final session without enthusiasm or illusions. This definition which, under better circumstances, would have made me so happy leaves me sad considering the evils it will bring in its train because of the feelings it has aroused."[6] But most members of the majority believed that the minority opposed a truth of the faith with merely "scruples about opportuneness and the political situation."[7] At the last moment, French majority members wrote to the pope, arguing that a phrase should be added to exclude any of the gallican views held by the minority. Pius IX forwarded this note to the drafting deputation, adding an allusion to the bad faith of the minority. The drafting deputation added the clause "and not from the consent of the church."[8]

After the council, the minority bishops were praised for their rapid acceptance of *Pastor aeternus* but rarely praised for their opposition to the council's work. The difficulties the French minority bishops posed for interpreters after the council become clear from an examination of their biographies and the orations at their funerals. In attempting to justify or explain the views of these bishops, most of their interpreters tended to minimize or explain away their subject's opposition to the schema and to emphasize his acceptance of *Pastor aeternus*.[9]

archdiocese of New Orleans, 18 January 1870, quoted in James Hennesey, *The First Council of the Vatican: The American Experience* (New York: Herder and Herder, 1963), p. 97; Augustus Martin to Napoleon Perché, then newly appointed coadjutor bishop of New Orleans, 12 March 1870, quoted in ibid., p. 127.

5. Aubert, *Vatican I*, p. 110; see also Roger Aubert, "Documents concernant le tiers parti au concile du Vatican," in *Abhandlungen über Theologie und Kirche*, Festschrift für Karl Adam (Düsseldorf: Patmos-Verlag, 1952). pp. 241–59.

6. Aubert, *Vatican I*, p. 232.

7. Georges Dejaifve, *Pape et évêques au premier concile du Vatican* (Brussels: Desclée de Brouwer, 1961), p. 54.

8. Aubert, *Vatican I*, pp. 229–30. Council members also wished to disavow two French brochures that had attacked the council's liberty. The two, *Les derniers jours du concile* and *Ce qui se passe au concile*, were circulated during the last few months of the council (Roger Aubert, *Le pontificat de Pie IX (1846–1878)*, in Augustin Fliche and Victor Martin, Series Histoire de l'église depuis les origines jusqu'à nos jours, no. 21 [Paris: Bloud et Gay, 1952], p. 358).

9. See, for example, Joseph-Abel Guillermin, *Vie de Mgr Darboy, archevêque de*

Paralleling this attempt by biographers to excuse or overlook the opposition of their subjects, there emerged a tendency to oversimplify the position the minority had actually held during the council. In his historical work, Theodor Granderath presents the views of the minority bishops in a negative and oversimplified light. Cuthbert Butler describes the minority more sympathetically, but he does not understand fully the depth of their objections to a definition. Fernand Mourret, writing in 1919, presents the French minority as simply inopportunists, not basically opposed to the doctrine of papal infallibility itself. This interpretation is repeated forty years later by Jean-Rémy Palanque. Recently August Hasler has argued that many

---

Paris (Paris: Bloud et Barral, 1888), pp. 56, 124; Joseph Foulon, *Histoire de la vie et des oeuvres de Mgr Darboy, archerêque de Paris* (Paris: Poussielgue Frères, 1889), pp. 47–48; Auguste R. M. Dubourg, *Oraison funèbre de Mgr Augustin David, prononcée à l'occasion de l'inauguration solennelle de son tombeau dans la cathédrale de Saint-Brieuc* (Saint-Brieuc: René Prud'homme, 1891), p. 35; Etienne Lelong, *Oraison funèbre de Monseigneur Frédéric-Gabriel-Marie-François de Marguerye, ancien évêque de Saint-Flour, d'Autun, Chalon et Mâcon, chanoine du premier ordre du chapitre de Saint-Denis.* (Autun: Michel Dejussieu, 1876, p. 46; François Lagrange, *Vie de Mgr Dupanloup, évêque d'Orléans,* 3 vols. (Paris: Poussielgue Frères, 1883–84), 3:143–44, 154, 185; Charles Cotton, *Oraison funèbre de Mgr Jacques Marie Achille Ginoulhiac, archevêque de Lyon et de Vienne, primat des Gaules* (Lyon: P. N. Josserand, 1876), pp. 38–43; A. Justice, *Mgr Guilbert et le parti catholique* (Paris: P. Lethielleux, 1898), pp. 154–55; Georges Bazin, *Vie de Mgr Maret, évêque de Sura, archevêque de Lépante, primicier de l'insigne chapitre de Saint-Denys, doyen et professeur de la Faculté de Théologie en Sorbonne,* 3 vols. (Paris: Berche et Tralin, 1891), 3:210–30, 462; L. F. Besson, *Vie de son éminence Mgr le Cardinal Mathieu, archevêque de Besançon,* 2 vols. (Paris: Bray et Retaux, 1882), 2:262–63, 265–68, 276; Henri Boissonnot, *Le Cardinal Meignan* (Paris: Victor Lecoffre, 1899), pp. vi, 32, 261, 308; Charles Place, *Pieux souvenir de son éminence le Cardinal Place,* with a Notice Biographique by unnamed author (Paris: Victor Lecoffre, 1895), pp. xxxii–xxxiii; F. M. A. Cabrières, *Eloge funèbre de sa grandeur Mgr Etienne Emile Ramadié, archevêque d'Albi* (Montpellier: J. Martel Aîné, 1884), pp. 24–28; Gustave Chevallier, *Mgr Rivet, évêque de Dijon* (Dijon: L'Union Typographique, 1902), pp. 170–73; Jean Romain Tapie, *Oraison funèbre de son éminence le Cardinal Thomas, archevêque de Rouen* (La Rochelle: Noel Texier, 1894), pp. 16, 37; F. J. E. Bonnefoy, *Oraison funèbre de son éminence le Cardinal Thomas, archevêque de Rouen* (La Rochelle: Rochelaise, 1894), p. 40. Others attack the interpretations of eulogizing biographers: *La vérité sur Mgr Darboy: Etude précédée d'une lettre à S.E. le Cardinal Foulon* (Cien: Paul Pigelet, 1889), pp. 6–12, 28, 78; Victor Pelletier, *Mgr Dupanloup: Episode de l'histoire contemporaine, 1845–1875* (Paris: Haton, 1876), pp. 100–103; Justin Fèvre, *Le centenaire de Mgr Dupanloup* (Paris: A. Savaète, 1903), pp. 105–6; Michel Ulysse Maynard, *Mgr Dupanloup et M. Lagrange son historien* (Paris: Société Générale de Librairie Catholique, 1884), p. 286; Albert Keller, *La fin du gallicanisme et Mgr Maret son dernier représentant* (Alençon: Veuve Félix Guy, 1900); Jean François Bergier, *Supplément à la vie du Cardinal Mathieu, en son vivant archevêque de Besançon* (Besançon: J. Bonvalot, 1883), pp. 2–3, 13, 207–8, 223–42, 329–30.

minority bishops were not inopportunists but had substantive arguments against the definition. But he simply dismisses their postconciliar thought. All of these positions oversimplify the thought of the French minority by ignoring a part of it.[10]

Recent discussion has seen an increasing interest in accurately understanding the position of the minority bishops. Some of this interest follows the kind of insight expressed by Charles-Henri Maret: "The minority has triumphed in its defeat." Roger Aubert notes that many minority bishops thought their work had succeeded in restraining the extremes of the ultramontanists. And Gustave Thils asks, "But without this minority, to what extremes would the fathers have gone?" Georges Dejaifve praises the minority bishops for their theological wisdom: "While admitting that some bishops might have been tinged with gallicanism, one cannot, without an astonishing lack of perception or even of common sense, declare that *all* the bishops, especially the more eminent ones in the minority group, had heretical tendencies. Rather, one must praise their theological foresight and well-informed pastoral judgment when they gave warning of the dangers which later appeared." And Yves Congar notes that present interpretations see the minority bishops as prophetic, "like the vanguard of Vatican II."[11]

Within this atmosphere of heightened interest, two studies that

---

10. Theodor Granderath, *Histoire du concile du Vatican depuis sa première annonce jusqu'à sa prorogation d'après les documents authentiques*, 3 vols. (Brussels: Librairie Albert Dewit, 1907–14), 3, 2:54–56, 119–21, for example; Cuthbert Butler, *The Vatican Council: The Story Told from Inside in Bishop Ullathorne's Letters*, 2 vols. (London: Longmans, Green and Co., 1930) 1:260–68, 2:144; Fernand Mourret, *Le concile du Vatican d'après des documents inédits* (Paris: Bloud et Gay, 1919), pp. 159, 288–89, 301; Jean-Rémy Palanque, *Catholiques libéraux et gallicans en France: Face au concile du Vatican, 1867–1870* (Aix-en-Provence: Editions Ophrys, 1962), pp. 180–81; August Hasler, *Pius IX. (1846–1878), Päpstliche Unfehlbarkeit und 1. Vatikanisches Konzil*, 2 vols. (Stuttgart: Anton Hiersemann, 1977), 2:447–51.

11. "La Minorité a triomphé dans sa défaite" (Henri Maret in personal notes written to himself after the Council, cited by Bazin, *Vie de Maret*, 3:218); see also the words of Pancraz Dinkel, bishop of Augsburg, to Friedrich von Schwarzenberg, cardinal, archbishop of Prague, 15 November 1870: "The decree should be called a victory for the minority rather than for the majority" (quoted in Granderath, *Histoire du concile du Vatican*, 3, 2:199). Roger Aubert, "L'ecclésiologie au concile du Vatican," in Bernard Botte et al., *Le concile et les conciles* (Gembloux: Editions de Chevetogne and Editions du Cerf, 1960), p. 272, n. 48; Gustave Thils, *L'infaillibilité pontificale: Source—conditions—limites* (Gembloux: J. Duculot, 1968), p. 176; Dejaifve, *Pape et évêques*, p. 143, Yves Congar, "Bulletin d'ecclésiologie," *Revue des sciences philosophiques et théologiques* 60 (1976):288.

focus on the role of the English and American bishops present some sympathetic analysis of minority views.[12] In addition, an early study of the Italian minority bishops and a more recent study of those from Germany focused additional attention on the minority's thought, and the latter provides a helpful theological analysis.[13] Hasler's study of the council somewhat through the eyes of the Old Catholic movement provides another interpretation of the minority as a whole, though it lacks a detailed understanding of the thought of individual minority members. Aubert, however, through studies of key members of the French minority, has greatly increased historical information about them. Finally, additional understanding of the French minority bishops came from the one important study on them, that of Jean-Rémy Palanque.[14] To his largely historical analysis of the activities and general perspectives of the French minority, I wish to add this theological study of their position.

Procedures of This Study

This study will seek to understand and evaluate the thought of the French minority bishops on infallibility. The first step—understanding their thought—will occupy the bulk of the study. The second step—evaluating their thought—will be the work of the final chapter.

In my effort to understand the thought of the French minority, I will focus first on a paradox that puzzled earlier evaluators: Why did the French minority at first oppose the definition of papal infallibility yet subsequently accept *Pastor aeternus*? The search for an answer to

12. Frederick J. Cwiekowski, *The English Bishops and the First Vatican Council* (Louvain: Publications Universitaires du Louvain, 1971); Hennesey, *First Council of the Vatican*.

13. Nicola Menna, *Vescovi italiani anti-infallibilisti al concilio Vaticano* (Napoli: A. Intravaja, 1958); Klaus Schatz, *Kirchenbild und päpstliche Unfehlbarkeit bei den Deutschsprachigen Minoritätsbischöfen auf dem I. Vatikanum* (Rome: Università Gregoriana Editrice, 1975).

14. Hasler, *Pius IX*. In addition to his many works on the council, Roger Aubert has also done several studies of Dupanloup and one of David: *Dictionnaire d'histoire et de géographie ecclésiastiques*, s.v. "Dupanloup (Félix Antoine Philibert)," and "David (Augustin)"; "Monseigneur Dupanloup au début du concile du Vatican," *Miscellanea Historiae Ecclesiasticae*, Congrès de Stockholm, 1960 (Louvain: Publications Universitaires de Louvain, 1961); "Mgr Dupanloup et le Syllabus," *Revue d'histoire ecclésiastique* 51(1956):79–142, 471–512, 837–915. Palanque, *Catholiques libéraux et gallicans en France*.

this question will occupy three parts. After introductory background on the council and the minority within it, I will look first at the early training and thought, the convergence and common fears of the French minority. In the second part, I will lay out the three cases they made against the definition of papal infallibility. In the third part, I will lay out the two cases they offered subsequently in favor of the acceptance of *Pastor aeternus*.

In discussing the position of the French minority bishops in these latter two parts, I intend to show their theological perspective as a coherent, unified vision. Although present in their thought, this vision eludes observation if one focuses solely on the ideas of a single bishop or speech. The great advantage of studying the twenty-two as a group is that it allows us to piece together a unified picture from the various contributions of each member. The major sources for the study of the thought of the French minority bishops are their own writings. I use their books, pamphlets, diaries, sermons, correspondence, council speeches, and the minutes of minority meetings to throw light on their understanding of infallibility.

In the second step of the study, I will interpret and evaluate their thought on infallibility. I will argue that the central emphasis of their thought is the ecclesial character of infallibility. When this central emphasis is recognized, the thought of the group in both opposing the definition of papal infallibility and eventually accepting the decree makes sense. Finally, I will evaluate the strengths and weaknesses of the bishops' thought on the ecclesial character of infallibility in the context of contemporary theological discussion.

In this book I do not present an extensive discussion of gallicanism, the French church, ultramontanism, French government, the First Vatican Council, or ideological currents of the nineteenth century. I presume that the reader has a general knowledge in these areas, available in a large number of studies. Nor do I attempt to analyze every written primary source by the French minority bishops. Such a task is more appropriate for a purely historical study, and it would also have made the amount of material to be handled unmanageable. Instead, I offer a theological analysis of the French minority's core or central writings relating to infallibility. Finally, I do not undertake an extensive review or evaluation of secondary literature on the French minority bishops, the First Vatican Council, or related subject matters. By analyzing theologically the core sources, I hope to offer fresh perspective on a group whose thought has not often been a focus of attention.

Values of This Study

I hope that this study can make a contribution to several important areas of thought.

First, the study of the French minority helps us to improve our understanding of the First Vatican Council and the meaning of its decree on papal infallibility. André Duval notes the importance of enriching "the documentary file of Vatican I, still far from completion." Yves Congar also believes that further studies of the history of the First Vatican Council are important. Along with other recent theological developments, he writes, they invite us to a new reception of the work of the council:

> The excellent historical works of an Aubert, a Pottmeyer, a Schatz, etc., on the one hand, even certain questions raised and discussed by H. Küng, lastly, the ecumenical dialogue: all invite us to a new "reception" of the dogma of *Pastor aeternus,* a "reception" under new conditions thanks to a more comprehensive and better balanced ecclesiology, with a deeper knowledge of history, particularly that of the relationship of the Roman See with the East . . . thanks, finally, to a better hearing of the *altera pars* than the unsatisfactory one under Pius IX. This will render justice to the more enlightened members of the minority.[15]

In this study, then, I hope to add to the understanding of the work of the First Vatican Council and thus enable the kind of new reception of which Congar speaks.

A contribution to such understanding of the First Vatican Council can throw light as well on the contemporary discussion about the doctrine of infallibility and the whole exercise of authority in the church, a discussion that is very important both for Roman Catholic theology and for the ecumenical dialogue among Christian communions.

Finally, the study of the French minority bishops will help improve our understanding of the part dissent and disagreement play in the development of doctrine. The French minority were first re-

---

15. Georges Darboy, "Le journal de Mgr Darboy au concile du Vatican (1869–1870)," ed. André Duval and Yves Congar, *Revue des sciences philosophiques et théologiques* 54 (1970):417; Congar, "Bulletin d'ecclésiologie," p. 288.

proached, then misunderstood and ignored. Yet their understanding of infallibility contributed to the final shape of *Pastor aeternus*, and their vision of the church can teach us much today. Does this not have something to say to us about the way we should treat theologians with whom we disagree?

Texts in Translation

At the request of the publisher, I have provided translations of all quotations that were originally in French or Latin and have used a consolidated footnote style. For quotations drawn from archival manuscripts or French diocesan newspapers, I also provide the quotation in its original language in the footnote because most readers would not easily have access to those sources. Most of the quotations in their original language can also be found in an earlier version of this study, "The French Minority Bishops of the First Vatican Council and the Ecclesial Character of Infallibility," my Ph.D. dissertation at the University of St. Michael's College in 1980, now on microfilm at the National Library of Canada, Ottawa.

The French translations were made by Sister Eleanor Breen, C.S.J., former associate professor of French at the University of St. Michael's College, working in discussion with me about the theological implications of the material. Charles Principe, C.S.B., associate professor of French at the University of St. Michael's College, also supplied helpful advice for the translation of many passages. I translated the Latin quotations myself, working in close collaboration with Richard Toporoski, associate professor of classics at the University of St. Michael's College. Included in these translations from Latin are the texts of the proposed conciliar schema on papal primacy and infallibility as well as the text of *Pastor aeternus*. I am very grateful to my colleagues for their generous assistance in this translation work.

Sometimes a passage is used to make two different points. At other times, it is used at the end of a section to refresh the mind of the reader or to illustrate an interpretation I am offering. In all such cases, I do not note that the passage has been used before; I simply repeat it.

Finally, summaries of preceding material conclude each section and chapter.

Acknowledgments

My interest in this topic took shape during my doctoral studies in theology at the University of St. Michael's College. It became clear that an understanding of the doctrine of infallibility was an essential element in ecclesiology and an important issue within contemporary ecumenical dialogue. The study of *Pastor aeternus* from the First Vatican Council was important for such understanding. An examination of the unique and relatively ignored position of the French minority bishops seemed to me a valuable way to deepen understanding of the context in which the decree had been passed. Eight months of research in the libraries and archives of Paris provided the necessary documentation of their views unavailable to North American readers. Later insights allowed me to revise my original manuscript. Throughout this process, I have been grateful to Harry McSorley, professor of theology in the Faculty of Theology at the University of St. Michael's College. His sound ecclesiological perspective, his continuing support of my work, and his critical suggestions for revision have been constant sources of help to me.

I am also grateful to Yves Congar, O.P., with whom I had the privilege of discussing my study when I first began research in Paris. His suggestions helped shape the entire study.

Thanks are due as well to François Vigan, archivist of the Archives de l'Archevêché de Paris, and to the staffs of the following libraries and archives: John M. Kelly Library in the University of St. Michael's College and John P. Robarts Library in the University of Toronto; the Newberry Library in Chicago; the Mullen Library of the Catholic University of America; the Library of Congress; the libraries of the journal *Etudes* and of the Institut Catholique in Paris; and the Bibliothèque Nationale and the Archives Nationales in Paris.

Finally, thanks also are due to my husband, Michael Vertin, for his encouragement and his careful reading of the manuscript at all stages.

This study is dedicated to my parents, James and Joan O'Gara, in appreciation for their continuing encouragement of my theological work.

MARGARET O'GARA, *Faculty of Theology*
University of St. Michael's College
Toronto School of Theology

Triumph in Defeat

Introduction

————◆●▶————

The First Vatican Council makes good drama. Like a great play, it called forth deep passions and brilliant speeches. It was filled with major themes and minor subplots. It gave prominence to great orators but found space as well for a chorus of less notable figures and even for a crowd of journalists, diplomats, and onlookers standing by in the wings. It took place with the eyes of the world upon it. And it built to a crashing climax in its definition of the primacy and infallibility of the pope, voted on and promulgated in the midst of a violent rainstorm that filled the council hall with reverberations of thunder and flashes of lightning.

Most of this study of the First Vatican Council will focus on the arguments and the concerns of one group of actors within this drama, the French minority bishops. Before focusing on them, it is important to review a basic outline of the events of the council in which they played a role and to learn about the cast of characters that made up the group.

The Shape of the Story

Although Pius IX had consulted the cardinals of the Curia on 6 December 1864 about calling a council, it was not until 26 June 1867 that his decision to do so was announced to the bishops on the occasion of their visit to Rome for the feast of the martyrdom of Saints Peter and Paul. On 29 June 1868 he issued a pastoral letter convoking the council, *Aeterni Patris,* in which he notes that a "fearful tempest now torments the church" and that "evils afflict society." He elaborates on these problems:

1

For violent enemies of God and men have assaulted and trampled upon the Catholic Church, its salutary doctrine, its venerable power, and the supreme authority of this Apostolic See. They have treated with contempt all sacred things; plundered ecclesiastical goods; harassed in all manner of ways bishops, highly esteemed men dedicated to the sacred ministry, and laymen distinguished for their Catholic dispositions; suppressed religious orders and congregations; widely circulated infamous books of all kinds, harmful periodicals, and pernicious sects of various types; taken from the hands of the clergy almost everywhere the education of unfortunate young folk; and what is still worse, entrusted this education in not a few places to teachers of harmful error.[1]

Because of these problems, he explains, he has judged a council opportune. By the time the council finally opened on 8 December 1869, the bishops had had considerable time to anticipate the event and to elaborate their hopes and their fears for its results.

At its start, the council adopted procedural rules that gave the pope the right to propose topics for discussion. The bishops could make written suggestions of topics, which were given to a special congregation that proposed the conciliar agenda; its recommendations were reported to the pope, who made the final decision. Conciliar business was conducted in general congregations and in more formal public sessions that concluded each stage of the council. Bishops who wished to speak about a question under consideration at a general congregation gave notice beforehand to the presidents of the council, and they were then called in the order of ecclesiastical rank. If a schema under discussion needed revisions before it could be passed at a general congregation, it was referred to one of four deputations, on faith, ecclesiastical discipline, religious orders, and Eastern churches and missions, each with twenty-four elected bishops. These deputations worked with a consultative group of theologians to revise the schema in light of oral and written suggestions from the council members.

By the time the council met, it was becoming clear that the bishops were deeply divided over whether infallibility of the pope should even come up for consideration. An important test in judging the extent of that division was the election of the members of the

---

1. Joannes Dominicus Mansi, *Sacrorum conciliorum nova et amplissimi collectio*, 53 vols. (Graz: Akademische Druck u. Verlagsanstalt, 1961), 50:1251C-D; given in English in John F. Broderick, trans. *Documents of Vatican I, 1869–1870* (Collegeville, Minn.: Liturgical Press, 1971), pp. 13–14.

Deputation on Faith, which took place in a general congregation on 14 December. Bishops intent on a definition of papal infallibility maneuvered this vote in such a way as to ensure that not one bishop from the minority who was known to oppose the definition was placed on the deputation. Within less than a week of the council's opening, then, the minority were already edged out of an important decision-making group; they began to feel that they were being treated unfairly and that the council lacked sufficient liberty.

The first major business of the council was the discussion of the proposed schema on faith, which began on 28 December and ended on 10 January 1870. The schema then went for revision to the Deputation on Faith, came back to the council members for further discussion on 18 March, and was passed unanimously by 667 bishops in public session as *Dei Filius* on 24 April.[2] During the period of revision, the bishops spent some of their time in general congregations discussing church discipline and canon law.

But outside the meetings, they continued to debate among themselves the question of defining papal infallibility. Only if the bishops petitioned for it would this topic be included in the conciliar proceedings because it had not been designated as a purpose of the council. Nevertheless, the theologians had prepared a chapter on the question, to be ready for use if called for. Many were ready to begin calling. On 23 December, just two weeks after the council began, the inner circle of those committed to defining papal infallibility met to prepare a petition requesting that papal infallibility be defined by the council. By the end of January, this petition had received about 380 signatures. About 100 other bishops signed alternative petitions that also supported the definition of papal infallibility by the council.

Bishops from different countries who were opposed to such a definition met together in the start of an international commission of the minority to formulate a counterpetition. Disagreement among these minority members, however, led to the formulation of five counterpetitions, which together gleaned some 140 signatures. One of these was from 32 French bishops and a few Portuguese and Eastern rite bishops. Dated 12 January, it argued that a definition of papal infallibility was unnecessary and would furnish new arms to the enemies of the church.

Then, on 22 February, a new concern arose for the minority

2. Mansi 51:429B–436B.

bishops when the original regulations were changed to state that closure on discussion could be called with a majority vote of the bishops after a subject had been discussed at length. The minority especially disliked the effects of this ruling because it meant that a general discussion of a schema could be ended by vote so that henceforth only sections of the schema could be discussed, not its entirety. The minority bishops began to feel that their responsibility as judges of the faith was being undermined and the council's freedom seriously undercut. They believed that for a definition of the faith, sufficient time for discussion and moral unanimity among the bishops were required. Again letters of protest were sent, with twenty-nine French bishops and one Eastern rite bishop signing a protest letter on 1 March.

Meanwhile, the bishops had a great bulk of reading material to ponder. On 21 January the long schema on the church drafted by the theologians was circulated to the bishops; most of it never came up for consideration on the council floor, but its publication in early February in European newspapers increased fears of a church-state conflict over the work of the council. On 22 February, the sessions of the general congregations were suspended to allow the deputations to catch up with their work, and the bishops were invited to respond in writing to the schema on the church. On 9 February, the congregation for the consideration of topics had met and decided to respond favorably to the petitions requesting a definition of papal infallibility. This decision was confirmed by the pope; on 6 March it was announced publicly that papal infallibility would be considered for definition and the chapter prepared in advance on the topic was distributed.[3] The council members were given ten days to respond in writing to this chapter; when a protest was raised that the time was too short, the deadline was extended until 25 March.

When the general congregations resumed on 18 March to finish work on the schema on faith, they did so amidst a rumor that papal infallibility would be proclaimed by acclamation on 19 March. During March more petitions were circulated, now asking that the question of the papacy might come up right after the completion of the first schema on faith. When the council presidents did not favor these petitions, the majority bishops appealed directly to Pius IX,

3. Mansi 51:539A–553A, 701C–702A.

who granted their request. So as soon as *Dei Filius* was passed, the council presidents announced on 29 April that the question of the papacy, including the pope's primacy and infallibility, would be considered immediately, without first discussing the ten chapters on the church, which had preceded this topic in the original schema. In protest, on 4 May twenty-five French bishops complained that this decision in fact violated the rules. And then on 8 May, seventy-one bishops, including twenty-three French, signed a last general protest against the change in the order of discussion which the 29 April announcement signaled. They argued that the consideration of the papacy before a discussion of the church was illogical and would lead to a distorted treatment. But, they continue, "We have been taught by an experience sufficient—and more than sufficient—that, far from entreaties of this kind being respected, they have up to this point been regarded as worthy not even of a response." Palanque calls this protest "the last cry of the minority. On 13 May, the debate opened; the supreme combat began; but the minority knew in advance that it had lost." As Felix Dupanloup, bishop of Orléans, had written in his diary in March, "What sadness! This settled prognosis, through so many indignities and lies, is like dying a slow death."[4]

On 9 May, the bishops were given the revised schema on the papacy, which had been prepared in response to their written comments. All of the public speeches addressed this schema during the next few months, until the amended form was put in the hands of the bishops on 2, 9, and 16 July. All the speeches cited in this study refer to this text distributed on 9 May; it is printed in translation in the Appendix.

The first set of debates on this schema opened in a general congregation on 13 May, when the schema as a whole was addressed. During this period discussion focused on the opportuneness of defining papal infallibility. Discussion was ended on 3 June by a majority vote for closure; the minority bishops protested this vote the next day because it prevented many who had planned to speak from doing so. The minority complained that bishops in council had a right not only to vote but to give the reasons for their vote when a definition of faith was involved. Nevertheless, the discussion on the

---

4. Mansi 51:730A; Palanque, *Catholiques libéraux et gallicans en France*, p. 166; Félix Dupanloup, Journal, entry of 23 March 1870, quoted in Hasler, *Pius IX*, 1:168, n. 45.

primacy, considered in three chapters, was begun on 6 June; it ended on 14 June, and on 15 June began the discussion of the last chapter in the proposed schema, on infallibility of the pope; this ended on 4 July. The voting on amendments proposed by the Deputation on Faith in response to conciliar speeches began on 2 July, and it continued on 9 July, when the deputation suggested additional amendments to the schema, which were finally accepted. After the speech of Vincent Gasser, bishop of Brixen, on 11 July, in which he explained the deputation's rationale for the schema and the proposed amendments, the general congregation held its final vote for the schema as a whole, with 451 voting *placet*, 88 *non placet*, and 62 *placet iuxta modum*.

One more crisis remained for the minority at the council. On the evening of 15 July, a group of minority bishops obtained an audience with Pius IX, in which they pleaded with him for a concession that would allow the minority to vote in favor of the schema. Pius IX made no concession. Instead, the Deputation on Faith decided to introduce a final clause to the definition, "and not from the consent of the Church," which pushed the definition further in the direction the majority desired. This amendment was accepted in the general congregation on 16 July; and on 18 July, with the backdrop of a great thunderstorm, the council met in public session and passed the final text of *Pastor aeternus*, printed in translation in the Appendix. The final vote was 533 *placet*, 2 *non placet*; but some 70 bishops did not attend the public session. It was their last protest. For them, the drama had ended in tragedy; they had nothing left to do but go home.

Soon the rest went home as well. On 19 July war was declared between France and Prussia. Some attempts were made to continue the conciliar sessions in late August and early September, with about 120 council members attending. But after Rome was invaded by the Italian army, Pius IX issued a letter on 20 October 1870 suspending the council indefinitely. The story thus came to an anti-climactic close.

Some Actors in the Story

Many members of the council were opposed to the definition of papal infallibility and thus found themselves in the minority. But it is difficult to determine the exact number of bishops who remained in the minority throughout the council all the way through the vote on

18 July. Eighty-eight voted *non placet* on 13 July, but only two voted *non placet* on 18 July. I count as certain members of the minority only those two and the following: the fifty-five who signed the 17 July letter explaining their absence from the final session; Aimé Guilbert, bishop of Gap, whose signature seems to have been left off the copy of this first letter but appeared in the later copy; the eight bishops who wrote individual letters excusing themselves from the 18 July session;[5] and seven others—George Errington, archbishop of Trebizond; Gustave de Hohenlohe, Bavarian cardinal at the Vatican; John MacHale, archbishop of Tuam; François de Mérode, archbishop and pope's almoner; David Moriarty, bishop of Kerry; Luigi Puecher-Passavalli, apostolic preacher; and Joseph Rauscher, cardinal, archbishop of Vienna—whose membership in the minority was made clear by their actions.[6] This gives a total of seventy-three definitely in the minority through the session of 18 July; but there are probably some others whose absence was unexplained.

I have defined as the French minority bishops those twenty-two Frenchmen who met together, maintained their opposition to the definition of papal infallibility throughout the council, and absented themselves from the final vote on 18 July because they still felt bound in conscience to vote *non placet*. Other French bishops also opposed the definition of papal infallibility, and many even attended the meetings of the French minority throughout most of the council. They did not, however, continue their opposition until the end, and hence they are not included in this study.[7] Two of them—Jean Lyonnet, archbishop of Albi, and Jean Devoucoux, bishop of Evreux—left the council early because of ill health. Others seemed to hesitate in their opposition, either voting with the minority only until 13 July or dropping away before that. A handful helped to form a small third or center party.

In this study, then, I focus on the role played by the twenty-two French minority bishops in the drama of the First Vatican Council. A brief sketch of each of them is important before we turn to their common efforts.

Jean-Pierre Bravard (1811–76), bishop of Coutances and Avranches,

5. Mansi 52:1325A–1327A, 1327C, 1324A–C, 1327A–1328A.
6. Butler, *Vatican Council*, 2:159–60; Aubert, *Vatican I*, p. 231.
7. See Palanque, *Catholiques libéraux et gallicans en France*, pp. 148–51, for a discussion of these bishops and the reasons for their withdrawal from the minority group.

was ordained for the diocese of Sens, where he was made vicar general in 1858. Consecrated a bishop in 1862, he devoted himself to encouraging the work of religious communities. Bravard went as far as the doorway of the council chamber on 18 July 1870, but he decided he could not enter. He resigned his episcopal seat because of illness in 1875 and died the following year.

Jean-Baptiste-Irénée Callot (1814–75), bishop of Oran, was ordained in 1838 and taught on the theological faculty of Maison des Chartreux in Lyon. Callot was a close friend of Maret and his circle. His consecration to the episcopate in 1867 was delayed by the Vatican because of his gallican reputation. Callot was obliged to write a letter stating his submission to the *Syllabus* and the Vatican's liturgical directives. He was a strong opponent of the definition of papal infallibility at the council.

Charles-Théodore Colet (1806–83), bishop of Luçon, was ordained in 1831 in Versailles. In 1838, he became François Rivet's secretary in Dijon, later serving as his vicar general, and the two men developed a close friendship. Made bishop in 1861, he later became the archbishop of Tours, entering the archdiocese in 1875. Colet served as secretary for the French minority meetings, providing us with excellent documentation on the discussions among minority members. In addition, at Rivet's suggestion, he wrote his "Souvenirs du concile du Vatican" as a personal prolegomenon to the copy of the minutes. This work gives us a fairly good picture of the atmosphere of the council as seen through minority eyes, as well as Colet's own hesitations about its plans to define papal infallibility.

Pierre-Paul de Cuttoli (1826–70), bishop of Ajaccio in Corsica, was the youngest of the French minority bishops. Ordained in 1851 after seminary training at Saint-Sulpice in Paris, he became Georges Darboy's secretary in 1855. Named a bishop only in December of 1869 during the council, he seems simply to have followed the thought of his teachers and his mentor, the archbishop of Paris. Because of Darboy's position, however, we can surmise that this former secretary was fairly involved with the minority struggle. By the end of 1870 de Cuttoli was dead from an illness.

Georges Darboy (1813–71), archbishop of Paris, was the leader of the French minority bishops at the council. Ordained at Langres, he taught philosophy, Scripture, and theology at the diocesan seminary until coming to Paris in 1845. There he continued to teach, on the theological faculty of the Ecole des Carmes, and he became titular vicar general before his consecration as bishop of Nancy in 1859. He was made archbishop of Paris in 1863 and became involved in a lengthy controversy with the Vatican in 1867 over his jurisdictional rights within his own diocese. The Vatican's bad treatment of Darboy probably confirmed his developing gallican tendencies. Darboy was an extremely intelligent man. He was deeply involved in French political questions and eventually was made a senator. By every account he seems to have been withdrawn, almost cold, in temperament but with the brilliance, energy, and courage to see the weaknesses in the council's plans for a definition and to direct the work of the minority against it with acumen and vigor. His journal reveals his continuing impatience with the Vatican and the council. Darboy met a violent end. Refusing to flee Paris when the Commune came to power, he was imprisoned because of his position in the church and, after a mock court-martial on 24 May 1871, he was executed that night. He fell to the ground pardoning and blessing his executioners.

Augustin David (1812–82), bishop of Saint-Brieuc, was an influential member of the French minority group. After his training in Lyon at a Sulpician seminary, he joined the religious community of Chartreux. A good preacher and musician, he was also well educated, particularly in archaeology and the early history of the church. In 1857 he became vicar general in Valence and in 1862 was consecrated bishop of Saint-Brieuc. He came to the support of Maret when the latter's book was under attack and involved himself energetically in support of government concerns, causing the defeat of Charles de Montalembert's bid for the Corps Législatif in 1863. David's stance against ultramontanism irritated his clergy, who petitioned the pope for a definition of papal infallibility; they were sharply rebuked by David in a confidential letter which became public. David had strong theoretical objections to the definition of papal infallibility.

Félix-Antoine-Philibert Dupanloup (1802–78), bishop of Orléans, probably best represented the thought of the French minority bishops and served as their spokesman. Intensely involved with ecclesiastical, political, and educational issues of his day, he served as a major defender of the church and liberalism in Europe. Dupanloup was a man of great warmth, intensity, and drama. After study with the Sulpicians in Paris, he was ordained in 1825, having already become a well-known catechist. He was appointed catechist to the

children of the royal family and was made superior of the minor
seminary of Saint-Nicolas du Chardonnet. There he developed the
educational philosophy for which he became famous. Involved in the
deathbed reconciliation of Talleyrand to the church, Dupanloup in
1845 plunged into the controversy surrounding the liberty of the
church to teach in France. In 1849, Dupanloup was consecrated
bishop of Orléans, where he improved seminary education and
catechesis. By 1854, he was intervening continually in public affairs to
defend the church against both enemies of religion and the ultramontanists. This was his habitual stance. Neither a radical nor an
original thinker, Dupanloup had the ability to find a means of compromise in concrete situations. He believed that the church's best interests were served by its adaptation to some modern ideas, and this
moderate, liberal position enabled him to mediate between the
church and the society on many issues. He became a major figure in
France, where he was made a member of the French Academy in 1854
and a senator in 1875. His moderate interpretation of the *Syllabus*
won him an international reputation, and his position of importance
made him a natural center of opposition and spokesman for the
minority bishops at the council. His opposition to the definition of
papal infallibility was based on his central life concern: preventing
the rupture of relations between the church and modern society. It
was this concern that underlay his energetic proliferation of hundreds of sermons, books, and pamphlets on education, politics, pastoral care, and spirituality; it was this concern which gave his sermons and writings an intensity and appeal even when they lacked
original thought. Dupanloup's journal at the council gives us an intimate picture of this concern and completes our sense of him as a man
of action, dynamic and enthusiastic in his untiring devotion to the
good of the church in a changing time. After the council, he involved
himself increasingly in politics. Leo XIII wanted to make him a cardinal, but Dupanloup's sudden death put an end to this plan.

Paul-Georges-Marie Dupont des Loges (1804-86), bishop of Metz,
was ordained in 1828 after his seminary training at Saint-Sulpice in
Paris. The vicar general of the diocese of Orléans in 1842, he became
bishop of Metz in 1843, where he encouraged theological education
and religious orders. Though a timid and grave man, Dupont des
Loges came to public attention for his strong stands against both the

French government and the German government, which annexed the area of his diocese after the Franco-Prussian War.

Joseph-Alfred Foulon (1823-93), bishop of Nancy, studied at Saint-Nicolas du Chardonnet in Paris under Dupanloup; he completed his seminary training at Saint-Sulpice in Paris, then continued his studies at the Ecole des Carmes and the Sorbonne. After his ordination in 1847, he taught on the faculty of Saint-Nicolas du Chardonnet and then Notre Dame des Champs. Consecrated a bishop in 1867, Foulon worked to improve the intellectual preparation of his clergy. Not a strong opponent of the definition of papal infallibility, he yet believed it inopportune. A man of wisdom and moderation in ecclesiastical and political affairs, he was made archbishop of Besançon in 1882, archbishop of Lyon in 1887, and cardinal in 1889. His scholarly biography of Darboy gives us insight into both subject and biographer.

Jacques-Marie-Achille Ginoulhiac (1806-75), bishop of Grenoble, was a scholar of significance and an influential member of the French minority bishops. After ordination in 1830, he was appointed to the faculty of the seminary at Montpellier. Vicar general of Aix in 1839, he became bishop of Grenoble in 1853. Ginoulhiac published several major studies in theology, the New Testament, and apologetics, including a study of ecumenical councils. He stressed the communal nature of the teaching office given to the apostles, and his speeches at the council contain some of the minority's most carefully developed arguments. Highly respected by the French minority for his learning, he was made archbishop of Lyon during the council.

Aimé-Victor-François Guilbert (1812–89), bishop of Gap, served as professor and rector of several seminaries before becoming vicar general of Coustances. He was consecrated to the episcopate in 1867 and became famous for his receptivity to modern ideas. Guilbert emphasized the value of democracy, and he urged the church to adapt itself to modern political forms when possible. He published three editions of a theological and apologetic work. He was transferred to Amiens in 1879, to Bordeaux in 1883, and in 1889 was made a cardinal.

Flavien-Abel-Antoine Hugonin (1823-93), bishop of Bayeux and Lisieux, studied at Saint-Sulpice in Paris and the Ecole des Carmes before his ordination in 1850. He received his doctorate four years

later and became director of seminary training at the Ecole des
Carmes. He also was first a student and then taught theology at the
Sorbonne, joining the circle around Maret. A serious scholar and
thinker, Hugonin published several studies in philosophy and law.
The Vatican asked him to denounce the ontologism it found in his
works before naming him a bishop in 1866, after which he maintained an attitude of a certain independence toward Rome.

Félix-François-Joseph Barthélémy de Las Cases (1818–80), bishop of
Constantine, a French colony in Africa, was an energetic opponent
of the definition of papal infallibility. After serving as vicar general to
the bishop of Périgueux, he was consecrated bishop in 1867. He resigned his episcopal seat in August of 1870 because of ill health or a
scandal, but he was later appointed a canon of the First Order of the
Chapter of Saint-Denis.

Charles-Henri Maret (1805–84), titular bishop of Sura, was the best
theologian among the French minority bishops. After studies at
Saint-Sulpice in Paris, he was ordained in 1830 and served in various
diocesan administrative jobs for ten years. In 1841 he became professor of dogmatic theology at the Sorbonne, and eventually he was
made the dean of its theological faculty. Interested in the adaptation
of the church to modern society, he used the thought of Bossuet and
others to develop a moderate form of gallicanism as a means to this
adaptation. He was a constant opponent of the rise of ultramontanism in France, and he was quite successful in influencing the French
government to choose many episcopal candidates with gallican leanings. Maret had written several philosophical studies before the
council, but he began to plan a major work that would defend and
explicate a Catholicism adapted to modern ideas. He published the
first part of this work, his study on councils, on the eve of the First
Vatican Council. In it, he emphasized that infallibility is found in the
accord of pope and bishops. This book generated great controversy
before the council, and after the council Maret was asked to retract
some of his ideas. Finally he did so and withdrew the book from sale.
In 1882 he was named titular archbishop of Lépante. It is difficult to
avoid the conclusion that Maret's contemporaries did not give his
theological work the credit it deserved.

Frédéric-Gabriel-Marie-François de Marguerye (1802–76), bishop of
Autun, was ordained in 1825 after seminary training with the Sulpicians in Bayeux. Eventually a vicar general at Soissons, he was made

bishop of Saint-Flour in 1837 and was transferred to Autun in 1852. His promulgation of the 1854 teaching on the Immaculate Conception gives us a sense of how minority bishops struggled to interpret the procedures involved in this teaching.

Jacques-Marie-Adrien-Césaire Mathieu (1796–1875), cardinal, archbishop of Besançon, was the only cardinal among the French minority bishops during the council. He was a well-educated but somewhat calculating and temperamental person. Ordained in 1823 after study at Saint-Sulpice in Paris, he was appointed vicar general in Paris in 1829, bishop of Langres in 1832, and archbishop of Besançon in 1834. Mathieu had enormous influence in both French and Roman political circles, bringing about a good number of the episcopal nominations made in France after 1860. A cardinal in 1850, he was liked at Rome for his defense of the temporal sovereignty of the pope and his stand on the independence of the church from government control. Mathieu was uneasy that his role as nominal chief and host of the French minority meetings would offend the Vatican, and he absented himself twice at key moments of the conciliar proceedings, probably because of this uneasiness.

Guillaume-René Meignan (1817–96), bishop of Châlons, was a figure of some significance in biblical studies. Ordained in 1840 after seminary training at Mans, he had studied in Paris, Munich, and Rome before he was thirty. In 1861 he joined the theology faculty at the Sorbonne to teach Scripture, in 1863 he became Darboy's vicar general, and in 1865 he was consecrated a bishop. One of the few French minority bishops who had any real understanding of the depths of the historical question as it affected biblical studies, Meignan did not succeed in integrating these insights into his own work. Most of his biblical studies are apologetic refutations of new biblical critical methods or exegetical studies of the messianic prophecies. The writings of Albert Loisy suggest that Meignan was a man of some cowardice, somewhat insincere in his refusal to reveal publicly his understanding of the complexities of the biblical question or to support Loisy in his struggle. But Meignan was a benevolent person, troubled by the untimeliness of the definition of papal infallibility. He became bishop of Arras in 1882, archbishop of Tours in 1884, and cardinal in 1892.

Charles-Philippe Place (1814–93), bishop of Marseille, was a lawyer and professor of history before beginning his seminary studies in

Rome in 1847. Ordained in 1850, he joined the Lazarist community. Made superior of the minor seminary at Notre-Dame des Champs in 1861 and an auditor of the Rota in 1863, Place was consecrated a bishop in 1866. A reflective and somewhat taciturn person, Place was opposed in his stand against papal infallibility by his ultramontanist priests both before and after the council in rather notorious affairs. A liberal in the circle of Dupanloup, Place was made archbishop of Rennes in 1878 and cardinal in 1886.

Etienne Ramadié (1812–77), bishop of Perpignan, a man of fiery temperament, was one of the definition's most stubborn opponents. He received his seminary training at Montpellier and was named bishop in 1865. Not a speculative person, Ramadié was loyal to his circle of friends around Maret. He praised Maret for courage in publishing the controversial book on councils, and he praised Dupanloup after his death.

François-Victor Rivet (1796–1884), bishop of Dijon, was a close friend of Colet. A professor before his ordination in 1819, Rivet became a bishop in 1838. Rivet was outspoken in his opposition to the definition of papal infallibility, which seemed to him to contradict the seminary training he had received early in the century.

Jean-Pierre Sola (1791–1881), bishop of Nice, was the oldest of the French minority bishops, but his age did not prevent him from energetic opposition to the definition at the council. Ordained in 1816, he was a pastor until 1857, when he was named to the episcopate. He resigned his seat in 1877 and died four years later.

Léon-Benoît-Charles Thomas (1826–94), bishop of La Rochelle, was ordained in 1850 after study with the Sulpicians at Bourgogne and Paris. A vicar general of Autun in 1856, he was made a bishop in 1867. An outspoken liberal, Thomas urged the church to adapt to modern ideas. He saw in the encyclical *Immortale Dei* of Leo XIII a confirmation of liberalism. Made the archbishop of Rouen in 1883, Thomas became a cardinal before his death.

PART I

The French Minority Bishops in Common

The Common Cause

*Background and Convergence of the
French Minority Bishops*

———◆——

Surprisingly little time elapsed from the opening of the First Vatican
Council before the French minority bishops began meeting together
to plan their strategy of opposition to the decree on papal infallibility.[1] How did a disparate collection of French bishops converge
so quickly into a well-organized minority group gathered around a
common cause?

A search for the roots of that rapid convergence requires a look at
their early training, friendships, and ideological ties. A glance at their
organizational structure gives clues to their motivations and their
leaders.

Seminary Education

Although the effects, for good or ill, of seminary education on the
views of the French minority should not be exaggerated, some explanation of their views can nevertheless be found here. Funeral
orators or biographers, some trying uneasily to justify the gallican
tendencies of their subjects after these tendencies were no longer respectable, often lay blame for them on a seminary professor or manu-

---

1. Within a week after the council's beginning, Dupanloup was involved in forming an international committee of minority bishops; the French minority began meeting soon after that, or even shortly before (Palanque, *Catholiques libéraux et gallicans
en France*, pp. 152–53).

al that was tainted with "the indelible gallican mark."[2] And in his last testament de Las Cases, after insisting that he had really opposed the definition during the council, explains simply that he was "brought up on anti-infallibilist doctrines."[3]

All twenty-two minority bishops received their seminary training before 1853, when the encyclical *Inter multiplices* changed seminary training in France.[4] All twenty-two did their seminary studies in the interval from just before 1816 (when Sola, the group's eldest, was ordained) to 1851 (the year of ordination for the youngest, de Cuttoli). Probably all but one studied in France. What kind of training did they receive on the issue of papal infallibility and related questions?[5]

In France, seminary education had behind it that tradition of thought on relationships among church and state, pope and bishops, called gallicanism. Although this tradition can be traced back to medieval times, it had been given classic formulation by Jacques Bossuet, theologian and bishop of Meaux, and the Four Articles of 1682, after which it became the common theological opinion of the clergy of France.[6]

The French Revolution was a turning point for theological education in France. Certain sociological practices or bases that had favored the development of a gallican ecclesiology disappeared, and now the church needed to moderate its gallican stand to gain sup-

2. Boissonnot, *Le Cardinal Meignan*, p. 32, writes thus on Jean Bouvier, a manual writer who became bishop of Mans.

3. Mansi 53:1042C.

4. This encyclical contained "a very clear repudiation not only of gallicanism, even moderate gallicanism, but also of all those opposed to the ultramontanist current for any reason whatever, and these opponents were not taken in by it" (Aubert, *Pie IX*, p. 276). See also Aubert, *Pie IX*, p. 298.

5. I have not been able to learn where Bravard, Colet, de Las Cases, and Sola received their seminary training. Place attended seminary in Rome. For a discussion of seminary education in France in the period preceding the First Vatican Council, see Roger Aubert, "La géographie ecclésiologique au XIXe siècle," and J. Audinet, "L'enseignement *De Ecclesia* à St Sulpice sous le Premier Empire, et les débuts du gallicanisme modéré," in Maurice Nédoncelle et al., *L'ecclésiologie au XIXe siècle* (Paris: Editions du Cerf, 1960), pp. 11–55, 115–39; Xavier de Montclos, *Lavigerie, le Saint-Siège et l'église de l'avènement de Pie IX à l'avènement de Léon XIII (1846–1878)* (Paris: Editions E. de Boccard, 1965), pp. 27–75; Jacques Gadille, *La pensée et l'action politiques des évêques français au début de la IIIe République, 1870/1883*, 2 vols. (Paris: Hachette, 1967), 1:31–40.

6. For a discussion of gallicanism, see *Dictionnaire de théologie catholique*, s.v. "Gallicanisme," by M. Dubruel; Martimort, *Le gallicanisme*; Aimé Georges Martimort, *Le gallicanisme de Bossuet* (Paris: Les Editions du Cerf, 1953).

port in Rome.[7] But the rise of ultramontanism in France, although swift, did not dominate the seminaries until *Inter multiplices*. From just after the Revolution until 1853, the most widely used manuals were those of Louis Bailly and Jean Bouvier and the *Théologie de Toulouse;* Darboy thought Bailly was the most popular.[8] All had gallican tendencies, though they were moderate, less strong than the gallicanism of Bossuet. Professors further moderated the manualists' views, so that the seminary of Saint-Sulpice in Paris, for example, can be said to have been teaching a semigallicanism—a kind of moderate gallicanism—in the nineteenth century, with ultramontanism increasing in influence.[9]

In 1810–11, for example, Pierre-Denis Boyer in teaching his course on the church at Saint-Sulpice tried to avoid the dangers of the extremes of both ultramontanism and gallicanism. He taught that the pope is the voice of the church and the center of unity, but he is not infallible. Only ecumenical councils are infallible. To represent the church, the pope needs the subsequent approbation of the bishops, whose office is divinely instituted. But the question of papal infallibility remains open because the articles of 1682 had not pronounced against it.[10]

A generation later, in 1845, M. Philipin de Rivière taught his course on the church at Saint-Sulpice. While demonstrating the constant orthodoxy of the popes, he remained neutral on the question of papal infallibility, showing the strengths and weaknesses of both the

7. Aubert, "La géographie ecclésiologique," pp. 12, 14. De Montclos sees a decline in ecclesiastical studies even before 1789 (*Lavigerie, le Saint-Siège et l'église*, p. 77). See also Audinet, "L'enseignement *De Ecclesia* à St-Sulpice," p. 116.

8. Louis Bailly, *Theologia dogmatica et moralis,* 9 vols. (Dijon, 1789) (vol. 9 contains appendices on notes of the church and civil laws). His *Tractatus de Ecclesia* (Dijon, 1771) was also important. Jean Baptiste Bouvier, *Institutiones theologicae ad usum seminariorum,* 6 vols. (Mans, 1834). *Théologie de Toulouse,* 6 vols. (Toulouse, 1828), was a revision, under the direction of Benoît Hippolyte Vieusse, of its predecessor, the *Théologie de Poitiers.* Georges Darboy, "Des leçons théologiques du P. Perrone," *Le correspondant* 20 (25 November 1847):524; Darboy indicates Bailly's popularity though he favors the manual of Giovanni Perrone. See also *Dictionnaire de théologie catholique,* s.v. "Bailly, Louis," by E. Dublanchy.

9. Aubert, "La géographie ecclésiologique," pp. 15–16. De Montclos finds Bailly gallican and hence out of touch with the times (*Lavigerie, le Saint-Siège et l'église*, pp. 39–40). Gadille calls the nineteenth-century phenomenon "semigallicanism" (*La pensée et l'action politiques des évêques français,* 1:47). Audinet prefers "moderate gallicanism" (L'enseignement *De Ecclesia* à St-Sulpice," p. 115).

10. Audinet, "L'enseignement *De Ecclesia* à St-Sulpice," pp. 115–39.

gallican and ultramontanist positions. He felt the question could be freely debated; he himself declined to take a position.[11]

So if gallicanism was taught in the seminaries of France in the first half of the nineteenth century, it was not the political gallicanism associated with royal or parliamentary politics,[12] but at most a moderate theological gallicanism, in which the rights of bishops were emphasized, papal infallibility was not considered self-evident, and such issues were treated within the context of the infallibility of the church. In 1859, Thomas Gousset, cardinal, archbishop of Reims, writes to Pius IX, "In the seminaries the Four Articles are no longer taught; most of the theology professors, however, present them to the students as optional opinions that one may equally accept or reject, without any danger, to which there can be not even the slightest objection."[13]

Philipin's course with its moderate approach to the issue of papal infallibility typifies the Sulpician teaching of that period.[14] Sulpicians were of special importance in theological education because of their widespread influence in seminary training. The Sulpicians tried for a long time to stem the ultramontanist tendencies affecting ecclesiastical life in France.[15] Although their gallicanism can be exaggerated, their reverence for seventeenth-century practices and especially for Bossuet kept that tradition alive.[16] At least ten of the twenty-two French minority bishops trained with Sulpicians, eight of them at Saint-Sulpice in Paris, and the teachers of a few others were also noted for gallican views.[17]

11. De Montclos, *Lavigerie, le Saint-Siège et l'église*, pp. 40–45.

12. Aubert, *Pie IX*, p. 306, n. 1. Darboy notes that the monarchy's policy toward the church had the result that "the clergy is less gallican than ever" ("Des conciles récemment tenus en France," *Le correspondant* 27 [25 November 1850]:212).

13. J. Gousset, *Le cardinal Gousset, archevêque de Reims: Sa vie, ses oeuvres, son influence* (Besançon: Bossanne, 1903), quoted in de Montclos, *Lavigerie, le Saint-Siège et l'église*, p. 44.

14. De Montclos, *Lavigerie, le Saint-Siège et l'église*, p. 44.

15. Aubert, *Pie IX*, p. 300. Henri Icard, superior general of Saint-Sulpice, however, disagreed with the suggestion that Sulpicians were gallican; see Hennesey, *First Council of the Vatican*, pp. 201–2.

16. Aubert, "La géographie ecclésiologique," p. 15. Aubert also attributes the moderate gallicanism of some nineteenth-century American seminaries, especially that of Baltimore, to the Sulpician training received by many American bishops.

17. In addition to those eight who attended Saint-Sulpice in Paris, de Marguerye and David also were trained by Sulpicians. At the seminary of Montpellier, Ramadié was taught a gallican position (Cabrières, *Eloge funèbre de Ramadié*, p. 25). Ginoulhiac

Consider, then, the stir caused in France when, in 1852, Pius IX placed Bailly's manual on the Index. It caused "quite a strong reaction," according to Xavier de Montclos; Rivet, one of the older bishops of the group who had used Bailly for his training, was astonished.[18] Since 1815, the ultramontanists had been gaining ground in the seminaries through the distribution of the works of Joseph de Maistre, Félicité de Lamennais, Prosper Guéranger, and others. But *Inter multiplices* assured the victory of ultramontanism.[19] Seminaries began to adopt the manual of Roman theologian Giovanni Perrone[20] or to correct the older French manuals of Bouvier and the *Théologie de Toulouse* "in accordance with the remarks put forward by a few Roman theologians." In addition, ultramontanist polemical literature was substituted for the accustomed reading of Bossuet, the Maurists, and writers of Port-Royal. Since France did not have canonical faculties of theology, French seminary professors were required to pursue their higher studies in Rome, which furthered the entry of Roman ideas into French seminaries after 1853.[21] Even the Sulpicians fell into line; in 1856 the Sulpician superior, Joseph Carrière, traveled to Rome to assure the pope of the society's orthodoxy, and at his return, a critic complains, the society was "forced to make new concessions to the Roman doctrines."[22] At Carrière's death, Pius IX assured an ultramontanist successor.[23]

But if these developments after 1852 touched profoundly the lives of the twenty-two, they occurred after the formation of the bishops'

---

attended and taught at the same seminary. The training Guilbert received at Coutances would have had a Sulpician spirit (Gadille, *La pensée et l'action politiques des évêques français*, 1:33). Meignan studied under Bouvier, the author of the manual with a moderate gallican viewpoint.

18. De Montclos, *Lavigerie, le Saint-Siège et l'église*, p. 40; Chevallier, *Rivet*, p. 173.

19. Aubert, "La gèographie ecclésiologique," pp. 17–25, 46. By ultramontanism, I mean the tendency to emphasize or exaggerate the rights and privileges of the pope in relationships between pope and bishops or between the church and national governments. For a discussion of the rise of ultramontanism in nineteenth-century France, see Aubert, *Pie IX*, pp. 262–310; Butler, *Vatican Council*, 1:35–78.

20. Giovanni Perrone, *Praelectiones theologicae*, 9 vols. (Rome, 1835–42). For a study of Perrone's thought, see Walter Kasper, *Die Lehre von der Tradition in der römischen Schule* (Freiburg: Herder, 1962), pp. 29–181.

21. Aubert, *Pie IX*, p. 300.

22. Jean Wallon, *Premier mémoire sur l'église de France* (N.p., n.d.), quoted in Palanque, *Catholiques libéraux et gallicans en France*, p. 65.

23. Aubert, *Pie IX*, p. 300.

early theological opinions, when moderate gallicanism was a respectable position or even, as Ramadié's funeral orator reports, "above dispute."[24]

A Network of Relationships

For some, friendships or experiences would play a greater role in their theological position than seminary training. Ramadié's funeral orator claims that the bishop was "dominated" by personal ties, and Palanque suggests the same about de Cuttoli and Foulon. Place studied for the priesthood in Rome, but he hardly held ultramontanist views. He even tried to suppress the ultramontanist movement of priests in his diocese in the "Marseille affair."[25] In his early days as a seminary professor, Darboy taught that the pope was infallible.[26] But his experience as archbishop of Paris—especially his poor treatment at the hands of the Vatican[27]—led him to endorse a practical gallicanism as the more appropriate stance.[28] According to Palanque, "The question of infallibility with regard to dogmatic matters interests him less than that of the rights of bishops. . . . He lives in the concrete."[29]

Palanque is correct when he notes that no party of opposition was organized in France before the council, if by a party one means an organized chain of command with a common strategy for group action. But there were friendships and other contacts among the minority bishops long before the council was held. Palanque in his biographical sketch of the minority finds most of the twenty-two bishops involved in a string of such relationships.[30] Ramadié was

24. Cabrières, *Eloge funèbre de Ramadié*, p. 24.

25. Ibid.; Palanque, *Catholiques libéraux et gallicans en France*, pp. 145, 148; for details of the "Marseille affair," see pp. 138–40.

26. This claim is made by Foulon, *Histoire de Mgr Darboy*, p. 47, and confirmed by Aubert in *Pie IX*, p. 307.

27. For an account of the controversy between Darboy and the Vatican, see chapter 2 at notes 49–52; see also M. R. Durand, "Mgr Darboy et le Saint-Siège," *Bulletin de la Société d'Histoire Moderne*, ser. 2, 7 (December 1907): 6–8, (January 1908):9–11; Palanque, *Catholiques libéraux et gallicans en France*, pp. 23–25. Letters of Darboy and others involved in this incident are available in "Monseigneur Darboy et le Saint-Siège: Documents inédits," *Revue d'histoire et de la littérature religieuses* 12 (1907):240–81.

28. Aubert, *Pie IX*, p. 307.

29. Palanque, *Catholiques libéraux et gallicans en France*, p. 23.

30. Ibid., pp. 64–65, 142–48.

named to his episcopal seat through the influence of Maret, as were a good number of other bishops with gallican leanings, most notably Darboy.[31] Ramadié also was a friend of Dupanloup, as were Colet, Thomas, and Sola. Dupont des Loges had been the seminary comrade of the bishop of Orléans, Place his secretary and vicar general, Foulon and Hugonin his students. Meignan, Ginoulhiac, David, de Las Cases, and Callot joined Ramadié in an interested circle around Maret. Foulon was a friend of Hugonin, Colet of Rivet.[32] Colet and at least three others had served as secretary or vicar general for another minority group bishop: he for Rivet, de Cuttoli for Darboy, Place for Dupanloup, Thomas for de Marguerye. Maret, Hugonin, and Meignan had been colleagues at the Sorbonne in 1863.

The list of relationships could continue, and doubtless some of them went unrecorded. But these suffice to show that although the twenty-two bishops were not organized as a group before the council, yet they were part of a network of clerical and episcopal relationships.

It was an active network. Friends of Maret formed "a closely knit network of opponents to Roman politics," in continual contact by letter.[33] And a random entry in Dupanloup's journal notes, "100 letters dictated, and sealed."[34] He often dictated to two secretaries at once while writing himself as well or rose in the middle of the night to work after only a few hours of sleep.[35] This network of relationships was the background out of which naturally emerged the defense of Dupanloup's *Observations sur la controverse soulevée relativement à la définition de l'infaillibilité au prochain concile* by many, such as de Marguerye and Place, and even the more limited support for Maret's book, *Du concile général et de la paix religieuse*, from Ramadié

31. Aubert, *Pie IX*, pp. 305–7.

32. Colet calls Rivet his "closest friend [ami le plus intime]" and explains that he "encouraged me to undertake this work [m'a encouragé à entreprendre ce travail]" when he begins to set down his "Souvenirs du concile du Vatican," 4AI, 2, 20, fol. A, Archives de l'Archevêché de Paris.

33. Aubert, *Pie IX*, p. 306.

34. Félix Dupanloup, *Journal intime de Monseigneur Dupanloup*, ed. L. Branchereau (Paris: P. Téqui, 1902), entry of 16 January 1864, quoted in Aubert, "Dupanloup."

35. Dupanloup archival holdings bulge with the numerous letters he wrote and the many additional ones he received; see Aubert, "Dupanloup" for their location. Some have been published: *Lettres choisies*, ed. François Lagrange, 2 vols. (Paris: Jules Gervais, 1888); *Mgr Dupanloup. Lettres de direction sur la vie chrétienne*, ed. H. L. Chapon (Paris: P. Lethielleux, 1905).

and Meignan. And it was also from this network that the future minority would be formed.

But more than personal ties held the network together; the minority bishops shared ideological bonds which in many cases caused the developing personal ties. Two streams of thought, the moderate gallicanism defined above and liberalism, distinguish the two schools of thought among the twenty-two.

Around Maret, professor and dean of theology at the Sorbonne and avid supporter of the government, were gathered a circle of supporters who sympathized with his gallican viewpoint.[36] Others remained independent of his circle but shared his gallican tendencies or exercised their own gallican influence. A different line of thought was exercised by Dupanloup, liberal spokesman for the reconciliation of the church with modern society, around whom another group gathered. Others were liberals but remained independent of the Dupanloup circle.[37]

Liberals and gallicans at first had little in common, and on many occasions each group even opposed the views of the other. Although many friendships crossed ideological lines, Dupanloup and Maret had little enough sympathy with each other that the bishop of Orléans called the appearance of Maret's book a "most regrettable complication," a "calamity." He demanded that Maret not preach at the episcopal retreat lest his own position be damaged.[38]

But ultramontanism proved an enemy strong enough to break down the barriers between the two groups. With the support of the imperial government, which feared Roman influence, both groups began to harbor a grievance against the Vatican for endangering their rights as bishops.[39] The gallicans saw Rome as a dangerous influence threatening the divinely established constitution of the

36. This division follows that of Palanque, who lists the circle around Maret as Callot, David, de Las Cases, Ginoulhiac, Meignan, and Ramadié, in *Catholiques libéraux et gallicans en France*, p. 142.

37. Palanque lists gallican independents as Bravard, Darboy, de Cuttoli, de Marguerye, Mathieu, and Rivet (ibid.). Aubert is perhaps more accurate when he notes Darboy's powerful influence over others (*Pie IX*, pp. 307–8). Palanque lists the circle around Dupanloup as Colet, Dupont des Loges, Foulon, Hugonin, Place, Sola, and liberal independents as Guilbert and Thomas.

38. Dupanloup, *Journal intime*, quoted in Palanque, *Catholiques libéraux et gallicans en France*, p. 64; see also n. 14.

39. Aubert, "La géographie ecclésiologique," p. 48.

church.[40] The liberals, once champions of ultramontanism,[41] now began to fear an infallible pope whose pronouncements in the style of the *Syllabus* against liberal ideas would assume even more weight and drive an irreversible wedge between modernity and the church.[42] Aubert summarizes, "Opponents to absolutism in the church as well as in the state, these latter [liberals] were now apprehensive of what Archbishop Sibour had already denounced as an 'idolatry of spiritual power'. They feared especially a solemn definition of papal infallibility which would reinforce the authority of the *Syllabus*, of the bull *Unam sanctam*, and of other documents which set forth politico-religious views incompatible with modern mentality."[43] Thus, notes Palanque, the two schools of thought were different in origin, characteristics, and ideas, "and . . . the reasons of the gallican opposition differ wholly from the reasons of the liberal opposition. One group combats personal and separate infallibility in the name of the bishops' rights; the other opposes absolute infallibility in the name of modern society, insisting above all on the inopportuneness of a definition."[44] The liberals continued to oppose the Empire and government-supporting bishops, but by the late 1860's a rapprochement between the two groups was under way.[45] Thus, if there was no organized French caucus ready to move into action as a minority party at the start of the council, the earlier debates and issues had succeeded in classifying tendencies such that strange bedfellows were ready to make common cause.[46]

Maret was the only thinker in the group to unite gallicanism and liberalism into a systematic theological synthesis, according to de Montclos. He continues:

But, to varying degrees, the idea of moderating the exercise of papal authority in order to safeguard the fundamental liberties of modern society was shared by the majority of the French minority bishops. A number of them had no fundamental objection to raise against the doctrine of papal infallibil-

40. Palanque, *Catholiques libéraux et gallicans en France*, p. 61.
41. Aubert, "La géographie ecclésiologique," p. 48.
42. Palanque, *Catholiques libéraux et gallicans en France*, pp. 61–62.
43. Aubert, "La géographie ecclésiologique," pp. 48–49. Marie-Dominique Sibour had been archbishop of Paris until 1857.
44. Palanque, *Catholiques libéraux et gallicans en France*, p. 64.
45. Aubert, *Pie IX*, pp. 308–9.
46. De Montclos, *Lavigerie, le Saint-Siège et l'église*, p. 433.

ity; but they feared above all that, should this doctrine be defined, a movement would be endorsed which would convey, along with ultramontanism,
a whole set of absolutist and reactionary theories; that is, that the pope who
had challenged the modern world with the *Syllabus* would be held exempt
from all error.[47]

For the French minority, the defense of modern ideas made necessary the attack on ultramontanism.

Thus with a similar theological education behind them, a network
of relationships among them, and a common enemy before them,
the twenty-two were ready for the decision recounted by Colet in his
"Souvenirs du concile du Vatican:" "that there be imposed on them
a mission painful, difficult, but very useful to the church."[48]

Becoming a Minority

Before the start of the council, Hugonin writes to Darboy, "I am
really afraid that we are going to the Council without having made
the slightest preparation together."[49] But his hopes for some preconciliar minority organization were not well realized in France.

The liberals were increasingly drawn to the circle of Maret in their
common fear, but they disapproved of Maret's decision to publish
his major work with its moderate gallican theory on the eve of the
council. In response to rumors of an impending definition, they condemned the public discussions of such matters in the press. Journalists discuss disagreements among the bishops with "supreme indis-
cretion," writes Dupanloup when he finally breaks his own silence.[50]
He follows with a virulent attack on Louis Veuillot, the journalist
whose *L'Univers* had become "an instrument of combat"[51] for Rome:
"You make short work of questions of doctrine and discipline, you
set yourself as judge among the bishops, in order to disgrace some

47. Ibid., p. 434.
48. "qu'une Mission pénible, difficile, mais fort utile à l'Eglise leur était imposée"
(Colet, "Souvenirs du concile du Vatican," fol. N).
49. Bazin, *Vie de Maret*, 3:73, quoted in Palanque, *Catholiques libéraux et gallicans
en France*, p. 75. In n. 64, Palanque argues convincingly that the writer, unnamed by
Bazin, was Hugonin.
50. Félix Dupanloup, *Observations sur la controverse soulevée relativement à la définition de l'infaillibilité au prochain concile* (Paris: Charles Douniol, 1869), p. 6.
51. Aubert, *Pie IX*, p. 298.

and dominate others. . . . You insult, denounce and banish from Catholicism all Catholics who do not think or speak as you do. . . . No one has ever merited more than you these harsh words of holy Scriptures: *Accuser of the brothers!*"[52] Meignan would write to his priests and seminarians in April 1870, "Let the decisions of the church and of the Holy Father, when he gives commands, be our rule, not *L'Univers*."[53]

Preconciliar organization among the twenty-two bishops was impeded by the different ideologies and by the strife within each diocese between a liberal or gallican bishop and his usually ultramontanist clergy. Even the religious orders, whose ongoing common life and structured organization might have provided a catalyst or a base for organizing the minority in France, remained ultramontanist, divided, or uninvolved.[54] The German professor Ignaz von Döllinger writes to Maret of his hopes for some organization among the French minority: "Among the German bishops who will come to the Council, some will make common cause with the French bishops, if the latter form a nucleus of resistance against the ultramontane party and its favorite dogma."[55] And Dupanloup's trip to Germany in the summer of 1869, where he met Döllinger for the first time, was "an attempt at concerted action."[56]

But if little organizing or strategizing was carried out in France before the council, the French did not delay plans long after their arrival in Rome. By early December of 1869, those French bishops hesitant to define papal infallibility were meeting regularly at the palace of the Duke of Salviati, Mathieu's residence during the council.[57] "We already have our right and our left," writes Foulon on

52. Félix Dupanloup, *Avertissement adressé par Mgr l'évêque d'Orléans à M. L. Veuillot rédacteur en chef du journal "l'Univers"* (Orléans: Ernest Colas, 1869), pp. 2–3.

53. Boissonnot, *Le Cardinal Meignan*, p. 286. The same position was taken by the liberal newspaper *Le correspondant*; see Palanque, *Catholiques libéraux et gallicans en France*, pp. 97–103.

54. In some dioceses, bitter quarrels erupted between bishop and clergy, such as in Place's diocese of Marseille; see Palanque, *Catholiques libéeraux et gallicans en France*, pp. 138–40 see also pp. 50–51.

55. Ignaz von Döllinger to Henri Maret, 18 March 1869, quoted in Bazin, *Vie de Maret*, 3:86.

56. Palanque, *Catholiques libéraux et gallicans en France*, pp. 62, 109.

57. Ibid., pp. 152–53.

the opening day of the council. The council historian, Theodor Granderath, confirms this report: the "diversity of sympathies dominated conciliar activity and especially the relations of the fathers among themselves; it became involved in all of the other matters and was the source of all the differences of opinion." This division first seemed most evident among the French and then spread to characterize the other bishops at the council as well. Bernard Ullathorne, bishop of Birmingham, writes, "Of course, as I told you before I left England, the outside of the council is an arena of policy and intrigue."[58]

Less homogeneous than the council's majority, the minority was really a group of groups. While all of the national groups that made up the minority shared many common motives, the particular concerns of each played an important role in shaping the opposition offered by the minority as a whole to *Pastor aeternus*. Aubert characterizes the French group by their hostility to absolutist tendencies. In fact, the different preoccupations of the French and German groups, he explains, led the two to have little contact with each other, and "their very pronounced national character prevented them from becoming a rallying point for bishops of other countries who sympathized with their point of view." It was to unify the many minority groups into one that plans for an international committee headed by Joseph Rauscher, cardinal, archbishop of Vienna, were laid, although this committee never fulfilled its purpose adequately.[59]

If a few French bishops opposed a definition of papal infallibility because of their loyalty to the French government, reasons of conscience formed the basis of opposition for most of the minority, which, Aubert says, "their opponents did not often want to recognize."[60] Darboy, who tells fellow bishops at the council that he wishes to discuss matters that bother his conscience, was typical.[61] Many were troubled to find themselves thus bound in conscience to be the minority at a great council, because precisely their argument against *Pastor aeternus* was that it threatened the divinely established need for unity between pope and bishops in proclaiming dogma.

58. Joseph Foulon to abbé Tapie, 8 December 1869, quoted in Aubert, *Pie IX*, p. 325; Granderath, *Histoire du concile du Vatican*, 2:321–22; Aubert, *Pie IX*, p. 325; Bernard Ullathorne to Dr. Northcote, Ullathorne's theological adviser, 8 February 1870, quoted in Butler, *Vatican Council*, 1:238.

59. Aubert, *Pie IX*, pp. 327, 329.   60. Ibid., p. 328.

61. Mansi 52:155C.

Now they found themselves in disagreement with the pope and other bishops over the need to agree! What went unnoticed, writes Colet in his "Souvenirs," "is the account of the moral suffering of these 137 bishops condemned by their conscience to stifle continually the feelings of their heart, and to oppose the desires of a revered and beloved Pontiff for whom they would have given their lives." And he quotes de Las Cases in conversation with Antonio du Luca, cardinal and council president, on 21 December 1869: "I love the Church and the Holy See too much not to tell you in all simplicity, Your Grace, the great sorrow which today's session has caused me."[62] David cites the worries of his conscience and the obligations of his office as reasons for his conciliar remarks, and Colet blames his early departure on his uneasy conscience. After the council de Las Cases writes: "During the Council, to allow my conscience to speak, I imposed silence on my heart, not without great distress. My heart was suffering from not being in agreement on this point with His Holiness Pius IX, while my conscience laid upon me the strict duty of defending what I then believed to be the truth."[63] Bravard tells his diocese that he spent many nights in tears because of his sadness at seeming a rebel, but "my conscience was stronger than my grief."[64]

In his council speech, Bravard complains about the attitude shown toward the minority. "In truth, I am seeking the things which are better sincerely, and with an upright heart and an unfeigned conscience; my conscience bears me this witness," he comments hotly. He is annoyed by the accusations of the majority: "We admit your good faith, admit also ours." He continues:

For you have heard some, most reverend fathers, who did not at all hesitate to say to opponents of the schema that if they were either a little learned in theological matters, or meek and humble of heart, or not blinded by the gifts of princes, not led to enormous honors and by an accursed hunger for gold,

---

62. "c'est le récit des souffrances morales de ces 137 Evêques condamnés par leur Conscience à marcher constamment sur leur coeur, et à contrarier dans ses désirs un Pontife vénéré [sic] et bien aimé, pour lequel ils auraient donné leur vie" (Colet, "Souvenirs du concile du Vatican," fol. Q. "J'aime trop l'Eglise et le St. Siège pour ne pas vous dire en toute simplicité, Mgr, l'affliction que me fait éprouver la Convocation de ce jour" (ibid., fol. V). This seems the correct rendering of the sentence, although the word *affliction* is somewhat unclear in the manuscript.

63. Mansi 52:71C, 53:1018B, 1042C.

64. "ma conscience a été plus forte que ma douleur" (Jean Bravard, quoted in "Nouvelles et faits religieux du diocèse," *Revue catholique (Semaine religieuse) du diocèse de Coutances et Avranches* 3 [14 April 1870]:454).

if they had feared Greeks even when bearing gifts, or were not hypocrites, as
the Arians were, when they speak about obedience and devotion and love
toward the Holy See and the pope: certainly, most certainly along with
themselves [the accusers] they [the opponents] would applaud the schema
and the infallibility of the supreme pontiff.[65]

Mathieu also defends the minority's good faith,[66] and David asks,
"Why should we, who hold a contrary opinion with an unwilling
heart, but because conscience commands it, because reason commands it, why should we be brought under suspicion?"[67] Ginoulhiac
is strong in his criticism of a suggestion to limit prematurely the discussion of papal infallibility. Such a suggestion is unsuitable, he
argues, because it lumps minority bishops who oppose the schema
together with Protestants and heretics, rather than recognizing that
their objections are products of a faith shared with supporters of the
definition.[68] Before the opening of the council, he had insisted that
each bishop must speak his mind freely, even if he knows his view is
not shared by other bishops or the pope. "No pretext can dispense us
from this duty," he had warned.[69]

For the twenty-two, the role of minority in which their consciences placed them was indeed "a painful mission."[70]

Leader of the French Minority

Speculation about the identity of the French minority's leader re-
volved around several figures.

Thomas Gousset, cardinal, archbishop of Reims, calls Mathieu
"invisible leader of the gallican Church,"[71] and it was Mathieu who
presided over the minority meetings at the Salviati palace, evidently
because of his ranking position as sole cardinal in the group. But his
enthusiasm for any obvious role with the minority was low. His
biographer notes that the cardinal found himself "presiding over an
assembly which gradually adopted its own style, and was in time
reputed to be the center of the opposition to the definition of papal
infallibility. This role was repugnant to his character, to his feelings,

---

65. Mansi 52:308A–C.
66. Ibid., col. 724A.
67. Ibid., col. 988B.
68. Ibid., col. 218B.
69. Jacques Ginoulhiac, *Le concile oecuménique* (Paris: C. Douniol, 1869), p. 49.
70. "une Mission pénible" (Colet, "Souvenirs du concile du Vatican," fol. N).
71. Bergier, *Supplément à la vie du Cardinal Mathieu*, p. 210.

to his well-known past history. . . . Rather than dominating his group, he was swept along by it."[72] "But he was too hesitant in making decisions, and had neither the character nor the soul of a leader," comment J. Brugerette and E. Amann.[73] Dupanloup complains of Henri Bonnechose, cardinal, archbishop of Rouen, and of Mathieu, "Our two cardinals have done their utmost to divide us, to split us up, to prevent us from coming together."[74] Mathieu's reserve for the work of the minority may be the best explanation for his mysterious absences at two key moments during the council.[75]

Dupanloup could easily have compensated for any lack of enthusiasm Mathieu felt about leading the French minority. The exuberant bishop from Orléans felt called to become the center of protest against Roman centralization and its opposition to modern society's concerns. "All his activity—all his agitation, one should say—was focused on this goal," says Aubert. Before the council, Dupanloup had begun extensive correspondence with Rome, with other bishops, and with foreign theologians. Soon after arriving at Rome, he plunged into a series of feverish organizing activities, using his residence as a base of operations. The Vicomte de Meaux writes of him, "The leader of the opposition in the council took counsel with his companions at arms and his lieutenants in order to carry on the campaign." Some had speculated that Dupanloup would arrive in Rome as the head of an organized party, but the ambassador from Austria explains in a letter why those in Rome were showing surprisingly little apprehension toward Dupanloup's possible leadership: "They rely a great deal on the fact that Latin has been ruled the exclusive language at the Council. Now, the French bishops in general speak Latin very badly, and Bishop Dupanloup in particular, little or none; so, they feel confident that, despite his well-known verve, he will not succeed in expressing himself so as to convince his hearers and persuade many of them to adopt his views."[76]

72. Besson, *Vie de Mathieu*, 2:262–63.

73. *Dictionnaire de théologie catholique*, s.v. "Vatican (Concile du)," by J. Brugerette and E. Amann.

74. Félix Dupanloup to Augustin Cochin, 11 January 1870, quoted in Aubert, "Dupanloup au début du concile," pp. 113–14. Bonnechose would become a leader in the third or center party.

75. A variety of explanations—excuses, Palanque suggests—were given for Mathieu's absences by different people (*Catholiques libéraux et gallicans en France*, p. 153).

76. Aubert, "Dupanloup au début du concile," pp. 105, 97, 106, 103, 99, n. 11.

In fact, Dupanloup found that his position among the French bishops was less appreciated than he had hoped. Darboy notes in his journal that many were irritated by Dupanloup's *Observations sur la controverse soulevée relativement à la définition de l'infaillibilité au prochain concile.*[77] In the attempt by minority bishops to elect representatives to the Deputation on Faith, Dupanloup finished second to Ginoulhiac even among the bishops assembled at the Salviati palace, which put him at fourth place in the final vote of all the French bishops. But this did not discourage him from his activities,[78] which he continued throughout the council. Aubert suggests that these activities may have done more harm than good to the cause of the minority, but still Dupanloup was an important influence within the group and the standard-bearer for liberal ideas.[79]

But it is to Darboy, the reserved but energetic archbishop of Paris, that the credit for leadership of the French minority must go. Having learned the dangers of Roman absolutism through a bitter experience of papal intervention in his diocese, Darboy was prepared to exert organized tenacity in galvanizing the resistance of French minority bishops to a definition of papal infallibility. His opposition sprang from the conviction of conscience.[80] Before the council, Jean-Pierre Mabile, bishop of Versailles, had written, "If Bishop Darboy is not the acknowledged leader of this coalition, he is its soul and center." Emile Ollivier, French premier during the council, confirmed Darboy's exercise of leadership in France before the council.[81] Darboy's silence during preconciliar debates over the definition of papal infallibility gave him the freedom to seize leadership in Rome. He was less the spokesman for an organized group than the leader of many groups within the minority, Palanque notes.[82] De Las Cases would write to him later, "Your strength has been not in the imposition of your will, but in the direction that you gave us while acting as if you were following the direction we were giving you." Darboy's

---

77. Darboy, "Le journal," entry for 1 December 1870, p. 419.

78. Aubert, "Dupanloup au début du concile," pp. 108–9.

79. Aubert, "Dupanloup."

80. *Dictionnaire d'histoire et de géographie ecclésiastiques*, s.v. "Darboy (Georges)," by François Guédon.

81. Jean-Pierre Mabile, bishop of Versailles, in an 1867 memorandum, "La réaction gallicane," quoted in Aubert, *Pie IX*, p. 307; Emile Ollivier, *L'église et l'état au concile du Vatican*, 3d ed., 2 vols. (Paris: Garnier Frères, 1879), 2:91–95, 142–45, 236–39.

82. Palanque, *Catholiques libéraux et gallicans en France*, p. 64.

journal of his days in Rome reveals his deep involvement in key leadership activities. Writing on the French minority, Aubert comments
that it was "presided over, without much drive, by Cardinal
Mathieu, enlivened by the passion of the fiery bishop of Orléans, but
directed in fact, with circumspection and perspicacity, by Darboy."[83]

Two other bishops exercised important leadership of the French
minority during the council. Ginoulhiac, the respected theologian
from Grenoble who was made archbishop of Lyon in June during
the council, served as French representative—along with Darboy
and Dupanloup—to the international committee of all minority
groups in the council. David, the bishop of Saint-Brieuc, with "a
knowledge of Christian antiquity superior to that of the average
French bishop,"[84] was listed along with Darboy, Dupanloup, and
Ginoulhiac as an opposition candidate from France to the Deputation on Faith.

Departure before the Vote

Throughout the council, the French minority worked against the
definition of papal infallibility. In letters, speeches, and private conversation, in petitions, conciliar motions, and papal audiences, they
tried to prevent the passage of the definition.[85]

By the last days before the vote on 18 July, the French minority
bishops had realized that their opposition would probably not succeed in defeating or further revising the schema. Before the session
of the final vote, the French bishops who had been opposing the
definition gathered to discuss what stance they should take. Mathieu
feared that a *non placet* vote would be useless and would appear as
bravado in front of the pope. He also reported rumors of a plan to
heckle or deride publicly those who voted *non placet*.[86] Some of the
bishops who had worked against the definition throughout the

83. Félix de Las Cases to Georges Darboy, 4 July 1870, quoted in Aubert, *Pie IX*, p.
328, n. 1; Darboy, "Le journal," pp. 417–52; Aubert, *Pie IX*, pp. 327–28; see also the
editorial comments of Duval in Darboy, "Le journal," p. 418.

84. Aubert, "David."

85. For the details of the French minority's actions during the council, see Palanque, *Catholiques libéraux et gallicans en France*, pp. 152–76; cf. Aubert, *Vatican I*; Butler, *Vatican Council*.

86. Colet, "Copie des procès-verbaux rédigés par Mgr Colet des séances tenues par
les évêques de la minorité," 4AI, 2, 3°, fol. 71, Archives de l'Archevêché de Paris.

council decided to end their opposition, and they voted for *Pastor aeternus*.[87] Others argued that scandal would result from *non placet* votes. In addition, they believed, "a definition of faith promulgated despite the opposition of a considerable minority will suffer discredit."[88] They feared that *non placet* votes would cause a schism. Thus they argued that it would be better "to absent oneself from the session, if one does not believe oneself able in conscience to approve the Constitution."[89] One bishop reported that he would have to abstain rather than vote *non placet* because he had heard that *non placet* voters would be listed in the press and his diocese did not favor his taking such a stand.[90] After these discussions, which lasted through more than one meeting, "the great majority at the meeting voted for abstention."[91] But they resolved to make no final decision until the international committee of minority bishops had met.

At the international gathering, Darboy was not present because he was ill. Ginoulhiac and Dupont des Loges joined Louis Haynald, archbishop of Kalocsa, Hungary, in arguing that the minority should cast *non placet* votes publicly. But Dupanloup, arriving late, argued that the other council members would not believe a minority vote of *placet* and that the faithful would be scandalized by a minority vote of *non placet*.[92] The minority should abstain, he concluded, by absenting themselves from the plenary session. Mathieu and Josip Strossmayer, bishop of Djakovo, Croatia, also urged this course, and the international group finally voted in its favor.

The French minority thus joined other minority bishops in staying away from the public session of 18 July 1870. The minority accompanied their abstention with a letter to Pius IX, explaining that their

87. In this study, the French minority bishops are understood to include only the twenty-two Frenchmen who met together, maintained their opposition to the definition of papal infallibility throughout the council, and absented themselves from the final vote on 18 July 1870 because they would still have been bound in conscience to vote *non placet*. Hence I have not regarded bishops who finally voted for the definition to be true members of the minority.

88. "du discrédit qui frappera une définition de foi promulguée malgré l'opposition d'une minorité considérable" (Colet, "Copie des procès-verbaux rédigés par Mgr Colet des séances tenues par les évêques de la minorité," fol. 70).

89. "de s'abstenir d'assister à la session, si on ne croit pas pouvoir en conscience approuver la Constitution" (ibid.).

90. Ibid., fol. 71.

91. "la grande majorité de la réunion vote [*sic*] pour l'abstention" (ibid.).

92. Mourret, *Le concile du Vatican*, p. 307.

filial piety would not permit them to vote *non placet* before him.[93] Most of the twenty-two French minority bishops left Rome on the evening before the public vote, the rest within the next few days. On his way home, Dupanloup writes to a friend, "This momentous decision was taken despite all opposition."[94]

Conclusion

When they arrived at the council, the French minority bishops already shared a network of friendships and a common background of seminary training with a moderate gallican viewpoint. They also shared a dissatisfaction with the growing ultramontanist trends in the church, and they found a response to these trends in liberal or gallican ideas. Troubled in conscience at the prospect of a definition of papal infallibility, they quickly made common cause under the leadership of Darboy with the bishops of other countries who opposed the definition. At the council's end, they still felt bound not to support the definition, and so they left the council rather than vote against their conscience.

93. Mansi 52:1325A–1327B.
94. Félix Dupanloup to Augustin Cochin, 20 July 1870, quoted in Mourret, *Le concile du Vatican,* p. 316.

The Common Thought

Some Theological Presuppositions

――――――◆●►――――――

It is a strange theologian who would speak of the eucharist in the same manner that a mathematician discusses logarithm tables, writes the young Darboy. Theology should address the heart and intelligence, not only the logical sense.[1]

The other bishops of the French minority would have agreed. For most of them, theological views were shaped through interaction with concrete issues during times of change. As Darboy had suggested, the minority gave attention to more than the logical sense in their theology. The results formed a vibrant but coherent set of perspectives that served as important presuppositions for their later reflections on papal infallibility.

Several issues are important as background for understanding the position taken by the French minority bishops at the First Vatican Council. Their general attitude toward the relationship of church and state, especially in France, shaped many of their pastoral concerns about the effects that a definition of papal infallibility might have. Their theological understanding of the role of the bishop and of the ecumenical council formed important presuppositions for these bishops as they approached an ecumenical council within their own lifetime. These understandings in turn shaped their attitude toward the newspapers with their rumors about the upcoming council. The bishops' view of the pope and his temporal power was another factor in their thought. Finally, their understanding of infal-

1. Darboy, "Des leçons théologiques," pp. 534–35.

libility before arriving at the First Vatican Council forms important background for their conciliar behavior, as do their preconciliar efforts at puzzling over the problem of continuity and change in dogmatic teaching.

Spiritual and Temporal Orders in the Modern World

"The questions thus in agitation in France were of the religious-political order, rather than of the theological; they were questions of the relations of Church and State, of kinds of government, of theories on the ideal rights of the spiritual power in face of the civil," writes Butler.[2]

On such questions, the French minority bishops tried to steer a moderate course. They were aware of the dangers of an irreligious age, yet they knew that the church must adapt to the times. Between these two general concerns falls a spectrum of views on which the twenty-two can be located.

Protective of the church's interests, many minority bishops emphasized its independence from government interference. Dupont des Loges explained his opposition to the government's policy on the *Syllabus* and *Quanta cura* in a letter to Jules Baroche, government minister for worship, in which he stresses that the church's independence in the spiritual domain provides the foundation for its liberty to teach. If a government attributes to itself the authority to permit or to forbid promulgation of a papal teaching, it thereby constitutes itself the supreme judge in the spiritual order. Dupont des Loges dismisses with derision any support for government policy based on appeals to the gallican tradition of the superiority of general councils over the pope. Such an appeal, he believes, fails to note that the present government council is composed of laity from different religions or no religion who set themselves above the doctrinal decisions of the pope and bishops, thereby ignoring the Concordat's protection for the free exercise of Catholicism in France.[3]

Others echoed this concern for the liberty of the church. According to Colet, the church has rights which it cannot always exercise

2. Butler, *Vatican Council*, 1:72.
3. Paul Dupont des Loges to Jules Baroche, 10 January 1865, quoted in Félix Klein, *L'évêque de Metz, vie de Mgr Dupont des Loges, 1804–1886* (Paris: Charles Poussielgue, 1899), pp. 195–96.

but will never renounce. Two decades before the council, Darboy notes the importance of the reestablishment of local councils for the preservation of the church's freedom in France. For him, these councils parallel "the reception of the Council of Chalcedon." The liberties of the gallican church did not include the freedom to hold councils "except at the good pleasure of the king," often refused: "This is what gallicanism wanted. Well, if there is one thing it can boast about today, it is having reached the antipodes of the promised land. And, besides that, after two centuries of marching ahead—and with what humiliations! The clergy is less gallican than ever: this is the actual result."[4] Darboy's concern was the preservation of true liberty for the church and its bishops. He opposed any theory, including forms of gallican theory, that threatened such liberty.

Minority bishops continued to stand guard for the liberty of the church in France long after the council and the Empire ended,[5] but they did not object in principle to the French government or its institutions. Christianity does not preach any specified form of government, many maintained, and it condemns only those forms that are opposed to the church's mission for the salvation of souls.[6]

Some bishops believed that Christianity or the church was the source of good political order. The world had learned such principles as equality and fraternity from Christianity, claims Dupanloup. Thomas also believes that the church can take credit for all actions leading to human benevolence. Catholicism responds to human nature and its social needs, Guilbert writes. To ensure the state's existence and security, human beings need more than reason: they need a religion that can command their consciences to fulfill patriotic and moral obligations.[7]

4. Colet, "Souvenirs du concile du Vatican," fol. A; Darboy, "Des conciles récemment tenus," pp. 203, 212.

5. E.g., Flavien Hugonin, *Du droit ancien et du droit nouveau* (Paris: Victor Palmé, 1887), pp. 39–122; Joseph Foulon, Charles Place, et al., *Exposé de la situation faite à l'église en France et déclaration des éminentissimes cardinaux* (Besançon: H. Bossanne, 1892), p. 3 (the other authors were Julien Desprez of Toulouse, Benoit Langénieux of Reims, and François Richard of Paris).

6. E.g., Flavien Hugonin, *Discours de S.G. Mgr l'évêque de Bayeux et Lisieux au Congrès des Associations Ouvrières Catholiques à Caen* (Bayeux: Octave Payan, 1886), pp. 8, 11; Charles Colet, "Lettre circulaire prescrivant des prières à l'occasion des élections," *La semaine religieuse de la ville et du diocèse de Tours* 10 (12 February 1876):705; see also Charles Place, *Lettre de l'archevêque de Rennes à M.le Président de la République* (Rennes: H. Vatar, 1880), p. 5.

7. Félix Dupanloup, *L'église et le progrès social*, cited by Henri Edouard Dutoit,

Ideally, church and state should live in accord, Dupanloup writes in 1845. Accord between the temporal and the spiritual should also be reflected in intellectual life. Sola hopes for an end to the conflict between science and religion. Nature is "God's book," he reminds a group of young students. Christian philosophy should meet the challenges of the modern age, writes Hugonin in 1893. In an attempt to meet such challenges, Meignan examines and evaluates the beginnings of German critical biblical exegesis in the introduction to his study of David. In earlier works in which he had examined biblical criticism, he had maintained that science and faith are not in conflict over human origins, finding proofs for this harmony in the historical character of Genesis, the unity of the human species, and the possibility of a primitive unity within human language.[8] So the idea of concord between church and state was enlarged to envision a similar concord between faith and reason, religion and science.

But the immediate practical implications of harmony between church and state commanded more attention from minority bishops than did such theoretical themes, and many went farther than simply advocating the peaceful accord of the spiritual and the temporal. Maret was one bishop who advocated, not just tolerated, the French form of government during the Empire. His thought on infallibility cannot be understood without attention to the social side of his

---

Dupanloup (Paris: Desclée de Brouwer et Cie, 1933), p. 528; Léon Thomas, *Deuxième Congrès des Catholiques de Normandie: Discours de S.G. Mgr l'archevêque de Rouen* (Rouen: Mégard et Cie, 1885), pp. 14–15; Aimé Guilbert, *Sur l'avenir social du catholicisme* (Amiens: Delattre-Lenoel, 1881), p. 15; see also Georges Darboy, "Lettre pastorale à l'occasion de l'encyclique *Quanta cura* en date du 8 décembre 1864," in *Oeuvres pastorales*, 2 vols. (Paris: Adrien le Clere, 1876) 1:412.

8. Félix Dupanloup, *De la pacification religieuse* (Paris: J. Lecoffre, 1845); Jean Sola, *Discours prononcé à la distribution des prix du lycée de Nice* (Nice: Caisson et Mignon, 1873), p. 6; Flavien Hugonin, *Lettre de Mgr l'évêque de Bayeux et Lisieux sur l'enseignement de la philosophie aux professeurs de nos établissements diocésains* (Bayeux: Octave Payan, 1893), pp. 6–7; Guillaume Meignan, *David, roi, psalmiste, prophète, avec une introduction sur la nouvelle critique* (Paris: Victor Lecoffre, 1889). The introduction aroused negative comment, so Meignan requested Leo XIII to examine it. Leo's examiner concluded, "I would not have signed the introduction, but I see nothing there to criticize" (*Dictionnaire de la Bible*, s.v. "Meignan, Guillaume René," by Octave Rey). See also Meignan, *Les évangiles et la critique au XIXe siècle* (Paris: Victor Palmé, 1870); Meignan, *Le monde et l'homme primitif selon la Bible* (Paris: Victor Palmé, 1869). Despite his advanced understanding of critical biblical exegesis, however, Meignan seems to have kept much of it out of his books. Alfred Loisy recounts a long discussion with Meignan, shortly before he was made a cardinal, which suggests the archbishop was very cautious, even devious (*Mémoires pour servir à l'histoire religieuse*

work. During his early attempts to reconcile faith with reason and Catholicism with the needs of the times, Maret had believed that the thought of Lammenais would prove a solution. But gradually his view shifted, so that by 1852 he had rejected the ultramontanism in Lammenais.[9] For Maret, according to his biographer, the great question of the nineteenth century was the general conciliation of orthodoxy and liberalism, a conciliation that would allow the church to operate in the modern world without regarding modern thought as the enemy of orthodoxy. In his 1862 memorandum to the bishops, Maret notes that the great task of the century—"to reconcile science with faith, liberty with religion, legitimate progress with Catholic Christianity"—would remain unfinished until the church took account of modern thought. Catholic liberalism, writes Maret, respects the freedom of all orthodox opinions. It professes moderate views on the nature and exercise of authority and accepts frankly, "without regret and without turning back," the conditions of modern society and the position in which it places the church and the clergy.[10]

Outdated church procedures worried Maret. He argued that giving bishops a series of secret propositions about modern errors with no chance for public discussion contrasted badly with procedures of civil institutions and might lead some to revolt against the church. Although it is not by nature an absolute monarchy, the church "has for some centuries increasingly tended to assume the form of an absolute monarchy: everything is in the hands of Roman congregations composed almost exclusively of Italians."[11]

In light of such concerns, Maret's alarm at the appearance of the *Syllabus* is easy to understand. The treatment of the church-state relationship especially distressed him because it seemed to require

de notre temps. 3 vols. [Paris: Emile Nourry, 1930–31], 1:224–32). I am grateful to Daniel Donovan for bringing this passage to my attention.

9. An account of Maret's intellectual development is available in R. Thysmans, "Le gallicanisme de Mgr Maret et l'influence de Bossuet," *Revue d'histoire ecclésiastique* 52 (1957):401–65. On Lammenais, see Peter Stearns, *Priest and Revolutionary: Lammenais and the Dilemma of French Catholicism* (New York: Harper & Row, 1967).

10. Henri Maret, *Mémoire* (21 September 1862), cited in Bazin, *Vie de Maret*, 2:240, 246, 261–63.

11. Ibid., pp. 252–53; ibid., quoted in Palanque, *Catholiques libéraux et gallicans en France*, p. 30. A typographical error in Palanque leaves some doubt as to whether he is quoting Maret directly or paraphrasing.

Catholics to oppose French political structures that he regarded as legitimate. He writes to Pius IX, "These aspirations to intellectual freedom, to freedom of conscience, of the press, of worship, are not bad in themselves; it is only their abuse which is bad."[12]

Another bishop who defended the French form of government, now that of the Third Republic, was Guilbert. Less negative than many Catholics about the French Revolution and democracy, Guilbert even finds some justification for democracy in the Scriptures.[13] He argues that democracy, a torrent with good and bad, carries the modern world along with it. Democracy eliminates the shocking inequality of privilege and treats people as equals before the law, as before God, he notes with approval. Guilbert echoes other minority bishops, however, when he sees the church as the means of salvation for the providential current of democracy. Only the church gives the true meaning of liberty, equality, fraternity.[14] In fact, he argues, what people love about the modern world finds its source in the Gospel.[15]

His openness to the modern age led Guilbert to emphasize repeatedly that the church should not dictate any specified political form.[16] He spoke out often, sometimes alone, urging the French church to abandon opposition to the government and work instead for laws favorable to the church.[17] He even wrote a catechism lesson to be read from diocesan pulpits, in which he instructs Catholics on their right and duty to vote and warns them only to refrain from voting for an enemy of religion.[18]

But it is Dupanloup's interpretation of the *Syllabus* and of *Quanta*

12. Henri Maret to Pius IX, 29 January 1865, cited in Bazin, *Vie de Maret*, 2:329, quote on p. 334.

13. Aimé Guilbert, *La démocratie et son avenir social et religieux*, 2d ed. (Bordeaux: Feret et Fils, 1886), pp. 5–8. Guilbert finds support for democracy in Matt. 23:8 and Gal. 3:27–28.

14. Ibid., pp. 11, 13–16.

15. Aimé Guilbert, *Lettre pastorale et mandement de Mgr l'évêque de Gap à l'occasion de son entrée dans le diocèse* (Gap: Delaplace, 1867), p. 8; see also Guilbert, *La démocratie et son avenir*, pp. 15, 35; Guilbert, *La crise religieuse et la pacification* (Amiens: Delattre-Lenoel, 1880), pp. 22–23; Guilbert, *Abolition du concordat et séparation de l'église et de l'état* (Bordeaux: Duverdier et Cie, 1885), pp. 17–18.

16. Aimé Guilbert, *Lettre de Mgr l'évêque de Gap à un sénateur sur la crise religieuse présente* (Gap: J. C. Richaud, 1879), pp. 3–4; see also Guilbert, *L'église et la République: A MM. les sénateurs, les députés et les électeurs* (Gap: J. C. Richaud, 1879), pp. 2–7.

17. *Dictionnaire de théologie catholique*, s.v. "Libéralisme catholique," by C. Constantin.

18. Aimé Guilbert, *Des devoirs du prêtre touchant la politique et une leçon de catéchisme sur les élections* (Gap: J. C. Richaud, 1876).

cura that probably best represents the approach of most French minority bishops to the relationship of spiritual and temporal matters. His ability to mediate between the good of the church and modern ideas had been called into action before the *Syllabus* appeared in the construction of the Falloux law in 1850 and in his continuing defense of the pope's temporal power.[19] Dupanloup preferred to emphasize the common bonds between the church and modern society rather than the differences; he preferred the advantages of concrete and achievable guarantees to more thorough but theoretical stances. Dupanloup argues that the church adapts to the times in which it lives like a river that receives new streams and adapts to many climates. For him, Aubert argues, moderate paths seemed the only ones by which to ensure the successful defense of Catholicism in the modern world.[20]

Thus when Pius IX published the *Syllabus* and *Quanta cura*, Dupanloup leapt to the defense of a "true" meaning of the pope's words, distorted and misunderstood by the enemies of religion, exaggerated and manipulated by the (unnamed) ultramontanists.[21] Again he argues against two fronts, the irreligious and the intransigent pious, and portrays the latter as somehow betraying the pope by distorting his meaning.[22]

Although the twenty-two bishops did not always agree about the French government, certain general perspectives characterized their thought. While concerned to protect the interests of the church, most thought such protection was best achieved through some accommodation to modern ideas. Convinced of the necessity of religion and of the church for the proper functioning of even the temporal order, the group nevertheless tried to avoid a total identification of the church with any particular form of government. Some

19. Dupanloup was an architect of the Falloux law of 1850, which won for Catholics the right to set up primary and secondary schools and the right for qualified Catholics, including religious orders, to teach in them. His defense of the pope's temporal power in such works as *La souveraineté pontificale selon le droit catholique et le droit européen* (Paris: Lecoffre, 1860) won him international acclaim.

20. Félix Dupanloup, *Lettre sur le futur concile oecuménique* (Paris: Charles Douniol, 1868), pp. 18–19; Aubert, "Dupanloup."

21. Félix Dupanloup, *La convention du 15 septembre et l'encyclique du 8 décembre* (Paris: Charles Douniol, 1865). This brochure was translated into the major European languages and received the approbation of Pius IX.

22. This interpretation follows that of Aubert, "Dupanloup." For a lengthier dis-

could defend such modern ideas as increased liberties and democracy; most could support Dupanloup in his moderate path of interpretation for the embarrassing *Syllabus*.

Devotion to the Pope and the Temporal Sovereignty of the Papacy

Devotion to the person of the pope and defense of the temporal sovereignty of the papacy were two themes often combined in the work of the French minority bishops. On each theme, their position is almost unanimous. Most took opportunities to reaffirm personal devotion to Pius IX and to defend the papacy's right to temporal power.

"Let us love the Church, let us love the pope!" Foulon exhorts his diocese at the death of Pius IX. "It is no longer possible to make a distinction between these two loves." Before the council, Foulon refers to the pope as "the common father of pastors and the faithful"; he sees the chair of Peter as the "center of unity and truth." Dupanloup also teaches the importance of the pope for Catholicism. In his edition of Bossuet's catechism, Dupanloup holds that Christ established the pope as head of the church and gave him a primacy of honor and jurisdiction over the other bishops.[23] Darboy, whose relationship with the Vatican remained stormy for years, could still plan to preach at a retreat:

At the first level of the hierarchy is the sovereign pontiff. For this great and venerable authority, we all profess the most profound respect. Our feelings toward it are consistent with all that the councils have defined about it, particularly the Council of Florence, in the magnificent terms which you all know. It is in these same terms that we love to express our thoughts; surely no one can demand that we go beyond this. . . .—I will dwell no more on

---

cussion of Dupanloup's interpretation of the *Syllabus*, see Aubert, "Mgr Dupanloup et le Syllabus."

23. Joseph Foulon, "Lettre pastorale prescrivant des prières à l'occasion de la mort de notre saint père le Pape Pie IX et pour l'élection de son successeur," in *Oeuvres pastorales de Monseigneur Foulon*, ed. François Jules Demange, 2 vols. (Nancy: Société Nancéienne de Propagande, 1882), 2:195; Foulon, "Lettre pastorale à l'occasion du cinquantième anniversaire de la première messe de notre saint père le Pape," ibid., 1:34, 36; Félix Dupanloup, *Le catéchisme chrétien: Suivi d'un sommaire de toute la doctrine du symbole, par Boussuet* (Orléans: Blanchard, 1865), p. 30.

this subject so that one may not suspect, in the courteous and affectionate expressions which I shall use about an authority which I venerate and love, concerns which are beneath me.[24]

And David, who would defend himself against other reproaches by referring to his own "strong gallican convictions, all so well-known, so firmly established, and so old," still showed "filial reverence toward the pope," in the view of his funeral orator. David mentions the "kindness" of the pope in a letter to his diocese; he complains that the *Syllabus* was misunderstood. Even an explanation of the limits on papal power becomes a compliment to the pope in David's explanation: "We know the limits which the power of Peter should not exceed, our doctors have passed this conception on to us. The ocean itself has its boundaries in its plenitude, Bossuet said magnificently, and if it went beyond them it would become a deluge which would devastate the universe."[25]

Because France drew on its troops to help Pius IX maintain control over the Papal States until the outbreak of the Franco-Prussian War in 1870, the question of the papacy's temporal sovereignty was important in France. Just as they were devoted to Pius IX, the French minority also agreed in their defense of his rights to temporal power, which they supported as a means to maintain his freedom.

24. "Au premier degré de la hiérarchie est le Souverain Pontife. Nous professons tous, pour cette grande et vénérable autorité, le respect le plus profond, et nous avons d'elle des sentiments conformes à tout ce que les Conciles en ont défini, surtout le Concile de Florence, dans les termes magnifiques que vous connaissez tous. C'est dans ces mêmes termes que nous aimons à exprimer nos pensées; personne ne peut assurément exiger que nous allions au-delà. . . .—Je n'insisterai pas davantage sur cet article, pour que l'on ne soupçonne pas, dans les expressions courtoises et affectueuses que j'emploirai [*sic*] vis-à-vis d'une autorité que je vénère et que j'aime, les [*sic*] préoccupations d'esprit qui sont au-dessous de moi" (Georges Darboy, Notes for Retreat Conferences, IDVIII, 1, Archives d'Archevêché de Paris). This manuscript seems to be written in the first person as sermon notes, although it also contains another hand, perhaps that of a secretary. One wonders if Darboy is not defending himself against the continuing accusations of Pius IX against him; see below, at nn. 49–52.

25. "convictions gallicanes tout [*sic*] si notoires, si arrêtées et si vieilles" (Augustin David to unnamed correspondent, 11 December 1861, F192.575, Archives Nationales, Paris). Jean Marie Bécel, *Oraison funèbre de Mgr David, évêque de Saint-Brieuc et Tréguier* (Vannes: Galles, 1882), p. 10; David, Circular Letter to Diocese, 26 May 1870, *La semaine religieuse du diocèse de Saint-Brieuc et Tréguier* 3 (4 June 1870):343; David, *Oraison funèbre de Pie IX* (Saint-Brieuc: L. Prud'homme, 1878), p. 19; David, Sermon on the Papacy for the Feast of the Chair of St. Peter, 18 January 1851, quoted in M. R. Durand, "Communication de M. R. Durand—Mgr David, évêque de Saint-Brieuc (1862–82) et le concile du Vatican," *Bulletin de le Société d'Histoire Moderne*, ser. 3, 5 (23 April 1911):44.

For the pope to maintain the independence of his spiritual power, David argues, he must maintain his temporal power.[26] Dupanloup also defended the pope's temporal sovereignty for many years.[27] For the pope to fulfill his role as judge, he must be free of pressure, Dupanloup writes in his 1860 work on the question. Even after the events of the war, he maintains that religion, necessary to France, is linked to the independence of the pope.[28]

Many minority bishops tied temporal sovereignty to Christian doctrine. Foulon believed that it was the work of God's providence, ensuring the pope his power and freedom. Citing de Maistre, Mathieu argues that spiritual and temporal power, although distinguishable in theory, mix inevitably in practice. Also tying temporal sovereignty to Christian doctrine, Darboy argues that it is a historic right and an institution necessary at the time: "If it is not a dogma of faith, it is at least a truth which cannot be denied without error, nor combated without fault, since it is affirmed by the pope and the bishops, natural judges of the question."[29]

One minority bishop disagreed with the unquestioning support others gave to the papacy's temporal sovereignty. In a memorandum to the bishops, Maret writes that the Roman government has committed grave faults against French and Italian citizens. It has not always understood the great movement to restore nationality and liberty in both France and Italy.[30]

The French minority bishops repeatedly expressed personal devo-

26. Augustin David, *Le combat d'Auvours* (Saint-Brieuc: L. Prud'homme, 1874), p. 4; see also Paul Dupont des Loges, Address at Diocesan Synod of 1858, in *Oeuvres choisies*, ed. L. Willeumier (Paris: Charles Poussielgue, 1901), pp. 171–72.

27. An annotated bibliography of Dupanloup's works on temporal sovereignty of the pope is available in Aubert, "Dupanloup."

28. Dupanloup, *La souveraineté pontificale*; Dupanloup, *Discours de Mgr l'évêque d'Orléans prononcé à l'Assemblée Nationale sur l'indépendance nécessaire du Saint-Siège et les calomnies répandues dans ces derniers temps contre le clergé* (Paris: Charles Douniol, 1871), p. 14.

29. Joseph Foulon, "Allocution au clergé de Nancy avant le départ pour le concile," in *Oeuvres pastorales*, 1:62; Césaire Mathieu, *Le pouvoir temporel des papes justifié par l'histoire: Etude sur l'origine, l'exercice et l'influence de la souveraineté pontificale* (Paris: Adrien le Clere, 1863), p. 676; Georges Darboy to Pius IX, 1862, quoted in Foulon, *Histoire de Mgr Darboy*, p. 238. Theologians inclined to multiply truths closely tied to dogmas of the faith might find Darboy's view a useful deterrent because few would wish to defend Darboy today—slightly more than a century after his widely held opinion was expressed.

30. Henri Maret, *Mémoire* to bishops (21 September 1862), cited by Bazin, *Vie de Maret*, 2:265.

tion towards the pope, even when they disagreed with him. And although not many would go as far as Meignan, who believed that God punished France for its failure to defend the papacy, still these bishops generally supported the pope's temporal power.[31]

The Attack on Journalists

Although many of the French minority bishops supported certain newspapers,[32] they frequently criticized journalists in general and especially Louis Veuillot and his paper, *L'Univers.*

The minority defended jealously their right as bishops to judge doctrine; they resented any infringement of that right by journalists. Because *L'Univers* discusses questions to be treated at the council, David ridicules it for having erected "contempt for episcopal authority into a system in which lay people set themselves up as judges when there is question of proclaiming a dogma."[33] Trying to assuage the fears of his diocese before the council, Meignan writes, "Fear neither the words of our enemies, nor those of certain journalists who take upon themselves a mission which they do not possess." Guilbert advises his listeners to seek information about the church from bishops and the pope, not from journalists or theologians who lack mandate. Bravard goes further, saying the newspapers are full of false news. Looking in newspapers or pamphlets for news about the council, he suggests, shows one to be not only imprudent but less than a true child of the Church.[34]

31. Guillaume Meignan, Pastoral Letter for Lent 1871, cited by Boissonnot, *Le Cardinal Meignan*, p. 308.

32. Different French minority bishops were associated with *L'ère nouvelle, Le correspondant*, and *L'ami de la religion.*

33. Augustin David to diocesan clergy, confidential letter, 20 April 1870, quoted in Durand, "Mgr David et le concile du Vatican," p. 46. This letter was later divulged to the public—through the author's intention, Durand suggests (p. 45).

34. "Ne croyez ni à la parole de nos ennemis, ni à celle de certains publicistes, qui se donnent une mission qu'ils ne possèdent pas." (Guillaume Meignan, "Lettre circulaire et mandement de Mgr l'évêque de Châlons, à l'occasion de son départ pour le concile oecuménique du Vatican," *La semaine champenoise* 4 [4 November 1869]: 454); Guilbert, *Abolition du Concordat et séparation de l'église et l'état*, p. 21; see also Flavien Hugonin's remarks at a diocesan meeting, cited by "Nouvelles diocésaines," *La semaine religieuse du diocèse de Bayeux et Lisieux* 5 (21 November 1869):748; Jean Bravard, "Lettre pastorale et mandement de Monseigneur l'évêque de Coutances et d'Av-

Dupanloup frequently criticizes journalists for their discussion of papal infallibility before the council's start, a discussion he feels places pressure on the bishops.[35] Many years before his direct attack on Veuillot, Dupanloup had forbidden teachers under his authority to read *L'Univers* and had made an unsuccessful attempt to have the paper condemned by the French bishops.[36] On the eve of the council, Dupanloup attacks Veuillot's journalism for its failure to make important distinctions, for its party spirit, and for its condemnation of Catholics who disagreed with *L'Univers*. Dupanloup is surprised that Veuillot should raise the question of papal infallibility before the council begins, and he charges that his own entrance into its public discussion is caused by the editor's faulty treatment of the question.[37] But Dupanloup's complaints did not prevent others from criticizing his behavior; many fellow bishops criticized his *Observations* not for its views but for the expression of those views in a public journalistic style.[38]

Colet writes that minority bishops at the council were attacked by Catholic newspapers approved by Rome, and "a sort of crusade was organized for the purpose of stirring up against them the priests and the faithful of their respective dioceses." He adds, "The situation was certainly painful."[39]

In short, minority bishops often opposed newspapers and journalists because they considered news treatment of the council to be misleading and an invasion of episcopal rights.

---

ranches, au clergé et aux fidèles de son diocèse, pour le Carême de 1870," *Revue catholique (Semaine religieuse) du diocèse de Coutances et Avranches* 3 (10 March 1870):373; see also Mathieu's criticism of the newspapers as information sources in Mansi 52:723D.

35. Dupanloup, *Observations sur la controverse*, p. 5; see also p. 8, as well as the articles signed François Beslay but written by Dupanloup's vicar general François Lagrange, according to Aubert (*Vatican I*, p. 82). They are described by Palanque, *Catholiques libéraux et gallicans en France*, pp. 78–79. Although he incorrectly attributes them to Dupanloup, they certainly would have received the bishop's approval.

36. Aubert, "Dupanloup." Aubert believes that this effort made Rome suspicious of Dupanloup for what was perceived as an attempt to restrain ultramontanism.

37. Dupanloup, *Avertissement à Veuillot*, pp. 4–19.

38. Aubert, "Dupanloup au début du concile," pp. 102–3.

39. "une sorte de croisade fut organisée en vue de soulever contre eux les prêtres et les fidèles de leurs diocèses respectifs." "La situation était assurément pénible" (Colet, "Souvenirs du concile du Vatican," fol. Q).

The Authority of the Bishop

Denying the rights of the bishop can be just as heretical as denying those of the pope's.[40] This warning of Ramadié to his diocese summarizes a central concern in the theological perspective of the French minority: the divinely constituted authority of the bishop.

The bishop is "judge of the faith." More than any other episcopal task, that of judging was stressed by the French minority. "As judge, he pronounces and defines," writes David in one of the many discussions of this role.[41] The certitude of their right to judge doctrine, especially at an ecumenical council, stood behind much of the minority's unhesitating opposition to the will of the majority at the council.

Many combined the right to judge with other episcopal responsibilities. Ginoulhiac, for example, reflects on the pastoral epistles and notes that the bishop teaches, judges, and governs. The bishop guards the church and its holy rules; he is the image of the risen Christ.[42]

As judges, Darboy maintains, the bishops interpret the Gospel, source of the church's beliefs. This means, Dupanloup points out,

40. Etienne Ramadié, cited by "Nouvelles du diocèse," *Semaine religieuse du diocèse de Perpignan* 1 (27 November 1869):796.

41. David to diocesan clergy, 20 April 1870, cited by Durand, "Mgr David et le concile du Vatican," p. 45. Among the many who assert that the bishop is judge are Colet, "Souvenirs du concile du Vatican," fol. N; Dupont des Loges, "Pastorale retraite" (1869), in *Oeuvres choisies*, p. 325; Flavien Hugonin, Teaching for the Council, cited by Stanislaus Touchet, *Mgr Hugonin, évêque de Bayeux et Lisieux: Sa vie, sa mort et ses funérailles* (Bayeux: S. A. Duvant, 1898), p. 46, n. 1; Meignan, "De son départ," p. 453; Charles Place, "A l'occasion de son prochain départ pour le concile oecuménique," *La semaine liturgique de Marseille* 8 (21 November 1869):836; Ramadié, cited by "Nouvelles du diocèse," p. 797. A reference to the role of bishop as judge almost always serves as a declaration of an episcopal right, though Mathieu follows such an assertion with a comment on papal rights: "There is before him, above him, another judge, another guide who directs him." Mathieu is defending his reading of *Quanta cura* in *Sénat: Discours prononcé par S. Em. le Cardinal Mathieu, sénateur, dans la discussion de l'adresse* (Paris: Charles Lahure, 1865), p. 9.

42. Jacques Ginoulhiac, *Les épîtres pastorales, ou réflexions dogmatiques et morales sur les épîtres de saint Paul à Timothée et à Tite* (Paris: Victor Palmé, 1866), pp. 5, 60–63. Deepening Ginoulhiac's point, Rivet writes that Christ, assisting the bishops, is guard and judge in his church in "Sur l'église," in Jacques Migne, ed., *Collection intégrale et universelle des orateurs sacrés*, 2d ser., vols. 68–99 (Paris: Petit-Montrouge, 1856–66), 84(1856):103. Darboy says that Christ is "the supreme bishop of our souls" in his Pastoral Letter on the Occasion of Entrance to the Archdiocese of Paris, in *Oeuvres pastorales*, 1:233.

that bishops have a right to teach. Bishops have the right to speak in council, David asserts against his opponents. But this right does not extend to priests or to the laity.[43]

David also emphasizes another task of the bishop closely related to judging: the bishop gives witness or testimony of the faith of those he represents. David writes that the bishop, "as witness . . . attests the faith which he has found not only in his diocese, but in all the regions where he has lived in close contact with Christian souls." Colet also relates the two roles of witness and judge: "Consequently the bishops who make up the Council are, above all, witnesses. They testify to and certify what has been received as dogma and professed until now. But they are also judges, with this reservation, however, that their judiciary power should not go beyond their power as witnesses."[44]

The mission of the apostles was to express the unity of the whole church and of local churches with Christ, writes Ginoulhiac. The apostles represented the corporate nature of the church, and the bishops continue their double work of knowledge and charity.[45] It is to the group of apostles that assistance is guaranteed, Rivet maintains.[46] Preservation of apostolic doctrine is thus maintained by communion with the body of the churches and principally with the

43. Darboy, On the Occasion of Entrance to the Archdiocese of Paris, p. 234; see Dupanloup's comments on the small catechism in Mansi 50:718B–724C; ibid., 52:988B; David to diocesan clergy, 20 April 1870, cited by Durand, "Mgr David et le concile du Vatican," p. 45; see also Dubourg, Oraison funèbre de David, p. 37.

44. David to diocesan clergy, 20 April 1870, quoted in Durand, "Mgr David et le concile du Vatican," p. 45. "Les Evêques qui composent le Concile sont donc avant tout témoins. Ils déposent et constatent ce qu [sic] ont reçu comme dogme et professé jusqu'ici. Mais ils sont aussi Juges, sous cette Réserve pourtant que leur pouvoir judiciaire ne doit pas dépasser leur pouvoir de témoins" (Colet, "Souvenirs du concile du Vatican," fol. N). On the bishop as witness, see also Hugonin, Teaching for the Council, cited by Touchet, Hugonin, p. 44; on Ramadié's understanding of his witness role, Cabrières, Eloge funèbre de Ramadié, p. 28.

45. Jacques Ginoulhiac, Les origines du christianisme, 2 vols. (Paris: A. Durand et Pedone Lauriel, 1878), 2:261; Ginoulhiac, Oraison funèbre de Monseigneur Marie Nicolas Fournier, évêque de Montpellier (Montpellier: Auguste Seguin, 1835), pp. 3–4. Alfred Loisy notes a certain levity in Meignan's approach to apostolic succession. As the bishop was playing billiards with an Algerian priest, he struck him on the shoulder and exclaimed, "To think, my good friend, that we are the successors of the apostles!" (Loisy, Mémoires, p. 224, quoted in Albert Houtin and Félix Sartiaux, Alfred Loisy: Sa vie, son oeuvre, bibliog. and bio-bibliog. index by Emile Poulat [Paris: Editions du Centre National de la Recherche Scientifique, 1960], p. 271).

46. Rivet, "Sur l'église," pp. 106–7. Rivet cites Matt. 28:18–20 to show that assistance is promised to the apostles as a group.

church of Rome, Darboy explains: "If we ask you to listen to our teaching with a docile and trusting ear, it is because we are in communion with the churches of the Catholic world, and principally with the Roman Church, their center of unity and their indefectible sovereign; and since the episcopate forms one single body of united members, our fraternal relations with the leading pastors witness to our orthodoxy and guarantee the purity of our doctrine."[47] The bishop also holds a divine right to govern or legislate for the church, French minority bishops often state.[48]

Perhaps the attitude of episcopal independence shared in varying degrees by all the French minority bishops is best manifested by the lengthy controversy between Darboy and the Vatican, which began in 1864, touched off by a series of incidents related to the bishop's jurisdiction within his diocese.[49] Appeal was made to Rome, and Darboy was reprimanded, but on 1 September 1864 he responds with a lengthy self-justification, charging that the Vatican complaints were vague, hasty, and suspicious. He continues with a defense of episcopal rights, maintaining that normally a bishop has the right to judge cases in his diocese without an appeal to Rome: "The regularly established bishops are judges, under the control of the Holy See, and sole judges of what is needful or harmful to the spiritual interests of their dioceses." In his own diocese, "by divine right," the bishop "is the judge and a good judge until there is proof to the contrary"; an appeal to Rome should be made only for extraordinary reasons. In opposing the usurpation of episcopal authority, Darboy says, he is rendering a true service to the church and to the Apostolic See.[50]

Darboy continues his outspoken opposition to Vatican interference, and relationships worsen when Pius IX makes further accusations against him. Remaining dissatisfied with Darboy's counterevi-

47. Georges Darboy, Pastoral letter on the occasion of entrance to the diocese of Nancy, in *Oeuvres pastorales*, 1:10; see also Darboy, "Lettre pastorale sur le prochain concile," in *Oeuvres pastorales*, 2:407, and Joseph Foulon, who emphasizes more than Darboy a submission to the pope in "Lettre pastorale pour la prise de possession du siège épiscopal de Nancy et de Toul," in *Oeuvres pastorales*, 1:5.

48. Colet, "Souvenirs du concile du Vatican," fol. A; Joseph Foulon (to Félix Dupanloup?), 24 March 1869, AB XIX 524, Archives Nationales, Paris; Hugonin, Teaching for the Council, p. 44.

49. See Chapter 1, n. 27, for references on the controversy between Darboy and the Vatican.

50. Georges Darboy to Pius IX, 1 September 1864, quoted in "Monseigneur Darboy et le Saint-Siège," pp. 244, 247–52, 254.

dence in his own support, Pius IX criticizes Darboy on 26 October 1865 for holding opinions "entirely opposed to the divinely established primacy of the Roman pontiff over the universal Church," opinions like those of Febronius. Darboy answers in a simple defense, "I am full of respect and devotion toward your person, and . . . I have no other doctrine than that of the Church." A visit to Rome seemed to end the issue, but on 16 June 1868 the pope's letter of reproach was printed in Canada and then reprinted in France. Darboy was furious and was certain that the letter had been leaked from the Vatican.[51] The Vatican expressed regrets for the leak. With these events fresh in his memory, Darboy soon was making plans to return to Rome for the council.[52]

The French minority bishops believed that the role of the bishop was "brazenly misunderstood" in their time, and they intended to defend it.[53] They emphasized the right of the bishop to judge doc-

51. Pius IX to Georges Darboy, 26 October 1865, cited by Palanque, *Catholiques libéraux et gallicans en France*, p. 24; Darboy to Pius IX, 1 January 1866, quoted in "Monseigneur Darboy et le Saint-Siège," p. 265; Darboy to Giacomo Antonelli, cardinal and secretary of state for Pius IX, 25 August 1868, ibid., p. 273.

52. Palanque notes that, despite its apology, the Vatican probably did reveal the pope's letter of reproach in an effort to compromise the reputation of the independent archbishop of Paris (*Catholiques libéraux et gallicans en France*, p. 25); but compare *Dictionnaire d'histoire et de géographie ecclésiastiques*, s.v. "Darboy (Georges)," by François Guédon. Darboy's notes show that he knew of the rumor that he would never be made cardinal (Darboy to Antonelli, cited in "Monseigneur Darboy et le Saint-Siège," p. 277). But he never fell sway to the mediation efforts by Henry Manning, archbishop of Westminster, that would have rewarded Darboy with a cardinal's hat in return for a public submission (Durand, "Mgr Darboy et le Saint-Siège," p. 10). The editors of his journal charge Darboy with a proud and independent attitude approaching inflexibility (Darboy, "Le journal," p. 420, n. 7). But there is room for another, more admiring interpretation of the fearless archbishop when we consider, for example, what he wrote to Ernest Armand, envoy of the French ambassador to Rome, on 8 March 1869: "I could accept a favor from the Holy Father, but not beg for it: I am the sort of person who can give himself, not one who may be bought" ("Monseigneur Darboy et le Saint-Siège," p. 279). Darboy would write in his journal at the council: "Archbishop Manning seems to fear that the definition of papal infallibility will not be voted for unanimously. He tells me that I could do much *to bring about this unanimity*. Without it, they will not dare to proceed. He gives me to understand that this would be advantageous for me.—I answered him that I would be concerned neither with pleasing nor displeasing; that given the attitude which the Holy See has taken toward me by its odious publication, I cannot show hostility, because that would be seen as spite, which is beneath me; nor can I make concessions and perform acts of courtesy, because that would be attributed to ambitious considerations, which I disdain" ("Le journal," entry for 6 December 1869, pp. 420–21).

53. Etienne Ramadié, "Oraison funèbre de Monseigneur le Cardinal de Rohan-Chabot," in Migne, ed., *Collection intégrale et universelle des orateurs sacrés*, 84:764.

trine after thorough discussion with other bishops in which they witness or testify to their faith and that of their dioceses. They understood that through such witness, a bishop represented in his testimony the faith of his entire community. In addition, the French minority bishops noted their part in governing the church—each ordinarily independent within his own diocese, as Darboy emphasized, but in communion with other bishops and with the pope, thus succeeding to the mission of the apostles. R. Thysmans draws attention to a positive aspect of Maret's theology, which also characterized the French minority bishops as a group: they had "a very keen sense of the bishop and of the place which is his by divine right within the constitution of the Church."[54] This emphasis on the role of the bishop was one of the most characteristic aspects of the group's theology.

Hopes for the Council

Announcement that a council would be held drew great hope initially from the French minority bishops. Not only did they rejoice at the failure of the ultramontanists to prevent a council, but some even felt that its calling was in part their personal accomplishment.[55] Even when rumors of a possible definition of papal infallibility began to worry the minority, they continued to share their hopes for the council with their dioceses. Many believed the troubled state of the world made the council necessary.[56] Dupanloup listed the Enlightenment, rationalism, the French Revolution, and other social changes as causes necessitating a council. Not all of these were evils, but the nineteenth century was more agitated than most, Dupanloup believed, and contemporary errors were the main source of evils.[57]

54. Thysmans, "Le gallicanisme de Mgr Maret et l'influence de Bossuet," p. 465.

55. Palanque, *Catholiques libéraux et gallicans en France*, pp. 70–71. Palanque says that both Dupanloup and Maret considered themselves partly responsible for the calling of the council. Maret's entire theology was based on the consensus of pope and bishops in judging doctrine, and he recommended that councils be held periodically (Henri Maret, *Du concile général et de la paix religieuse*, 2 vols. [Paris: Henri Plon, 1869], 2:389–409).

56. Georges Darboy, "Lettre pastorale sur le prochain concile," in *Oeuvres pastorales,* 2:403; see also Charles Place, "Pour la publication de l'indulgence plénière, en forme de jubilé," *La semaine liturgique de Marseille* 8 (4 July 1869):502; Colet, "Souvenirs du concile du Vatican," fol. A; Foulon, "Allocution au clergé de Nancy avant le départ pour le concile," *Oeuvres pastorales,* 1:49–50.

57. Félix Dupanloup, *Lettre de M. l'évêque d'Orléans au clergé et aux fidèles de son*

The upcoming council, however, would not condemn the modern world. Reassurance of this point constituted a focus for many of the minority bishops. Meignan believes the council will not worsen the propositions of the *Syllabus*, nor will it condemn necessary modern developments or define matters best left undefined. "Entrust these sensitive issues to the infallible wisdom which has its seat in the Vatican, to the eminently prudent and practical minds of your bishops, who know the present bases for possible reforms and for the good that must be facilitated rather than impeded," he writes.[58] De Marguerye expresses hope that the council will address the problems of the modern world and of religious liberty, and Ginoulhiac believes that the council should undertake a reconciliation between the church and the modern world.[59]

In addition, many bishops tried to calm fears arising from rumors of division among themselves or from claims about the future council's outcome.[60] Fears that the pope will annul or absorb the episcopate, that he regards himself as personally infallible and superior to

---

diocèse à l'occasion des fêtes de Rome et pour leur annoncer le futur concile oecuménique (Paris: Charles Douniol, 1867), p. 14; Dupanloup, *Lettre de Mgr l'évêque d'Orléans au clergé et aux fidèles de son diocèse avant son départ pour Rome* (Paris: Charles Douniol, 1869), pp. 10–13. But Meignan thinks the biggest danger in Christian society is ignorance of Christianity by its enemies (Address to diocesan priests, quoted in Boissonnot, *Le Cardinal Meignan*, p. 242).

58. Guillaume Meignan to Jules Baroche, government minister, 29 July 1868, cited by Boissonnot, *Le Cardinal Meignan*, p. 271; Meignan, "De son départ," p. 454. For assurances that the council will not condemn the modern world, see also Darboy, "Lettre pastorale sur le prochain concile," pp. 413–15; Flavien Hugonin, Speech at Departure for the Council, cited by J. Laffetay, "Départ de Mgr l'évêque de Bayeux pour le concile," *La semaine religieuse du diocèse de Bayeux et Lisieux* 5 (21 November 1869):741; Place, "A l'occasion de son prochain départ pour le concile oecuménique," p. 836; Ramadié, cited in "Nouvelles du diocèse," *Semaine religieuse du diocèse de Perpignan* 1 (27 November 1869):798; Léon Thomas, "Lettre pastorale à l'occasion de son départ pour le concile oecuménique," *Bulletin religieux du diocèse de la Rochelle et Saintes* 6 (20 November 1869):243–46.

59. Frédéric de Marguerye to Félix Dupanloup, 18 May 1867, AB XIX 526, Archives Nationales, Paris; Ginoulhiac, *Le concile oecuménique*, p. 109, though Ginoulhiac makes clear that his understanding of such a reconciliation would involve a change on the part of modern society to accord with the church, not vice versa; for Bravard's hopes for the council, see his council speech in Mansi 52:306A–C.

60. For example, Augustin David, "Sur la cinquantaine de S.S. Pie IX," *La semaine religieuse du diocèse de Saint-Brieuc et Tréguier* 2 (3 April 1869):230; see also Charles Place, "Sur le prochain concile oecuménique," *La semaine liturgique de Marseille* 8 (14 February 1869):183, 186; François Rivet, Farewell Discourse on the Council, cited by Chevallier, *Rivet*, pp. 161–62.

councils, that the council will define new points of doctrine or points not certain to Catholic theologians: all of these are unnecessary because they reflect neither the pope's plans nor the church's ordinary conduct, Ginoulhiac assures his readers. After reconciliation between the church and the modern world, a reunion with "schismatic churches and separated communions" would be possible, Ginoulhiac believes, and Dupanloup hopes for the same unity with Christian "separated brothers" and even with Jews.[61] The council will stand as a great vision of unity, Dupanloup predicts, not divided into schools or parties, not forgetful of France's contributions to the church. The council's sole aim is peace in truth and charity, and perhaps this great spectacle of living unity will draw other Christians to reunion.[62]

The French minority bishops shared hopeful expectations about the council before its start. Convinced that the problems of the modern world necessitated the council's convocation, they were just as convinced that it would not condemn the modern world. In fact, they believed that the council promised peace and union between the church and the world, the church and other Christian groups.

The Nature of the Ecumenical Council

Discussions of a council's nature by the French minority bishops show the importance they placed on this aspect of the church. An ecumenical council, Dupanloup writes, is the "Catholic church assembled to do with more splendor the work which it accomplishes each day scattered over the whole earth, namely the transmission to men and the authentic interpretation of the dogmatic and moral truths contained in the Gospel revelation." The church assembled to teach: this understanding of a council is echoed by Ginoulhiac, who defines a council as "a legitimate assembly of bishops gathered to deliberate and to pronounce in common on questions having for their principal object faith, morals or the discipline of the church." Only bishops have a right to be seated at a council, to deliberate, and to pronounce, Ginoulhiac believes; but others may be invited, even heretics. The council is convoked and presided over by the pope or

---

61. Ginoulhiac, *Le concile oecuménique*, pp. 89–108, 109; Dupanloup, *Sur le futur concile oecuménique*, pp. 46–57.

62. Dupanloup, *Avant son départ*, pp. 6–10; Dupanloup, *Le futur concile oecuménique*, p. 261.

his legates, Bravard notes, and it must invite at least all bishops in communion with Rome.[63] Ecumenical councils have a divine origin, Ginoulhiac stresses, and only those assembled in Christ's name and with his authority "form his Church and exercise apostolic power."[64] Councils combat heresy or evil, and they reform the church.[65]

Dupanloup expects the upcoming council to be the most perfect representation of the church ever held. He ties this concept of representation to the nature of a council: "Ecumenical councils are, I have said, the solemn assizes of Catholicism, the general assemblies of the teaching Church. The pope convokes all the bishops of the world; they come from all quarters of the Christian universe. With the pope who is their leader and who presides over them, they represent all the churches, and, consequently, the universal Church." Colet states the point simply: "The Council is the representative of the whole Church, but it is not itself the Church."[66]

Many French minority bishops emphasized that a council manifests the corporate nature of the church and of its teaching office. The bishops in council and the pope cannot decide anything without each other, Bravard notes. He recounts the biblical story of the Council of Jerusalem, the first ecumenical council, where "all the apostles . . . pronounced the judgment," and he continues:

As soon as an error appeared, attacking the faith, the Church, its authority, moral doctrine or laws, the peace of nations was troubled; the successor of Peter, in concert with emperors and kings, or on his own initiative, convened the bishops in conciliar assemblies. There, they prayed, they searched Scripture and tradition, they studied, they sought truth and they established it with irrefutable proofs; then, the bishops judged, anathematized heresies and schisms, took the most appropriate measures for preserving intact the

---

63. Dupanloup, *Sur le futur concile oecuménique*, p. 10; Ginoulhiac, *Le concile oecuménique*, pp. 1, 25; Jean Bravard, Pastoral Letter on the Council, *Revue catholique (Semaine religieuse) du diocèse de Coutances et Avranches* 2 (17 June 1869):603 (see also Dupanloup, *Sur le futur concile oecuménique*, p. 11).

64. Ginoulhiac, *Le concile oecuménique*, p. 9.

65. Bravard, "De son prochain départ pour le saint concile du Vatican," *Revue catholique (Semaine religieuse) du diocèse de Coutances et Avranches* 3 (2 December 1869):149; Félix Dupanloup, "Speech at the Catholic Congress of Malines," *Catholic World* 6 (February 1868):592. The church is the only society that can reform itself without revolutions, Dupanloup says, because the deposit of faith serves as a principle of reform (*Sur le futur concile oecuménique*, pp. 14–19).

66. Dupanloup, *Le futur concile oecuménique*, p. 10. "Le Concile est la représentation de toute l'Eglise, mais il n'est pas l'Eglise elle-même" (Colet, "Souvenirs du concile du Vatican," fol. N).

revealed doctrines, and, the pope having sanctioned all these decrees, it was God himself who thus announced to men what they should believe and observe.

Ginoulhiac states the point concisely: "The pope presides; the emperors attend; the bishops judge." If the pope did not preside, the council would not be "the true and real representation of the universal Church." But all the bishops judge and interpret. Called by Christ in Matt. 18:20, they are gathered in his name, and thus he is present with them so that they form "a living and unique body, charged with the government of the Church," Ginoulhiac explains. Sometimes this permanent governing body manifests itself in the form of a council. Guilbert agrees: "The sovereign pontiff, with his brother bishops—be they assembled in council or even dispersed—speaks to the whole spiritual world." Although not necessary, councils are good because "in unanimous opinions and common efforts there is a plenitude of light and authority which settles uncertain minds in a better way, and inspires everyone with a fuller respect," Darboy believes.[67]

The French minority bishops believed that councils were reliable legislative assemblies. Even by human standards, Meignan argues, a council should raise expectation of good resolutions: its members are wise, free of earthly ambitions, aided by the Gospel, theology, saints, and prayer.[68] A council presents Gospel teaching that will be persuasive for its hearers: "Assisted by the Holy Spirit, they investigate the formulations most capable of making Christian truth attractive; and while sacrificing nothing contained in the sacred deposit that they are to hand on, following their predecessors' example, to future ages in its timeless integrity, they strive to teach evangelical doctrine as revealed by Jesus Christ: strong but gentle, indisputable but persuasive."[69] A council "will not be carried away and decree, in enthu-

67. Bravard, On the Council, pp. 603–4; (see also Dupanloup, *Sur le futur concile oecuménique*, p. 11; Maret, *Du concile général et de la paix religieuse)*; Ginoulhiac, *Le concile oecuménique*, pp. 29–35, 6. Ginoulhiac also refers to the biblical account of the Council of Jerusalem. Aimé Guilbert, *La divine synthèse, ou l'exposé dans leur enchaînement logique des preuves de la religion révélée* (Valognes: G. Martin, 1864), p. 282; Darboy, "Des conciles récemment tenus," p. 216; see also Darboy, "Sur le prochain concile," pp. 407–8.

68. Guillaume Meignan, "Du prochain concile oecuménique," *La semaine champenoise* 3 (13 February 1869):658–59; see also Bravard, "Pour le Carême de 1870," p. 355.

69. "Assistés du Saint-Esprit, ils étudient les formules les plus capables de faire

siastic fervor, a penalty so terrible as that of anathema. Five or six hundred bishops assembled to deliberate on matters involving such serious interests will not lose their temper and settle them by sheer force, disdaining to listen to and calm any scruples that might be felt, even when respectable and modestly presented," Darboy assures his diocese before the council. And Dupanloup describes a somewhat unreal detachment from worldly cares that will characterize the upcoming council, when "all rumors will die, all rash interferences will cease, all imprudent actions will disappear."[70]

Many of the French minority bishops emphasized the necessity of study at a council. Bishops in council "reread the commentaries of the great doctors of East and West, they examine the traditions of all churches throughout the world," writes Meignan.[71] The assistance of the Holy Spirit "dispenses us neither from work, nor study, nor from any means by which we can and even should try to discover exactly what God wants of us," notes Bravard, who would complain about the lack of books available at the council. Pope and bishops are not "inspired," writes Ginoulhiac. "They are only the guardians and interpreters of divine revelation handed down by the apostles. Moreover, God does not direct his Church by continual miracles. His action within the Church is hidden beneath nature's action."[72]

The emphasis on study at an ecumenical council was tied closely to another theme: the importance of adequate discussion. Darboy's account of the first two councils illustrates the high value he and his hearers placed on conciliar discussion:

At the Council of Jerusalem, which was the first of the councils and served them as model, they consulted together, although all the members of that

---

goûter la vérité chrétienne; et sans rien sacrifier du dépôt sacré qu'ils doivent, à l'exemple de leurs devanciers, transmettre aux âges futurs dans sa perpétuelle intégrité, ils s'efforcent d'enseigner la doctrine évangélique telle que Jésus-Christ l'a révélée forte, mais douce, indiscutable, mais persuasive" (Meignan, Pastoral Letter for Lent 1870, *La semaine champenoise* 4 [26 February 1870]:691).

70. Darboy, "Sur le prochain concile," pp. 417–18; he continues, "Has the Church ever handled souls with this off-handedness, and will it begin to do so tomorrow?" Dupanloup, *Observations sur la controverse*, p. 55; see also p. 4.

71. Meignan, Pastoral Letter for Lent 1870, p. 691.

72. "ne nous dispense ni du travail, ni des études, ni d'aucun des moyens, par lesquels nous pouvons, nous devons même chercher à connaître exactement ce que Dieu veut de nous" (Bravard, "Pour le Carême de 1870," p. 371); Jean Bravard to abbé Croulebois, 13 March 1870, *Revue catholique (Semaine religieuse) du diocèse de Coutances*

august assembly were personally infallible, and all were able to express their opinion, even after the most authoritative opinion had been given. An ecumenical council was held three centuries later, where it was a question of defining and formulating the faith of the church regarding the consubstantiality of the Word, in other words of affirming the divinity of Jesus Christ, the fundamental dogma of Christianity, a dogma for which several million martyrs had died . . . they did not vote by acclamation. This precedent, to mention only this one, my dearest brothers, ought to reassure you: today in Rome we shall not fall short of what they were at Nicea, fifteen centuries ago, and the approaching council will not blight its work by suppressing discussion.[73]

Bravard also describes the detailed examination given to even the smallest expressions of doctrine at the council. Dupanloup believes that councils arrive at their decisions only after research, long debates, and scruples, and Ginoulhiac even welcomes difficulties that had to be discussed because they show that the final acceptance of the council is not the result simply of complacency.[74] A council need not rush to its decisions. Why rush, asks Ramadié, when centuries are available to the church? Ginoulhiac also takes a long-range view of the work of councils. It took four councils to develop an orthodox understanding of Christ. "So, what one council began, another finishes," he explains. "And if a new council does not meet, the Church itself completes it, at the opportune time, under the action of the Spirit of God. Because the *Spirit of truth* was not promised to the apostles for a time and only in particular circumstances, but to dwell with them eternally."[75] Bravard agrees about the necessity of "long prayers, much reflection and intensified research, advice and precautions of every kind"; the council proceeds at "such a wise, slow pace" because its decisions are "for eternity."[76]

---

et Avranches 3 (31 March 1870):423 (see also Mansi 52:306D; Ginoulhiac, *Le concile oecuménique*, pp. 40–41.

73. Darboy, "Sur le prochain concile," pp. 417–18. Darboy followed the neoscholastics in regarding the apostles as personally infallible.

74. Jean Bravard to abbé Croulebois, 5 January 1870, *Revue catholique (Semaine religieuse) du diocèse de Coutances et Avranches* 3 (13 January 1870):242–43; Dupanloup, *Sur le futur concile oecuménique*, p. 12; Ginoulhiac, *Le concile oecuménique*, p. 139.

75. Etienne Ramadié, Pastoral letter for Lent 1870, *Semaine religieuse du diocèse de Perpignan* 2 (26 February 1870):136; Ginoulhiac, *Le concile oecuménique*, p. 115.

76. "de longues prières, de réflexions et de recherches multipliées, de conseils et de précautions de toute nature" (Bravard, "Pour le Carême de 1870," p. 355); "une si sage lenteur" (ibid., p. 357); "pour l'éternité" (Bravard, quoted in "Nouvelles et faits religieux du diocèse," p. 453).

For the French minority bishops, the council was one divinely constituted means of fulfilling the church's teaching and governing mission. It manifested in a particular time and place the ongoing tasks of pope and bishops to carry out this mission, and it served as a representation of the whole church. The council's representative character was especially important to the French minority bishops. For them, the bishops attending a council represented the faith of their own dioceses and hence together embodied the whole church's faith. In addition, the corporate nature of a council mirrored the church's communal nature and manifested the communal locus of the Holy Spirit's assistance in preserving evangelical teaching. They anticipated that bishops of an ecumenical council would be reliable in their disinterested wisdom, zealous in their detailed study, prolonged and careful in their deliberations, working hard and long to arrive at decisions that must endure for centuries.

Infallibility of the Church and of the Ecumenical Council

No discordant note broke the agreement of the French minority bishops on the infallibility of the church and of the ecumenical council.

The French minority emphasized the church's infallibility. Both before and after 1870, Guilbert teaches that the church is "the official and infallible guardian" of the deposit of revelation.[77] Its infallibility can be proved from the Scriptures, but its unity is sufficient to establish its infallibility.[78] The church is the only infallible interpreter of Scripture and tradition, says Ginoulhiac, which allows it to conserve revelation.[79]

Christ dwells within the church and protects it from error, ex-

77. The quotation is from Guilbert, *La divine synthèse, ou l'exposé dans leur enchaînement logique*, p. 284; but both of his later editions, while adding to this point, include it: *La divine synthèse, ou l'exposé au double point de vue apologétique et pratique de la religion*, 2d ed., 3 vols. (Gap: J. C. Richaud, 1875), 2:272; and *La divine synthèse, ou l'exposé rationnel au double point de vue apologétique et pratique de la religion révelée suivie de monde et Dieu*, 3d ed., rev., 2 vols. (Bordeaux: Feret et Fils, 1889), 1:213.

78. Guilbert, *La divine synthèse, ou l'exposé dans leur enchaînement logique*, pp. 284, 286.

79. Jacques Ginoulhiac, *Histoire du dogme catholique pendant les trois premiers siècles de l'église et jusqu'au concile de Nicée*, 2 vols. (Paris: Auguste Durand, 1852), 1:iii–vii.

plains Rivet, who finds promise of this protection in Matt. 28:20 and Matt. 16:18.[80] The church has promises of immortality, writes Dupont des Loges; it "personifies God made man" and thus possesses "the infallible certitude of its teaching," says Thomas: "The dogma of the permanent union of Jesus Christ with his Church corresponds in the order of redemption to the dogma of providence in the order of creation." The church is the mouth, the hand of Christ by which he continues the work of redemption. Because the church is the incarnate truth, human and divine, Christ guarantees it to be infallible in teaching. The church must be infallible to ensure the unaltered transmission of the deposit of faith, Dupanloup points out.[81]

Because the church is infallible, so are ecumenical councils: they express the teaching of the church. A council is the infallible organ of the church, Hugonin explains.[82] Although the church is always infallible, Place believes that the times of ecumenical councils are even "more glorious" for then "this privilege of its infallibility is called forth to shine with a more intense brilliance, when a greater exercise of this divine assistance is solicited."[83] It is God who is the basis for confidence in ecumenical councils:

The visible majesty of these assembled pontiffs is nothing compared to the invisible majesty of the one of whom they are the representatives and the ministers and who, faithful to his word, will be present among them, governing their hearts, enlightening their deliberations, directing their votes, communicating to their decrees the infallible brightness of his own light, and making use of their great collective voice to obtain for truth a testimony whose tone, brilliance, and power can rouse the inertia of consciences and awaken the sleeping echoes of the Christian world.[84]

80. Rivet, "Sur l'église," pp. 101–3; see also Dupanloup's edition of the Bossuet catechism, Le catéchisme, p. 30, which cites the promises in Matt. 16:18 and 18:20; Frédéric de Marguerye, "Lettre pastorale pour l'établissement d'une association diocésaine en faveur de l'oeuvre des séminaires et des écoles," in Migne, ed., Collection intégrale et universelle des orateurs sacrés, 84:672, which refers to the use of Rom. 8:31; Dupanloup, "Le futur concile," p. 11, which refers to Matt. 28:19a, 20 and John 20:21b.

81. Paul Dupont des Loges to diocesan clergy, 8 December 1865, cited by Klein, Vie de Dupont des Loges, p. 197; Thomas, "De son départ," pp. 230, 241; Dupanloup, Sur le futur concile oecuménique, p. 8.

82. Flavien Hugonin, cited in "Nouvelles diocésaines," p. 748. These are a reporter's rendition of Hugonin's words.

83. "plus glorieux"; "ce privilège de son infaillibilité est appelé à briller d'un éclat plus vif, où cette assistance divine est sollicitée à s'exercer davantage" (Place, "De son prochain départ," p. 834).

84. "La majesté visible de ces Pontifes assemblés n'est rien auprès de la majesté

The presence of Christ in the church and the assistance of the Holy Spirit are "the foundation of the infallibility of the church, its invincible force and the very principle of its life," concludes Place.[85] Bravard went further: "The authority of ecumenical councils is, in effect, divine, it is infallible like God Himself."[86] And Ramadié writes: "The human element is present, for that is the law adopted by God's providence: he made the Church with men, as he made Adam with earth; but just as he vivified this earth with the divine breath of his mouth, so does he vivify with life and direct the holy assembly by his Holy Spirit. The word of God is faithful: his promises are sure. . . . When the Church speaks, it is Jesus Christ, that is God, who speaks."[87]

David also emphasizes God's assistance to an ecumenical council: "After all the reasons have been heard, all the testimonies recorded, after the council has deliberated with maturity and liberty, then the Church, through the mouth of its leader, pronounces and defines. At that moment, every other voice must be silent; the Holy Spirit is present, according to the promise of Jesus Christ; the Church teaches; the world bows and believes: God has spoken."[88] Darboy writes, "Whatever the council does or decides, faith teaches us that

invisible de Celui dont ils sont les représentants et les ministres, et qui, fidèle à sa parole, sera présent parmi eux, gouvernant leurs coeurs, éclairant leurs délibérations, dirigeant leurs suffrages, communiquant à leurs décrets l'infaillible clarté de sa propre lumière, et se servant de leur grande voix collective pour procurer à la vérité un témoignage dont l'accent, l'éclat et la puissance puissent remuer l'inertie des consciences et réveiller les échos endormis du monde chrétien" (ibid.).

85. "le fondement de l'infaillibilité de l'Eglise, sa force invincible et le principe même de sa vie" (ibid., p. 835).

86. "L'autorité des Conciles oecuméniques est, en effet, divine, elle est infaillible comme Dieu lui-même" (Bravard, On the Council, p. 604).

87. "Que l'élément humain s'y trouve, c'est la loi adoptée par la Providence de Dieu: il a fait l'Eglise avec des hommes, comme il fit Adam avec de la terre; mais de même qu'il vivifia cette terre du souffle divin qu'il tira de sa bouche, ainsi il anime et dirige par son Saint-Esprit la sainte assemblée. La parole de Dieu est fidèle: ses promesses sont assurées. . . . Quand l'Eglise parle c'est Jésus-Christ, c'est-à-dire Dieu, qui parle" (Ramadié, Pastoral Letter for Lent 1870, p. 135).

88. "Après que toutes les raisons ont été entendues, tous les témoignages recueillis, après que le Concile a délibéré en toute maturité et liberté, alors l'Eglise, par l'organe de son Chef, prononce et définit. En ce moment, toute autre voix que la sienne doit se taire; l'Esprit-Saint est présent, selon la promesse de Jésus-Christ; l'Eglise enseigne; le monde s'incline et croit: Dieu a parlé" (David, Circular Letter to Diocese, 26 May 1870, *La semaine religieuse du diocèse de Saint-Brieuc et Tréguier* 3 [4 June 1870]:342).

this will be well done and well decided." Ginoulhiac speaks explicitly of the infallibility of a council: "Since these councils are assured of the presence of Jesus Christ himself, since they are instructed by the Holy Spirit, and since in their decrees, whether dogmatic or disciplinary, they have the right to say: *It has seemed good to the Holy Spirit and to us,* their authority is thus divine, sovereign and infallible: sovereign with respect to the government of the Church, infallible in their decisions dealing with faith and morals."[89]

To show the link between ecclesial and conciliar infallibility, some minority bishops emphasize the quality of consensus between bishops and pope in a conciliar decision, which for Maret is the locus of the council's infallibility: "Infallibility . . . is present only in the concurrence and the agreement of the pope with the bishops, the bishops with the pope; and the absolutely binding rule of the Catholic faith, under the sanction of the penalties directed against heresy, resides also in this concurrence and this agreement of the two elements of spiritual sovereignty." Ginoulhiac also notes that "it is on the authority of these decrees made *in common* that the firmness of the belief and the tradition of the Church rests."[90]

Many minority bishops offered clarifications of the assistance granted to a council, or the promises of this assistance. If the assistance of Christ is assured to "his Church dispersed throughout all the countries of the world," how much more is it assured "when it meets in order better to harmonize its efforts and assert more forcefully its moral teaching and its dogmas," writes Rivet.[91] Thomas notes that

89. Georges Darboy to A. Surat, archdeacon of Paris, 20 April 1870, *Collectio Lacensis: Acta et decreta sacrorum conciliorum recentiorum* (Freiburg im Breisgau: Herder, 1890), 7:1407; Ginoulhiac, *Le concile oecuménique,* p. 12. For additional discussions of ecclesial or conciliar infallibility, see Darboy, "Des conciles récemment tenus," pp. 213–14; de Marguerye, "Marie a été conçue sans péché," in Migne, ed., *Collection intégrale et universelle des orateurs sacrés,* 84:710; David, Circular Letter to Diocese, 6 January 1870, p. 123; Flavien Hugonin to a government minister, 17 July 1866, F[19] 2.500, Archives Nationales, Paris.

90. Maret, *Du concile général et de la paix religieuse,* 1:xx–xxi; Ginoulhiac, *Le concile oecuménique,* p. 14. He is referring to Celestine here, but he had first cited Matt. 5:14, 28:19–20, and Eph. 9:14.

91. "son Eglise dispersée dans tous les pays du monde"; "lorsqu'elle se réunit pour mieux concerter ses efforts, affirmer plus fortment [*sic*], sa morale et ses dogmes" (François Rivet, Farewell Discourse on the Council, quoted in "Chronique diocésaine," *La chronique religieuse de Dijon et du diocèse* 5 [20 November 1869]: 1032; see also Dupont des Loges, "Pastorale retraite" [1869], p. 325; and Meignan, "Du prochain concile oecuménique," p. 659).

there were many misconceptions about this assistance. Some think that the church claims to be inspired, with its popes as prophets; that it believes a superhuman light allows it to discover unknown dogmas or to recall forgotten ones; that it regards itself as a living Mount Sinai. "And yet such is not the mind of the Church," he explains: "All that it [the church] maintains is that from the moment it is engaged in making a decision, in combating an error, in defining such or such a point of the doctrine of Jesus Christ, God is with it, not so much to open the way as to guide it and to support it; he prevents it from erring in the expression of the faith, but he does not convey this expression himself. To sum it all up in one word, the Church's infallibility is a kind of assistance, not inspiration."[92]

In short, the French minority bishops agreed in holding that divine assistance ensured the infallibility of both the church and its ecumenical councils. Many of them thought councils were infallible because of the representative role of the bishops assembled, who embodied together the faith of the whole church by testifying to the faith of their dioceses. Hence the council was seen as an organ or exercise of the church's infallibility.

Continuity and Change in the Understanding of Dogma

The French minority bishops were puzzled by the problem of change in the understanding of dogma, and they did not develop a coherent theological explanation for it. In general, they emphasized the continuity of dogma at the expense of what later theologians would call its development.

Dogma emerges from an immutable church, they taught. Unchanging in its victory over evil, in the structure of its ecumenical councils, the church, "like a building solidly built on rock, has defied the storms," Bravard exclaims: "Always one, always the same, it con-

92. "Tout ce qu'elle [the church] affirme, c'est que du moment où elle s'occupe de prendre une décision, de combattre une erreur, de définir tel ou tel point de la doctrine de Jésus-Christ, Dieu est avec elle, non pas tant pour lui frayer la route que pour la guider et la soutenir; il l'empêche de se tromper dans l'énoncé de la foi, mais il ne lui communique point cet énoncé lui-même. Pour tout résumer d'un seul mot, le caractère de l'infaillibilité de l'Eglise, c'est une assistance et non point une inspiration" (Thomas, "De son départ," p. 241).

tinues to appear to the human race what it was, from its beginning, all holy, apostolic, without innovation or change in what was entrusted to it by Jesus Christ."[93] This emphasis on the church's immutability in teaching is reflected in the contrast Darboy draws between church law and dogma: "It is true, the institutions of purely ecclesiastical law have not retained the same character of immutability as dogma and moral teaching. They correspond, in effect, to the human and exterior part of the Church." And Dupanloup notes that the deposit of divine revelation must be transmitted without alteration; doctrine is preserved always pure and the same in the church, according to Ginoulhiac.[94]

Councils cannot create new dogmas: frequent emphasis on this insight formed another part of the French minority's stress on the continuity of dogma. For Colet, a council merely professes dogma already received and confessed by the church: "Consequently the bishops who make up the Council are, above all, witnesses. They testify to and certify what has been received as dogma and professed until now. But they are also judges, with this reservation, however, that their judiciary power should not go beyond their power as witnesses. In their capacity as judges, their role is not to invent dogmas; but to interpret and explain them."[95] Dupanloup agrees: "The church does not create dogmas, it proclaims them." Guilbert asserts that all Christian doctrine is found in Scripture and tradition; the church "has the right neither to add to it nor to subtract from it":

It has never claimed the right to create a new dogma. Its first principle is to admit only what has been believed everywhere, always, and by everyone, *quod ubique, quod semper, quod ab omnibus creditum est*. And in its dogmatic

93. "semblable à un édifice solidement établi sur le roc, a défié les tempêtes." "Elle, toujours une, toujours la même, continue de se montrer au genre humain ce qu'elle fut, dès son origine, toute sainte, toute apostolique, n'ayant rien innové, ni rien changé à ce qui lui fut confié par Jésus-Christ" (Bravard, On the Council, p. 605; see also Bravard, "De son prochain départ," p. 150; Jean Bravard, *Distribution des prix au petit-séminaire et collège diocésain de Valognes* [Valognes: G. Martin, 1854], p. 4).

94. Darboy, "Des conciles récemment tenus," p. 216; Dupanloup, *Sur le futur concile oecuménique*, p. 8; Ginoulhiac, *Histoire du dogme catholique*, 1:iii.

95. "Les Evêques qui composent le Concile sont donc avant tout témoins. Ils déposent et constatent ce qu [*sic*] ont reçu comme dogme et professé jusqu'ici. Mais ils sont aussi Juges, sous cette Réserve pourtant que leur pouvoir judiciaire ne doit pas dépasser leur pouvoir de témoins. En leur qualité de Juges, ils n'ont pas à faire les Dogmes; mais à les interpréter et à les expliquer" (Colet, "Souvenirs du concile du Vatican," fol. N).

judgments, it has no other purpose than to clarify more exactly debated points of doctrine. Thus it is that, amid attacks by heresy, it has formulated many truths successively and with stricter accuracy; but these truths were already part of Catholic teaching, before the formal decision of the Church, as one becomes readily aware when going back through the centuries.[96]

The proclamation of the dogma of the Immaculate Conception might have been expected to test severely a nondevelopmental picture of dogma. Nevertheless, Dupanloup's discussion of this proclamation shows how deeply rooted was his conviction of the continuity of dogma. Noting that the church does not honor error, he explains, "As soon as a doctrine is universally received throughout the whole Church, that is enough to allow one to declare with certainty that it is true and that it derives from divine revelation and from the early teaching of the Church.[97] Like other dogmas, that of the Immaculate Conception was proclaimed only after it was clear that the belief was universally held throughout the church; the proclamation simply pronounced with certitude that the belief was true. De Marguerye also emphasizes that a definition of dogma by the Apostolic See "is not at all the creation of a new belief. . . . This doctrine already existed in the Church, it formed part of the sacred deposit entrusted to its care; all its dogmatic formulation does is surround it with the brilliant light of faith by which it will be inaccessible henceforth to every attack." De Marguerye notes that not all thirteenth-century theologians believed in the Immaculate Conception, but explains that now new lights allow it to be seen. But these new lights are reliable precisely because they draw on the unchanging faith of the church. Darboy's lengthy reflection on the possibility of a conciliar definition summarizes the emphasis the French minority bishops placed on the continuity of dogma:

First, as far as new definitions are concerned, if the ecumenical Council ordains explicit belief in matters which until now could be denied without

96. Dupanloup, *Observations sur la controverse*, p. 7; Guilbert, *La divine synthèse, ou l'exposé dans leur enchaînement logique*, pp. 285–86; see also Rivet, Farewell Discourse on the Council, p. 1033.

97. Félix Dupanloup, "Instruction sur l'Immaculée Conception de la Très-Sainte Vièrge," in *Défense de la liberté de l'église*, 2 vols. (Paris: Régis Ruffet et Cie, 1861), 2:239. Dupanloup continues by noting that the medieval debates on this doctrine prove that it was already held then or at least was believed worthy of serious consideration. He justifies Thomas Aquinas' failure to hold the doctrine by arguing a disjunction between his thought and his practice in regard to it.

being heretical, it is because these things would already be certain and generally believed in; for in these matters the bishops are witnesses who verify, and not authors who invent. For a truth to become an article of faith, it must have been revealed by God and contained in the deposit which the Christian centuries guard faithfully and pass down from age to age without change. Now there can be no doubt that five or six hundred bishops will not testify before the world to having found, in the beliefs of their respective churches, what is not there. If they therefore propose, in council, truths to believe, it is because they already exist in the monuments of tradition and in the common teaching of theology, and thus they are not a novelty.[98]

A few attempts to explain the phenomenon of changes in understanding can be found in discussions of dogma. Dupanloup notes that the church does not change even when all around it changes. At a council, for example, the eternal truths are recalled "to make them, if possible, yet more clear and more firm; to defend the sacred deposit against all innovation, but also against all weakening." But if truth demands that the church never change, charity demands that it always change, in order to meet the needs of the times. "That is why there is an unchangeable side and a changeable side to religion," he explains. The church preserves and adapts at the same time.[99] Thomas explains the phenomenon of change in dogmatic formulations as a development and spreading of the truth of the dogmas without changing them: "To preserve revealed doctrine without alteration or compromise, yet at the same time to develop and spread its light; to unite the immutability of the faith to a continual progress in sacred science: such is the mission of the Church envisioned as a doctrinal power." Truths, then, do not change, but they are ascertained, elucidated, expanded, understood better.[100] Maret gives precision to an understanding of development when he suggests that a definition must be a regular speculative development of anterior belief, as was

98. De Marguerye, "Marie a été conçue sans péché," p. 710; Darboy, "Sur le prochain concile," pp. 410–11.

99. Dupanloup, *Avant son départ*, p. 15; Dupanloup, *Sur le futur concile oecuménique*, p. 38.

100. "Conserver sans altération et sans mélange la doctrine révélée; mais en même temps développer et propager sa lumière; unir l'immutabilité de la foi à un progrès continuel dans la science sacrée, telle est la mission de l'Eglise envisagée comme puissance doctrinale" (Thomas, "De son départ," pp. 242–43). Meignan might have found room for a theory of development from his work on the church's recognition of the messianic prophecies in the Old Testament, but his interests were more narrowly apologetic; a list of his work in this area is available in O. Rey, "Meignan, Guillaume René."

the definition of the Immaculate Conception. There is development, he explains, but it must be from same to same or the immutability and divinity of the church's constitution will disappear.[101]

A strong emphasis on the continuity and immutability of church and dogma characterized the thought of the French minority. A few efforts were made to explain the changes in the understanding of a dogma, but they were not typical. The French minority bishops did not succeed in formulating a coherent theological explanation of development.

Conclusion

Strong in their convictions, the French minority bishops approached the First Vatican Council with a tendency to adapt to modern political developments, though not to modern journalistic style. Though personally devoted to the pope and his temporal power, they were fiercely convinced of the important role of the bishop in the church. Bishops were judges in the church who represented the faith of their diocese and who as representatives embodied the corporate character of the church when they gathered in ecumenical council. The French minority bishops believed that God gave infallible assistance to the church as a whole and that ecumenical councils were enabled to exercise infallibility to preserve the unchanging Christian message and to proclaim it in a way persuasive for the day. These bishops struggled to maintain their hopes for the upcoming council, repeating these hopes to members of their dioceses and to their own fearful hearts.

101. Maret, *Du concile général et de la paix religieuse*, 2:379, 1:344.

3

The Common Fear

Apprehension about a Separate, Personal, Absolute Papal Infallibility

—————◄•►—————

Rumors and fears played important roles in shaping the drama of the First Vatican Council. Rumors filled the air before and during the council, and they helped to mold the fears of the minority bishops of the council. The French minority bishops heard the rumors, they read them, they wrote of them nervously to each other in private letters. Gradually, these rumors helped to weld them together by implanting a common fear that the council would proclaim the separate, personal, absolute infallibility of the pope.

Rumors

Published just a month before the opening of the council, Dupanloup's *Observations* launched a heated discussion:

The discussion takes place in the market square; everyone takes part in it, and fashionable ladies begin to argue about it during intermissions at the Opera! All discussion in the marketplace is by nature intemperate: and this one follows suit. A mob of pamphleteers and second-rate writers began to abuse the arguments of the masters and to add to them their own disordered ideas. Doctrinal, official, *ex cathedra* infallibility in faith and morals does not suffice for them; they must have an absolute, unconditional, unlimited, universal infallibility; an infallibility inspired, individual, scientific, political, governmental: this would mean that the pope could not fall into any error, public or private. The excess of words accompanies and increases the excess of ideas; irrationality calls to its aid invectives, recriminations, insulting gossip, denunciations, everything in language which could arouse terror.[1]

1. Ollivier, *L'église et l'état au concile du Vatican*, 1:488–49.

Popular discussion of papal infallibility had not begun in the marketplace, of course. Certain theologians held ultramontanist positions which could be drawn on for more popular presentations. In his "Souvenirs," Colet criticizes the work of the theologian François-Xavier Schouppe, who, he claims, sees the church as "the society of the faithful governed by the sovereign pontiff." In preparatory notes before the council, the moderate superior of Saint-Sulpice in Paris, Henri Icard, would write:

It is said by men of a certain school that the pope is at the same time the source of all jurisdiction and of all doctrinal infallibility. He alone teaches the universal Church and the bishops have no other mission than to transmit to the faithful the doctrine which they receive from the Apostolic See. The majority of bishops have no other infallibility than that which God has given to the majority of the faithful, passive infallibility, which consists in letting themselves be taught and in adhering to the doctrine of the sovereign pastor. . . . They think that they glorify and exalt the head of the Church by separating him in this way from the rest of the pastors, almost—as I said one day to a nuncio, Bishop [sic] Sacconi—as though one thought he honored the head of an important person by detaching it from the neck and raising it above the prone body.[2]

When the ultramontanist Prosper Guéranger, abbot of Solesmes, published two works in response to critics of papal infallibility,[3] he at least specified some tests or conditions by which the *ex cathedra* quality of a papal statement could be detected. But William George Ward, editor of the *Dublin Review,* complained that such conditions were limitations on the scope of *ex cathedra* pronouncements[4] and denounced as minimizers those who did not agree with him. Some ultramontanist theologians busied themselves with defending as *de iure divino* extreme theses formulated by Gregory VII or Boniface VIII, while others wanted to extend the limits of the privilege of infallibility to include all papal encyclicals or papal statements on reli-

2. "La Société des Fidèles gouvernés par le Souverain Pontife" (Colet, "Souvenirs du concile du Vatican," fol. C); Henri Icard, Preparatory Notes for the First Vatican Council (winter 1868–69), quoted in Aubert, *Pie IX,* p. 302. Icard was theological adviser at the council for Victor Bernadou, archbishop of Sens. Carlo Sacconi, cardinal, was papal nuncio in Paris.

3. Prosper Guéranger, *De la monarchie pontificale* (Paris: Victor Palmé, 1870); and *Défense de l'église romaine contre les accusations du R. P. Gratry* (Paris: Victor Palmé, 1870). The former work answered Maret's *Du concile général et de la paix religieuse*; the latter answered Alphonse Gratry, a priest of the Oratory, who early in 1870 wrote a series of letters that questioned papal infallibility and raised the issue of Honorius.

4. Butler, *Vatican Council,* 1:75.

gious matters, even those of a somewhat political nature.[5] It is not hard to understand Icard's dismay when he surveyed the work of such theologians.

More extreme and yet more widespread in influence were the popular expressions of devotion to the person of the pope. Veuillot writes, "We all know certainly only one thing, that is that no man knows anything except the Man with whom God is for ever, the Man who carries the thought of God. We must unswervingly follow his inspired directions." In his *L'Univers,* Veuillot printed hymns in which the pope was substituted for God as the object of devotion, such as

> To Pius IX, Pontiff-King:
> Father of the poor,
> Giver of gifts,
> Light of hearts,
> Send forth the beam
> Of your heavenly light!

or

> Pius, steadfast energy of [all] things,
> Remaining undisturbed in yourself
> Give the words of life that govern
> The lambs, the sheep, and the world.[6]

The words of Heb. 7:26 about Christ were attributed to the pope; *Civiltà cattolica,* the Roman Jesuits' periodical, remarked, "When the Pope thinks, it is God who is thinking in him";[7] Jean-Baptiste Berteaud, bishop of Tulle, represented the pope as "the Incarnate Word continuing itself"; and Gaspard Mermillod, auxiliary bishop of Lausanne, preached on "the three incarnations of the Son of God": in the womb of the virgin, in the eucharist, and in the old man of the Vatican.[8] *Civiltà cattolica* augmented this trend when, claiming to represent the view of most French Catholics, it argued that papal infallibility should be defined, by acclamation if possible, in a council

5. Aubert, *Pie IX*, p. 302. It was Ward who wanted a papal bull every morning with his *Times.*

6. Louis Veuillot and hymns quoted in Butler, *Vatican Council*, 1:75–76. The first hymn is the sequence for Pentecost; the second was used at None, attributed to St. Ambrose.

7. Ibid., p. 77.

8. Aubert, *Pie IX*, p. 303.

of brief duration and general accord.[9] And Colet notes that the doctrine of papal infallibility was given further encouragement at the level of popular piety by the Jesuits' use of the pulpit, the press, the confessional, and religious associations.[10] In short, a tremendous outburst of popular devotional feeling toward the pope was given often exaggerated expression.

The widespread interest in papal infallibility did not go unobserved by the French minority bishops. They began to repeat the popular rumors to each other. In April of 1867, Rivet writes to Dupanloup that "some overwrought minds" are thinking "of having the assembled bishops declare the *personal infallibility of the pope* a dogma of the Catholic faith."[11] Rivet confesses that he prefers the Liguorian affirmation of *Doctor,* and he continues, "Let us beg God to spare us this" because it would bring "internal strife and incalculable external problems."[12] Another writer tells Dupanloup:

They discussed in this way some definition or other regarding the infallibility of the pope and the subordination of the State to the Church. In my opinion this would be the source of great dangers. I am not a gallican; I do not accept *in entirety* any of the Four Articles of 1682, not even the first one; but I have studied these sensitive questions too much not to feel how difficult it is to see and to express the truth regarding them in precise, clear terms capable of clarifying misunderstandings and overcoming objections. They hide numberless *historical and political* stumbling blocks which can only be avoided by infinite precautions. How imprudent would it not be to consider them in so brief a session where reflection and discussion would be impossible![13]

Dupanloup tried to remain calm when first hearing these rumors; he writes to a priest, "*I know that he thinks as we do concerning the inopportuneness of certain decisions* of which you have spoken to me; but I do

9. The *Civiltà cattolica* article of 6 February 1869 is available in Aubert, *Vatican I,* pp. 261–69.

10. Colet, "Souvenirs du concile du Vatican," fol. C.

11. "certains esprits ardents"; "de faire déclarer par les Evêques réunis comme dogme de la Foi Catholique *l'Infaillibilité personelle du Pape*" (François Rivet to Félix Dupanloup, 29 April 1867, AB XIX 524, Archives Nationales, Paris). Palanque suggests, incorrectly, that this letter was written by Hugonin, in *Catholiques libéraux et gallicans en France,* p. 66, n. 22.

12. "des Luttes Intestines, et des difficultés extérieures incalculables" (Rivet to Dupanloup, 29 April 1867).

13. "On a parlé ainsi de je ne sais quelle définition, sur l'infaillibilité du Pape et sur la subordination de l'Etat à l'Eglise. Il y aurait là, je crois, de très graves dangers. Je ne

not believe that any such intentions are under consideration at Rome."[14] But Place writes Dupanloup that a rumor has arisen that the bishops will be presented in Rome with prepared decrees, and another correspondent writes, "Bishop Place has many worries which I believe, alas, only too well justified."[15]

Others began to hear the rumors about plans to proclaim papal infallibility. Although the Protestant Edmond de Pressensé writes in 1867 in the *Revue chrétienne,* "It is certain that the coming Council is a concession to the moderating tendencies in the bosom of Catholicism," in 1868 he would write, "It is certain that the most outrageous ultramontane theses are going to be promulgated as dogma." Maret hears that a decree has already been prepared before conciliar discussion has even begun. A correspondent writes him from Rome:

> The Council will be a stormy one. . . . Papal infallibility is still on the agenda and there is a possiblity there of great danger. . . . There will be eight hundred prelates, three-quarters of whom are absolutely old-fashioned, who will be ready to accept anything brought forward by the Vatican. I greatly fear that our bishops will be powerless and that, unless one fights them mercilessly, the Jesuits will triumph. More than ever one can foresee a sweeping reaction resulting in the destruction of everything leading to progress, to new ideas. We are plunged into the heart of the Middle Ages.

Another letter comments: "Who can foresee the outcome of the Council on which we had built such marvelous hopes? There is everything to be feared when we see what is written and professed by such people as Archbishop Manning!" Maret was well aware of the dangers of ultramontanism. In 1857, he had addressed a *Mémoire* to

---

suis pas gallican; je n'admets *absolument* aucun des quatre articles de 1682, pas même la premier; mais j'ai trop étudié ces questions délicates pour n'avoir pas senti combien il est difficile de voir, et d'exprimer la vérité sur ces matières, en des termes précis, lumineux, propres à détruire les malentendus, et à résoudre les objections. Il y a là d'innombrables écueils *historiques et politiques* qu'on ne peut pas éviter sans des précautions infinies. Quelle imprudence ne serait-ce pas de s'y engager, dans une assemblée aussi courte, où la réflexion et la discussion seront impossibles?" (unnamed correspondent to Félix Dupanloup, 1 May 1867, AB XIX 524, Archives Nationales, Paris).

14. François Lagrange, *Life of Monseigneur Dupanloup,* trans. and abridged by Mary Elizabeth Herbert (London: Chapman and Hall, 1885), pp. 302–3. This letter is typical of Dupanloup's early responses to the rumors.

15. Charles Place to Félix Dupanloup, n.d., AB XIX 524, Archives Nationales, Paris; Marquise de Forbin d'Oppède (née Roselyne de Villeneuve-Bargemon, daughter of a prefect of the Restoration, married into an important family of Provence) to Félix Dupanloup, November 1868, quoted in Aubert, *Vatican I,* p. 73.

the minister of worship on "the ultra-Catholic party" demonstrating "the moral, social and political dangers" with which that "party" threatened France. It wants to restore a theocracy in which the pope "possesses the divine right of true political jurisdiction throughout the whole world, a jurisdiction which will make him sole arbitrator in the great social and even political problems." He maintained that it was a strong party, including respectable bishops and talented writers, and above all enjoying the support of Rome with its "tradition of a universal dictatorship." In his book on councils, Maret shows the same concern about an extreme party, claiming that a new group hoped to see defined as dogma the thought of one school on papal infallibility. Maret had unwittingly prophesied the difficulties his book would face in Rome in 1857, when he commented darkly that gallican ideas once respected and rewarded by Rome were increasingly likely to be placed on the Index.[16]

A common rumor that spread among some French minority bishops claimed that a definition of papal infallibility would pose political dangers. Montalembert tells of Rivet's apprehensions after the bishop's return from Rome: "He believes that the Roman prelates, bishops and cardinals incline rather to extending the scope of the *Syllabus* than limiting it." A correspondent writes to Dupanloup, "I read the exaggerations of overzealous men. . . . The definition of infallibility . . . what will it result in? The Emperor will be hurt: he will make it a pretext to withdraw his troops from Rome and the Italians will go in directly."[17] In 1857, Maret had recommended an "episcopalism allied to liberalism" to the minister of worship, with a recognition of the independence of secular power from the jurisdic-

16. Edmond de Pressensé, *La revue chrétienne* 14 (1867):573; 15(1868):700, quoted in Aubert, *Vatican I*, p. 73; unnamed correspondent to Henri Maret, 5 January 1869, quoted in ibid., p. 74; unnamed correspondent to Henri Maret, n.d., quoted in ibid., p. 73; Henri Maret, *Mémoire* (4 December 1857), quoted in Palanque, *Catholiques libéraux et gallicans en France*, p. 29; Maret, *Du concile général et de la paix religieuse*, 2:359; Maret, *Mémoire sur l'état de l'église en France*, quoted in Palanque, *Catholiques libéraux et gallicans en France*, p. 15. Maret's position was not helped by the antireligious publicity his book received. One anticlerical journal praised him as a serious and courageous man who fought against "the ancient and absurd claims of the doctrine of pontifical infallibility" (quoted in ibid., p. 84). Maret's book was not finally placed on the Index.

17. Charles de Montalembert to unnamed correspondent, 17 August 1867, quoted in Aubert, *Vatican I*, p. 71; unnamed correspondent to Dupanloup, July 1869, quoted in Lagrange, *Life of Dupanloup*, p. 360.

tion of the church and an affirmation of the principles of 1789 and of modern society.[18] The attempt of Napoléon Daru, French minister of foreign affairs, to inform the Vatican about the hesitations his and other European governments felt toward the conciliar discussions on the papacy served only to heighten the sense of impending political disaster for the French minority bishops.[19] As late as 8 July 1870, Darboy would write in his journal: "M. de Behayn [sic], secretary of the French embassy in Rome, on his return from Paris told me that spirits were still in turmoil over the question of infallibility. The Empress spoke to him about it with great emotion although she said that she would follow my advice. He adds that the Hohenzollern affair has just created a strong derivative of the Roman question and one has no idea how the quarrel will turn out."[20]

During the council, bishops continued to hear rumors, now of the dismay, indifference, and confusion among French Catholics regarding the work of the council. Meignan would receive several letters that convey the ongoing sense of extraconciliar agitation about which he and other minority bishops were informed. One correspondent writes to Meignan:

They are doing a lot of talking about the Council again; and almost all the scholars who discuss it do so with a phenomenal ignorance. If the dogma of infallibility is defined one can be certain that it will be accepted by very few, even by very few Catholics. I know from what pure sources the venerable bishops draw their convictions which overflow in their constant polemics; but, your Excellency, your profound wisdom surely shows you how preferable silence would be to such outbursts![21]

Another writes:

Here is what I feel I can give you as the real diagnosis of the situation we are in. There has been a considerable falling off of discussion: weariness, other business, etc.; the Council question is much less interesting. Pious people will accept whatever is done; those who are indifferent are uninterested; only knowledgeable Catholics continue to worry and to be very anxious about the outcome. However I feel sure that, except for a few individual defections, in a short time everything will settle down quietly. Memories are

18. Palanque's phrase to describe Maret's position, *Catholiques libéraux et gallicans en France*, p. 29.
19. An account of Daru's intervention is available in Aubert, *Vatican I*, pp. 172–78.
20. Darboy, "Le journal," pp. 447–48.
21. M. Vassard, president of the Reims tribunal, to Guillaume Meignan, 18 March 1870, quoted in Boissonnot, *Le Cardinal Meignan*, p. 289, n. 1.

short in France. Of course, the government is in favor of the minority. . . . Let them do what they will, decree what they will: if they exclude themselves from modern thought that is their misfortune. If they make decisions contrary to our right, we will just cancel them out: that's what they are saying.

The priests of Paris are moderate, he writes, with young priests more ardent than old ones in advocating papal infallibility. But the priests outside of Paris agree with the ultramontanist views of Veuillot's *L'Univers*. He continues:

We should make a few concessions: let us accept the power of the pope in which we have always believed but let us not introduce anything new into the faith. This is what I feel is the opinion of those who are most disinterested. As far as I am concerned, I have pulled myself together as well as I could and, following advice you gave me formerly, I try to be orthodox without casting into hellfire beforehand all those who disagree. When are you coming home? It looks as if the council will last forever.[22]

The writer goes on to report a drop in Mass attendance and a decreasing respect for episcopal authority.

Richard Whelan, bishop of Wheeling, writes in a note to Dupanloup during the council:

I am convinced that all the arguments which can be accumulated will have no effect with those who favor this doctrine. In one way or another they reject everything. Reasons mean nothing. Facts count for nothing. Difficulties for the future do not trouble them. They are not alarmed by the effect which the definition may produce among the faithful, nor of the outside opposition which it may arouse. . . . They want it; they have decided on it; nothing can prevent it (humanly).[23]

One of the most persistent rumors, both before and during the council, was that a decision on infallibility would be reached by acclamation. Colet confides in his "Souvenirs": "What worries me most since my arrival is the extent of the rumor, along with everything likely to make it appear absolutely true, that there was a very serious question of declaring the pope infallible by acclamation as had been advised and ardently recommended to the Council fathers, either by *Civiltà* or *L'Univers*. I don't know if this idea was really conceived and agreed upon; but twice I have witnessed attempts to carry

22. Joseph Bourret to Guillaume Meignan, 26 May 1870, quoted in Boissonnot, *Le Cardinal Meignan*, pp. 288–89.
23. Richard Whelan to Félix Dupanloup, 24 April 1870, quoted in Hennesey, *First Council of the Vatican*, p. 184.

it out, attempts which I opposed openly."[24] The ultramontanists denied later that they had ever considered such an acclamation, but from Icard's journal Mourret suggests there was some foundation for Colet's fears. The impact of such rumors was not lessened when Veuillot urged the bishops to hurry toward a definition so as to facilitate further progress: pontifical acts could replace conciliar discussion.[25] Colet reports the views of Pierre Parisis, bishop of Arras, which follow a similar direction: "The infallibility of the pope gives him what is necessary to deal with all the needs of the Church. It is up to him, therefore, by virtue of his infallibility, to define whatever concerns faith and morals and to establish disciplinary laws apart from and independent of any council session."[26]

Other bishops as well had heard of the hopes for at least a speedy definition. Place writes from Rome before the council of rumors that the bishops would be presented with prepared decrees upon their arrival.[27] One newspaper correspondent believes that "the supreme authority of the Council will soon reconcile opponents who are equally devoted to the cause of the Church and submissive in advance to its indisputable authority; the very vehemence of their differences only serves to bring out more clearly the filial submission with which the highest intelligences bow before its decisions."[28] But

24. "Ce qui m'affligea surtout, dès mon arrivée, ce fut d'y voir répandu, entouré de tous les caractères propres à lui donner une vraisemblance incontestable, le bruit que, conformément à ce qui avait été conseillé et vivement recommandé aux Pères du concile, soit par la *Civiltà*, soit par l'*Univers*, il était très sérieusement question de déclarer le Pape infaillible, par acclamation. J'ignore si ce projet a été réellement conçu et concerté; mais deux fois j'ai été témoin des tentatives faites pour en déterminer l'exécution, tentatives auxquelles j'ai résisté ouvertement" (Colet, "Souvenirs du concile du Vatican," fol. C).

25. Palanque, *Catholiques libéraux et gallicans en France*, p. 155, n. 87; Mourret, *Le concile du Vatican*, p. 135; Butler, *Vatican Council*, 2:34.

26. "L'infaillibilité du Pape lui communique ce qui est nécessaire pour faire face à tous les besoins de l'Eglise. Il lui appartient donc, en vertu de son infaillibilité, de définir tout ce qui a rapport à la Foi et aux Moeurs et d'établir les Lois de Discipline en dehors et indépendamment de toute Assemblée Conciliaire" (Colet, "Souvenirs du concile du Vatican," fol. A.).

27. Charles Place to unnamed correspondent, n.d., AB XIX 524, Archives Nationales, Paris. In a postscript intended only for the clergy, Place supports Dupanloup's attack on Veuillot.

28. "l'autorité suprême du Concile va bientôt mettre d'accord des adversaires également dévoués à la cause de l'Eglise et soumis d'avance à son indéclinable autorité; l'éclat même des divergences qui se produisent ne servira qu'à faire mieux ressortir la soumission filiale avec laquelle les plus hautes intelligences savent s'incliner devant ses

Maret would see this differently: his visit during the council to Filippo de Angelis, a cardinal president of the council, led to the conclusion that "the Holy Father is insistent on a decree on infallibility and will not let the bishops leave without his having obtained it."[29] Whether the rumor of a proposed definition by acclamation was based on a real plan of the ultramontanists or not, Colet writes, "What is certain, moreover, is that the fear of this irregular method of definition by acclamation has moved minds to be unfavorably disposed at least as much as the question itself, and this from the very opening of the conciliar proceedings."[30]

Darboy writes from Rome that he will allow the council itself to correct and clarify the rumors and false newspaper reports about its proceedings.[31] Nevertheless, "the excesses of the New Ultramontanism . . . did exercise a profound influence on the atmosphere in which the Council was held."[32] The French minority bishops heard and repeated to each other the growing numbers of rumors about the council—rumors that the council would define a new doctrine on papal infallibility, that it would confirm the excesses of the ultramontanist school, that it would present the bishops with a completed text upon their arrival, that it would define by acclamation. Gradually these rumors drew a disparate collection of bishops together into a minority with one major bond: a common fear.

The Common Fear

The French minority bishops were united against any definition of separate, personal, or absolute papal infallibility. Because they believed that the upcoming council might head toward such a definition, they braced themselves for a fight. Because they believed that the conciliar schema actually proposed for definition a separate, per-

décisions" (unnamed correspondent from Rome, 28 November 1869, *La chronique religieuse de Dijon et du diocèse* 6 [4 December 1869]:35).

29. Quoted in Bazin, *Vie de Maret*, 3:198.

30. "Ce qui du reste est certain, c'est que l'appréhension de ce mode irrégulier de définition par acclamation a pesé au moins autant que la question elle-même, sur la disposition peu favorable des esprits, à partir de l'ouverture des travaux conciliaires" (Colet, "Souvenirs du concile du Vatican," fol. C).

31. Georges Darboy to A. Surat, 2 February 1970, *Collectio Lacensis* 7:1406.

32. Butler, *Vatican Council*, 1:77; see also Aubert, *Vatican I*, p. 73.

sonal, absolute papal infallibility, they fought against it to the last hour. All of the arguments that I will examine in the next three chapters had their basis in this common fear.

Because the fear of a separate, personal, absolute papal infallibility motivated the French minority so deeply, it is referred to again and again in their arguments against the schema. This point cannot be emphasized enough: the French minority believed that the question under debate at the council was whether to define the separate, personal, absolute infallibility of the pope. Because they believed that the schema did in fact propose such a definition, they opposed the schema. As we follow their arguments against the schema in the next section, we will see how much this understanding of the schema—whether correct or not—shaped their opposition to it.

Sometimes a bishop mentions or focuses on just one of the feared three aspects under discussion, such as a separate infallibility of the pope. But gradually the bishops came to see that all three aspects were interrelated and must all be opposed.

Concern about this issue is evident in David's letter in support of Maret's book: "We are here concerned with truth and with the most apparent and most serious of the Church's interests in the nineteenth century. In my opinion the point you are defending appeals to my most intimate and invincible convictions. *If a personal, absolute, separate infallibility were proclaimed I am convinced that it would be the greatest misfortune of modern times.*" Ginoulhiac writes to Dupanloup about a meeting in Rome before the council: "I am very worried about the probable purpose of the meeting we are to have in June. . . . From all sides I hear that it will be either the definition of the personal or at least the separate infallibility of the pope or that preparations will be begun toward this definition. . . . As far as I can see there is no more serious question today and the results of such a definition would be disastrous for the Church."[33] Again and again before the council, explicit fear of the definition of separate, personal, and absolute papal infallibility is expressed. Ginoulhiac, in his public writing, tries to calm those who fear that the council will define several points of doctrine that have not been required in the belief of those returning to the church, "or which do not even appear certain

---

33. Augustin David to Henri Maret, n.d., quoted in Palanque, *Catholiques libéraux et gallicans en France*, p. 144; Jacques Ginoulhiac to Félix Dupanloup, 31 January 1867, quoted in ibid., pp. 66–67.

to all Catholic theologians." But Dupanloup, in his *Observations*, confronts the fear more realistically. The present rumors raise serious issues, he says, because "it would mean proclaiming a new dogma, the dogma of the personal and separate infallibility of the pope." He cites Henry Edward Manning, archbishop of Westminster, in explaining that, if defined, the dogma would oblige Catholics to believe that the pope can pronounce alone, "OUTSIDE OF THE EPISCOPAL BODY, ASSEMBLED OR DISPERSED THROUGHOUT THE WORLD," and that he can define dogmas alone, "SEPARATELY AND INDEPENDENTLY OF THE EPISCOPATE, without any agreement of the bishops, explicit or implicit, antecedent or subsequent." If such a dogma were proclaimed, he hastens to add, it would not be new as though created, for the church does not create dogmas. "I say a new dogma," he continues, "in the sense that never, for eighteen centuries, were the faithful bound to believe this under pain of no longer being Catholic."[34]

That the council might define as dogma the ideas of one school of thought is a frequent theme also in the work of Maret. Denouncing the Vatican officials, he writes in 1867, "They would look to the bishops for a new lead in favor of the temporal power of the pope. They would like, above all, a declaration of the bishops in favor of a *personal, absolute, separate infallibility* of the sovereign pontiff." Two years later, he writes at the start of his book that one school of thought prevails in the church. In the system of this school, "dogmatic infallibility is a privilege wholly and exclusively personal to the pontiff; that is, it is a privilege of the pontiff when he is teaching alone and without any necessary agreement with the episcopate. Thus understood, infallibility is identical with the pure, indivisible, and absolute monarchy of the Roman pontiff. Spiritual sovereignty and its necessary attribute, dogmatic infallibility, belong to the pope and to him alone." But such a view should be discussed freely before the council, Maret believes, because it is not the only acceptable view of infallibility. He opposes papal infallibility only if it is equated with a system of pure, indivisible, absolute monarchy of the pope. "Pontifical infallibility is not denied but its true nature is clarified," Maret explains, describing his position. "We recognize and assert that, by his right to consult or to convene the episcopate, by the possibility

34. Ginoulhiac, *Le concile oecuménique*, p. 107; Dupanloup, *Observations sur la controverse*, p. 7; see also p. 16.

that it act always in agreement with him, the pope has, by virtue of divine command, the assured means of giving infallibility to his dogmatic judgments." He opposes papal infallibility only "inasmuch as his absolute monarchy and his personal infallibility are thus made a single entity, which seems to us to be in disagreement with Scripture, and with tradition, and with the acts of the general councils."[35] Meignan understands him: "Today all Catholics believe in the infallibility of the pope; Bishop Maret as well as M. Bouix. But while some desire a personal and separate infallibility, others have a different understanding of it."[36] It is against the school which understands papal infallibility as separate, personal, and absolute that Maret struggles, he says throughout his book. He fears that people will confuse this school of thought with Catholicism itself.[37]

During the council, French minority bishops continued to believe that acceptance or rejection of a separate, personal, and absolute papal infallibility was the choice that lay before them. David writes that the council must choose between infallibility "personal or isolated" or infallibility of the pope in union with the church.[38] Colet writes in his "Souvenirs" that a group supporting the definition of "the personal and independent infallibility of the pope" presented its *postulatum* and prevented opponents of a definition from appointment to preparatory deputations.[39] In a letter written during the council, Dupanloup summarizes one of his objections to a definition:

Yes, of course, the Church must have an infallible doctrinal authority; but must this authority be the pope *alone:* wouldn't the authority of the pope and of the bishops assembled be sufficient? . . . In a word: is infallibility in the Church infallibility of the Church, that is, the infallibility of the pope with the bishops, so that, in this way, the episcopate has a real and necessary part in the definition of the faith, at least by its consent, either formal or tacit, antecedent or subsequent? Or is it the infallibility of the pope *alone,*

35. Henri Maret, *Mémoire* (25 March 1867) to the Emperor, quoted in Palanque, *Catholiques libéraux et gallicans en France*, p. 67; Maret, *Du concile général et de la paix religieuse*, pp. xvii, xxvii.

36. Guillaume Meignan to *L'Univers*, 19 November 1869, quoted in Palanque, *Catholiques libéraux et gallicans en France*, p. 92, n. 127. M. Bouix is probably Marcel Bouix, who translated and commented on spiritual works.

37. Maret, *Du concile général et de la paix religieuse*, 1:130, 2:62, 2:359; Maret, *Mémoire* (21 September 1862), cited by Bazin, *Vie de Maret*, 2:260.

38. David to diocesan clergy, 20 April 1870, quoted in Durand, "Mgr David et le concile du Vatican," p. 46.

39. "l'infaillibilité personnelle et indépendante du Pape" (Colet, "Souvenirs du concile du Vatican," fol. I).

without any agreement of the episcopate necessary at all? This is the question: and M. de Maistre's argument does not touch on it.[40]

Dupanloup here argues that the choice facing the council demands an acceptance or rejection of separate papal infallibility. A correspondent of Maret writes in the same month that absolute papal infallibility is under consideration: "Whether or not absolute infallibility be defined, the damage [already done] is immense, almost irreparable. We have lost the sympathy of the educated classes and of intelligent men. The possibility of such a definition, either soon or in the remote future, is a sword of Damocles hanging over the heads of unbelievers whom this eventuality separates from us even farther. It is already unfortunate that the question has even been raised."[41]

In their discussions of the schema during the council, French minority bishops continued to show their conviction that a separate, personal, absolute papal infallibility was under consideration. In his argument against the schema shortly before the final vote, Ramadié says that if an infallible magisterium is necessary, "it does not seem necessary that Christ reserve it to the head alone of his mystical body. Obviously he could have decided that that infallible authority should reside in the body teaching with the head, and have established that in its exercise—which is the supereminent act of the Church's life—both the head should direct the body and the body should sustain the head." He suggests that perhaps the council should in fact consider condemning the idea of separate infallibility, which affirms a truncated body, and he even proposes the formulation for such a condemnation: "If anyone say that the Church's infallible magisterium, instituted by Christ, can be exercised either by the bishops separate from the Roman pontiff, or by the Roman pontiff separate from the bishops, let him be anathema."[42] Ginoulhiac challenges one speaker who, he believes, assigns to only one witness the tasks of safeguarding the deposit of faith and witnessing to it. On the contrary, he maintains, Christ commissioned many witnesses. De Las Cases contests the schema because it presents "an infallibility divided but separate and without any agreement [*consensus*], whether

40. Félix Dupanloup to Victor Dechamps, archbishop of Malines, 1 March 1870, *Collectio Lacensis* 7:1327A–B.
41. An Oratorian to Henri Maret, 17 March 1870, quoted in Bazin, *Vie de Maret*, 3:181.
42. Mansi 52:1016C, 1019B.

antecedent or concomitant or subsequent, of the bishops." David also speaks against the schema because he believes it teaches the separate, personal, absolute infallibility of the pope:

This is my thesis: In proclaiming definitions of faith, the supreme pontiff is never even to be thought of as endowed with infallibility separately from the teaching Church, by himself alone, even [when] speaking as supreme pastor. For either the teaching Church itself anticipates or solicits the pope's revered opinion, or it teaches with the pope when he teaches the universal faith, or it assents to the pope when he teaches prior to everyone. This is the law of the holy Church, this is the discipline of healthy theology, this is the authentic summary of our entire history.[43]

Callot fears that the schema's wording suggests an infallibility which resides exclusively in the pope in such a way that it is unable to reside in other subjects. Against such an opinion, Callot cites the teaching of Alphonsus Liguori that infallibility remains with the body of bishops whenever the Apostolic See is absent or occupied by a doubtful or heretical pope.[44] In his section on the attitude of inopportunists at the council, Colet writes: "Now since what has always been a matter of faith is that the sacred magisterium of the Church, made up of the pope and the bishops, assembled or dispersed, cannot err in matters of faith and morals and that the pope speaking in the name of the Church teaches the truth infallibly, it does not seem to me that one can logically conclude that the pope is personally and separately infallible. On the contrary, this doctrine seems a complete reversal of the preceding one."[45] Colet showed this concern in his second speech against the schema at the council, when he notes that it proposes a separate, personal, and absolute infallibility, which cannot be derived from indefectibility.[46]

In his conciliar speech, Darboy repeatedly refers to his belief that the schema proposes a separate, personal, absolute papal infallibility. It does not consider infallibility in general, he argues, since all believe

43. Ibid., col. 215D–216A, 338D, 988B–C.
44. Ibid., col. 1046A.
45. "Or de ce qu'il a toujours été de foi que le Divin Magistère de l'Eglise composé du Pape et des Evêques réunis ou dispersés, ne peut pas errer sur les questions intéressant la foi et les moeurs, et que le Pape parlant comme l'Organe de l'Eglise enseigne infailliblement la vérité, il ne semble pas que l'on puisse logiquement déduire que le Pape est personnellement et séparément infaillible. Cette doctrine apparaît au contraire comme le renversement de la précédente" (Colet, "Souvenirs du concile du Vatican," fol. N).
46. Mansi 52:985A–B.

that the church is infallible; rather, it proposes to define as *de fide* that the pope "by himself alone" is infallible and that this privilege extends as widely as does the church's infallibility. To prove his contention, he continues:

> For it should be noted that that infallibility always admitted by everyone, i.e., that infallibility which resides uniquely in the common consensus [*consensus*] of the bishops joined to the supreme pontiff, as the invincible and irresistible force of decrees or dogmatic decisions commanding the faith of all, both faithful and pastors, is not treated in the schema. On the contrary, what is treated—even if the thing is not proclaimed openly—is the personal, absolute, and separate infallibility of the pope.

Darboy again exhibits his understanding of the schema later in the speech when he notes that if the doctrine of the pope's personal infallibility is to be defined, it should be clearly explained and held in moral unanimity by fathers of the council. Speaking on the schema's inability to attract other Christians, he asks, "Surely a personal and independent infallibility will not raise extinct churches of the African coast from the tomb, or raise from sleep that East, which once flourished with so much talent and strength?" Later he exclaims, "And they hope that by this definition of personal and separate infallibility everything can be healed, faith can immediately be strengthened in everyone and morals changed for the better! . . . Therefore it is not enough to declare the pope to be infallible personally and apart from the bishops."[47]

The minority continued to find foundation for their fears during the council. Colet's minutes of the French minority gathering only one month before the final vote give a terse report on the meeting between David and Pius IX: "But after having declared that it was the duty of the bishops to teach defined doctrine without mitigating it, His Holiness let it be understood that he would not consent to having infallibility subjected to any rule as to its subject, nor limited in its object."[48] A report like this helps us to understand why the French minority's fears continued throughout the council. Dupan-

---

47. Ibid., cols. 157D–158A, 159D, 160D, 161B–C.

48. "Mais après avoir déclaré qu'il était du devoir des Evêques d'enseigner la doctrine définie sans la mitiger, Sa Sainteté a donné à entendre qu'Elle ne consentirait pas à ce que l'Infaillibilité fût assujétée [*sic*] à aucune règle quant à son sujet, ni restreinte dans son objet" (Colet, "Copie des procès-verbaux rédigés par Mgr Colet des séances tenues par les évêques de la minorité," fol. 64; see also Palanque, *Catholiques libéraux et gallicans en France*, p. 175, n. 209).

loup sums up the atmosphere well in a random journal entry: "Many
. . . say: 'I would rather die than see all this.'"[49]

The French minority bishops did not apply the terms *separate, personal,* or *absolute* to their opponents' position on papal infallibility
without some clear reflections on the precise meaning of these terms.
In a description of the "absolutist" school, Maret examines its belief
in a separate, personal, absolute papal infallibility. What does this
school mean by these terms? By *personal,* Maret explains, this school
does not conceive infallibility as attached "to the human person."
Rather, infallibility, as attached "to the pontifical person, to the pontiff, becomes, in this sense, personal." By *absolute,* this school means
"without condition, or rather with conditions which no one can or
should verify," Maret continues, noting that the school is divided
over the conditions and signs of infallible teachings. By *separate,* this
school means "the attribution of this divine privilege to the pope,
exclusive of any agreement of the bishops in pontifical decisions,
whether this agreement be antecedent, concomitant, or subsequent;
whether it be expressed or tacit."[50] Maret shows in these clarifications
that he understands his opponents' position in a somewhat nuanced
way.

Dupanloup also reveals a nuanced understanding of his opponents' position. He claims that he uses *personal* in exactly the same
way as do supporters of personal papal infallibility; but he opposes
their position of "personal infallibility," which he describes as

the infallibility active in the pope alone, and through him to the teaching
Church to which he communicates it; the infallibility of the pope, I no longer say "separately" as this word has been rejected, although the English expression (apart from) has this same meaning, but independently, since this
formula is acceptable, independently of the episcopate assembled or dispersed: there you have the position [of Dupanloup's opponents] and what I
understand by personal infallibility.

He continues by noting the distinction of his correspondent between the private person and the public person: "You say: 'It is not
to a *private* but to a *public* person that infallibility was promised.' The
personal infallibility of which I spoke is the infallibility of the public
person of the pope."[51] Dupanloup wants his opponents to grasp that

49. Dupanloup, Journal, entry for 25 April 1870, quoted in Hasler, *Pius IX,* p. 168,
n. 47.

50. Maret, *Du concile général et de la paix religieuse,* 2:71.

51. Félix Dupanloup to Victor Dechamps, 1 March 1870, *Collectio Lacensis* 7:1327B–C.

he has understood their position clearly and nevertheless opposes it.

Finally, Rivet mirrors a common view of the French minority in his council speech. He grants the unclear meaning of the terms *personal* and *absolute* but argues that, because these terms were widely used in discussion, the council must refer to them. Opposition to the definition comes from people who believe in the church's infallibility but would not be able to believe in the pope's personal and absolute infallibility. Public opinion must be taken into account, Rivet argues, even when it is wrong.[52] Rivet here recognizes that widespread discussion of the definition has confused the exact meaning of the proposed schema in the public mind. But since that discussion has convinced people that the personal and absolute infallibility of the pope is under consideration, he points out, the council cannot afford to ignore this conviction.

Despite their many differences, the French minority bishops worked together because of their common fear that the council would define the separate, personal, absolute infallibility of the pope. This fear proved a powerful bond of union, which impelled them to elaborate a common vision and a common plan of action.

Conclusion

The French minority bishops formed their opposition to the definition of papal infallibility in an atmosphere of exaggerated personal devotion to the pope and alarming rumors about the council's purpose. They came to believe that the council would consider a definition of the separate, personal, absolute infallibility of the pope. A few showed that their understanding of such a definition included at least some of the nuances their opponents used to defend the position. Nevertheless, the French minority opposed the definition of separate, personal, absolute infallibility of the pope, and their common fear of such a definition continued to shape their opposition to the proposed schema throughout the council. These bishops believed that the conciliar schema proposed for definition as *de fide* the separate, personal, absolute infallibility of the pope, and proceeding on this understanding of the schema they formed their case against it. Had their understanding of the schema been different, their arguments would have been different as well.

52. Mansi 52:50D–51C.

PART II

The French Minority Bishops Against the Definition of Papal Infallibility

4

On Timeliness

Papal Infallibility as Proposed Should Not Be Defined

———— ◀●▶ ————

Why did the French minority bishops oppose the definition of papal infallibility? The answer to this question can be found in the cases the minority built against the proposed definition.

The Systematic Framework of the Arguments

The French minority bishops opposed the proposed schema's definition for a variety of reasons, expressed by the arguments found within their books, letters, journals, sermons, and speeches written before and during the council. If systematic theologians believe that they will hear, in addition to these arguments, an explicitly articulated, systematic framework for these arguments, they are mistaken. The French minority did not often reflect upon the general principles or systematic framework that underlay their specific arguments; in fact, only a few bishops advert explicitly to it. Nevertheless, systematic theologians can discern that such a framework stands behind all of the French minority's arguments and shapes them into a unified system of thought. Because it is for the most part unrecognized, its presence in the thought of an individual minority bishop can go unnoticed; it stands out only when the arguments of the group as a whole are studied. And only then can we gain an understanding of why the French minority opposed the definition of papal infallibility.

Three questions synthesize the general concerns to which the French minority's arguments responded: (1) Is the proposed teaching true? If yes, (2) Is the proposed teaching definable? If yes, (3)

Should the proposed teaching be defined? These three questions form a systematic set by which to differentiate the positions on the definition of papal infallibility held by each bishop at the First Vatican Council. Indeed, these questions could be used to differentiate and classify the position of any member of any ecumenical council concerning any proposed definition. Council members who answered each of the three questions affirmatively for the proposed teaching thereby placed themselves in the group supporting the definition of the proposed teaching at that time. So the majority from the First Vatican Council, for example, can be equated with those members who would have answered *yes* to each of these three questions if asked them explicitly. On the other hand, opponents of the proposed teaching's definition, such as the French minority at the First Vatican Council, would have answered *no* to at least one of these questions if asked them explicitly.

The French minority at the First Vatican Council can be further distinguished by the number of questions they answered negatively. A *no* to the third question reveals only mild opposition; a *no* to the second and third questions shows stronger opposition; and a *no* to all three questions evidences the strongest opposition. We can begin to attain a more thorough understanding of the many arguments of the French minority when we organize their arguments with this tool. Thus, some arguments aimed to show that the teaching on papal infallibility—as the French minority understood the schema's presentation of that teaching—should not be defined. It was untimely or, to use a frequently misunderstood term, inopportune. Another set of arguments went further; bishops who used these arguments believed not merely that the definition was untimely but that it was impossible: not merely that the teaching should not be defined but that it could not be defined. Finally, a third set of arguments was made by bishops who believed not merely that the teaching was untimely, nor even that it could not be defined, but also that it was untrue.

The French minority bishops made three cases against the proposed definition of papal infallibility: a case against its timeliness, a case against its definability, and a case against its truth. Each case, made up of several often interrelated arguments, forms the basis for one chapter in this section, starting with the mildest case of opposition and moving toward the strongest.

Explicitation of the Systematic Framework

A few of the French minority bishops seemed at times to grasp reflectively the systematic framework behind their thought, or at least to suggest some hint of such a grasp. These bishops spell out two or three of the questions around which they group their arguments.

On the issue of pontifical infallibility, Colet writes, there are two questions: its opportuneness and its definability. Ginoulhiac, noting the importance of careful deliberation at a council, writes that bishops at a council must concern themselves with the question of "definability or the certainty of the revelation of the dogma itself," as well as with "opportuneness" of a definition in light of 1 Cor. 6:12 and 1 Cor. 10:22. Ginoulhiac notes firmly that the church "does not obey mystical thoughts, speculative ideas or so-called suitability, almost always arbitrary; she makes up her mind after a well-thought-out conviction brought about by a clear providential indication whose proof lies only in a real and urgent necessity or in what is of general, incontestable and practical use." The three questions are again made somewhat explicit by Maret, who asks whether a definition of the dogma of separate, personal, absolute papal infallibility is possible and opportune, noting that it would have to be found in Scripture and tradition as revealed. He concludes with a reflection on the truth and definability of the teaching: "So these privileges are not truths expressly, formally, clearly revealed in divine Scripture; they are not confirmed by ancient, perpetual, constant, unanimous tradition; they cannot, therefore, become the object of the divine Catholic faith; thus they cannot be defined as dogma.[1]

Dupanloup discusses the three questions in letters written to members of the majority at the council. In a letter to Manning, he draws attention to the Council of Trent's concern with timeliness, even when the matter itself in question was considered certain. He notes two questions, though his second question raises obliquely the issues of both definability and timeliness:

When they were debating the tiresome question of residency at the Council of Trent, first of all they divided the question in two thus:

1. Colet, "Souvenirs du concile du Vatican," fol. C; Ginoulhiac, *Le concile oecuménique*, p. 44; Maret, *Du concile général et de la paix religieuse*, 2:368.

1. Is residency of divine right?

2. If the theologians, on being consulted, declare, *unanimously*, that it is of divine right and if the fathers confirm this opinion, SHOULD the Council define it and erect it as an article of faith?

They realized then, that it might be inopportune to define a certain and revealed truth! . . . As far as I am concerned, I cannot believe that in its most serious decisions, the Church is dispensed from considerations of prudence and from the charity of sparing people's feelings! In following this inspiration so worthy of it, moreover, it merely imitates the example of our divine master who said to his apostles: "I have many other things to say to you but you cannot bear them now."[2]

In a letter to Victor Dechamps, archbishop of Malines, Dupanloup spells out the three questions more clearly. He writes that "with regard to every dogmatic definition, but especially to the one that you are considering, there are two questions: the dogma itself that they wish to define, the question of opportuneness." Dupanloup adds that the issue of opportuneness has always been raised by councils, and he accuses Dechamps of having misunderstood the extent and import of the second question of opportuneness. He divides this issue into two aspects: "first of all the very definability of the dogma, that is, the theological and historical problems involved; then, a second still more serious consideration, the consequences and the dangers that could follow in its wake." Dupanloup then provides a summary of the three-question framework, which I have found behind the thought of the French minority as a whole:

Thus, in the last analysis, there were, regarding the requested definition, several very distinct questions: as in every proposed definition three things had to be examined: the truth to be defined, the definability, and the definition itself. The discussion of the truth I have reserved until the Council in case the question arises; I have brought forward all the chief difficulties surrounding the definability; I have shown what consequences and dangers could follow on the definition. There is my whole case.[3]

Dupanloup hints at the importance of distinguishing among the three questions when he notes that Dechamps confuses the two

2. Félix Dupanloup, *Réponse de Mgr l'évêque d'Orléans à Mgr Manning, archevêque de Westminster* (Paris: Charles Douniol, 1869), pp. 14–15.

3. Dupanloup to Dechamps, 1 March 1870, *Collectio Lacensis* 7:1321C–D. For Dupanloup, as well as for other minority bishops, the term *inopportune* refers to both the second and third questions that I have found to differentiate their concerns. Because of this meaning for *inopportune*, I have used the term *timeliness* to indicate precisely the concerns inherent in the third question only, which this chapter treats.

questions of infallibility and opportuneness, lumping together in-opportunists (that is, in my usage, those who question its definabil-ity or its timeliness) with those who oppose the thing itself (that is, its truth). In addition, he says, Dechamps confuses sovereignty with infallibility.[4] This suggests another characteristic of the French minority bishops: although only a few made explicit the systematic framework of the group, all at least discerned the differences in-volved in the three questions.

I have shown the underlying systematic framework of the French minority's arguments and their occasional explicitation of this framework. Now let us examine the first of the three cases which they made against the definition: the case against its timeliness.[5]

Unity of Belief and the Good of the Church

The French minority bishops believed that definition of papal in-fallibility would endanger the church. Callot typifies this view when he praises Pius IV and Charles de Lorraine, cardinal, archbishop of Reims at the time of the Council of Trent, both of whom showed concern at that council for the church's welfare: "For they knew that to define a certain article, it is not sufficient that it be believed, in-deed even that it be proved true and revealed; but it is required that it not be dangerous to the Church. They knew this definition to be an act of the government of the Church, an act which, the more im-portant it is, the more prudence it requires." A definition of papal infallibility would produce a great wound in the church, Callot be-lieves, and others agree with him. Bravard shows his fears when he comments: "May this God be pleased not to use this experience to castigate Europe for all its infidelities, or delight in this occasion in order to incite schisms, renew hatreds in the Church, snatch away the Catholic faith from our peoples just as once he snatched it away from both Africa and Asia!"[6] Ginoulhiac believes that a definition

4. Ibid., cols. 1326B–1327A.

5. I have arranged the points in each case through a series of subheadings which group together arguments or insights that make the same general point. In some cases, of course, an individual argument does not share in all of the aspects of other arguments in its group, but its intent seems the same, or it has most of the characteris-tics shared by other arguments of its group. My intention is not to provide an exact set of mutually exclusive categories with my subheadings, but rather to reflect the range of arguments actually used, with all of their many shades of difference.

6. Mansi 52:618D, 619B, 307D.

would be disastrous for the church because it would harm the church's unity and even lead to schism.[7] Callot also thinks that a definition will set Catholics against each other, and he remembers the comment of de Lorraine, "that Catholics already had enough to do and more, disputing with heretics, and that Catholics ought not to be set against one another."[8] Colet believes "that the question of pontifical infallibility was not matured enough to be imposed without danger on the weakened faith of the faithful accustomed to believe only in the infallibility of the church.[9] Dupanloup and Mathieu fear that the German Catholics would be upset or even led to schism by a definition, and Bravard warns the council, "The Christian people were not so greatly desirous as you think for the doctrine about the supreme pontiff to be defined."[10]

David was also worried about the dangers the definition would bring for the church. The schema deals with the foundation of the church, he maintains; but if any human society were to proceed as the discussion suggests, he would fear lest the whole edifice fall and bury the participants in its ruins. Of course, the church will endure because it has God's protection, but passage of the proposed schema would open it to injury from heretics and schismatics. Emphasizing only one aspect of the truth, he warns, could do harm to the present and future church:

How the state of the Church at this time is to be bewailed. For if in our texts and speeches we show only one face of the truth, we are not taking counsel for the good of the Church and for truth itself; but what has already often happened because of the fault of times and men, what God has already often permitted, that will be able to return again in the future. This would also be harmful for our holy Church especially in these days, when authority is everywhere attacked, even in its legitimate exercise, and *a fortiori* its possible excesses.[11]

7. Ginoulhiac to Dupanloup, 31 January 1867, cited by Palanque, *Catholiques libéraux et gallicans en France*, p. 67.

8. Mansi 52:618C.

9. "que la question de l'infaillibilité pontificale n'était pas assez mûre pour que l'on prît sans danger en imposer la croyance à la foi affaiblie des Fidèles accoutumés seulement à croire à l'infaillibilité de l'Eglise" (Colet, "Souvenirs du concile du Vatican," fol. K).

10. "Lettres de l'abbé Dupanloup—Projet de réedition de l'*Ami de la Religion*" (dossier), 4BI, 7, Archives de l'archevêché de Paris; Besson, *Vie de Mathieu*, 2:268; Mansi 52:307A.

11. Mansi 52:73A, 73C–D, 596A.

Public opinion in the church is opposed to a definition of papal infallibility, Rivet points out, and such opposition comes, not from any depraved or impious mind, but "from the conscience formed by reasoning, from the consideration of the usual results of civil and ecclesiastical history, from the great power of contemporary ideas, and finally—and it is not absurd to say this—from that contrary opinion that has already been implanted in the mind from one's most tender years." Such people believe in the church's infallibility, but they would not be able to believe in the pope's personal and absolute infallibility, especially since many doctors of the faith have disputed among themselves over this point. Public opinion, even when it is wrong, must still be taken into account, Rivet believes, citing the practice of France, following the principle, "The laws must be lived before being codified." He continues: "Nothing therefore, as is right, should be prescribed under penalty either to be believed or to be done unless the mores and common opinion have first been formed regarding this thing: otherwise both opinion and mores will rise up stubbornly and try to shake off indignantly an imposed yoke." Rivet's argument here for prior agreement by the church seems to be a practical one: without such agreement preceding a formal decision, the decision will be unenforceable and even likely to stir up revolt. Rivet thinks that the Council of Trent had given attention to such prior agreement. He cites as another example the procedure of Pius IX in defining the Immaculate Conception: although "he had long ago been informed of the wishes, so to speak, of the entire Church," the pope solicited the views of bishops and theologians and asked for prayers. "It even seemed to such a supreme pontiff that in matters of religion one ought always to act not rashly but with very cautious opinion," Rivet explains, adding the words of Christ in John 16:12 to illustrate further his point.[12]

Other French minority bishops share the view that agreement among church members on a belief should precede a formal definition of the belief so as to avoid harming the church. Darboy exclaims: "On the other hand, for authority to flourish and function efficaciously, it is necessary not only that it be affirmed but also moreover that it be accepted. Therefore it is insufficient to declare that the pope personally and separately from the bishops is infallible;

12. Ibid., cols. 51B–C, 52C–D. I think Mansi's *cautissime* should be *cautissima*.

what is required is that he be accepted as such by everyone in order that he not exercise his office in vain." The mere proclamation of an infallible authority does not suffice for effective teaching of beliefs, Darboy maintains, using the response to the *Syllabus* as an example. Public opinion should not dominate church behavior, but neither should it be ignored.[13] Along the margin of his copy of the schema, in the section on the antichrist, Meignan writes: "I should prefer a milder introduction: it is a matter of bringing back to the Church an immense crowd of Christians who are leaving it and of not driving them away by harsh language. . . . We must proceed by way of exposition. Ignorance, the preponderance of material interests, love of comfort and security: these are the great ills of the century. . . . One finds few antichrists or falsifiers of doctrine in my diocese."[14]

Callot returns to the Council of Trent and to de Lorraine, who asked Pius IV to drop from the agenda the question of the preeminence of pope over council, "lest there be given an occasion of writing various pamphlets from both sides, and of calling into doubt the authority of the Apostolic See." A definition of papal infallibility could have similar detrimental effects, he argues, and could hurt the unity of the church. A council definition should be suited to aid church unity, likely to promote obedience among all church members, says Ginoulhiac. In addition to showing the unity among council members, he maintains, a definition should be able to elicit positive response from believers. He cites Pius VI that the pope must always attend to the ways that his declarations will affect the faithful and notes the similarity of the times to those of Pius VI: "It is therefore to be regarded as both a principle and an utterly sacred rule that, for the successor of St. Peter to be able after mature examination to arrive at the declaration of a doctrine, he must be certain that the voice of the first pastor will not lack the docility of those who hear." The council members should also ask themselves

whether we are not simply confident but are certain that the docility not only of the simple faithful but of those who hear in general will not be lacking to the formula that has been handed down to us, as Pius VI used to say. Is not the time in which we are living comparable to that time in which the supreme pontiff was speaking? Are not the mental confusions, the freedom given to errors, the current license given to doctrines a kind of extension of

13. Ibid., cols. 161C, 162A.
14. Boissonnot, *Le Cardinal Meignan*, p. 292.

those things which were disturbing the world at that time and were evident in the world? Is not this time the very time of uproar and, as it were, of universal madness? Who, therefore, would inspire the confidence of this docility in a time of madness? Who would affirm whether more evil or good would come from the enunciations of a formula such as is being presented?[15]

Other bishops from many lands have indicated similar concerns, and Ginoulhiac believes that their views must be taken into account by the council.

Some French minority bishops thus felt that the council should not define papal infallibility because its definition would hurt the church. Many Catholics would not agree with such a definition, and their opinion should not be ignored. A definition should be capable of eliciting positive reception by the whole church, and such reception is served best by attention to the state of opinion among believers about the teaching.

Freedom in Theological Opinion and Unanimity in Definitions of Faith

"The Church, in its councils, has always defined only what the needs of the times and of souls demanded," Dupanloup argues against the definition of papal infallibility. That an unnecessary definition should not be made constituted another argument made by several French minority bishops. The proposed definition, argues Meignan, involves "a thousand problems" and is inopportune. A definition is inopportune when unnecessary, he continues; "now, why would that of infallibility be timely now when faithful, priests, and bishops all obey with so great unanimity the orders, even the desires of the sovereign pontiff?"[16] The very fact of actual unity in obedience to the pope seems to Meignan an argument against spelling out the need for such obedience.

Darboy makes a similar point in his discussion of the practical consequences of adopting the proposed schema. The doctrine of personal papal infallibility should not be required for belief "save in order that there might be a closer unity in the Church and a stronger central authority, and thus that a more efficacious remedy be provided

15. Mansi 52:618C, 908B, 909B–C.
16. Dupanloup, *Reponse à Manning*, p. 14; Boissonnot, *Le Cardinal Meignan*, pp. 298–99.

for all evils." Of course, in the church there has always been a central authority under which the unity of faith and communion exist—to say less would indicate a centuries-old lack in the church. "Therefore there remain unshaken both the unity of doctrine and also of communion, and the central authority of the supreme pontiff, which blossomed and flourish quite apart from any dogmatic definition of infallibility," he points out. This unity and central authority should be served, not as we imagine or reason it should be, but as instituted by Christ and understood by the fathers. But unity would not be stronger with a stronger central authority; on the contrary, a tightening can cause things to perish, to be stopped up. Darboy contrasts the unity among free men with the unity among slaves under a tyrant: "Thus in morals, the unity of men acting freely and boldly under the law is less constrained and more honorable than is the unity of slaves sluggishly spending their lives under the will of a tyrant."[17] Thus the central authority instituted by Christ, which does not separate bishops from pope nor pope from bishops, should be kept lest the actual unity in the church which it has furthered be destroyed.

Rivet carries the argument against the schema further, saying that a definition was not only unnecessary, but useless. The purposes it would fulfill have been achieved for hundreds of years without a defined dogma, Rivet contends, citing the condemnation of Jansenism, the discipline against the Napoleonic church, and other examples.[18] What use would a definition now serve after such an established practice?

Callot urges the importance of an atmosphere of freedom on debated questions. After showing the uncertain state of the issues raised in the schema, he argues that this complex question should be left open precisely to foster obedience: "But I believe that in such serious and intricate questions it is in the interest of the universal Church, the peace of Christianity, and the obedience of the provinces (to speak with Cardinal de Lorraine) to allow the same liberty and not to resolve the doubts, which, as the most holy prelate says, at one and the same time foster humble and paternal rule on the part of superiors and more ready obedience on the part of inferiors." He repeats this opinion later, expressing his hope that the council adopt a

17. Mansi 52:160A–C.   18. Ibid., cols. 54D–57A.

milder definition than that in the schema "so that, the sacred primacy and the necessity of true obedience to the Holy See having been solemnly safeguarded, both wise liberty and true peace may still remain in the Church."[19]

The conviction that the definition was unnecessary or useless is closely related to the belief that unanimity was necessary for the effectiveness of a definition. As Callot argues that an unresolved question should remain undefined lest its definition discourage obedience, so Ginoulhiac argues that a definition should spring from the unanimous opinions of council members so as effectively to promote church unity, since matters of faith are not like topics considered by civil legislatures. "Who does not know that in councils of the Church things are done differently than in assemblies or in public and civil meetings, and that for councils of the Church others' material plurality of votes is not enough?" he asks. The history of councils shows great efforts and plans to achieve virtual unanimity, he continues, and this is because of the importance given to unanimity by Paul by which "he wants us to stand united in one spirit as fellow laborers for the Gospel of faith."[20]

Unanimity so that the definition would be effective was desired by other French minority bishops as well. They feared that lack of unanimity in a definition would render it ineffective or worse. A correspondent of Maret echoes the bishop's own fears when he wonders if the majority, proud of its numbers and tired by the resistance of the minority, plan a coup d'état that will leave "Catholic consciences prey to cruel doubts." Charity requires councils always to act "with one accord," writes Maret, "because then unity reigns in minds, laws are more respected and more efficacious and the practice of good is easier."[21] Meignan believes that the words of a definition should be exact, not exaggerating the truth of the doctrine of infallibility; thus the unanimity necessary for the definition to achieve force will be restored.[22]

19. Ibid., col. 619A–C.   20. Ibid., col. 908B–C.

21. Unnamed correspondent to Henri Maret, 25 February 1870, quoted in Bazin, *Vie de Maret*, 3:171; Maret, *Du concile général et de la paix religieuse*, 2:417.

22. Mansi 52:1015B–C. We can probably assume that Mathieu also argued for unanimity, since a popular writer, Jean-François Bergier, attacks those who maintain the need for unanimity among the council members in his polemical biography, *Supplément à la vie du Cardinal Mathieu*, p. 13. His book berates Besson's *Vie de Mathieu* for its sympathetic presentation of the cardinal and his views.

This argument by the French minority bishops, then, emphasized the importance of freedom of opinion in the church whenever possible. Dogmatic definitions should be made only when necessary. Many of the bishops noted that such an approach actually encouraged compliance with what definitions were made, and some emphasized the need for unanimity to secure such compliance.

Haste and Public Opinion

Before the council, Ginoulhiac had reassured his readers that decisions would not be taken in haste. If one council lacks time to reach the certitude necessary for definition, another council will complete its work. Emphasizing the length of time needed to arrive at a definition, he reminds his readers that the orthodox understanding of Christ needed four councils for its development:

Thus, what one council has begun another finishes. And if a new council does not assemble, the Church itself finishes it, at an opportune moment, under the inspiration of the Spirit of God. For the *Spirit of truth* was not promised to the apostles for a time and only for special occasions but he was to stay with them always and ceaselessly to teach them all truth. And Jesus Christ did not promise his apostles and through them, the Catholic episcopate, to be with them only when they were gathered together in his name, but to be *with* them, teaching and baptizing, *always, even to the consummation of the world.*[23]

Since no excuse can be found for rushing, a council loses credibility among the faithful if it seems to have acted hastily, argues Bravard, who complains frequently about the suddenness with which the question of papal infallibility has been introduced. Although it was not in the bull of convocation, "suddenly, unexpectedly, we find ourselves at other things which regard the Roman pontiff." Bravard's fear focuses not on the procedural issue itself but on the bad effects this unexpected emphasis may have on public opinion. An opportunity for calumny against the Vatican will be introduced, leading some to suggest that the council was called for the sole but unannounced purpose of proclaiming papal infallibility. Why should the bishops seem "agitated" before the people, when the promises of

23. Ginoulhiac, *Le concile oecuménique*, pp. 115–16.

Christ have been made to the church, the ship "which, though always shaken by waves, is never overwhelmed, and joyful and triumphant rows toward the eternal shores?"[24] Because of the suddenness with which the question of papal infallibility has been introduced, discussion of the schema which proposes its definition would be imprudent.

Other French minority bishops will argue on procedural grounds that haste invalidates definition. But Bravard knows the importance of the slow deliberation about which Ginoulhiac had written and thus sees the bad effects a hasty definition would have on public opinion of the definition.

Reunion of Separated Christians

An important argument against the timeliness of the schema emphasized the difficulties it would raise for the reunion of the church. A definition of papal infallibility would hardly be inviting to Protestant, Anglican, and Orthodox Christians, French minority bishops argued.

A look at their view of Christians who were not in communion with Rome should precede consideration of their argument.

Some expressed the standard apologetic criticisms of Protestants.[25] Bravard sees Protestantism as the immediate source of many evils in society; it gave birth to confusion, incertitude, revolution, and other intellectual and moral evils. To Meignan it is a cause of rationalism because it gives no authority to dogma. Guilbert argues that the Protestant churches have lost their dignity before the public, and he continues polemically: "Ecclesiastical discipline, the priesthood, the creed itself are governed by the will of a czar, by the laws of a secular parliament, by the decree of a woman!"[26]

The guide for seminarians' study in Dupanloup's diocese explains that Protestantism has three principles: that Scripture is the sole rule of faith, that private inspiration and free examination are the means

---

24. Mansi 52:306C–D, 307C.

25. Most French minority bishops call Anglicans *Protestants*.

26. Bravard, On the Council, p. 605; Guillaume Meignan, *La crise protestante en Angleterre et en France* (Paris: Charles Douniol, 1864), p. 6; Guilbert, *La divine synthèse, ou l'exposé au double point*, 2d ed., 1:287.

to interpret it, and that admission of the fundamental articles of revelation suffices for membership.[27] Dupanloup himself believes that
the negation of all doctrinal authority in the church, and hence the
belief in the absolute liberty of examination, form the gravest
dogmatic difficulty with Protestantism; further, he believes that
these traits are often mistakenly confused with rationalism. He also
blames Protestantism for the largest division in Christian society.[28]

Despite this analysis of their weaknesses, Dupanloup shows a
positive attitude toward Protestants. "Protestants hold us in esteem.
. . . They live in peace with Catholics: is this not a better situation?
. . . Where there is self-esteem, there is a proper regard of self, one
respects oneself as being sincere. Why not leave to God the question
of good faith?" he asks.[29] Throughout one pastoral letter, he addresses Protestants and Orthodox as "separated brothers,"[30] and he
does not blame them for the divisions in the church; they are merely
innocent victims: "I can distinguish between errors that begin and
errors that end, between those responsible for them, the guilty, who
willfully sow error, and the innocent victims, those of good faith,
who through the centuries have remained attached to these errors."[31]
Meignan also objects to unfair accusations against Protestants. In the
margin of his copy of the conciliar schema, he writes:

If you would reflect upon it, the general sense of the paragraph is as follows:
The single source of all contemporary errors is that the teaching of the
Church has been replaced by private judgment: whence rationalism, natural-
ism, materialism. Of course, I do not deny that whoever rejects the magisterium of the Church loses a firm support and is exposed to many errors; but I
fear that German, English and French Protestants, who are not materialistic
or pantheistic, will accuse the Vatican Council of teaching that all Protestants are atheists.[32]

27. *Programmes pour les études ecclésiastiques et conseils aux jeunes prêtres sur l'étude des différentes branches de la science sacrée: Rédigés conformément aux ordonnances de Mgr Dupanloup, évêque d'Orléans, pour l'usage de son clergé* (Orléans: Ernest Colas, 1875), pp. 48–49.
28. Dupanloup, *Sur le futur concile oecuménique*, p. 53; Dupanloup, *Le futur concile oecuménique*, p. 14.
29. Emile Faguet, *Mgr Dupanloup: Un grand évêque* (Paris: Hachette et Cie, 1914), pp. 90–91.
30. Dupanloup, *Sur le futur concile oecuménique*, pp. 46, 47, 51, 54, etc.
31. Ibid., p. 57; see also *Unitatis redintegratio* 3 in Walter M. Abbott, ed., *The Documents of Vatican II* (New York: Guild Press, 1966), p. 345.
32. Boissonnot, *Le Cardinal Meignan*, p. 292.

Hugonin also shows a positive attitude toward both Orthodox and Protestants. Orthodox and Catholics hold in common the authority and perpetuity of the church, the existence of the priesthood, the teachings of the theologians, and the decrees of the first six ecumenical councils. "Ignorance, political interests, and a sterile immobility have always been the great obstacle to their return," he continues.[33]

Hugonin also hopes for a reunion with Protestants, which he regards as more likely than at the time of the Reformation because "time, reflection, knowledge have considerably diminished the dogmatic differences which separate us."[34] Hugonin does not believe that the beginnings of Protestantism were as bad as Catholics often see them: "Primitive Protestantism was not merely a capricious rebellion against the established Church nor the result of a petty jealousy between two rival orders or an excessive violent reaction against real disorders. It was born of the personal thought of Luther; it is the fruit of the painful labor of a zealous soul and of a tormented conscience which were seeking tranquillity and peace."[35] Nevertheless, Hugonin believes the teaching of Protestantism to be radically irreconcilable with that of Catholicism. Its central dogmas are justification by faith and the uselessness of good works; from these come the suppression of the priesthood and its replacement by a ministry of the Word, the rejection of sacraments and ceremonies, belief in an invisible church, and the negation of the pope's supremacy.[36] But he believes also that these dogmas are widely abandoned by popular Protestant teaching, thus paving the way for a possible reunion through the upcoming council: "Now, we gladly proclaim that those doctrines still preserved in the formulas of faith are usually abandoned in the scientific and commonplace teaching of the doctors of

33. "L'ignorance, les intérêts politiques et l'immobilité stérile ont toujours été le grand obstacle à leur retour" (Flavien Hugonin, Pastoral Letter on Jubilee for the Council, *La semaine religieuse du diocèse de Bayeux et Lisieux*, 5 [13 June 1869]:375).

34. "le temps, la réflexion, la science ont considérablement amoindri les oppositions dogmatiques qui nous séparent" (ibid.).

35. "Le protestantisme primitif ne fut pas seulement une révolte capricieuse contre l'Eglise établie, ni l'effet d'une jalousie mesquine entre deux ordres rivaux, ou l'excès d'une réaction violente contre des désordres réels. Il est né de la pensée personnelle de Luther; c'est le fruit du travail douloureux d'une âme ardente et d'une conscience tourmentée, qui cherchent la tranquillité et la paix" (ibid.).

36. Ibid., p. 376.

the Reform. . . . So, the abyss separating us from Protestants is at
least partly bridged. . . . We are confident, our very dear brothers,
that the sight of Catholic unity rendered more evident by the
ecumenical Council will exert a salutary attraction on our separated
brothers."[37]

One of the most frequently made arguments against the schema's
timeliness was its detrimental effects on reunion of the church. Darboy suggests that a new definition of faith would perhaps increase
the obstacles blocking the return of "our dissenting brothers." His
awareness of these obstacles would have been heightened by several
years of participation in an exploratory dialogue on the possibility of
reunion with the Anglicans.[38] Darboy suggests that the schema's passage would hardly aid reunion with other Christians:

Surely a personal and independent infallibility will not raise extinct churches
of the African coast from the tomb, or raise from sleep that East, which once
flourished with so much talent and strength? Surely it will not be easier for
our brothers, that is, the apostolic vicars (whatever on the contrary will be
taught here), surely it will not be easier for them to lead pagans, Muhamma-
dans, and schismatics to the Catholic faith if they should teach precisely that
the pope by himself alone is infallible? Surely the proposed definition will
not add courage and strength to Protestants and other heretics to come to
the Roman Church and set aside now all prejudices and hatreds?[39]

Mathieu as well believes that the schema will prolong the separation
of Anglicans from reunion with Rome; Rivet fears that it will make
the return of Protestants and Orthodox more difficult; and the biographer of Dupont des Loges attributes this view to the bishop as
well. Maret, too, believes that the definition would deepen the division within the church, a division that already weakens the church's

---

37. "Or, nous le proclamons avec bonheur, ces dogmes conservés encore dans les
formules de foi, sont généralement abandonnés dans l'enseignement scientifique et
vulgaire des docteurs de la Réforme. . . . Donc, l'abîme qui nous séparait des Protestants est au moins en partie comblé. . . . Nous avons confiance, Nos Très Chers Frères,
que le spectacle de l'unité catholique rendue plus évidente par le Concile oecuménique
exercera sur nos Frères séparés une salutaire attraction" (ibid., pp. 376–77).

38. Darboy, "Lettre pastorale sur le prochain concile," *Oeuvres pastorales*, 2:411;
"Darboy: Concile," 1DVII, 4, Archives de l'Archevêché de Paris. A note in this dossier
says that Darboy had a major position in talks between Edward Pusey, an Anglican
theologian in the Oxford Movement, and French bishops that had been in progress
from 1866 until the council.

39. Mansi 52:160D–161A.

ability to accomplish its mission.[40] Colet hopes that the council will
not define papal infallibility because it will make more difficult the
reunion with a small sect in his diocese, the Petite Eglise of Vendée.[41]
This sect was in schism with Rome because it did not recognize the
episcopal power of the pope and his right of immediate jurisdiction.[42] Colet believes that its members should rejoin the Catholic
church and obey their bishop, but he treats them with indulgence
and gentleness.[43]

Dupanloup often speaks of his hope for reunion with separated
Christians, and he uses this as an argument against the timeliness of
the schema. In a way rare for his time, Aubert argues, Dupanloup
was open to the problems of Catholic churches in other countries
and to the reunion of the church. Why repel Protestants by insults,
Dupanloup asks, instead of drawing them by virtues and enlightening them by reason? This is a better means to encourage peace as
well. In a pastoral letter before the council, Dupanloup expresses his
hope that the council will heal the divisions in the church, which are
weakening the Gospel's credibility, drawing energy away from the
mission work of the church, and isolating the Orthodox churches.
"Who does not see . . . that union, the return to unity, is for the
certain good of souls, that it is the manifest will of God, and that it
would be the salvation of your churches?" he asks.[44]

Dupanloup argues against the timeliness of the definition of papal
infallibility in part because of the grave difficulty which the personal
infallibility of the pope would pose for the return of "our separated
brothers" to the one church. Would one add a new difficulty to the
Orthodox churches, saying to them, Dupanloup asks ironically, "A
ditch separates us; we are going to turn it into an abyss." In his imag-
inary address to the Orthodox he continues:

Until now you have refused to recognize the simple primacy of jurisdiction
of the Roman pontiff; we are going to oblige you, to begin with, to believe

---

40. Besson, *Vie de Mathieu*, 2:268; Mansi 52:54C; Klein, *Vie de Dupont des Loges*, p.
243; Maret, *Du concile général et de la paix religieuse*, 2:387–88.
41. Mansi 52:653B.   42. Palanque, *Catholiques et gallicans en France*, p. 172.
43. Mansi 52:653B–C.
44. Aubert, "Dupanloup"; Faguet, *Mgr Dupanloup*, p. 90; Dupanloup, *Sur le
futur concile oecuménique*, pp. 47–48, 50. Dupanloup even hopes that the council will
inspire the conversion of the Jews (p. 56).

something entirely different, to accept something that until now Catholic doctors themselves have not acknowledged: we are going to erect into dogma a much more obscure doctrine—as far as you are concerned—in both Scripture and tradition, than the very dogma not yet believed in by you, namely, the personal infallibility of the pope, alone, "INDEPENDENTLY AND SEPARATELY FROM THE BISHOPS." It is under those conditions that we are proposing an understanding between us.

When the schism arose between East and West, councils were the means by which definitions were reached; no one then was inclined to define papal infallibility. Thus a definition would further postpone the reunion with separated Christians, for Orthodox as well as Protestants, many of whom desire reunion even though they deny the authority of the church.[45]

Thus French minority bishops opposed the definition of papal infallibility in part because they believed it would impede reunion with Protestants, Anglicans, and Orthodox. Some even gave an unusually positive assessment of the teachings of those groups. But even without such a positive view, many bishops echoed Dupanloup's question: Why repel rather than draw and enlighten?

The Modern Spirit

Definition of papal infallibility is untimely, argued the French minority bishops, because it is woefully out of touch with the modern spirit. This part of their argument was well remembered by their biographers and funeral orators. Colet contested the opportuneness of the definition, according to one eulogy, because he feared that the modern spirit of revolt would find the doctrine too difficult and arouse hostility against the church.[46] Dupanloup's awareness of the unacceptable impression of absolutism which papal infallibility was giving led to the publication of his *Observations*, comments Aubert. The views of Lagrange, Dupanloup's vicar general and later his biographer, can be taken as a good indication of the understanding held as well by the bishop of Orléans, Aubert believes. The real danger,

---

45. Dupanloup, *Observations sur la controverse*, pp. 15, 16, 17–20. The phrase "INDEPENDENTLY AND SEPARATELY FROM THE BISHOPS" is quoted from Manning.

46. Charles Emile Freppel, *Oraison funèbre de Mgr Colet, archevêque de Tours* (Angers: Germain et G. Grassin, 1884), p. 21; see also Klein, *Vie de Dupont des Loges*, p. 243.

Lagrange writes, is less the triumph of a theological doctrine than the triumph of certain tendencies which the proclamation of the doctrine as dogma exaggerates. He lists these unfortunate effects: "Its immediate results, whether on all the non-Catholics whose point of view has not been seriously enough considered by Rome, whether in the usual government of the Church and this exorbitant Italianism which has done and can still do so much harm to the Church, whether lastly, on those tendencies so opposed to the reconciliation between Catholicism and modern society that we are seeking because it is true as well as necessary." The need to reconcile Catholicism with modern times and the failure of the definition to accomplish this reconciliation lead Lagrange to conclude, "The question is, therefore, very extensive, much more extensive than Bossuet's gallicanism." Seeking support for Dupanloup, he urges those Catholics who are friends of liberty and "who can see absolutely no use of applying to the present day what *L'Univers* called, a few days ago, traditions of the Middle Ages" to defend Dupanloup resolutely and always in "the great struggle in which he is engaged."[47]

The definition is not for the good of the church because it is out of touch with the times, says Rivet. In the modern day, people resist legitimate authority and want some part in determining their own government. Though the church need not bow to modern ideas for their own sakes, it should attend to them for the sake of the flock.[48] Darboy also notes that the definition contradicts the spirit of the times in Europe, where the church is in exile from congresses, public assemblies, schools, laws, and families. On all of those modern men who would throw off as burdens the customs of the past, the definition would impose "a new and therefore heavy burden"; those weak in faith are being overwhelmed "as it were, with a new and not sufficiently opportune dogma, doctrine which thus far has not yet been defined, a doctrine which has suffered not a few wounds in the present discussion." The definition will not heal a world that is sick, sick not from ignorance of truth but from flight from truth.[49]

Meignan is dismayed to discover that a fellow bishop is out of touch with the times. He writes in his journal: "I have talked with

47. Aubert, "Dupanloup au début du concile," pp. 98, 105, n. 36; François Lagrange to Augustin Cochin, 5 January 1870, quoted in ibid.
48. Mansi 52:53C–D.
49. Ibid., col. 161B.

the bishop of Gibraltar, a very intelligent man. He is firmly convinced about infallibility. He has read *Janus* and has not been at all influenced by it. Only if the bishops of Germany and France declare that infallibility is inopportune will he go along with them, for away there on his rock he is not enough in touch with the state of the world."[50]

The modern problem of unbelief formed the focus for some opposition to the schema. Rivet fears that the definition of papal infallibility will prevent the return of those whose faith is weak or rebellious, and the bishops will be blamed at the final judgment for their failure to draw people to salvation.[51] His funeral orator explains that Ramadié also opposed the definition out of concern for "hesitant souls, deluded minds" for whom a gallican position provided easiest access to truth.[52] A definition of papal infallibility is not useful, Maret writes. It would make it difficult for those outside of the church to return, and it would cause difficulties for those within the church who already love the pope. A definition would manifest the church's uncertainty about the locus of sovereignty; it would arouse the world's hatred and even fear of a possible political rivalry from the church.[53] Meignan asks: "Will those outside the Church, those who reject the authority of Christ and of the Word of God, be converted? They must be brought back not through threat of anathema but through the beauty of truth and of charity." Enemies of the church will take the opportunity to restrain it even more. "Neither the times nor the circumstances urge that the burden of faith be made to weigh more heavily on the shoulders of those Christians who already refuse to carry it at all," Meignan concludes sadly.[54]

The council should inspect carefully the state of the world, Darboy argues, and it will find that the schema is unable to correct the world's evils.[55] Dupont des Loges writes of his fears that, "Humanly speaking, this Council doesn't seem able to respond to universal hopes. A great deal is expected from this solemn gathering to remedy the ills of the Church and of society; and so far I see nothing to

50. Quoted in Boissonnot, *Le Cardinal Meignan*, p. 281, n. 1.
51. Mansi 52:54A–B.
52. Cabrières, *Eloge funèbre de Ramadié*, pp. 25–26.
53. Maret, *Du concile général et de la paix religieuse*, pp. 380–85.
54. Boissonnot, *Le Cardinal Meignan*, p. 299.
55. Mansi 52:160C–D.

promise great things and great results." In 1862, Maret had noted that giving a secret list of modern errors to bishops, with no chance for public discussion, manifests a procedure that contrasts badly with free civil institutions; it could lead souls to revolt. Such a constrast seems to stand behind Dupanloup's agitation when he berates Dechamps for ignoring reality, for failing to observe the times. In examining the opportuneness of defining the dogma of papal infallibility, Dupanloup argues, the council should look at the state of souls in general. He recalls nonbelievers, schismatics, Protestants, and believers weak in their faith and adds that many other bishops share his hesitations about troubling souls. The definition could speed a church-state separation at a time when many countries, not resting on God's promises, are in a state of unrest and when government leaders are not favorable to the church.[56]

Some believe that, since the principle of authority is not respected in modern civil society, Dupanloup continues, its exaltation in the church will save the world. But, he adds ironically, "To believe that by proclaiming the infallibility of the pope you are going to turn back the revolution is, in my opinion, one of those illusions despairing people sometimes hold, in human societies, on the eve of deadly crises." In fact, revolutionaries do not care about the plans of the ultramontanists to save society, says Dupanloup, and he gives his own recommendations for that task. The church should develop its holiness, knowledge, charity, and zeal. It should dissipate, by clear formulas, all of the errors that devour modern people, and it should show further that there is no incompatibility between them and the church. "That is how we will bring back these times which are running away from us and how we will be able to save society which is crying for help in the voice of all its suffering people and in all its perils," he concludes.[57]

The argument against the timeliness of the definition because of its disregard for modern concerns was perhaps one of the most insightful arguments made by the French minority bishops. A comment from a letter of Ullathorne sheds some light on why they found

---

56. Rough copy of Paul Dupont des Loges to Comte de Chambord, 17 January 1870, quoted in Klein, *Vie de Dupont des Loges*, pp. 239–40; Maret, *Mémoire* (21 September 1862), cited by Bazin, *Vie de Maret*, 2:252–53; Dupanloup to Dechamps, 1 March 1870, *Collectio Lacensis* 7:1327D–1330B.

57. *Collectio Lacensis* 7:1330C–D.

themselves so isolated in their sensitivity. "The majority represents the Curia Romana, Italy, Spain, Belgium, Ireland, South America. It is composed of men who have not come into conflict with the unbelieving mind, or into contact with the intellectual mind of the time."[58] Unbelief and the modern spirit: their knowledge of these two realities provided the French minority with one of their most convincing arguments against the timeliness of the definition.

Hostility from Civil Governments

Some French minority bishops feared that definition of papal infallibility would arouse hostile reaction from civil governments.

After the definition of the Immaculate Conception, Ginoulhiac had expressed his fears that a definition of papal infallibility would incite hostility among intelligent people and among those concerned with politics. Mathieu was afraid that the French troops guarding Rome might retreat if the pope's infallibility was defined. Darboy tried to suggest the possibility of such a withdrawal to Camillo de Pietro, cardinal, archbishop of Albano, using Alfred du Boys as his messenger. He had told the pope that the liberties of France aided Catholics, and he was in regular contact with French government officials during the council. He wrote to Napoleon III requesting that he intervene in the council to inform it of the possible dangers from a definition of papal infallibility.[59] In conversation with the Prussian minister Harry von Arnim, Darboy said that a common action by governments would be necessary and useful, and that such action should contest the council's legitimacy.[60]

Darboy hints at these fears of political dangers in his council talk when he suggests that the definition of papal infallibility would be used by supporters of church-state separation as an occasion to further their aims. Although the church does not depend on human support, yet it need not feel obligated to reject such civil support from society where available, he points out.[61]

58. Bernard Ullathorne to David Moriarty, bishop of Kerry, 3 February 1870, quoted in Butler, *Vatican Council*, 2:29.

59. Jacques Ginoulhiac (to Félix Dupanloup?), 31 January 1867, AB XIX 524, Archives Nationales, Paris; Besson, *Vie de Mathieu*, 2:268; Darboy, "Le journal," p. 436, n. 78; Guillermin, *Vie de Darboy*, p. 247. Darboy's letter to Napoleon of 26 January 1870 is in *Collectio Lacensis* 7:1551A–1552C.

60. Darboy, *Le Journal*, p. 440, n. 98.   61. Mansi 52:161D, 162A–B.

Dupanloup also feared trouble from governments if papal infallibility were defined. Before the council, he had written, "The measures that the Emperor's government saw fit to take when this document [the *Syllabus*] appeared can easily portend the line of conduct it will follow if analogous doctrines were proclaimed by the Council."[62] He gives a fuller picture of his fears in his *Observations*, which argues against a definition of papal infallibility in part because of its effects on governments. A definition would revive old fears in Protestant countries about the power of the pope over their Catholic citizens, and these countries would become suspicious of Catholics. But Catholic countries as well are full of anger at the church, and the church should not ignore governments in its deliberations.[63]

A definition would give pretexts for raising ancient hostilities, Dupanloup believes, pretexts for which history gives some unfortunate confirmation. Even though small in number, for example, there have been weak and ambitious popes. Governments would remember such popes if a definition were made and wonder: What are the objects of this personal infallibility? What are its limits? Who determines them? Do not spiritual matters touch on temporal matters? "Consequently, will not the proclamation of the new dogma seem, not to skillful theologians, but to governments who are not theologians, to consecrate in the pope, as regards incompletely defined and often undefinable matters, an unlimited sovereign power over all their Catholic subjects and thus cause, for the governments all the more ready to take offense, the fear of an always possible abuse of this power?"[64]

And there would be some basis for these fears, Dupanloup points out, because several famous bulls have tended to give rise to such an interpretation, such as *Unam sanctam, Ausculta fili* of Boniface VIII, and the bull excommunicating Henry VIII. "I am sad . . . when I recall the great and painful events of history; but those whose shallowness and temerity arouse these burning questions force us to act in such a way," he comments. But would a definition render such events impossible in the future? "Who then will hinder a new pope from defining what several of his predecessors have taught: that the

---

62. Félix Dupanloup to a correspondent in Rome, n.d., quoted in Faguet, *Mgr Dupanloup*, p. 91.
63. Dupanloup, *Observations sur la controverse*, pp. 21–24.
64. Ibid., pp. 25–26.

vicar of Christ has a *direct* temporal power over princes; that he is within his right if he sets up or deposes sovereigns; that the civil rights of kings and of nations are subject to him." In the eyes of the governments, a definition of papal infallibility would place all religious beliefs, as well as civil and political laws, in the hands of a single man. Such ideas are "far from being abandoned" in certain Roman journals, Dupanloup notes, citing from such a journal, which he does not name. He does not question the right of the church to proclaim the eternal laws of justice to governments as well as to citizens, but here a different matter is involved. In short, the present time is full of perils for such a definition. "Would one wish to put on the agenda throughout the whole of Europe, the separation of Church and State? . . . For what reason?"[65]

Concern over the political dangers for the church and for Catholic citizens thus was another argument used by the French minority against the timeliness of the definition.

Open to Misunderstanding

The proposed schema defining papal infallibility could be easily misunderstood, the French minority bishops argued as part of their case against its adoption.

For Meignan, the proposed schema does not make clear that dogmatic statements taught infallibly must express the faith of the whole body of bishops. If this point is not clarified, people will think that separate infallibility of the pope has been defined, and calamities and scandals will ensue. If the schema does not make clear that the pope receives no new inspiration, then heretics will accuse the church of teaching that popes are the originators of dogma, Ginoulhiac warns.[66]

In addition, the schema tends to confuse the infallibility of Christ, the apostles, and the church with each other, Ginoulhiac believes. Ramadié fears that the schema will actually serve to weaken some papal authority: "I fear lest in this way, by affirming the necessity of infallibility to maintain obedience, we weaken the authority of the

---

65. Ibid., pp. 26, 28–29; see also Aubert, *Vatican I*, p. 118.
66. Mansi 52:1015B–C; 905C–906A.

supreme pontiff when he is not speaking *ex cathedra*. Let us not say therefore that it is necessary that authority be infallible in order to maintain obedience."[67]

Maret had believed that most Catholics would misunderstand the limits of papal infallibility: "This man would become for the faithful a sort of *God-man*. Consequently could his *absolute* infallibility be kept within the bounds of matters of faith? By a very natural inclination would not Catholics tend to extend it to everything, at least to all moral, social concerns and, therefore, every political matter closely associated with them?" On the eve of the council, he writes again of the misunderstanding a definition would cause for the majority of people. "In the light of a pope, infallible in himself, the man would disappear." This misunderstanding would tempt the pope to exceed his rightful authority.[68] Darboy also fears that, if the definition does not more clearly determine the scope of its object and of personal infallibility, it could suggest that the pope will include political issues within the scope of his moral teaching sphere.[69] But Sola cynically believes that this misunderstanding is precisely what its proponents desire as a support to the pope's authority. "All this schema and everything connected with it is a joke," he comments to Chlodowig von Hohenlohe, chancellor of Bavaria, in December 1869. "They want the infallibility of the pope only to be able to add strength to the necessity of the temporal power."[70]

Dupanloup wrote at length about the dangers of misunderstanding to which a definition of papal infallibility would be subject. Not only would it be a burden to those weak of faith; it would also lead to confusion whenever the pope erred in making a statement that was not *ex cathedra*. In such a case, he could be judged, even deposed; but first the pope accused of error would try to show either that he had not erred or that he had not spoken *ex cathedra*. But how confusing this would be for consciences, Dupanloup exclaims, citing the example of Honorius. Dupanloup notes the difference between

67. Ibid., cols. 215C, 1019A.
68. Maret, *Mémoire* (25 March 1867), quoted in Palanque, *Catholiques libéraux et gallicans en France*, p. 67, n. 30; Maret, *Du concile général et de la paix religieuse*, p. 385–86.
69. Mansi 52:161C.
70. Palanque, *Catholiques libéraux et gallicans en France*, p. 154, n. 84.

the nuanced distinctions available to theologians and the simple grasp of the doctrine that will be available to most Catholics: "Doubtless here theologians will be able to distinguish the nuances and the fine points and to show that this is not exactly a definition, but how will the multitude of those who are not theologians discern that the pope who is fallible even as pope in such and such an act is no longer fallible in this or that other act? How will they understand that he can be infallible and yet, by great pontifical acts, *foment heresy*? In the eyes of the public, that will still be infallibility." And from the assumption that papal acts were always infallible, new problems for consciences would arise. People would feel obligated to make new acts of faith, and the enemies of the church would seize new occasions to attack Catholic doctrine.[71]

Without touching on the question itself, Dupanloup continues, he wants to point out the credibility problems which even a moderate version of the pope's personal infallibility would pose for the faithful: "What will astonish the faithful is how this immense privilege proves to be, first, that of which the definition is, it would seem from history, the least necessary, since the Church has been able to get along without it for eighteen centuries; secondly, that of its certainty, less established than that of the infallibility of the Church itself, since this has always been an article of faith, while the other has never been professed in the Church as a dogma." Proponents of personal infallibility themselves are unresolved about many questions related to their own positions, questions touching on the status of a heretical pope and the means for his deposition. A definition of this controverted doctrine would simply increase the practical difficulties surrounding the questions.[72]

In addition, a definition of papal infallibility will seem opposed to beliefs the faithful held before the council. It will appear to diminish the importance of the authority of bishops and councils; indeed, it will seem that the bishops are decreeing their own abdication. And other essential prerogatives of bishops would be lost, at least in practice. The bishops are judges of the faith; but would not a definition seem to recognize but one judge of the faith? "Their cooperation, antecedent or subsequent, will in effect no longer be in any way

---

71. Dupanloup, *Observations sur la controverse*, p. 41.
72. Ibid., p. 42.

necessary." How would the church show the faithful that the bishops are truly judges along with the pope? "What judgment can they hand down, then?—A decision of simple adherence, you say.—But would this decision be at least freely made? No; it is not free since they are obliged to accept.—Is it even necessary? No, it is not at all necessary, for the judgment of the pope is in itself, of obligation, independent of any acceptance by the episcopate." Again, Dupanloup calls attention to the difference between theologians and the understanding of the simple faithful: "The theologians can discuss and distinguish these points. But where will the faithful be, that great public which does not understand theological distinctions?"[73]

In addition, a definition would seem to undermine the belief that the bishops, with the pope, constitute the teaching church; it would seem to make the bishops not voices but simply "echoes." But the church's teaching is a testimony to revelation, and Catholics have always understood it to be "a testimony by all who are witnesses; it is the individual churches, giving testimony, by the very fact that they are witnesses, to the faith of the universal Church." The faithful will not easily understand a teaching that makes it unnecessary for bishops to give testimony to the faith of all their churches, that makes of the pope "the sole witness."[74]

When the French minority bishops argued that the schema on papal infallibility would be misunderstood, they had a variety of errors in mind: exaggerations of papal power, confusion of spiritual and temporal affairs, weakening of episcopal rights. Were they not accurate in foreseeing the popular misunderstandings to which this teaching would be subject?

Humility

A few arguments from humility were advanced against the schema. Callot cites in admiration the adage that the church best serves the papacy not by its proclamation but by obedience. And Darboy notes that the papacy is actually being hurt by a premature introduction of the question of papal infallibility because the pope is being forced to be judge in his own cause.[75]

73. Ibid., pp. 44–47.   74. Ibid., pp. 48–49.
75. Mansi 52:618B–C, 157B–C.

Conclusion

It is always opportune to declare what God wants men to know, Manning had remarked, but the French minority thought otherwise.[76] For them, the definition of papal infallibility was untimely, and this in itself seemed to constitute a good case against the definition.

It is important to remember what substantive arguments the French minority employed to make the general point about untimeliness. The definition would cause disunity; it would alienate Protestants, Anglicans, and Orthodox; it would drive modern people away from the church; it would be misunderstood and lead to attacks on the church. These are not light arguments; they show the inappropriateness of the judgment, so common among later eulogists of the minority, that the bishops were "merely" inopportunists. Even those bishops who made no case other than this one against the timeliness of the definition saw the case as a weighty one. They did not find their own case "mere."

One characteristic that emerges through all of the arguments is the link the French minority drew constantly between infallibility and the church as a whole. For them, infallibility was first a gift to the church, before its expression through council or pope; thus any definition of infallibility should be only for the good of the church, with the approval of the church. For the council to define a teaching on infallibility in a way and at a time that would hurt the church or drive people away from it seemed to the French minority a radical inner contradiction. For them, infallibility had an ecclesial character. This conviction emerges again as we examine the other two cases against a definition of papal infallibility.

76. Manning, cited in French in Dupanloup, *Réponse à Manning*, p. 13.

5

On Definability

Papal Infallibility as Proposed Cannot Be Defined

————◆◆▶————

In the last chapter, I set forth the systematic framework behind the thought of the French minority bishops with the help of three questions: (1) Is the proposed teaching true? If yes, (2) Is the proposed teaching definable? If yes, (3) Should the proposed teaching be defined? I then examined the arguments with which French minority bishops answered *no* to the third question, that is, arguments that the schema was untimely.

In this chapter I turn to the case used by some French minority bishops to answer *no* to the second question. Whereas the previous case against the schema was that it should not be defined, this case is that it cannot be defined.

Arguments against the definability of papal infallibility took two forms. One was simply that the definition as it was proposed in the actual schema could not be passed because of its inadequacies. The other suggested that papal infallibility was an inherently undefinable teaching. The two forms of this case were not always distinguished explicitly from each other by the French minority bishops, who often mixed them together in making an individual argument. But we should bear in mind the distinction between the two forms.

Necessity a Requirement for Definition

Several French minority bishops argued that a *de fide* definition by a council cannot be made if this definition is not necessary. One rule councils have followed, Ginoulhiac writes, is to define only when a definition is providentially or historically necessary. Dupanloup expands upon the requirement of the necessity of a definition. Why raise a controversy about the pope's authority, he wonders, at a time when it has never been more respected? In addition, if a definition of a dogma is necessary, how has the church formulated doctrine, condemned heresies, and brought forth theologians without it? "The Church is infallible, and until now the infallibility of the Church is all sufficient," he continues. "Are you afraid that in the future it will become insufficient and would you flatter yourself that those who will not believe in the infallibility of the Church united to the pope will more easily believe in the personal and separated infallibility of the pope?" Dupanloup seems to be raising a technical point. If the church has been able to operate authoritatively without a definition of papal infallibility, and if papal authority indeed is not even in doubt in the present, he is convinced that there is no strict necessity for such a definition. And without such a necessity, he sees no reason to define. "When the oak is two thousand years old, to look for the original acorn by digging under its roots would shake the entire tree!" he exclaims.[1]

Bravard makes the same point in his council speech. The definition is not necessary because the church has succeeded in defining heresy for centuries without the existence of a definition of papal infallibility. "And in our most recent days, I ask, what new error could bring the Church of Christ to destruction, so that there is need of the supreme pontiff to overturn that error with more abundant authority?" he asks rhetorically. Bravard believes that the formula of the Council of Florence would suffice to meet the church's need.[2]

This argument, then, focused on the importance of necessity for a definition. Since the church had defended itself successfully against heresy for centuries without the benefit of a definition of papal infallibility, such a definition hardly seemed a necessity to some of the

---

1. Ginoulhiac, *Le concile oecuménique*, p. 75; Dupanloup, *Observations sur la controverse*, pp. 9, 11–12; see also Dupanloup to Dechamps, 1 March 1870, *Collectio Lacensis* 7:1330D–1338A.

2. Mansi 52:307B, 308D–309A. The decree of the Council of Florence is available in Henry Denzinger and Adolf Schönmetzer, eds., *Enchiridion symbolorum: Definitionum et declarationum de rebus fidei et morum*, 32d ed. (Freiburg im Breisgau: Herder, 1963), 1307.

bishops. But they believed that definitions could be made only if they were necessary. Hence, they reasoned, papal infallibility could not be defined.

Freedom in Theologically Disputed Questions

Another argument against the schema's definability came from those French minority bishops who saw the schema as the opinion of a theological school rather than the faith expression of the whole church. Only the latter would be appropriate for a definition, they believed.

Colet believes that a definition should exclude mere scholarly opinion,[3] but he feels that the definition of papal infallibility itself has been "demanded by one school of thought." Its object is to establish as an article of faith "a doctrine formulated in terms which would give it, in the eyes of a great many, the character of an innovation."[4] Callot also objects to the schema because he believes it condemns one particular theological opinion on the relationship between council and pope. Callot wishes, not to agree with this opinion, but to defend it as a possible orthodox view that should not be excluded in a definition, and he cites the Council of Trent in its refusal to condemn such an opinion. "I propose therefore that, following the footsteps of Pope Pius IV, the Vatican Council at least does not condemn that doctrine harshly," he argues. Dupanloup also cites the Council of Trent in arguing against the definition of one school's opinion. Rather than cause division among the bishops, Pius IV withdrew the issue of the pope's role from discussion and ruled that no decisions should be taken that were not unanimous. Dupanloup understands that Trent thus chose not "to proclaim as dogmas opinions, however worthy they be, yet still only matters of debate among the doctors." Dupanloup also notes that Bossuet defended the pope's primacy but maintained silence on his infallibility, which he saw as a disputed question among the schools.[5]

3. Mansi 52:984D–985A.

4. "demandée par une Ecole. . . . une doctrine formulée en des termes qui lui donnaient, aux yeux d'un grand nombre, le caractère d'une innovation" (Colet, "Souvenirs du concile du Vatican," fol. Q).

5. Mansi 52:617C–619C; Dupanloup, *Observations sur la controverse*, pp. 12–13.

Ramadié believes that the tradition is silent on the question of papal infallibility, and he does not think that the merely scholarly supposition of the pope's infallibility should be raised "to the dignity of a dogma." David extends this argument to include those who lived in the church's past. If the church defines papal infallibility, it will thereby condemn many past theologians and councils—indeed, the majority of Christians—who have not held this view: "It surely is totally without doubt that never in history, never in the history of our dogmas, has the Church done anything like this, namely struck a doctrine of this kind with an anathema, and condemned at least materially so many and such great men commendable for both virtue and knowledge, men who were not considered courtiers except when they died for the supreme pontiff himself."[6]

In the last chapter, we saw an argument made from freedom in theological opinion as part of a case against the schema's timeliness: it is not for the good of the church to stifle free discussion. Here a similar argument is made in another case, that against the schema's definability: a definition cannot express the view of just one theological school, because then it is not fulfilling the function of a *de fide* definition, namely, to express the faith of the whole church.

Binding Quality of Scripture and Tradition

A frequently recurring argument against the definability of papal infallibility involved the binding quality of Scripture and tradition for definitions of the faith. If Scripture and tradition contained a teaching, it could be defined; if they did not, its definition was impossible.

Many of the French minority bishops draw on Scripture and tradition to make their arguments, but several make explicit the more formal principle that underlay their use of those sources. Colet notes that bishops exercise their teaching role, first, by examining the testimony given by apostolic tradition and by themselves, and, second, by deciding whether a dogma unites the three indispensable conditions for definition. Colet lists these conditions as those "of universality, of perpetuity and of unanimous consent."[7] The assumption

6. Mansi 52:1018D, 993B–C.

7. "de l'universalité, de la perpetuité, et du consentement de tous" (Colet, "Souvenirs du concile du Vatican," fol. N).

here is the need for a witness of the dogma in the church's past as well as its present. Callot also believes that a definition must note the views of past thinkers. The opinions of great men of the past against papal infallibility should not be condemned, and the freedom to hold such views ought to be respected by the present council. In fact, he believes that doubts based on the history of diverse views itself will impede the certainty necessary for defining: "I expect that doubts, especially historical ones, over many things will prevent the absolute certitude communicable at another time and necessary for proclaiming dogmas of faith."[8]

Darboy also requires the witness of Scripture and tradition before a dogma can be defined, saying, "It is necessary to prove the devised and refined formula of the definition by arguments that are solid and exclude all doubt." To fulfill this need for certainty, several requirements would have to be met. First, the doctrine of personal infallibility must be contained in Scripture "interpreted always in the same sense, and in the tradition of every age." Then it must be admitted always by fathers, doctors, bishops, and theologians and admitted not only by some but "morally by everyone." In addition, the doctrine must accord perfectly with all of the discussions and acts of authentic ecumenical councils, and it cannot be impugned by historical facts or by pontifical acts. Finally, the doctrine must be shown to be among those that are discernible and definable by a council united to the pope, that is, it must be admitted as revelation by all, everywhere, always.[9] But, Darboy concludes, the proposed schema does not meet these requirements.

Dupanloup often notes the binding quality exerted by Scripture and tradition upon any proposed definition of the faith. There are difficulties with papal infallibility, he writes, which arise from the past and from "historical facts." Is the tradition unanimous on the question of papal infallibility? Is history without embarrassment? To such questions, Dupanloup believes, the council must give lengthy and sensitive study. A definition of papal infallibility would engage the past, for "if the pope is infallible, he always has been." All decisions meeting the definition's conditions would, retroactively considered, be seen to have been infallible. Would this mean that St. Cyprian did not believe in the pope's infallibility because he resisted

8. Mansi 52:619B.   9. Ibid., col. 159A–B.

St. Stephen? Apart from the controversy itself about Honorius, did the Third Council of Constantinople, and hence the church of his day, consider the pope to be subject to error when he addressed the churches on a matter of faith, and themselves competent to condemn him? Dupanloup raises a similar question about the attitude of Leo II and notes that the council would have to pronounce on this question. In fact, "with the usual circumspection of the councils," it would have to undertake "a complete review of history." He leaves aside the well-known difficulties raised by Vigilius and Liberius and notes the Council of Vienne's condemnation of Pascal II. Did Pascal's contemporaries, and Pascal himself, believe that a pope could fall into heresy? "Will they say that an implicit heresy, and yet one deserving of anathema, in a great pontifical act, is no proof against infallibility when this act is not a definition *ex cathedra*? But how can the multitude understand these distinctions?" Dupanloup wonders.[10] Dupanloup is convinced that the council must study the historical precedents; it cannot close its eyes to these issues although it will not be easy for the bishops to engage "in this study of the most sensitive facts of history, in the discussion and the dissection of the texts of Scripture and of tradition." But, since the difficulties "are there, recognized, noted, embarrassing a great many learned and sincere minds," the council must deal with them. Dupanloup accuses Dechamps of incomplete historical work. In response to the claims of Dechamps that theology is unanimous on the question of papal infallibility, Dupanloup produces a list of theologians and schools that have held contrary opinions.[11]

Many French minority bishops cited the need of a definition of the faith to agree with both Scripture and tradition. Their conviction that the proposed schema did not find support in these formed one of their strongest arguments in opposition to its passage.

Difficulties with the Definition's Formulation

Several bishops argued against the definability of the dogma by attacking the actual formulation of the proposed schema. For them,

10. Dupanloup, *Observations sur la controverse*, pp. 31, 38–40.

11. Dupanloup to Dechamps, 1 March 1870, *Collectio Lacensis* 7:1325B, 1331A, 1333A–D.

the definition of papal infallibility as it was formulated in the schema was impossible.

For a dogma to be defined correctly, Darboy argues, the formula must be shaped carefully. But several difficulties plague the actual schema. First, vague terms are used, which lead to unanswered questions, such as the nature and conditions for the exercise of the pope's supreme teaching role. Second, the framers of the schema do not make clear whether or not they eliminate the consent of the bishops in the making of definitions of the faith. "If the former, if they eliminate, they do something both unheard-of and intolerable; if the latter, they proclaim a thing that is ancient and accepted by everyone, [and so are] contending laboriously against an absent enemy." But whatever its position, the schema at least should state it clearly. Similarly, the schema does not determine the object of papal infallibility, except to declare that it is the same as that of ecclesial infallibility, which, however, remains undefined. A further logical deficiency arises from the difference between ecclesial infallibility and papal infallibility. The former is exercised within the proper limit of its object; it involves the common consent of the bishops and the holiness of the church, which ensures freedom from sin. But the schema makes no attempt to argue that the pope himself is holy and thus impeccable.[12] In short, Darboy maintains, the schema in its formulation contains many imprecisions that render its aim unclear and therefore, in some sense, unexecuted.

Ginoulhiac finds in the schema not only inadequacies in wording but also important omissions. To provide a correct understanding of Peter's primacy, he points out, the schema should discuss the apostles and the sense in which one can speak of an apostolic primacy and dignity. Apostolic succession should be discussed, as should the question "whether the supreme pontiff alone is the true and proper successor of the apostles, or at least in what sense," since "all of antiquity is a witness that in teaching and at the same time in governing, the bishops are the true successors of the apostles." But on the election, call, mission, and dignity of the apostles, on their governing and ruling the church, Ginoulhiac concludes, the schema is silent.[13]

Dupanloup warns that the council will have to determine the con-

12. Mansi 52:158B–159A.   13. Ibid., col. 215B.

ditions of infallibility, "for to define the infallibility of the pope, without stating precisely and defining the conditions of this infallibility, would be to define nothing, because it would be defining too much, or not enough." Writing before the council, he lists the difficulty of defining the conditions of an *ex cathedra* act among the theological difficulties, not with the dogma itself, but with what he calls its opportuneness. The schools dispute the conditions of the *ex cathedra* act; how will the council decide among their opinions? "It will have to undertake the heavy task of making a choice, in a dogmatic and absolute way, among all these theological opinions by approving some, rejecting others: but on what certain, clear and undisputable bases can it rely for all that?" he wonders. Again, the schools dispute about what exactly constitutes an *ex cathedra* act. Must the pope express his intention of teaching *ex cathedra*? Must he consult the bishops? Surveying a variety of views, Dupanloup cites the extreme opinion of Georg Phillips, an Austrian canon lawyer who believes that

the definition *ex cathedra* does not require the pope to consult anyone whatsoever: not the Council, nor the Roman Church, nor the College of Cardinals. The German doctor goes still farther: according to him, *the pope does not have to reflect with mature consideration; neither must he study the question carefully in the light of the written and the traditional Word of God; nor does he have to seek counsel of God in prayer before making a pronouncement. Without any of these conditions, his decision would be nonetheless valid, as valid, as binding on the whole Church as if he had observed all the precautions dictated by faith, piety and common sense.*[14]

Dupanloup wonders whether the council will decide among these views. "And how, once again, would one go about establishing these limitations? Where are they clearly set out in Scripture? Where can they be found in the so varied and so contradictory teaching of the theologians? What opinions will be proclaimed dogmas? Which ones heresies?"[15]

Another theological difficulty for defining cited by Dupanloup arises from the pope's double role as private doctor and as pope. To

14. Dupanloup, *Observations sur la controverse*, pp. 31–33; on Phillips, see *Dictionnaire de théologie catholique*, 1:877–78, Tables 3:3611; see also Gary Lease's review of Hans Schneider, *Der Konziliarismus als Problem des neueren katholischen Theologie* (Berlin: Walter de Gruyter, 1976), in *Journal of Ecumenical Studies* 15 (1978):747.

15. Dupanloup, *Observations sur la controverse*, p. 35.

discern in which role a pope is speaking is difficult for theologians themselves. Who would decide this question? History is filled with disputes over whether or not a heretical pope taught heresy *ex cathedra*, Dupanloup continues, citing Stephen and Honorius. Noting the continuing division over the acts of these popes, Dupanloup concludes that only the church can decide such questions: "One must often revert, in fact, to a decision of the Church." Dupanloup raises the possibility as well that a pope might err through fear or imprudence. All of these issues must be studied and resolved by the council if it defines papal infallibility, Dupanloup thinks, but "can one believe that solving all these problems would be light work for the Council?"[16]

Dupanloup's arguments here are against the definability of papal infallibility because they raise issues he does not think a council could resolve easily or at all. For him, these issues—the conditions, nature, and history of *ex cathedra* acts—would need resolution by any council defining papal infallibility as a dogma. Since he also suggests that some of these issues are really insoluble, his argument here becomes a strong one against the definability of papal infallibility.

Other French minority bishops argued more mildly against the definability of papal infallibility in their attack on the formation of the schema, stating that papal infallibility as formulated in this schema could not be defined. Place makes one such argument, though against the formulation on primacy. He does not like the phrasing "ordinary and immediate episcopal power" in the schema because it tends to diminish and confuse the pope's power and because these words were not used by the early fathers of the church. Place prefers the formulation of the Fourth Council of the Lateran or the Council of Florence to that of the schema, which he thinks is not useful, opportune, or necessary. In fact, he says it is almost necessary that the council avoid such language.[17] Callot also opposes the schema's formulations that seem to subordinate bishops to the papal office. He believes that such formulations imply it unorthodox to hold that the church, that is, the body of bishops, is superior to the pope, especially in doctrinal matters: "For if all the pastors not only individual-

16. Ibid., pp. 35–37.
17. Mansi 52:605C–606D; see also David's argument, col. 594A. The decree of the Fourth Council of the Lateran is available in Denzinger-Schönmetzer 811; the decree of the Council of Florence, in ibid., 1307.

ly but also collectively are bound by the duty of hierarchical subordination toward the supreme pontiff, then the body of them,
which is nothing other than all the pastors taken together, is inferior
to the supreme pontiff, and hence a general council—which is the
body of the pastors gathered together in one assembly—is lower
than the pope." But Trent allowed as orthodox the view that the
body of bishops, is superior to the pope, Callot believes, and he
advocates the clarification of the relationship between pope and
bishops. In another speech, Callot again criticizes the wording of the
schema for suggesting that infallibility resides exclusively with the
pope in such a way that it cannot exist in other subjects. Against such
a view, Callot cites the opinion of Alphonsus Liguori that infallibility remains with the body of bishops whenever the pope's chair is
vacant or occupied by a doubtful or heretical pope. Callot believes
that in such circumstances infallibility remains in the teaching
church, or rather, the body of bishops, because "the Church, the
supreme rule of faith, can never fall, otherwise the whole [church]
could slip into heresy."[18] Callot requests a clarification that would
show the duty of a pope to consult with a council in making doctrinal decisions, rather than exercising infallibility alone or expecting a
divine revelation.

Colet also argues against the definability of papal infallibility by
attacking the formulation of the schema. He believes that the schema
introduces such ambiguity into its discussion of the pope's infallibility that it could be subject to an interpretation exactly opposite to its
meaning, which would lead to difficulties among theologians, clergy,
and laity.[19] In his "Souvenirs," Colet notes the rising interest in defining papal infallibility. He believes that a definition should be
formulated "in terms which allow the defined truth to be presented
as clearly founded on Sacred Scripture and tradition." But "the formula under which the doctrine was presented gave it an air of novelty," he explains.[20] Colet suggests a change in the formula that would
eliminate the suggestion that the pope defines in solitude, or that his

18. Mansi 52:617D–618A, 1045C–D, 1046A; see also David's argument, cols. 993D–
994A.
19. Ibid., col. 984C–D.
20. "dans des termes qui permissent de présenter la vérité définie, comme claire-
ment fondée sur l'Ecriture Sainte et la Tradition" (Colet, "Souvenirs du concile du
Vatican," fol. N); "la Formule sous laquelle la Doctrine était présentée lui donnais
[*sic*] un air de nouveauté" (ibid., fol. K).

faith would be in contradiction to that of the college of bishops. His proposal would add the words, "after justly required investigation, he brings forth from the faith of the teaching Church"; this proposed addition, Colet explains, "is a pure historical assertion of the way of acting that is joined in an indissoluble way to all judgments *ex cathedra* regarding faith and morals."[21]

One objection to the definability of papal infallibility referred to its isolated treatment in the schema. Ginoulhiac, for example, wants the infallibility of the church treated in the schema before papal infallibility is introduced, so as to instruct the faithful and eliminate false understanding. The schema should treat the founding of the church, its nature and qualities, before launching into a discussion of its members and visible head. And if it is true, as the schema alleges, that the church is threatened by the gates of hell, should not the church's institution and perpetuity be discussed for the sake of the dignity of the church? In addition, the use of just one Scripture text, Matt. 16:18, will not be sufficient for everyone to understand the promises made by Christ to Peter alone. Bravard also believes that ecclesial infallibility should be discussed before papal infallibility. Darboy notes that the schema does not develop logically, for it treats papal primacy first, unlike the theological tracts. David also believes that a consideration of the church should precede that of papal infallibility. "Certainly no theology course in your memory ever proceeded in this way," he notes.[22]

Meignan also attacks the formulation of the schema, finding its claims are misleading. He argues that testimonies it uses from fathers and councils supporting the claim to papal infallibility contain textual problems, are not pertinent, or have been taken out of context, "so that the tradition appears rather not so much elucidated as obscured." The interpretation of these texts should be done by a special committee, Meignan believes; yet instead, speakers are making false, exaggerated claims about them and thereby weakening the case. In short, he is uneasy with the methods of argument used to base the claim of papal infallibility. In addition, "an ecumenical council should not seem ignorant of present-day exegesis," he writes.[23] De Las Cases also objects to the interpretations the schema

21. Mansi 52:986A.   22. Ibid., cols. 215C, 214A–C, 305C, 157A–B, 72D.
23. Ibid., col. 1013A (see also David's argument, col. 594B–D); col. 1013B; Guillaume Meignan, Personal Notes, quoted in Aubert, *Vatican I*, p. 186.

gives to many texts from Scripture and the history of theology. False conclusions are drawn from some texts, he believes. For example, the reference to "Feed my sheep" in John 21:17 is used to support the immediate ordinary episcopal jurisdiction of the pope. The words of Luke 22:32, "I have prayed for you," are said to support separate papal infallibility. But neither conclusion can be drawn from these texts, argues de Las Cases, using Augustine, Ambrose, and Chrysostom to support his point. The schema also uses texts in such a way as to twist their meaning. It cites councils, but it does not make clear that papal infallibility could be denied freely at these councils. De Las Cases gives lengthy exposition from Bossuet, Gerson, Aquinas, and Gregory the Great. He denounces any distortion of history or historical texts: "To deny historical facts or destroy them with the most trifling hypotheses, to shun the words of the most ancient and renowned fathers or else to interpret them in a new way, as we often see done, to introduce new prerogatives as though they were very old, while in the most certain documents of history the ancient Church was utterly unaware of them—what else would this be but to take up the side of the skeptics themselves?" He summarizes his argument: "Seeking the glory of the prime See in the simplicity of truth, let us build up on a firm rock an impregnable monument of Catholic dogma regarding the Church, against which arguments, whether historical or theological or conciliar, will avail nothing."[24]

The French minority bishops' arguments against the wording of the formulation were directed against the definability of papal infallibility as it was presented in the proposed schema. Some, such as Dupanloup, suggested that so many problems would accompany any such definition that they could never be overcome and hence no definition would really be possible. Others, such as de Las Cases, maintained at least that the definition as proposed used such unclear or misleading arguments that it failed to accomplish the task it wished to achieve.

Procedural Irregularities

One of the constant tasks of the minority, Colet writes, was to struggle against "everything that might possibly question the validity

24. Mansi 52:339B–342C.

and the canonicity of conciliar decisions."[25] Many French bishops claimed that procedural irregularities were so great that they invalidated any definition the council might pass.

Complaints about the acoustical qualities of the hall in which conciliar proceedings took place form a recurring, slightly amusing chorus in the writings of the French minority bishops that finally points to a somewhat serious problem for them. Dupanloup writes to Giacomo Antonelli, "The definite wish of the Holy Father, repeatedly expressed, is that the discussions of the Council be serious and free. Now, in such a room these discussions will not even be possible."[26] Maret complains that the acoustics are inadequate.[27] Colet notes that the consciences of many bishops were troubled especially since the meeting room lacked "all the necessary conditions for a discussion chamber."[28] The great majority of council participants, he reports, could not hear. This seems to have been the experience of Dupont des Loges, who read and reread the acts of the Council of Trent in the early days of the Vatican sessions because he could not hear the discussions. Before acoustical repairs were made, the meeting room was "an annoying confusion of echoes," he says. And Rivet writes from Rome, "Unfortunately one can hardly gain anything from the discussions because of the height even more than because of the size of the Council chamber."[29]

Some of the French minority believed that the acoustical difficulties, as well as other physical and procedural problems, undermined the validity of the council's work. Mathieu, his biographer reports, feared that the heat in Rome, the fatigue, and the absence of many council participants would undermine its authority. For Darboy these mechanical difficulties amounted to an argument against the

25. "tout ce qui aurait été de nature à faire révoquer en doute la validité et la canonicité des décisions conciliaires" (Colet, "Souvenirs du concile du Vatican," fol. Q).

26. "La volonté expresse et itérativement exprimée du St. Père est que les discussions du Concile soient sérieuses et libres. Or, dans une salle pareille, elles ne seront pas même possibles" (Félix Dupanloup to Giacomo Antonelli, 19 December 1869, quoted in Colet, "Souvenirs du concile du Vatican," fol. T).

27. Bazin, *Vie de Maret*, 3:176.

28. "toutes les conditions nécessaires pour être un lieu des Discussions" (Colet, "Souvenirs du concile du Vatican, fol. D; cf. fol. K).

29. Klein, *Vie de Dupont des Loges*, p. 241; Paul Dupont des Loges to Abbé Dieu, 26 January 1870, quoted in ibid., p. 242; François Rivet to Abbé Leboeuf, 22 March 1870, quoted in Chevallier, *Rivet*, p. 175.

liberty, and hence the validity, of the council; he complains of being "robbed of freedom of speech, since one can't be heard in the Council room."[30] A major area of his concern centered on discontent with the procedural rules of the council. He complains on 2 December 1869 about the pope's appointment of the council's officers, "to the detriment of the Council which, evidently, seems less free." Darboy discusses complaints about the rule with other bishops. He notes that "the entire assembly is dissatisfied and openly complains," and "many say among themselves that our liberty has, in fact, been suppressed." As late as July 1870, Darboy shouts from his place against a proposal to vote on a part of the document for which the council members did not have copies.[31]

Some minority bishops found the council rules arbitrary, tending to favor the views of the Vatican. Colet complains, "The vices of the Council's organization, the arbitrary measures authorized by its regulations, the impatience of the majority and the inexperience of the presiding officers combine to form a totality of circumstances susceptible of giving rise to irremediable abuses."[32] He finds that supporters of a definition of personal, independent papal infallibility blocked from the deputations those opposing a definition; "but a victory gained by such means could only prejudice the interests of the question itself." The rules diminished the liberty of the council, he complains, and so did the means of piecemeal distribution of the printed schemas and other materials. In addition, council members could communicate formally only by addressing the whole assembly or by submitting written comments.[33] Although he will not call it moral pressure, Dupanloup writes, he is disturbed that bishops are being asked to judge a question before it is debated. And his diary records another kind of complaint about the conciliar procedures. In early June, he writes, "If the voting were secret, the great majority

30. Besson, *Vie de Mathieu*, 2:268; Darboy, "Le journal," pp. 427–28; see also Aubert, *Vatican I*, pp. 142, 215; Mourret, *Le concile du Vatican*, p. 136.

31. Darboy, "Le journal," pp. 419, 421, 423, 447.

32. "Les vices d'organisation du Concile, les mesures arbitraires qu'autorisait son Règlement, les impatiences de la Majorité et l'inexpérience des Présidents formaient un Ensemble de Circonstances susceptibles de donner lieux à des abus irrémédiables" (Colet, "Souvenirs du concile du Vatican," fol. Q).

33. "mais une victoire obtenu par de tels moyens, ne pouvait que préjudicier aux intérêts de la question elle-même" (ibid., fol. I); ibid., fol. D.

would be against." And the next day, he notes, "If voting secret, majority is for inopportuneness."[34]

Darboy also focuses on wider procedural problems in his conciliar speech when he discusses the origin of the schema. He wishes to consider whether things were done correctly, and he begins by noting that the chapter on papal infallibility forms the hinge of the schema. In fact, the question of papal infallibility is uniquely the focus of the entire council, both because of the importance of defining for any council and because other questions are smaller or predetermined by it. Yet the question was not in the pastoral letter of convocation; it has arisen from promotion, even demagoguery, by clergy and laity outside the council. Bishops have feared to resist this pressure; they have been unduly influenced to introduce the question of papal infallibility, which seems to detract from their dignity and liberty. The bishops should not only be free; they should seem to be free.[35]

In short, concludes Darboy after a few other points, the procedure surrounding the question's introduction makes its definition impossible at the time because such a definition would lack proper moral authority: "Given that it has arisen under these conditions and been introduced in this way, we cannot, in my opinion, address and define this question of infallibility, without by that very action laying open an unhappy pathway for the jestings of the impious or even for objections diminishing the moral authority of this council."[36]

Writing before the council, Ginoulhiac had emphasized the importance of liberty for an ecumenical council. Because they had not provided the opportunity for free deliberation and free voting, he argued, the Councils of Rimini and of Ephesus were subsequently judged not to have been ecumenical councils. Ginoulhiac had found a technical reason for this: while the apostles as a group were guaranteed against error absolutely and unconditionally, the councils that followed them are not so protected; they must submit to the conditions of legislative assemblies.[37]

34. Dupanloup to Dechamps, 1 March 1870, *Collectio Lacensis* 7:1335C; Dupanloup, Journal, quoted in Hasler, *Pius IX*, 1:160–61, n. 25.

35. Mansi 52:156A–157A.

36. Ibid., col. 157C.

37. Ginoulhiac, *Le concile oecuménique*, p. 46. On the Council of Rimini and the

This concern for correct and free procedure haunted the consciences of the French minority. For them to communicate their perspective to the majority members of the council, "one had to overcome difficulties which the condition of the conciliar hall and the regulations of the Council seemed to render insurmountable," concludes Colet. Concern over these procedural problems led them to fear that the council's acts would be considered "invalid because of irregularities."[38]

Need for Consensus of the Church

Many French minority bishops argued against the definability of papal infallibility because this teaching was not held by all of the churches. For them, definition of a dogma demanded the consensus of the whole church.

To define a dogma of the faith, Callot argues, the views of all of the churches must be considered. He hopes that the council members will not only note the pious joy present within his own diocese at the prospect of a definition of papal infallibility but also take into account their obligation "to so many churches whose most outstanding bishops have clearly shown difficulties and dangers." The hesitation of conscience felt by some at the prospect of a definition should stop others from proceeding with it, David argues, lest a heavy burden be placed on the shoulders of those with hesitations. Not all churches find the belief in papal infallibility universal, Meignan reports in his argument against its definability. In some churches, such as those in America, Germany, and Hungary, the belief in papal infallibility is not held by all, which explains, he thinks, the great uproar in those churches at the rumors of a possible definition.[39] Dupanloup reminds his reader that both the Council of Trent and Bellarmine taught that the force of a dogma comes from the consent of the churches [*ex ecclesiarum consensu*].[40]

Robber Synod of Ephesus, see Charles Joseph Hefele, *Histoire des conciles d'après les documents originaux*, 11 vols. (Paris: Letouzey et Ané, 1907–52), 1,2:934–46, 2,1:584–606.

38. "il fallait vaincre des difficultés que l'état de la salle conciliaire et les dispositions du Règlement de Concile semblaient rendre insurmontables" (Colet, "Souvenirs du concile du Vatican," fol. N); "infirmés à raison des Irrégularités" (ibid., fol. Q).

39. Mansi 52:619B–C, 73D–74B, 1014D.

40. Dupanloup to Dechamps, 1 March 1870, *Collectio Lacensis* 7:1336C.

For Colet, defining a dogma demands two-way interaction; he compares it to the coursing of blood: "For there are many very true things that cannot be defined as things that must be believed, without disturbing the faith of the faithful. Thus definitions are consistent with the nature of faith, which like blood in the body of the Church flows from the center to remote members and circulates from the remote members to the center." Ginoulhiac notes that no direct revelation or inspiration is given for defining dogma, and he warns that a definition should make this fact clear:

It is necessary that the formula of definition exhibit this character, for it is certain among theologians and even declared by supreme pontiffs themselves, namely, that there is a great difference between the infallibility of the apostles and the infallibility of the teaching Church. The former is the infallibility of direct revelation; the latter, of conservation; and in the magisterium of the Church the former [the apostles] are the originators, while popes together with bishops are custodians and depositories.[41]

He raises this point in his speech on the inadequacies of the schema, noting that it should clarify the meaning of the assistance of the Holy Spirit: "There should be added the source from which the supreme pontiff brings forth the doctrine that he proposed, namely, from the fonts of revelation, from the sense and faith of the universal Church, from the deposit of truth entrusted to it, which is certainly very easy to do." Not only Peter but all of the apostles were responsible for guarding the deposit of faith, Ginoulhiac points out. And he interprets the "I have prayed for you" of Luke 22:32 to mean that Peter and his successors draw forth from the faith of the universal church that by which they confirm the brothers.[42]

The belief that a dogma must express the faith of the whole church also emerges in the discussion of reception of teachings by Ginoulhiac and Dupanloup. Ginoulhiac explains that the decrees of local councils are regarded as authentic testimonies of faith of only the local churches. "The authority of these decrees is greater when these councils have not been questioned; and if they have been accepted and wholly approved by the other churches, it becomes incontrovertible." For Ginoulhiac here, the authority of dogmatic defi-

41. Mansi 52:985B–C, 905C. Ginoulhiac had shown a similar concern earlier, when he wrote, "In making dogmatic decrees, councils and popes are not inspired writers who are unable to make a mistake in anything" (*Histoire du dogme catholique*, 2d ed., p. xxxiii).

42. Mansi 52:906C–907A.

nitions is measured by the extent to which they express the faith of
the whole church. Hence only when a local council's definition is received by the whole church and thereby recognized as expressing its
faith can the definition be considered incontrovertible. Dupanloup
uses a similar principle when he explains, in a discussion of the proclamation of the Immaculate Conception, "as soon as a doctrine is
held universally throughout the entire Church, that is enough for
one to be able to pronounce with certainty that it is true and that it
has its source in divine revelation and in ancient teaching."[43] He
notes that this teaching was held from the medieval period.

Because the French minority bishops believed that a dogmatic
definition must express the faith of the entire church, they often argued for the necessity of unanimity in defining. That is, they saw
unanimity not only as a timely aid for proclamation of the definition,
as demonstrated in the last chapter, but as a requirement for the very
process of defining. Dupanloup reminds Martin Spalding of the
practice of the Council of Florence, as well as that of Trent, "which
never proclaimed dogmatic definitions except with moral unanimity
and which three times and with regard to three most serious questions did not continue discussions because of this lack of unanimity."
Maret also refers to the ancient practice of a council's reaching *de fide*
definitions only when council participants are unanimous.[44]

We can only speculate on what agonies of conscience these French
minority bishops underwent at finding themselves at odds with
other council members, convinced as they were that unanimity
among participants was the necessary sign that a proposed definition
really expressed the faith of the whole church. A conciliar definition
must be in the name of the entire assembly, Ginoulhiac had written
earlier; "everything ought to be treated *in common*, decided *in common*, or by a common suffrage." This requirement is based on the
unity of the episcopate, he explains, and on the witness of the Council of Jerusalem. The conciliar decree must be the real judgment of
both pope and bishops, he emphasizes. Councils have always fol-

43. Ginoulhiac, *Histoire du dogme catholique*, p. xxxiv; Félix Dupanloup, "Instruction sur l'Immaculée Conception de la très-sainte Vièrge," in *Défense de la liberté de
l'église*, 2:239.

44. Félix Dupanloup to Martin Spalding, archbishop of Baltimore, 25 April 1870,
Collectio Lacensis 7:1370A; Maret to the international committee of minority bishops,
cited by Bazin, *Vie de Maret*, 3:177.

lowed the procedure of demanding "the virtual unanimity of votes." If one demands the reason for this procedure, he continues, it is because unanimity testifies to the certainty of the church on the teaching proposed for definition: "We remark that since the doctrine of faith is a common, public deposit entrusted to all the bishops, when a certain number of bishops are opposed, in a general council and for reasons of dogma, to the definition of a matter of doctrine, there is reason to believe that public tradition or the teaching of the Church on this point has neither the clarity nor the degree of certainty requisite to its proclamation and its definition as an article of faith."[45]

When Darboy tells the council participants that a doctrine of personal papal infallibility must be admitted by effectively all of them if it is to be proclaimed, he reflects this desire of a great number of the minority for unanimity. The step of binding all Christians to a defined truth is such a grave responsibility, he explains, that the Council of Trent would define only if this moral unanimity was achieved. The faithful are given anxious consciences if the position of a sizable minority is set aside, he reasons, or if this raises doubts about the validity and authority of the council itself. Thus unanimity is a requirement of the correct definition of dogma.[46] Other French minority bishops expressed their concern for this point, we have seen, by viewing dogmatic definitions as expressions of the faith of the whole church or as binding only when received by all of the churches. Their emphasis on the requirement that a definition express the consensus of the church was related to their questions about poor procedures and, as we shall see, to their desire for certitude.

Clarity and Certitude

In the judgment of many French minority bishops, the proposed schema lacked the certitude and clarity that must characterize a definition of the faith. This lack for them constituted another argument against it.

Dupanloup wonders how Dechamps can ignore the problems in the schema; "it will not be possible for the Council to continue on to

45. Ginoulhiac, *Le concile oecuménique*, pp. 50–56, 79, 81.
46. Mansi 52:159C–160A.

a definition, before having clarified them all," he comments.[47] Must not this council—as have all previous one—deepen its understanding of the question with all its obscurities and shed light on them through its definition? Then the council cannot define papal infallibility without a thorough study of the historical material, he maintains. "How can you, yourself, have the courage to close your eyes to such perils?" he demands. Mathieu also opposed the schema because he felt historical and theological problems should have been resolved before its passage.[48]

Ginoulhiac emphasizes the clarity and certitude that characterize conciliar definitions. "Catholic doctrine is expressed in such a clear, precise manner as to leave no opening for doubt, no loophole for error," he had written before the council.[49] He continues to show this concern in his complaints about the inadequacy of the definition. Whenever a question arises as to the definability of new dogma, he says, arguments proportionate to the question at stake should be used. Ginoulhiac distinguishes between two kinds of revealed truths: those needed for the Christian life or the church's effective government and those not needed. The first are practical and can be validly demonstrated by argument; they include the articles of faith, sacramental doctrine, the existence of a divinely instituted hierarchy, and truths relating to the rule of faith. These truths are never doubted in the Catholic church; they belong clearly to those certainties mentioned by Vincent of Lérins. The second kind, however, more speculative or accidentally practical, have been debated widely and at length, but they are less necessary for Christian life or government. Examples of the latter include the procession of the Holy Spirit from the Father and the Son, and the Immaculate Conception.[50]

The *de fide* definition of a truth of the first, more practical kind demands many good arguments. The following degree of certitude must be established: "It must be established, namely, that that [claim] was never unknown in the Church, never obscured at least in a large part of the Church, never called into doubt by a great number

47. Dupanloup to Dechamps, 1 March 1870, *Collectio Lacensis* 7:1323A. He cites Melchior Cano's observation that blind defenders of the pope render him no help, nor do those who defend him by emotions and the heart rather than by knowledge and the truth (ibid., col. 1325A).
48. Ibid., cols. 1325B, 1324A–B; Besson, *Vie de Mathieu*, 2:268.
49. Ginoulhiac, *Histoire du dogme catholique*, 2d ed., 2:xxxiii.
50. Mansi 52:217B–C.

of Catholics, that that [claim] is properly one of the number of those truths of which Vincent of Lérins used to say that they belong truly and properly to the Catholic Church." This kind of certitude must be established before a definition can be made. But thus Ginoulhiac is disturbed because he believes that some wish to limit discussion on the question facing the council before such certitude is reached. Such limitation would not be well grounded, he argues, because it presupposes that all opposition to the schema is opposition to revelation. But this presupposition begs the question because the presence of the schema's teaching in revelation is precisely what is being debated.[51]

The emphasis on clarity and certitude as requirements for a dogmatic definition relates closely to other themes in the French minority's case against the schema's definability. In the last section, we saw Ginoulhiac call for unanimity as a sign of "the clarity or the degree of certainty required" in a dogmatic definition.[52] The concern for clarity and certitude also lay behind the desire for thorough historical study which Dupanloup expresses and behind the complaint by some French minority bishops that the question of papal infallibility was being settled before being thoroughly discussed. Callot makes this objection to the schema, claiming that certain words "seem to condemn opinions heretofore not condemned, and indirectly to define the question of infallibility before discussion of the fourth chapter."[53] Dupanloup had voiced the same complaint, when he expressed his anxieties over the procedures of the council.[54]

Concern for clarity and certitude also lay behind the repeated complaints about the speed with which the council was proceeding. Bravard emphasizes that councils should proceed slowly, making a judgment only after much study and deliberation.[55] Before his departure for Rome, he writes, "The works of the Council, however well-prepared they may be, can experience unforeseen delays; on occasion difficulties may arise whose knotted strands cannot be quickly disentangled by even the greatest wisdom and learning.[56] In his explana-

---

51. Mansi 52:217D–218B.
52. Ginoulhiac, *Le concile oecuménique*, p. 81.
53. Mansi 52:617D.
54. Dupanloup to Dechamps, 1 March 1870, *Collectio Lacensis* 7:1335C.
55. Bravard, On the Council, p. 604.
56. "Les travaux du Concile, quelque bien préparés qu'ils soient, peuvent éprouver des lenteurs imprévues; il peut surgir, à leur occasion, des difficultés, dont la sagesse la

tion of the length of the conciliar discussions to his diocese during Lent in 1870, he says: "Do not be surprised; it is a question here of such major interests that, before giving a ruling, the Church has need of long prayers, much reflection and intensified research, advice and precautions of every kind. It is the truth, it is the law, it is honor and holiness, it is God and his revelation, man and his immortality, it is all which gives strength and glory, joy and the goal of life: it is that which it is necessary to declare, defend, clarify, protect and develop."[57] Bravard defends the council's slow pace as "a wise delay," and he defends the slowness and hesitations of the minority with the query, "Do you know that what they will do, what they will decide regarding faith and morals will be done and decided for all eternity?"[58] With such an emphasis on the necessity of slowness, Bravard's complaint against another council participant who urged greater speed assumes more importance: "In civil assemblies men hasten to establish laws, because they are struggling about merely transitory and fleeting things. But in the Vatican Council when the question of defining dogmas is discussed, the things that are said and done are not for time but for eternity. Wherefore neither truth nor utility are hurt by reasonable and logical delay, because God is truth and God endures forever."[59]

Ginoulhiac explains that, if debated questions arise, "they will be widely discussed, examined from every angle, freely resolved, then presented to the world in a way that will enlighten and almost satisfy it." The councils have for guarantees the promises of Christ and the history of ecumenical councils. When debated or delicate questions arise, he explains, "even when they have not been beforehand the object of contradictory discussions, they will have been treated with enough scope in this holy assembly that it must be recognized that

---

plus grande ne saurait dénouer brusquement les inextricables noeuds" (Bravard, "De son prochain départ," p. 147).

57. "N'en soyez pas surpris; il s'agit ici d'intérêts si majeurs, qu'avant de statuer, l'Eglise a besoin de longues prières, de réflexions et de recherches multipliées, de conseils et de précautions de toute nature. C'est la Vérité, c'est le droit, c'est l'honneur et la sainteté, c'est Dieu et sa révélation, l'homme et son immortalité, c'est tout ce qui fait la force et la gloire, la joie et le but de la vie, c'est cela qu'il faut déclarer, défendre, éclairéir [sic], protéger et développer" (Bravard, "Pour le carême de 1870," p. 355).

58. "une sage lenteur" (ibid., p. 357). "Savez-vous que ce qu'ils feront, que ce qu'ils décideront sur la foi et sur la morale sera fait et décidé pour l'éternité?" (Jean Bravard, quoted in "Nouvelles et faits religieux du diocèse," p. 453).

59. Mansi 52:307A.

they had reached that state of certainty and of light that according to even the principles of St. Augustine they could be definitely decided upon by a general council." If one council lacks the time to arrive at such certitude and clarity, another council will take up its work in the future.[60] So Ginoulhiac as well emphasizes the need for enough time and discussion to achieve the required clarity and certitude. And David makes a similar point:

It is one of the glories of the Catholic Church never to make a truth the formal object of obligatory belief for the faithful without a deep and complete examination where every bishop, as an official witness to and judge of the faith, raises his voice freely to say, before God and before the Church, all that he has in his inmost soul, and from this rigorous examination, from this discussion which turns the light of truth on every aspect of a doctrine, there results a certainty superior to all human certainties.[61]

David feels the discussion must be lengthy and rigorous enough to allow the council to achieve a certainty superior to human certainty. Darboy as well, in his conciliar speech against the schema, complains that "time was not granted for explaining this complex question, for resolving the difficulties, and thus for wisely forming the conscience, as you rightly know and as was mentioned in today's congregation; whence it would be necessary to refrain from defining this point of doctrine."[62] In matters of such importance, Darboy points out, nothing is lost if a decision is postponed, whereas hasty action is dangerous.

Many French minority bishops looked for a degree of certitude and clarity in dogmatic defining which they could not find in the proposed definition. Their desire for certitude and clarity affected their concern about procedures, their desire for historical accuracy, and their reluctance to rush deliberations. In their opinion, a council was required to take whatever steps were necessary to insure an adequate degree of certitude and clarity.

60. Ginoulhiac, *Le concile oecuménique*, pp. 115–16.

61. "C'est une des gloires de l'Eglise catholique de ne jamais prendre une vérité pour en faire l'objet formel de la croyance obligée des fidèles, sans un examen approfondi et complet où chaque évêque, comme témoin officiel et juge de la foi, élève une voix libre pour exprimer, devant Dieu et devant l'Eglise, tout ce qu'il trouve au fond de sa conscience, et de cet examen rigoureux, de cette discussion qui expose l'une après l'autre à la lumière toutes les faces d'une doctrine, résulte une certitude supérieure à toutes les certitudes humaines" (David, Circular Letter to Diocese, 26 May 1870, p. 342).

62. Mansi 52:159B–C.

Conclusion

The French minority advanced a large number of arguments against the schema on papal infallibility in their case against the schema's definability. A definition must be necessary, it must be properly formulated, and it must be arrived at by correct conciliar procedures. A definition cannot be rushed, cannot side simply with one theological school, and cannot avoid resolving the difficult biblical, historical, and theological problems. And no definition can be made if it is not an expression of the faith of the whole church because the church's infallibility grounds a council's ability to define in the first place.

The French minority's arguments against the schema's definability took two forms. Mildly, some argued simply that the schema as it stood could never be passed because of its wording, its irregularities in composition, its lack of clarity, and its poor argumentation. More drastically, other arguments questioned the possibility of ever arriving at a definition on papal infallibility because of the unclarity of the Scriptures and the tradition on this point, the lack of necessity for any definition on this question, and the insoluble theological questions surrounding its clarification. But these two forms of argument are related; they both distinguish between the truth of a teaching and the means of ascertaining that truth, and they focus their complaints on the means, actual or hypothetical, that are taken.

As in the case against the schema's timeliness, so in the case against its definability, a common theme emerges: the ecclesial character of infallibility. Again and again, the French minority bishops draw links between infallibility and the church. The council in defining is bound not to contradict the tradition of the church, not to eliminate justified diversity of theological opinion in the church, not to define anything that has not achieved consensus in the church or is not necessary to the church or seems to isolate the pope from the church. Complaints against procedure and haste and specious argumentation all seem to have at their base the conviction of ecclesial infallibility: if infallibility is first given to the church as a whole, then a council or a pope could proceed infallibly only by doing everything necessary to discern the mind of the church as a whole on a question. It is the whole church, whose mind is expressed through Scripture, or tradition, or unanimous conciliar participants, or agreement among theological schools that, for the French minority bishops, is the recipient of Christ's promise of assistance in maintaining the truth of the Gospel. Conciliar defining, then, brings to expression the faith held infallibly by the church as a whole. If the church as a whole is not certain and undivided on a teaching, then its uncertainty and division are the best signs possible to the French minority bishops that the teaching *cannot* be defined as a dogma of the faith. Infallibility for them has an ecclesial character.

6

On Truth

Papal Infallibility as Proposed Is Not True

In this chapter I will examine the arguments of those French minority bishops who made a case against the truth of papal infallibility as it was proposed in the conciliar schema. Remembering the questions that set forth the systematic framework behind the thought of the French minority: (1) Is the proposed teaching true? If yes, (2) Is the proposed teaching definable? If yes, (3) Should the proposed teaching be defined? we can identify this last case against the schema as an answer of *no* to the first question. And as we have seen in Chapter 4, an answer of *no* to the first question demanded also an answer of *no* to the other two questions. Thus this last case against the proposed schema was most opposed to it since the case found that the schema lacked not merely timeliness, nor even definability, but also truth.

It is important to remember that this case did not maintain that the pope was in no sense infallible. Rather, it maintained that papal infallibility as it was proposed in the schema was false. In Chapter 3, we saw that the French minority bishops understood the schema to propose a papal infallibility that was separate, personal, and absolute. It was against this conception of papal infallibility that the last case against the schema proceeded.[1]

1. But we should remember that some of the French minority bishops showed that they grasped the nuances in the position that advocated a separate, personal, and absolute papal infallibility and nevertheless opposed this position; see Chapter 3. In addition, the views of some bishops seem to have changed. Darboy, for example, seems to have developed his opposition to papal infallibility only after coming to Paris (Foulon, *Histoire de Mgr Darboy*, pp. 48, 295; Palanque, *Catholiques libéraux et gallicans en France*, pp. 21–23).

Opposition from the Tradition

Some French minority bishops argued that papal infallibility as defined in the schema was false because they felt it conflicted with important parts of the church's tradition. Not only did the tradition fail to support the schema's claims, they believed, it actually contradicted these claims.

Ramadié begins his case against the schema with an argument from silence. He finds nothing in the church's theological tradition on papal infallibility: "And certainly the entire tradition proclaims that the primacy of the Roman pontiff was instituted by Christ; that prerogative is known at the beginning of the Church; numerous teachers offer frequent, clear, and firm testimonies about it. Regarding infallibility they are certainly silent." During times of persecution, a teaching on papal infallibility would have been a great aid to the church, he points out. "Why therefore were the fathers thus silent? Were they unseeing? What a remarkable thing! They frequently speak of primacy; of infallibility as it is in the schema, never. Of the former, clearly; of the latter, not even obscurely; of the former, explicitly; of the latter, not even implicitly."[2]

Ramadié does not think that papal infallibility is included in the doctrine of papal primacy. He knows that its inclusion would make papal infallibility part of the rule of faith. But the content of the rule of faith cannot be doubtful or uncertain; it must rather be universal, perpetual, and constant. Thus, he reasons, "so likewise, if at some time it [the Catholic church] neither knew nor held it, I do not know whether it could become a rule of faith." But fathers and theologians in the church's history not only fail to refer to papal infallibility—they write rather of papal primacy, papal authority, or the consensus of all the churches—in addition, some explicitly argue against papal infallibility as proposed in the schema. If the doctrine of papal infallibility was so necessary to the church, Ramadié wonders, why was it hidden? Why did Irenaeus, Tertullian, Augustine, and Vincent of Lérins teach recourse to the consensus of all of the churches, rather than to the pope's infallibility?[3] If Peter had been thought infallible, why would the Council of Jerusalem have searched as a group to re-

2. Mansi 52:1016D–1017A.
3. Ibid., col. 1017A–B. Ramadié lists Cyprian, Augustine, Jerome, and Basil among those who have opposed papal infallibility as proposed in the schema.

solve their problem, expressing their resolution in words "which express the union of the head with the members?"[4]

The tradition of the church affirms the magisterium as the pope united with the bishops, and the modern distinction between the head and members of the teaching church cannot be found, Ramadié argues. "Only the infallibility of the Church is treated, recourse is had to it everywhere, and—in the words of Bellarmine—ultimate judgment pertains to it."[5]

Some say that the schema represents a development of the tradition on papal infallibility and hence appropriate dogmatic progress, Ramadié notes. But he believes that such a perspective evaluates the historical evidence incorrectly. The tradition shows the church as a monarchy, but tempered, with head and members, like a human body. The fathers of the church may speak of head or members, but no father opposed them to each other. At the time of the Council of Constance a living monster appeared—a living head separate from a living body—and the council had to clarify its authority over the pope. But that led to further excesses and to the previously unimagined distinction between the pope as private doctor and the pope speaking with the aid of the church. Aquinas and Antoninus of Florence would not have envisioned that the pope should act without the consensus of the churches, Ramadié maintains; "this is a more recent question."[6]

In short, the tradition did not speak of papal infallibility "as it is in the schema," Ramadié maintains. "A definition by the supreme pontiff without that episcopal agreement did not occur to the ancient theologians." Thus although the schema does express a development in thought, this development does not do enough justice to the tradition of antiquity. More justice is done even by ultramontane theologians, he argues, who at least speak of a conditional infallibility, rather than one that is absolute.[7]

Meignan also believes that the tradition of theological reflection does not support the claims made for papal infallibility in the schema. He points out that papal authority has nothing to fear from the disputes in the schools over infallibility because it is "the common, likewise the most probable, opinion." But he goes on to discuss the

4. Ibid., col. 1017A–D.   5. Ibid., col. 1018A.
6. Ibid., col. 1018A–C.   7. Ibid., cols. 1018C–1019A.

difficulties he finds in the schema: "The texts of Scripture are not as clear as one says. . . . One can conclude nothing certain from the fathers and from the monuments of the first centuries. . . . We must not forget what happened to the letters of Pope Honorius that were rejected by the sixth Council. Let us think about all that."[8] In his conciliar speech Meignan, like Ramadié, uses an argument from silence: the fathers neither affirmed, nor even conceived, the infallibility of Peter's successor as proposed in the schema, "They left unmentioned the thing and the word," he notes, varying from Ramadié's view by claiming that the fathers do not affirm even a tempered monarchy in their conception of the church. The fathers believe that Peter's successor shepherds, governs, and teaches the entire church, and they claim a privilege of assistance for this task. "But whether a grace and privilege of this kind extends as far as separate infallibility: no really temperate man will certainly be seen to affirm [this] from the writings of the ancients, in my judgment." What the fathers teach can be reduced to the idea that "the Church cannot fall from the true faith, the Roman pontiff in an ordinary way strengthens [his] brothers." But whether the pope can err, the fathers, with a few exceptions, do not say and do not wish to say.[9]

In their practice, the fathers may have admitted a separate papal infallibility, Meignan continues, but the force of what they say comes to this: personal errors of the pope, if any, could be guarded against and the faith kept safe. Thus, although Meignan prefers not to speak of its development, "a doctrine of infallibility of this type already existed in antiquity, as if in seed, whence, with the passing ages, it grew up"; and if the schema proposed no more than this, perhaps he would not oppose it. But the schema misrepresents infallibility by presenting its belief as part of the ancient and universal faith; as thus proposed, the dogma of infallibility seems to be expressed less accurately. For in the medieval period, inerrancy rather than infallibility was more widely held, and papal infallibility was not considered a *de fide* teaching. Even by the time of the Council of Trent, the tradition of infallibility was not constant throughout the entire church. The very fact of the development in France of a doctrine of personal infallibility of the pope, as well as the deeply rooted movements of Feb-

---

8. Meignan, Written Remarks on the Schema, quoted in Boissonnot, *Le Cardinal Meignan,* p. 299.

9. Mansi 52:1013C–1014A.

ronianism and Josephinism in Germany, both give further testimony that "the doctrine of infallibility had not yet been commonly admitted."[10]

David uses the silence of the tradition on papal infallibility as a strong argument against the schema. Although some doctrines are held implicitly by the church and only later made explicit, he notes, this does not happen to the most fundamental of doctrines. And would not the personal infallibility of the pope be such a fundamental doctrine? Indeed, he says, such a doctrine would have been the hinge "on which the entire magisterium of the Church turns."[11] Thus the fact that a fundamental doctrine like the pope's personal infallibility has not been defined is proof that it should not be defined because it is thus shown to be not *de fide* teaching.

David finds two kinds of examples to argue his conviction that the tradition is silent on the doctrine proposed by the schema. The first includes sources that do not mention the personal infallibility of the pope, such as creeds, professions, catechisms, and especially the Catechism of Trent. The second includes councils or theologians that went through great trouble to ascertain the truth on a doctrine without ever suggesting a consultation with the infallible pope. He wonders sarcastically why someone did not say, "He holds, himself, the total and integral deposit of faith; he bears in himself the entire tradition, at least in necessary matters." He comments: "To err is certainly human, but this silence speaks to me in such a loud voice and with such great force that—I can say without any doubt—no other example of this kind of thing is found in the world, in the history of the Church." Even the Immaculate Conception, which David calls a speculative doctrine, was not proclaimed without extensive consultation, and it did not relate to the intimate life and essence of the church as does the schema under consideration.[12]

De Las Cases believes that the schema explicitly contradicts both the more probable theological opinion and the older tradition in the church; he finds it threatening to moral and even historical certitude.[13]

Maret finds the tradition a clear testimony to his conviction that infallibility is found only in the accord of pope and bishops.[14] All

10. Mansi 52:1014A–C.   11. Ibid., col. 989A.
12. Ibid., cols. 990C, 991A.   13. Ibid., col. 342C.
14. Maret's analysis, unlike those of some other French minority bishops, is very

orthodox theologians agree that the church is a monarchy tempered by aristocracy, Maret believes, but they disagree among themselves about how this works. The Bellarmine school teaches that the pope possesses a monarchy that is pure, indivisible, absolute, and unlimited; the school of Bossuet and Paris teaches that bishops, though subordinate to the pope, yet judge and govern with him. Maret believes that both Scripture and the history of the councils testify to his conviction that the French school is correct in its conviction that dogmatic infallibility demands accord of pope and bishops. In this view, he believes, gallicanism contains a base of eternal and necessary truth.[15]

Maret cites numerous scriptural passages to support his position, notably the story of the Council of Jerusalem at which, he argues, both Peter and James spoke freely and gave judgments. "The decree, conformable to St. Peter's opinion, was drawn up in the very terms given by St. James, and published in the name of all the apostles and priests," he points out.[16]

But the history of councils yields the greatest bulk of testimony for Maret. From Nicea, for example, he emphasizes the freedom of discussion and unanimity of decision. The force of the decisions came from the consent of the group, but when made they required submission. The same was true at the First Council of Constantinople, "which, by the adherence of Pope Damasus and the western bishops to its decrees on the faith, became the second general council." But the question was not settled by the Roman judgment, but rather with "a general acceptance and . . . the confirmation of the pope." Again at Ephesus, "the greatest authority, the supreme authority was, for Catholics as for heretics, for emperors as for bishops, for the pope himself, not the pope alone or with a limited number of bishops, but the pope with the episcopate, the pope forming, with all the bishops, one great whole." The papal legates, he notes, were asked to confirm the council's decision. Again this was true at Chalcedon, where meetings were held until the doubts of some hesitant participants were assuaged.[17]

---

lengthy; I will only summarize his views here and in my later discussion of his thought.

15. Maret, *Du concile général et de la paix religieuse*, 1:129–30, XXVI.

16. Ibid., pp. 132, 141–42. 17. Ibid., pp. 149–50, 166, 170, 183, 195, 229–30.

Maret continues with his analysis of the history of councils, finding always that their infallibility derives from the agreement of pope and bishops. The fifth council, in fact, did not adhere to the views of the pope, but he instead adhered to it, "and unity was arrived at by this ceding of the pope to the majority or to episcopal unanimity." This council proved "that the council can enlighten the pope." The only way to know the truth in questions of faith is through deliberation and common decision of the church's pastors, Maret summarizes. With this approach, Maret is well prepared to treat the Third Council of Constantinople, whose condemnation of Honorius embarrasses Maret's opponents in the Bellarmine school. He reviews their various attempts to explain away the problem of Honorius but finds himself dissatisfied with their explanations.[18] The seventh council did not receive the letters sent to it without further examination and judgment, and the eighth council did not hesitate to condemn Honorius again. Councils feel free to judge teachings of popes, using the criteria of Scripture, tradition, and earlier decisions of the church. And again Maret concludes from these histories: "Spiritual sovereignty, such as it appears in the history of nine centuries, is essentially made up of two elements: the papacy and the episcopate, without any curtailment of the legitimate submission of the bishops to the pope."[19]

Maret finds further demonstration in the Councils of the Lateran and of Lyons that the pope is not sole judge of the faith. Discussing the Councils of Pisa, Vienne, and Constance, Maret finds in them confirmation that the councils, while not absolute, yet have real authority. Bound by the Scriptures, tradition, the faith, and former decisions of the church, a council will have the highest regard for the opinions of its president, the pope, but it will not separate itself from the great majority of the church. The pope should pronounce in accord with the votes of the great majority of the council. Maret says that he will not examine for long "what would happen if the pope were obstinately to refuse to confirm the decisions of this great majority, and where there would arise from this refusal a conflict

18. Ibid., pp. 248, 270, 272, 292–93. "Is it possible," he marvels, "to see in this definite teaching, in these formal precepts spoken by a pope to the Eastern bishops and, indirectly, to the whole Church, the act of an individual doctor?" (p. 294). He refers here to a common ultramontanist view that Honorius acted as a private doctor when he taught his erroneous doctrine.

19. Ibid., pp. 339, 336–37.

which would seriously endanger both the faith and the Church." In such a case, Maret believes, the pope can be deposed.[20]

Although ultramontanists see the confirmation of their theories in the Council of Florence, Maret does not believe that it proclaimed the separate infallibility of the pope because such a proclamation would have contradicted the previous two council's decrees and threatened a change in the nature of the church.

Maret notes the many means used to arrive at decisions when the episcopate is dispersed, and he observes: "By these communications, these exchanges, these understandings, is formed, even without a general council, this common consent of the highest pastors, which has always been and will always be the absolute rule of faith both outside of as within the council. . . . Indeed, if the agreement of these most important pastors is the great rule of faith within general councils, this understanding will be equally necessary, throughout the church, to sanction what is the true faith." A tacit agreement with papal teaching by bishops is sufficient to express their judgment, since "it is impossible to admit that the great majority of bishops would not offer opposition and protests if, may God preserve us from this forever, an error were contained in a pontifical judgment." Bishops then, as a necessary consequence of their right to judge in council, also have a right to examine pontifical decisions made outside of council, comparing them "with the tradition of their churches and with the teaching of the faith." The pope cannot refuse to sanction decisions that represent the moral unanimity or the great majority of the bishops; if he does, he separates himself in fact from the church and ceases to be pope.[21] Maret's analysis of the nonconciliar decisions sums up his continual interpretation of the church's history of *de fide* decisions: such decisions emerge only from the concord of both the pope and the bishops. For Maret, the witness of history to this practice is indisputable.

Other French minority bishops used the tradition in milder ways to argue against the truthfulness of the schema of papal infallibility. Five years before the council, Dupanloup had written to Montalembert: "The Church is certainly divine but it is built on men." That is why the history of the church is filled with both light and shadows, he explains. "The pope himself, head of the Church, is in-

20. Ibid., pp. 351–71, 423–25.
21. Ibid., pp. 513, 516, 520, 540.

fallible when he speaks in its name, in conditions where infallibility is promised, but he is not impeccable." In his *Observations* written on the eve of the council, Dupanloup distinguishes between the personal infallibility of the pope held by Bellarmine and the "absurd, unconditional and all-embracing infallibility" of extreme theologians.[22] Even Bellarmine's form of personal papal infallibility, Dupanloup notes, would be an innovation. Dupanloup himself, it seems, found Bellarmine's understanding of papal infallibility acceptable, a *proxima fidei* truth. The day after his meeting in Malines with Dupanloup and Emmanuel von Ketteler, bishop of Mainz, Dechamps writes:

> Usually they try to say that Bishop Dupanloup is a mitigated gallican! Well! That is wrong. The bishop of Orléans believes in the infallibility of the head of the Church speaking *ex cathedra*. He . . . says, as does St. Alphonsus, that this truth is *proxima fidei* and that it only needs to be defined. . . . It is good to know that there are no longer any lingering traces of gallicanism and that the chief of the bishops of France, whose voice is the one most listened to, is as ultramontane as a Belgian, I mean that he is as Catholic as Catholicity itself.[23]

When Dupanloup wrote his *Observations*, he made it clear that his treatment did not include the question of papal infallibility itself, but rather what he called its opportuneness. "What I wish to expose quite simply in this article are these difficulties—without going to the very depth of the theological question. I am not discussing infallibility but the opportuneness of all this," he explains.[24] Yet in writing to Manning, he accuses him of holding "a *separate infallibility*, infallibility outside of and separate from the episcopal body," perhaps a version of that "absurd, unconditional and all-embracing infallibility" which he rejected in extreme theologians. And Dupanloup appeals to Dechamps in the name of the Bellarmine with whom he agrees, but now to remind Dechamps that Bellarmine grounded the force of dogma in the consensus of the churches. Since unanimity does not exist among council fathers, Dupanloup suggests, would not silence be wiser?[25]

22. Félix Dupanloup to Charles de Montalembert, quoted in Lagrange, *Vie de Mgr Dupanloup, évêque d'Orléans*, 3:154; Dupanloup, *Observations sur la controverse*, p. 42.

23. Victor Dechamps to R. P. Mauron, C.ss.R., 2 October 1868, quoted in Aubert, "Dupanloup au début du concile," p. 98, n. 6.

24. Dupanloup, *Observations sur la controverse*, p. 9; see also p. 29.

25. Dupanloup, *Réponse à Manning*, p. 13; Dupanloup to Dechamps, 1 March 1870, *Collectio Lacensis* 7:1336A–C.

It is hard to know whether Dupanloup found the schema's teaching on papal infallibility untrue. While he agreed with Bellarmine, he still found even Bellarmine's thesis not shared by the consensus of the churches that would give the unanimity required to define. And his agreement with Bellarmine, he makes clear, did not include ratification of a separate, personal, absolute papal infallibility, of which he accuses Manning. Did he understand the schema to reproduce Manning's view? We do not know, but his opposition to it suggests that perhaps he did think of it this way and hence that finally he also argued that it was not true.

The positions of two other minority bishops raise similar questions. Did they think the schema's teaching untrue, as well as not definable and untimely? We cannot be sure, though we can suspect that they too found the schema untrue. Colet would write after the council that he had always considered the doctrine in the schema theologically certain, yet he complains in his "Souvenirs" about the views of Manning, Dechamps, and Henri Plantier, bishop of Nîmes. Unlike them, he says, the Italian schema distinguishes between the pope as universal teacher and private doctor; it presents the pope's infallibility operating under conditions; and it locates infallibility within the sphere of the deposit of faith, thus envisioning the pope as judge of controversies. Which of these two views of papal infallibility did Colet believe the conciliar schema represented? Or does he speak of the conciliar schema as the "Italian schema"? He does not say precisely, but he does write that some promote a definition of the pope's personal and independent infallibility. And he comments that the pope's ability to teach infallibly as organ of the church does not mean that the pope is personally and separately infallible.[26] Finally, he writes a little later, "In the presence of a definition demanded by one school, and of which the purpose was to establish, as an article of faith, a doctrine formulated in terms which gave it, in the eyes of a great number, the character of an innovation, it was almost impossible that the passions of the polemics not give rise, on both sides, to deplorable excesses."[27] These complaints suggest that he, too,

26. Charles Colet, Circular Letter, 22 August 1870, cited by Freppel, *Oraison funèbre de Colet*, p. 21; Colet, "Souvenirs du concile du Vatican," fols. M, I, and N.

27. "En présence d'une définition demandée par une Ecole, et dont l'objet était d'établir, comme article de foi, une doctrine formulée en des termes qui lui donnaient, aux yeux d'un grand nombre, le caractère d'une innovation, il était à peu près impossi-

thought the schema was in error in its teaching, insofar as that teaching presented a papal infallibility that was separate, personal, and absolute.

And Colet had heard of Rivet's audience with Pius IX, an audience which would hardly hearten either of the French bishops. "I am infallible," said Pius IX to Rivet. "I have always believed and taught this," answered Rivet, "but under certain conditions." "Without conditions," was the pope's reply. "Then I will vote *non placet*," said Rivet. "I am obedient to the order of God," said Pius IX. "It is his will which leads me."[28]

In summary, we have seen that many French minority bishops drew on the tradition of theological reflection as an argument against the schema. Some found the tradition silent on papal infallibility, and even filled with quite different views on the infallibility of teaching in the church. Maret in particular emphasized these different views, but he drew them from an analysis of the practice and theory of ecumenical councils in the church's history. Finally, a few of the bishops did not clearly oppose the teaching of the schema, but their writings taken together suggest such an opposition from the way they use Bellarmine and other schools of thought to contrast with Manning and his colleagues.

Authority of Bishops Undermined

Some French minority bishops argued that the schema was false in its understanding of episcopal authority.[29] While their concern often sprang from a practical sense of the issue, their argument rested primarily on a theoretical base.

---

ble que les ardeurs de la polémique ne donnerent pas lieu, de part et d'autre, à des excès déplorables" (Colet, "Souvenirs du concile du Vatican," fol. Q).

28. The report of this audience of 12 July 1870 is in Palanque, *Catholiques libéraux et gallicans en France*, p. 175, n. 209.

29. Many French minority bishops who defended episcopal authority did not envision its extension to priests. Writing after the council on episcopal authority, Foulon points out to his diocesan clergy that the church "has solemnly condemned the error which claimed that this authority is possessed collectively by the bishop and his priests so that the bishop can legitimately exercise it only with a certain degree of dependence on his clergy" ("Lettre circulaire pour annoncer le convocation du synode diocésain," in *Oeuvres pastorales*, 2:128). The bishop received his power from God and the Apostolic See, Foulon explains. Others, however, such as Ginoulhiac, seem to see episcopal authority derived from its quality of representing a local church.

Sola argues that the pope is not the ordinary bishop for every diocese in the church, that is, he does not have ordinary episcopal jurisdiction in every diocese as the schema claims. If he did, then other bishops would really be only vicars-general, Sola reasons, but in the Acts of the Apostles Paul calls them bishops.[30] From this, Sola concludes that bishops truly are bishops in their own dioceses, receiving their episcopal power from the Holy Spirit, but that they are consecrated bishops for the good of the whole church and hence must labor under the pope's direction. Sola wants to call the pope's jurisdiction "pontifical" rather than "episcopal" to eliminate the confusion that might arise if a diocese seemed to have two bishops. As in a body, so in the church, each part must keep to its own job lest the shape of things be changed, resulting in ruin.[31] Although Sola's argument does not deal directly with papal infallibility, it nevertheless reveals his emphasis on the divinely instituted authority of bishops. To endanger its operation, he claims, threatens ruin.

Colet thinks that supporters of papal infallibility are motivated by society's need for ratification of the pope's authority but that the same need applies to the authority of bishops. But he thinks the ultramontanist school wishes "to diminish this authority and thereby to change the divine constitution of the church." The schema does not even mention bishops, he notes in disdain, even though it is they who are present at the council to determine the subject of the infallibility of the church.[32] Again in this brief argument we see how a defense of episcopal authority begins to affect the case against the schema's view of papal infallibility.

This also emerges in the argument of de Las Cases that the schema incorporates a faulty view of episcopal authority. The schema seems to give the pope the ordinary and immediate jurisdiction over each diocese, he complains, such that bishops would stay bishops in name only. It seems to show the pope as principle of all faith, as the font of all power; and it risks a tremendous confusion about authority within the diocese that Christ would never have intended. Finally, the schema does not provide for any oversight of the pope by the rest of the church or for conditions within which to operate. And in fact, de

30. Mansi 52:584B; see also Aubert, *Vatican I*, pp. 197–98.
31. Mansi 52:584B–C, 585A.
32. Colet, "Souvenirs du concile du Vatican," fol. C. "de diminuer cette autorité et de modifier ainsi la Constitution Divine de l'Eglise" (ibid.).

Las Cases concludes, to complete the pope's power, it introduces "an infallibility divided but separate and without any agreement [*consensus*], whether antecedent or concomitant or subsequent, of the bishops."[33]

In his controversy with the Vatican before the council began, Darboy also had shown a strong concern to oppose the confiscation of episcopal authority, believing he was thus serving both the church and the papacy itself. Darboy argued, "The regularly established bishops are judges, under the control of the Holy See, and the sole judges of what is needful or harmful to the spiritual interests of their dioceses." Palanque sees in this sentence the basis of Darboy's later conduct, including his stance against the schema: "That is the essence of his gallicanism: all his actions are merely a commentary on it." Palanque thinks that Darboy was interested, not so much in the question of infallibility as a dogmatic matter, but rather in the rights of bishops.[34]

In their arguments against the schema, then, several French minority bishops were motivated by a strong sense of episcopal authority, and they thought that the schema actually misunderstood or seriously threatened it.

Accord of Pope and Bishops

A common argument against the truthfulness of the schema based itself on a grasp of episcopal authority in teaching. Those who took this approach argued that the church's infallibility needed the agreement or accord of pope and bishops for its exercise.

Colet found that his belief in this need set him in opposition to the proposed schema. The minority found themselves in the position, Colet writes, of working to ensure that a definition, if it were made, would be clearly founded on Scripture and tradition. The church has not received new revelation: "Now since what has always been a matter of faith is that the sacred magisterium of the Church, made up of the pope and the bishops, assembled or dispersed, cannot err in matters of faith and morals and that the pope speaking in the name of the Church teaches the truth infallibly, it does not seem to

---

33. Mansi 52:338B–D.
34. Darboy to Pius IX, 1 September 1864, "Monseigneur Darboy et le Saint-Siège," pp. 254, 248–52; Palanque, *Catholiques libéraux et gallicans en France*, pp. 24, 23.

me that one can logically conclude that the pope is personally and separately infallible. On the contrary, this doctrine seems a complete reversal of the preceding one."[35] In their work at the council, Colet believes, bishops are witnesses to the faith they have received and judges. As judges, they examine apostolic tradition and their own testimonies and then decide whether a proposed teaching shows "the three indispensable conditions of universality, of perpetuity, and of the consent of all."[36]

Rivet also emphasizes the need for accord between pope and bishops. Assistance in teaching and consequent preservation from error are promised to the body of the apostles as a group in Matt. 28:18–20, he insists. The bishops, then, serve as guardians and judges in the church. The pope possesses a supremacy of jurisdiction and of honor; he governs, but with assistance of the bishops. This understanding leads Rivet to ask that the schema be changed to include the words, "making use of counsel and requiring the assistance of the universal Church," recognizing the pope's infallible exercise of infallible teaching authority only when he had consulted with the universal church.[37]

David is convinced that the gallican tenet which located the exercise of infallible teaching in the accord of pope and bishops remains a free theological opinion. Referring specifically to the Articles of 1682, he acknowledges that the act involved in their proclamation was justly condemned, but he maintains that the doctrine they expressed was not condemned. The gallican view "regarding the necessity of unity and agreement [*consensus*] between the supreme pontiff and the bishops in defining matters of faith" remains a free view in his opin-

35. Colet, "Souvenirs du concile du Vatican," fol. N. "Or de ce qu'il a toujours été de foi que le Divin Magistère de l'Eglise composé du Pape et des Evêques réunis ou dispersés, ne peut pas errer sur les questions intéressant la foi et les moeurs, et que le Pape parlant comme l'Organe de l'Eglise enseigne infailliblement la vérité, il ne semble pas que l'on puisse logiquement déduire que le Pape est personnellement et séparément infaillible. Cette doctrine apparaît au contraire comme le renversement de la précédente" (ibid.).

36. "les trois conditions indispensables de l'universalité, de la perpetuité et du consentement de tous" (ibid.).

37. Rivet, "Sur l'église," pp. 106–7; François Rivet, "Sur l'orgueil," in Jacques Migne, ed., *Collection intégrale et universelle des orateurs sacrés,* 2d ser., vols. 68–99 (Paris: Petit-Montrouge, 1856–66), 84:98; Chevallier, *Rivet,* p. 171. The phrase Rivet proposes is the Antonine formula, from the work of the fifteenth-century bishop of Florence, Antoninus Pierozzi; it specified conditions under which a pope would be without error.

ion. That is, the subject of infallibility need not be specified as an object of faith; it remains open to discussion in the theological schools. Moreover, David argues that, until thirty years before the council, the view that required accord of pope and bishops for definitions of the faith was the dominant view and gaining in favor. The present vogue is papal infallibility, he notes; "but there were also times in which the opposite opinion was morally universal."[38]

David had made no secret that his own view coincided with what he calls the older tradition. In 1857 he was attacking the ultramontane currents in France,[39] and in an 1859 letter to a government minister he criticizes the fatal spirit causing difficulties among the clergy, a spirit "which broke up precious traditions and the resources of an incomparable past."[40] And in 1861 he defends himself against other reproaches by appealing to his gallicanism: "My strong gallican convictions, all so well-known, so firmly established, and so old that they have been remarked upon at various times."[41] He supports Maret during the controversy over his book and writes to him: "We are here concerned with truth and with the most apparent and most serious of the Church's interests in the nineteenth century. In my opinion the point you are defending appeals to my most intimate and invincible convictions. *If a personal, absolute, separate infallibility were proclaimed I am convinced that it would be the greatest misfortune of modern times.*"[42]

At the council, David's point is simple: definitions of dogma need the pope acting in union with the bishops to be infallible. Until the present time, he notes, when Catholics were asked to identify the

38. Mansi 52:991B–C, 993B, 992B.
39. Aubert, "David."
40. "qui dissolvait les traditions précieuses et le moyen d'un passé incomparable" (Augustin David to unnamed government minister, 18 July 1859, F[19]2.575, Archives Nationales, Paris).
41. "Mes convictions gallicanes tout si notoires, si arrêtées et si vieilles qu'elles ont été adressées à diverses époques" (Augustin David to unnamed correspondent, 11 December 1861, F[19] 2.575, Archives Nationales, Paris). In 1851, for the feast of the chair of Peter, David had remarked, "We know the limits which the power of Peter should not exceed, our doctors have passed this conception on to us. The ocean itself has its boundaries in its plenitude, Bossuet said magnificently, and if it went beyond them, it would become a deluge which would devastate the universe" (quoted in Durand, "Mgr David et le concile du Vatican," p. 44).
42. Quoted in Palanque, *Catholiques libéraux et gallicans en France*, p. 144.

subject of infallibility, the constant response was, "This criterion of infallibility stands in the agreement [*consensio*] of the pastors with the supreme pontiff." But now the council is threatening to cut off the head from the body, which can normally be done only to a corpse; in a living body, the head rules the body, but the body sustains the head. In addition, the proposal of the schema seems to misrepresent the promises of Christ: "If at one moment of time the Church separated from its pontiff could be conceived to err; if on the one side stood the pope alone teaching truth, and on the other side the Church falsely holding the contrary, then would not the divine promises of Christ have failed?" The long-standing openness of the church on the question of papal infallibility, its refusal to take sides among the schools, can in itself be seen as providential, David suggests. Who can say that the older opinion, sufficient for orthodoxy so far in the church's history, is not still sufficient? And why place a burden upon those who share David's conviction after lengthy study?[43]

In his second speech, David pushes his point further to assert that "the power of the supreme pontiff has its limits"; to assert otherwise would be idolatrous. In his third speech, he is even clearer:

This is my thesis: In proclaiming definitions of faith, the supreme pontiff is never even to be thought of as endowed with infallibility separately from the teaching church, by himself alone, even [when] speaking as supreme pastor. For either the teaching Church itself anticipates or solicits the pope's revered opinion, or it teaches with the pope when he teaches the universal faith, or it assents to the pope when he teaches prior to everyone. This is the law of the holy Church, this is the discipline of healthy theology, this is the authentic summary of our entire history.

Here David underlines his vision of the pope's infallibility: it never operates apart from the teaching church, which either anticipates or draws forth the pope's opinion, or teaches that opinion with the pope, or assents publicly to the pope's teaching. He thinks the vast majority of believers throughout history held the following view: "The infallible magisterium of the Church consists in this, namely, the supreme pontiff, the vicar of Christ, and all the bishops who adhere to him." Thus it should not be condemned. The council faces

43. Mansi 52:73A, 74D, 73C, 74B.

a choice between the infallibility "personal or isolated" or the infallibility of the pope in union with the church.[44] David's own preference is clear.

De Las Cases was another French minority bishop who found the exercise of the church's infallibility in the accord of pope and bishops. He criticizes the schema's picture of the church as an absolute monarchy, maintaining that Christ gave leadership to twelve apostles, not just Peter. Hence the church is an aristocracy, de Las Cases maintains, "a multiplicity converging toward unity" and not "a unity absorbing multiplicity." Although Peter has a primacy of honor and of jurisdiction for the sake of the church's unity, he does not relate to the other apostles as his subjects, but as brothers. De Las Cases is afraid the schema undermines the role of the bishop with his twofold privilege of teaching and jurisdiction and thereby threatens the divinely established constitution of the church.[45]

In addition, de Las Cases complains, the schema presents a separate infallibility that operates without the consensus of the bishops, either antecedent, concomitant, or subsequent. He notes that Christ's words of command or promise in Matt. 28:19 and John 14:16, 26 were addressed to the body of the apostles. If the pope is the head of the church, the bishops are special members from whom the head receives its life.[46]

Guilbert also maintains that the accord of pope and bishops is not adequately demanded by the schema. He notes that the primacy of the pope is not that total and absolute power which Christ gave to his church as a whole. To the apostles as a group were addressed many of Christ's promises of assistance; the bishops share power with the pope. Thus they teach and govern as a group: "Therefore it is not the case that the power of the supreme pontiff is opposed to that power of the bishops which, in the universal Church, they all exercise conjointly with the successor of Peter, as legislators and judges of the faith."[47] Meignan as well stresses the importance of accord between pope and bishops in his letter before the council to Baroche, the government minister:

44. Ibid., cols. 592C, 988B–C, 989D. David to diocesan clergy, 20 April 1870, cited by Durand, "Mgr David et le concile du Vatican," p. 46.
45. Mansi 52:338A, 337C.
46. Ibid., cols. 338D, 339A.
47. Ibid., col. 620C–D.

I think that it is impossible to declare as an article of faith the infallibility of the pope *without and against the bishops*. The idea of a pope contradicting the entire episcopate, in a matter of faith, morals and discipline, is opposed by all the theologians. In such a case, the Church would no longer be a living body as the trunk would be separated from the head. I am persuaded that if one approaches these matters in the Council, the wisdom of the fathers will formulate nothing more than what I am setting forth for Your Excellency.

He further observes that the pope can be infallible only when he interprets truly the judgment of the episcopate, who judge with him. Later, in a defense of Maret, he writes, "Today all Catholics believe in the infallibility of the pope; Bishop Maret as well as M. Bouix. But while some desire a personal and separate infallibility, others have a different understanding of it."[48]

Darboy opposes the schema because he believes that it would define that the pope "by himself alone" is infallible, making his privilege extend as widely as does the church's infallibility. He reasons that the church's infallibility, residing in the consensus of pope and bishops, is already held by all Catholics, and hence it would present no need for definition and discussion. But the schema would go beyond the belief in infallibility already accepted by all and would endorse a separate, personal, absolute infallibility of the pope:

For it should be noted that that infallibility always admitted by everyone, i.e., that infallibility which resides uniquely in the common consensus [*consensus*] of the bishops joined to the supreme pontiff, as the invincible and irresistible force of decrees or dogmatic decisions commanding the faith of all, both faithful and pastors, is not treated in the schema. On the contrary, what is treated—even if the thing is not proclaimed openly—is the personal, absolute, and separate infallibility of the pope.[49]

Most notable for his view on the accord of pope and bishops was Maret, whose book sets forth this understanding of infallibility as its major thesis. We have seen his defense of this view through his study of the history of councils; but he also argues the thesis systematically.

48. Meignan to Baroche, 29 July 1868, quoted in Boissonnot, *Le Cardinal Meignan*, p. 271; ibid., quoted in Palanque, *Catholiques libéraux et gallicans en France*, p. 145; Guillaume Meignan to *L'Univers*, 19 November 1869, quoted in ibid., p. 92, n. 127.

49. Mansi 52:157D–158A. Earlier Darboy had referred to the bishops and pope as "natural judges of the question" of the pope's temporal power (Georges Darboy, *Lettre à M. l'abbé Combalot en réponse à ses deux lettres à Mgr l'archevêque de Paris* [Paris: Sagnier et Bray, 1851], p. 25). But he had also referred to the Apostolic See as "the infallible guardian of truth and the final guarantee of liberty of conscience" (Darboy to Pius IX, 9 October 1863, quoted in Foulon, *Histoire de Mgr Darboy*, p. 295).

Maret had argued his view on papal-episcopal relations for many years before the council, but his book stated it most clearly. He summarizes his views at the book's start:

The Church, let us believe, is a monarchy efficaciously tempered with aristocracy; and it also has a democratic character since the monarch and the aristocratic body which govern it come or can come as the result of an election. . . . Spiritual sovereignty is therefore made up of two essential elements; the principal one, the papacy; the secondary one, the episcopate. Infallibility which forms the highest power of spiritual sovereignty is also necessarily composed of the essential elements of the sovereignty. They are found, in an absolutely certain fashion, only in the agreement and concerted action of the pope with the bishops, the bishops with the pope; and the absolutely obligatory rule of the Catholic faith, under pain of the punishments due to heresy, is based, also, on this agreement and concerted action of the two elements of the spiritual sovereignty.

Maret believes that his view can be reconciled with a moderate ultramontanism, for he does not deny papal infallibility, but rather shows it in its true nature. "We recognize and assert that, by his right to consult or to convene the episcopate, by the possibility that it act always in agreement with him, the pope has, by virtue of divine command, the assured means of giving infallibility to his dogmatic judgments." Does he contest the authority of *ex cathedra* judgments, Maret asks, when he affirms with the great theologians that the pope's judgments are certain only when he employs the most certain means given him by God for avoiding error, that is, accord with the bishops? Maret contests papal infallibility only if it is identified with a system of pure, indivisible, absolute monarchy of the pope.[50]

Maret opposes the absolutist ultramontanist school, which sees papal infallibility as separate, personal, absolute. To some in this school the pope is the source of episcopal power, but Maret sees it in Christ's institution of the bishops as successors of the apostles. He finds contradictions within the notion of a separate, personal, absolute papal infallibility. If the pope can be suspected of heresy and deposed for refusing to call a council, how is his infallibility separate, personal, absolute? If the bishops truly judge with him at councils, this shows that his infallibility is not separate, personal, absolute. It is false to see acts of superior authority in the pope's confirmation of conciliar teachings: "It seems certain that free and spontaneous

50. Maret, *Du concile général et de la paix religieuse,* 1:xx–xxi, xxvii.

agreement with the pope and the moral unanimity of the bishops in conciliar decisions is the ordinary procedure which stands out in the history of general councils." After discussing further disagreements within the ultramontanist school, Maret notes that even Bellarmine said that the definitions of the faith depend principally on the apostolic tradition and the consensus of the churches. *"If the consent of the churches, 'consensus ecclesiarum,'* is the principal rule of faith, it is sometimes necessary to hold a general council which is the best means of bringing out and of establishing this consent. But this authority of the council renders unnecessary the absolute and separate infallibility of the pope." A group possesses more wisdom and force than an individual; in addition, an infallible individual would also have to be impeccable, which is impossible.[51]

The accord between pope and bishops is necessary to establish the rule of faith. The bishops can examine freely the teachings of the pope, in or out of council. If one bishop disagrees with papal teaching outside of council, the presumption is in the pope's favor, but if many disagree, a council would be called. If a disagreeing bishop becomes increasingly isolated in his view, his duty would be submission to the widespread view. The conditions for papal infallibility, then, are two: consult the church or the bishops, and, if necessary, employ a means by which a vote can be taken. If the church is consulted by the pope, he cannot err. All agree that, for an *ex cathedra* judgment, the pope must use the best means possible to arrive at the truth. But this means is the accord of the church and of the episcopate. "The only true proclamations *ex cathedra* are those which have the consent of the Church. Oh, Church of Christ, how beautiful you are in your multiple unity! In you resides the authority of Jesus Christ."[52]

Maret believes that the French school of theologians have combined respect for the papacy with a grasp of the way the bishops tempered the monarchy of the pope with aristocracy. Bossuet wanted to fight arbitrariness in church rule. He explained that the French bishops did not argue against papal infallibility; rather, they emphasized that the decrees of the Apostolic See are not irreformable and fully authoritative until the assent of the church has been reached. "This principle stated, the question of infallibility becomes purely

51. Ibid., 2:62, 33–37, 157–60, 174, 233, 236–57.   52. Ibid., pp. 272, 284–88, 299.

speculative and entirely useless. If one would explain in this way the declaration of the French clergy, I am persuaded that the bishops would place no obstacles to it," Maret writes in citing Bossuet.[53]

Maret's book ends with the observation, "There is no absolute and definitely final act of spiritual sovereignty without the agreement of the two elements which compose it. The pope has always at his disposition, in the agreement of the episcopate, the divine means of giving infallibility to his dogmatic decrees." A practical way to ensure regular discussion, Maret suggests, is in periodically held councils, since the purpose of councils is the formation of a common decision.[54]

53. Ibid., pp. 328–31.

54. Ibid., pp. 390, 417. R. Thysmans emphasizes the debt Maret owes to Bossuet in both general perspective and details ("Le gallicanisme de Mgr Maret et l'influence de Bossuet," pp. 401–65). By 1865, Maret had begun to study Bossuet's *Defensio declarationis,* and this became the major work of Bossuet from which he drew. He especially used Bossuet for his strong criticisms of the theories regarding judgments *ex cathedra* and for his distinctions on the judicial role of bishops (p. 410). His reliance on Bossuet leads him to make some historical errors in his analysis of councils, although he also corrects some of Bossuet's mistakes (p. 425). Maret shapes his discussion of past councils with an eye on the council that is about to meet, emphasizing the lay role, the right of the minority at Chalcedon until the final vote, and the perpetual need for church reform (p. 432).

Maret also brings in other perspectives, such as the view of the ultramontanists, with whom he hopes to find a compromise. He must strike a balance between the gallicanism of Bossuet and the changed perception of the pope's role in the nineteenth-century church (pp. 441–42). Thus he comes to his central thesis: the church's constitution is complex, such that neither pope nor bishops can act alone in defining the faith. But here again he follows Bossuet's "lively sense of the organic unity of the ecclesial body" in which head and members cooperate under the Holy Spirit (p. 450). But in the nineteenth century Maret had to take account of the clearer and more universal affirmation of certain papal privileges (p. 451). Hence for Maret the pope in a council has slightly more weight than he did for Bossuet, and the presumption is in his favor when the church is dispersed; a bishop alone with his doubts must submit (pp. 453–56). Thus Maret can accept papal infallibility in a certain sense, within the idea of the consensus of the two parts of the church. "He is infallible to whom God, by a special disposition of his supernatural providence and in virtue even of the authority which he confers on him, gives the certain means of being infallible. Now, the pope, and the pope alone, always has the right to consult the Church or the episcopal body," says Maret (*Du concile général et de la paix religieuse,* cited by Thysmans, p. 457). Thysmans writes, "This is the true sense of judgment *ex cathedra.* This, too, is the secret of conciliation between gallicanism and the moderate ultramontane doctors. Maret, more than Bossuet, came closer, with regard to infallibility, to the logical conclusion of their common principles; but their fears, conscious or not, regarding pontifical arbitrariness as well as certain conciliar facts and some weaknesses of the popes, prevented them from going farther" (p. 457). Maret accepted the possibility of a pope's falling into heresy; if he persisted in his error, he ceased to be pope and should

In February 1870, Maret sums up his view on the relationship between pope and bishop for distribution to the French minority caucus. There he notes that if the pope acting alone errs, the truth will be conserved by the body of bishops.[55]

Maret was not alone in arguing that infallibility is found only when pope and bishops agree. A good number of other French minority bishops—drawing on scriptural interpretation, the tradition's teaching about episcopal authority, or a common-sense idea that many heads are better than one—argued that the schema failed to locate infallibility correctly within the accord of pope and bishops.

Consensus of the Church

Other French bishops made a similar argument, but they stressed that the pope acted not only in accord with the bishops but also with the entire church. Sometimes it is difficult to distinguish between the two arguments; the difference is more one of emphasis than of ideas. But in this argument, the bishops maintained that the schema was inaccurate because it suggested that the pope could teach infallibly apart from the consensus of the church.

Colet complains that the schema moves from primacy to infallibility. But the prerogative of primacy belongs only to the successors of Peter, while that of teaching "pertains to the body of the teaching church, which consists of head and members." The link between primacy and infallibility should not be made as though known naturally or from mere logic. And infallibility should not be presented as though it inhered in the pope in the same way that primacy inheres in him. The pope is infallible only insofar as he is head of the Church's magisterium: "Insofar as he is head and center of the ecclesial magisterium, he cannot err either in preserving the deposit of divine revelation, or in teaching it, or in refuting the errors opposing it."[56]

---

be replaced; but his seat remained indefectible (ibid.). For Maret, the pope has the right to confirm conciliar decisions, and sometimes such confirmation is necessary to give the council incontestable authority; but Maret thinks that the pope cannot refuse confirmation if the canonical rules and conditions for ecumenicity are respected by the council (pp. 453–54).

55. Bazin, *Vie de Maret,* pp. 171–72.

56. Mansi 52:984A–B.

Colet raises this issue again when he notes that infallibility as presented in the schema, that is personal, separate, and absolute, also cannot be derived from indefectibility. When the pope defines, he is the asserter and custodian of the faith of the universal church. But the bishops also have the role of testimony to this faith; they also witness and judge, united to the pope, and they also are bound to guard revelation and the deposit of the apostolic tradition. "It is the role of the bishops also to give witness to the vicar of Christ about their teaching, just as about the faith of their sheep."[57] Colet emphasizes that both bishops and pope are bound by the faith of the whole church. Colet emphasizes the teaching and witness role of the bishops, but he believes that the teaching and witness they offer represents the faith of their local churches. Hence his emphasis is on their role in the context of the whole church.

Ramadié also argues against the idea that papal infallibility can be derived from papal primacy. He notes that Christ was not bound to give the pope infallibility in order to protect the magisterium from error. If an infallible magisterium is necessary, that does not mean that an infallible pope is necessary; Christ could have chosen to grant infallibility to the whole body of the teaching church, not just the head: "It does not seem necessary that Christ reserve it [the infallible authority of the magisterium] to the head alone of his mystical body. Obviously he could have decided that that infallible authority should reside in the body teaching with the head, and have established that in its exercise—which is the supereminent act of the Church's life—both the head should direct the body and the body should sustain the head." The two prerogatives of primacy and infallibility have different objects, different subjects, different limits; and "whatever may be the case regarding the doctrine of infallibility, it is obvious that the primacy of governance is more extensive than the primacy of teaching." The infallibility promised to the church is a seamless garment, not to be divided, Ramadié insists. Perhaps the schema might condemn a notion of separate infallibility, which affirms a truncated body, with the words, "If anyone say that the Church's infallible magisterium, instituted by Christ, can be exercised either by the bishops separate from the Roman pontiff, or by the Roman pontiff separate from the bishops, let him be anathema." At this suggestion,

57. Ibid., col. 985A–B.

dissenting views are heard in the council hall; Ramadié concludes with a plea not to divide the episcopacy into two parts.[58]

After noting that infallibility does not operate without consensus of the bishops, de Las Cases also moves to a discussion of *consensus ecclesiae*. From the tradition that the head receives life from its members, he says, comes the common teaching that "the consensus of the churches is the perpetual rule of faith." If Peter remained mouthpiece within this consensus, he argues, the other bishops remained "fathers and teachers." The definitions of the faith are produced by the whole group: "The body of doctrine was regarded as put together out of their collectivity; nor had it occurred to anyone that I know that such great power exists in the head apart from the body, rather than in the body and the head indivisibly joined by a fraternal bond." To say that the Roman church defines and defends the faith before all other churches, as the Greeks said at the Second Council of Lyons, does not mean that such defining is done independently of other churches, de Las Cases insists. In fact, the Greeks maintained that the consent of the other churches is necessary: "Nay more, since it [the Roman church] derives this function of defining before the others from the principle of full primacy, therefore it declares all the more openly that the agreement [*consensus*] of the other churches is necessary."[59]

De Marguerye notes that Christ instituted a teaching authority in the church and gave it the privilege of infallibility for proclamation of dogma but that this teaching authority proclaims beliefs that have always existed. The pope and the episcopal body can define, de Marguerye says. The Apostolic See has the following rights: "to proclaim the meaning of the divine Scripture, to proclaim the divine doctrine preserved by tradition, to formulate and to define a revealed truth; and it has the right to do this throughout all time whether it be a question of defending this truth against the attacks of innovators or merely of surrounding it with more brilliant splendor." But de Marguerye notes the criteria by which the church can judge the reliability of the pope's definition. In defining the Immaculate Conception, for example, the pope consulted the bishops, noted the popular demand for the dogma's definition, and established a committee for consultation. After so many precise measures have been taken, he continues,

---

58. Ibid., cols. 1016B–D, 1019D, 1019B.   59. Ibid., cols. 339A–B, 340C.

who would not recognize the infallible certitude of this judgment, which even humanly speaking cannot be suspected of error? "The holy Church acts in this way in matters of faith and of evangelical ethics: this is because the Spirit of God directs its decisions as well as all the acts leading up to them."[60] Again the stress is on the faith of the church; certain criteria are available to believers by which to check the pope's teaching and recognize in it their own faith.

De Marguerye's concern is similar to that of Thomas, who complains that the schema in its development neglects much of the tradition of councils, the practice of theologians, and the example of Jesus himself in its discussion. For how can the primacy of the pope be treated before the bishops are discussed? How can the magisterium of the pope be separated from the "magisterium of the universal Church"? He suggests an addition to the schema showing the church, governed by the successors of the apostles, as the corporate means willed by Christ for his followers to be joined together. In addition, Thomas wants to use the word *center* rather than *chief* in discussing the Apostolic See. Not only is this term better received and more frequently used in the tradition of the church, he believes, it also expresses better the Apostolic See's function as root of ecclesial unity. The church is like a circle with radii; its doctrines are like blood coursing through a body, running from center to the ends and back again. Thomas is also afraid that the schema does not give the bishops the emphasis they deserve; they are the lookouts of the city of God, the columns of the house, the judges of faith and morals.[61]

Ginoulhiac always stresses the link between the church as a whole and any expression of its faith. Writing on infallibility before the council, he notes, "At least, one would know that if the pope is infallible, he is not so without the episcopal body sharing in active infallibility, in an agreement through proper action both to determine the truths of the faith and to lay down the rules of universal discipline."[62] The bishops' presence at the upcoming council might manifest this, he suggests. He is alarmed at rumors that a definition of papal infallibility "*separate and without* any consent, expressed or tacit, of the episcopate" might be proposed at the council:

60. De Marguerye, "Marie a été conçue sans péché," pp. 710–12.
61. Mansi 52:506C, 507C–D.
62. "Du moins, on saurait que si le Pape est infaillible, il ne l'est pas en ce sens que le corps épiscopal ne participe pas à l'infaillibilité active, un concours par une action

Of course, one wouldn't dare go so far as to say that the pope is *everything*, that he is the *only* power in the Church, and that the agreement of the episcopate with the judgments of the Holy See is unimportant; but of necessity and in fact one would finally end up there. What kind of teaching body could teach only what only one doctor dictates? How would the bishops in council be judges of the faith, with a deliberative voice, when the voice, the vote of one individual suffices for everything?[63]

Confusion about faith or morals never takes over the universal church, nor the church of Rome, its center, he writes, again linking the papacy to the church as a whole.[64] The pope presides at a council, but the bishops judge, a role recognized from the first days of the church and formalized in the words the bishop uses for his assent to a council's decree. A council needs the assent of both the pope and the bishops to constitute its decision, "for this judgment is formulated by the agreement between the bishops and their head and only thereby has the authority proper to a decision of the council."[65]

Ginoulhiac's emphasis on the consensus of the church necessary for infallible teaching also emerges in his strong sense of the importance attached to the reception given to a teaching by the church as a whole. Councils should be composed of many bishops from all parts of the world, he writes, because otherwise they are less ecumenical, and then they really achieve their ecumenical status by the subsequent acceptance of the whole church: "And general councils at which there were not present bishops or delegates from different parts of Catholicism are less ecumenical in themselves than they have become by the subsequent acceptance of the universal Church." Ginoulhiac makes this point again in another way. A council is ecumenical only "insofar as it is recognized and accepted as ecumenical by the Church: not that this recognition communicates to the Council an authority that it would not have of itself; but the recognition declares and manifests the authority." He distinguishes between councils that are ecumenical in themselves, through adequate representation of the whole church, and those that become ecumenical

---

propre et à déterminer les vérités de la foi et à établir les règles de la discipline universelle" (Jacques Ginoulhiac to Félix Dupanloup (?), 12 May 1867, AB XIX 524, fol. 3, Archives Nationales, Paris).

63. Jacques Ginoulhiac to unnamed correspondent, 23 April 1867, quoted in Mourret, *Le concile du Vatican,* p. 40.

64. Ginoulhiac, *Histoire du dogme catholique,* 1st ed., 1:vii.

65. Ginoulhiac, *Le concile oecuménique,* pp. 35, 37.

through their subsequent recognition by the whole church. But in each case he ties dogmatic definitions to a base in the faith of the entire church: "And that is how one distinguishes between councils which become ecumenical through subsequent acceptance by the Church and those which are ecumenical of themselves. Thus, different from the Council of Nicea, the First Council of Constantinople became ecumenical only through its union with the council that Pope Damasus had held at Rome and through the acceptance which this pope made of it with the whole western church." He summarizes the distinction he has drawn: "So, in certain cases, the subsequent acceptance or approbation of the universal Church is an essential condition of the ecumenicity of a council, in other cases, it is only the seal." An analogous point can be made about the reception of conciliar decrees by the pope. But Ginoulhiac is inclined to the position that the pope is obliged to confirm the legitimate decrees of a council. He reasons that even without the pope, a council still speaks with authority because of the presence of Christ, who would not leave the church without the rule of faith, the infallible authority of the church.[66]

Ginoulhiac notes that the definition of the Immaculate Conception was not made without requests for it, the unanimous agreement of all of the bishops, the desires of the faithful, and the agreement with the church's tradition. To emphasize his understanding of the unity between papal declarations and the faith of the entire church, Ginoulhiac cites the words of Leo to Theodoret. Leo was happy that "the dogma defined first of all by his ministry, had been confirmed at Chalcedon by the *irrevocable* consent of all his brothers, and that, in this way, God had shown that it was truly from him that this teaching came, since having been formulated by the first of all the sees, it had been received by the judgment of the whole world."[67]

Ginoulhiac's stress on the need for the *consensus ecclesiae* for the exercise of infallibility stands behind one of his arguments against the conciliar schema. He agrees with the commentator who notes that the pope's infallibility is not separate, personal, or absolute. Ginoulhiac also agrees that the pope gives testimony and safeguards the faith; he is not inspired. But Ginoulhiac argues that this testimony and safeguarding takes place not in one but in many; Christ

66. Ibid., pp. 39, 64, 129–31.   67. Ibid., pp. 137–38.

established many witnesses: "Moreover, the ordinary force and reasonableness of testimonies rests, as you well know, not on the quality of one witness but on the conformity and concord of many. Therefore according to the ordinary law of providence this universal truth is not to be sought in one witness but in many." Citing Tertullian, Jerome, and Augustine, Ginoulhiac makes the same argument about the task of safeguarding the faith: "For not [just] one of the bishops but all the bishops have the right and duty to preserve the deposit of faith."[68]

In discussing the active infallibility of the church, the schema makes a fictitious separation in its exercise between the pope and those who with him and beneath him are active subjects of this divine prerogative, Ginoulhiac complains. The schema fails to make clear the unity of the bishops as a teaching body:

With all due respect to the most distinguished *relator*, upon hearing and applauding him I was astonished that he said nothing about the teaching body in the Church, about the apostolic college, about the unity of the apostolate under Peter and with Peter, to whom such great promises were made by Christ, nor about the unity of the episcopate manifesting the unity of the apostolate through the ages and so often celebrated by the fathers, and so often proclaimed and defended by the most illustrious men of all the schools, especially in this noble city.

The inseparable unity of the entire teaching body of the church in the act of defining should also be made more clear, Ginoulhiac argues.[69] In addition, the conditions present in the exercise of papal infallibility should be specified. Everyone agrees that "definitions of faith depend especially on apostolic tradition and the consensus [*consensus*] of the churches." But some conditions under which the pope defines infallibly should be indicated. They need not be lengthy, Ginoulhiac continues, just enough to show that papal infallibility operates under the condition of the consent of the church. He suggests such phrases as "with the counsel of his brothers" or "speaking as head of the Church, and with its counsel, and with its required testimony and assistance" or the Antonine formula.[70]

Many joined Ginoulhiac in his argument against the schema for its failure to show the need for the *consensus ecclesiae* in the exercise of

68. Mansi 52:215C–216A.
70. Ibid., cols. 907B–908A.
69. Ibid., cols. 216C–217A.

infallibility. Whether they stressed antecedent or subsequent consensus, formal or informal means of attaining consensus, these bishops all shared the deep conviction that no definition of the faith could be made if it did not spring forth from the faith of the church as a whole.

They did not, of course, envision an active teaching role for the laity. Their concern was rather with the necessity of the corporate witness by the body of the bishops in teaching. But by stressing the corporate and witnessing dimensions of this episcopal work, they hinted at the links of the body of bishops to the communion of the entire church with its many local churches. Yves Congar observes:

> When St. Augustine writes, *In cathedra unitatis doctrinam posuit (Deus) veritatis* ("God has set [the] doctrine of truth in the chair of unity") he is speaking, not of the Roman chair, as has been thought and said too often, but of each individual chair and of the totality of chairs existing in the *unitas*. It is in unity as such that the truth is kept. In conjunction with a supernatural, completely biblical and Christian anthropology there is here a principle of crucial ecclesiological implication, containing a valuable share of the truth, to be found in the Orthodox idea of *Sobornost*, itself an expression in ecclesiology of a primarily anthropological position. Right up to the time when a juridical and unilateral theory, dominated by the idea of the pontifical monarchy, was victorious, Catholic tradition preserved the idea that the real subject of infallibility is the *Ecclesia universalis*.[71]

It is the echo of that idea, faintly heard but still honored, that we can detect in the frequent arguments that the French minority made by appealing to the need for the *consensus ecclesiae*.

Conclusion

Some observers of the First Vatican Council have argued that at most only one or two bishops from the French minority actually found the schema false, but I have corrected this view.[72] Using a variety of arguments, a good number of French minority bishops made a case that the schema's presentation of papal infallibility was not true.

71. Yves Congar, "Remarks on the Council as an Assembly and on the Church's Fundamentally Conciliar Nature," in *Report from Rome II: On the Second Session of the Vatican Council*, trans. Lancelot Sheppard (London: Geoffrey Chapman, 1964), p. 186. Sheppard translates *doctrinam* as "a doctrine."

72. For example, Mourret, *Le concile du Vatican*, p. 159; Palanque, *Catholiques libéraux et gallicans en France*, pp. 180–81; see also discussion of the history of interpretation of the minority in the Preface.

They drew their arguments from their interpretation of past theologians and of councils, from their sense of the role of the bishop, their conviction that pope and bishops must be in accord for the exercise of infallibility. But the heart of their case is expressed in the argument that infallible teaching expresses the *consensus ecclesiae*. This is really the central concern of this case: the conviction that the schema wrongly separated the exercise of infallibility from its foundation and isolated it in one person.

At the same time, those who think that the French minority opposed any concept of papal infallibility must be corrected. Hasler links this view of the whole minority with the opinion that they later submitted to *Pastor aeternus* simply out of cowardice or evasive interpretation.[73] Hasler is correct in seeing the real arguments that minority bishops had against the definition. But he is incorrect in failing to note that before the council Maret, Darboy, Meignan, David, Dupanloup, Ginoulhiac, Colet, and others held a certain nuanced doctrine of papal infallibility. They envisioned that the pope could speak infallibly when he spoke in accord with the bishops, with Scripture and tradition, with the whole church. They did not find their view in the schema. But this nuanced view of papal infallibility held by the French minority bishops laid the foundation for their subsequent assent to *Pastor aeternus*, when they were able to satisfy themselves that the decree did not fundamentally contradict their earlier understanding of papal infallibility.

Again, more insistently than in either of the earlier two cases, there emerges the thread that runs through all of the arguments: infallibility has an ecclesial character. It was given first to the church as a whole, and only expressions of the faith of this whole church can be judged infallible. Does not this argument, more than any other, help us to explain that last desperate attempt on the part of the minority to reach a compromise just before the council's final vote?[74] The International Committee of the minority promised to end all of their opposition if the "full power [*plena potestas*]" would be eliminated from the schema, replaced instead with a summary of the French minority's constant arguments: "relying on the testimony of the churches [*innixus testimonio Ecclesiarum*]."

73. Hasler, *Pius IX*, 2:447–51, 474–505.
74. Palanque, *Catholiques libéraux et gallicans en France*, p. 175.

PART III

The French Minority Bishops for the Reception of *Pastor aeternus*

7

On Formal Authority

Obedience Requires Reception of Pastor aeternus

———◆●▸———

"My friend, I bless God for calling me to himself before the definition," murmured Jean Devoucoux, bishop of Evreux, as he lay on his deathbed attended by Bravard in the spring of 1870.[1] But Bravard and his fellow bishops in the minority found themselves facing the very situation that Devoucoux had been glad to avoid: after all of their arguments against it, the council had nevertheless passed a definition of papal infallibility. What should they do?

Although they had opposed the schema on papal infallibility, every one of the twenty-two French minority bishops adhered to *Pastor aeternus*.[2] Why did this group, so vehement in their opposition to the schema during the council, yet find themselves unanimous in their acceptance of *Pastor aeternus*?

The Systematic Framework of the Arguments

In the last section, we saw that a systematic framework underlay the thought of the French minority bishops' opposition to the schema, a framework that could be expressed in three cases that re-

1. "Mon ami, je bénis Dieu de m'appeler à lui avant la définition." Bravard reports Devoucoux's deathbed words in a speech quoted in *Revue catholique (Semaine religieuse) du diocèse de Coutances et Avranches* 3 (9 June 1870):588–89. Devoucoux met with the French minority as an active minority participant during the council until his health forced him to leave Rome in the spring of 1870; he died in his diocese on 2 May 1870.

2. A chronological chart of the letters and acts of acceptance of *Pastor aeternus* by the French minority is available in Gadille, *La pensée et l'action politiques des évêques français*, 1:114. Gadille's definition of the French minority includes a few more bishops than does my definition.

sponded to three questions. A systematic framework can also be discerned behind the thought of the French minority's arguments in favor of the reception of *Pastor aeternus*. Again the concerns that shape this systematic framework can be expressed by the responses to a set of questions: (1) Does the formal authority of *Pastor aeternus* require its reception? (2) Does the material authority of *Pastor aeternus* require its reception? These questions are simpler than the complex interlocking questions of the last part. They can be answered separately from each other, and an answer to one does not determine the answer to the other. Every French bishop found that he was able to answer *yes* to at least one of these questions.

The two cases for the reception of *Pastor aeternus*—the first based on its status and the second on its content—will be treated in that order in this chapter and the next.

Preconciliar Views on Formal Authority

Before the council's conclusion or even its start, many French minority bishops promised to accept whatever decisions it might make. Others noted as well the inherent formal authority which the council would have simply in function of its character as an ecumenical council of the church.

Bravard writes to his diocese that conciliar decisions always carry the stamp of God because his unerring wisdom directs councils. This forms the basis for the obligation which councils impose upon the conscience and moral conduct.[3] He writes to members of his diocese during Lent of 1870 that they should prepare themselves to accept the council's decisions because of its authority:

In the first place, you have to be ready to welcome both with mind and heart all the decisions of the Council. This we have already given you to understand: these decisions will be the infallible manifestations of the truth, and of goodness: you will not be able to refuse your acceptance of them both internally and externally without denying your belief as a Catholic. Councils are like sacred Scripture and tradition: the word of God; they are indeed only the continuation and the development of this word. We are bound to be attached to them as we are attached to these Scriptures and this tradition.[4]

3. Bravard, "Pour le Carême de 1870," p. 355.
4. "Premièrement, vous devez être disposés à accueillir et d'esprit et de coeur

When the council announces its decision, Bravard maintains, all discussions will cease, all doubts disappear. He promises his own immediate acceptance in advance to all decisions of the church.[5]

Ramadié also emphasizes that conciliar decisions are binding upon Christians. All Catholic hearts wait for these teachings happily, and every Christian mind prepares itself to say, "I believe!"[6] Thomas teaches that Christ protects the church from error, so that, "when the Church speaks, therefore, the Christian believes in its word with complete confidence." The Christian knows that the church is "the infallible mouthpiece of the truth which is from God, which is God himself revealing himself through his word."[7]

Before the First Vatican Council, Dupanloup teaches that because ecumenical councils represent the universal church, they have doctrinal infallibility. "That is why the decisions of the ecumenical councils have always ended all controversy and established the faith in the Church." Dupanloup promises in advance his obedience to whatever the upcoming council will decide: "Obedient in advance, and obedient until death, I adhere to the decisions of the head of the Church and of the Council: I adhere to them from the bottom of my heart and with my whole soul, whatever these decisions may be, whether consistent with or contrary to my own ideas, I have said this before and I say it again; whether they confirm or contradict my opinion." Dupanloup notes that the upcoming council will have its share of human imperfections, but that the Holy Spirit always directs such imperfections and turns them to the service of truth: "No one is Catholic without this faith which is my own and that is why I adhere

---

toutes les décisions du Concile. Nous vous l'avons déjà fait entendre: ces décisions seront la manifestation infaillible de ce qui est la vérité, et de ce qui est la vertu: vous ne sauriez leur refuser votre adhésion, et intérieure et extérieure, sans renier vos croyances catholiques. Les Conciles sont comme les saintes Ecritures et la tradition: la parole de Dieu; ils ne sont même que la continuation et le développement de cette parole. Nous sommes tenus de nous attacher à eux comme nous sommes attachés à ces Ecritures et à cette tradition" (ibid., p. 371).

5. "Nouvelles et faits religieux du diocèse," p. 454.

6. "je crois!" (Ramadié, Pastoral Letter for Lent 1870, p. 135).

7. "quand donc l'Eglise parle, le chrétien croit à sa parole avec une pleine confiance" (Léon Thomas, "La paix de l'âme chrétienne," *Bulletin religieux du diocèse de La Rochelle et Saintes* 5 [13 February 1869]:386). "l'organe infaillible de la vérité qui est de Dieu, qui est Dieu même se révélant par son Verbe" (ibid.).

in advance, why I submit and I am happy to adhere, joyful to submit. After having argued freely, worked hard, acted courageously, our submission will be our victory, and you will give us all the grace, oh, my God, to find peace in faith and joy in obedience. For our victory is our faith. *Haec est victoria, fides nostra.*—And the nation of the just is only obedience and love."[8] David writes to his diocese before the council's end, "We are quite sure that your faith will accept them [the conciliar teachings] without hesitation, that the voice of the Church, resounding on the lips of its head, will reach your heart and will find there only docility and love." Once pronounced, a conciliar decision is "irrevocable and immortal as is divine truth," he explains. "All arguments and all doubts vanish. Unity reigns in the bosom of the Christian family." Those who before the council had the right and duty to discuss now know only how to believe and to proclaim their belief. For "one is Catholic in mind and in heart only on condition of being able to sacrifice all personal opinions to the defined faith of the Church," David argues.[9]

David emphasizes that obedience is the proper response to an official decree made at the highest level of the church: "As soon as the final and official decree is lawfully pronounced, that is, according to the laws which the Church has always considered necessary for the ecumenical character of the councils, our obedience of mind and heart must be the same; for at this moment all doubts cease, everything becomes light, love, repose." Each Christian sacrifices his own thought to teach instead the eternal truth believed everywhere, unanimously, and always. "One no longer argues, one believes."[10] This emphasis on the sacrifice of one's own thought for the sake of obedience to the church's decision is echoed in Place's pledge of "the

8. Dupanloup, *Le futur concile oecuménique*, p. 11; Dupanloup, *Avant son départ*, p. 20. Dupanloup's pledge was cited frequently after the council by his admirers to show the bishop's good intentions despite his opposition to the schema at the council. The preconciliar pledges of many minority bishops received the same treatment.

9. "Nous sommes bien sûr que votre foi les acceptera sans hésiter, que la voix de l'Eglise, retentissant sur les lèvres de son Chef, arrivera à votre coeur et n'y trouvera que docilité et amour" (David, Circular Letter to Diocese [26 May 1870], p. 342). "Toutes les disputes et tous les doutes s'évanouissent. L'unité se fait au sein de la famille chrétienne" (ibid.). "on n'est catholique par l'intelligence et le coeur qu'à la condition de savoir sacrifier toute pensée personnelle à la foi définie de l'Eglise" (ibid.).

10. Augustin David, Circular to Diocese, 26 May 1870, cited by David himself in Mansi 53:1026C. (Although the dates of publication are the same, this circular is a different piece from that cited in the last footnote.)

profound and absolute obedience that our hearts vowed in advance to the infallible decisions of the Vatican Council, whatever they may be." Place bases his security on Christ's promise of presence to his church. Hugonin also pledges that he will accept with perfect docility all decisions the council might take. In 1865, Darboy says that if the pope made new decisions, Catholics—bishops, priests, and laity—would accept them all with the same submission they had exercised in response to his former decisions. To be a Catholic, he says, means to believe that ecumenical councils exercise their teaching right and can have only salutary effects.[11]

Writing on the authority of dogma, Meignan notes that the unvarying articles of faith determine what Catholics believe: "We have the decisions of the councils and of the sovereign pontiff received throughout the universal Church. Whoever rejects a single dogma so defined has ceased to be a member of the Church." Thus he maintains that Christian faith hails in advance whatever decisions the upcoming council will make. Meignan joins the other French minority bishops who pledge acceptance of the council's decisions before they are made, even though those decisions may not agree with the bishop's views argued during the council:

Of course, we will express our complete opinion; we will be there not as advisers only, since divine right invests us with the liberty and the authority of a judge; but here the judge is enlightened in the midst of peaceful discussions; he profits by the thoughts of his brothers, by the shock of ideas which produce light and his judgment is formed under the influence of the word of Peter and the inspirations of the Holy Spirit. Oh, our very dear brothers, we promise God to humble our own judgments, if it is necessary, before those of the Council.

But the work of study required of the bishops, Meignan says, corresponds to another work required of the laity: "the great obligation of preparing themselves to receive with docility, with confidence, all the oracles of the venerable synod."[12]

11. "l'obéissance profonde et absolue que nos coeurs ont vouée d'avance aux infaillibles décisions du Concile du Vatican, quelles qu'elles soient" (Place, "De son prochain départ," p. 835); Flavien Hugonin at a meeting cited in "Nouvelles diocésaines," *La semaine religieuse du diocèse de Bayeux et Lisieux* 5 (21 November 1869):748; Darboy, Notes for Retreat Conferences, 1DVIII, 1, Archives de l'Archevêché de Paris; Darboy, "Lettre pastorale sur le prochain concile," pp. 411–12.

12. Meignan, *La crise protestante*, p. 29; Meignan, Pastoral Letter for Lent 1870, p. 692. "Sans doute, nous dirons notre pensée tout entière; nous ne serons pas là seulement des conseillers, puisque le droit divin nous investit de la liberté et de l'autorité du

The French minority bishops attributed formal authority to the decisions of the First Vatican Council even before those decisions were made. They were convinced that all Catholics, including themselves, would be bound in faith to submit to the decisions. They based this conviction on their belief, elaborated in Chapter 2, that ecumenical councils were infallible because of Christ's promises to be present with his church. Some bishops explained their pledged acceptance as an act of obedience.

Most would have agreed with the opinion expressed by the famous layman Charles de Montalembert, who would die before the council reached its decision on papal infallibility. When close to death, Montalembert is asked what he will do if the council defines papal infallibility. Although opposed to such a definition, Montalembert replies that he will make an act of faith and simply submit. His questioner responds, "Oh! you will give external submission; but how will you succeed in reconciling this submission with your convictions?" But Montalembert replies: "I'll reconcile nothing at all. I shall submit my will as one submits it in all sorts of other questions of conscience. God will not ask me to understand, to contrive anything whatever, he will ask me to submit my will and my intelligence and I will submit them."[13] That the bishops, though participants at the council, held a view on their postconciliar role similar to that of this layman who had no vote at the council makes an interesting consideration in itself.

---

juge; mais ici le juge s'éclaire, au milieu de discussions pacifiques; il bénéficie de la pensée de ses frères, du choc des idées qui produit la lumière, et son jugement se forme sous l'influence de la parole de Pierre et des inspirations de l'Esprit-Saint. Oh! Nos Très-Chers Frères, nous promettons à Dieu d'humilier, s'il le fallait, nos propres jugements devant ceux du Concile" (Meignan, "De son départ," p. 454). "la grande obligation de se préparer à recevoir avec docilité, avec confiance, tous les oracles du vénérable synode" (Meignan, Pastoral Letter for Lent 1870, p. 692).

13. Quoted in Palanque, Catholiques libéraux et gallicans en France, p. 127; also in Pierre Michel Pagès, Mgr Dupanloup: Sa vie, ses écrits, sa doctrine (Paris: Delhomme et Briguet, 1895), p. 260, in a slightly abbreviated version. See also the comment of Lord John Acton when his bishop asked if he truly adhered to the First Vatican Council: "As the bishops, who are my guides, have accepted the decrees, so have I. They are a law to me as much as those of Trent, not from any private interpretation, but from the authority from which they come. The difficulties about reconciling them with tradition, which seem so strong to others, do not disturb me, a layman, whose business it is not to explain theological questions, and who leaves that to his betters" (Lord John Acton to Richard Simpson, editor of the Rambler, 10 December 1874, printed in John

Postconciliar Views on Formal Authority

After the council ended,[14] the French minority bishops explained their acceptance of *Pastor aeternus,* or argued for its acceptance by others, on the basis of its formal authority. The bishops made this argument from formal authority more frequently than they did the argument from material authority.

Minority bishops absent from the final vote on 18 July 1870 were made to understand that the Vatican desired a formal acceptance of *Pastor aeternus* from them. Most wrote to the pope, many using just a version of the simple formula of Colet, "Moreover I adhere with mind and heart to the first constitution *de ecclesia Christi* promulgated by your Holiness."[15]

Others discussed in more detail their understanding of the formal authority possessed by *Pastor aeternus.* The discussions at the council were not like ordinary battles because they were not determined by personal triumphs but by the victory of faith and of God's will, writes Dupanloup. Foulon writes that decrees of councils are to be received as dogmas "with the filial respect which they deserve and with the submission of mind and heart which they exact of all the Christian faithful."[16] In response to doubts expressed about the council's decrees, Hugonin responds, "The answer to these questions admits of no doubt. A pontifical and dogmatic bull is obliga-

---

Acton, *Lord Acton and His Circle,* ed. Francis Gasquet [London: Burns and Oates, 1906], p. 364).

14. Technically, of course, the council did not end but was given a recess by Pius IX on 20 October 1870. The expectation of further conciliar sessions may have influenced some French minority bishops in their acceptance of *Pastor aeternus.* Bravard, for example, notes, "This is not a complete treatise on the Church, studied and decided upon: it is only one section of what concerns the society of the faithful, instituted by our Lord; the remainder will come following conciliar deliberations" (Mansi 53:1028B); see also Aimé Guilbert to his diocese, ibid., cols. 1046D–1047A; Guillaume Meignan, "Lettre circulaire et mandement (28 July 1870)," *La semaine champenoise* 5 (5 August 1870):226; Charles Place to his diocese, Mansi 53:1036A.

15. Mansi 53:1018B–C; see also the acceptance letters of de Cuttoli, ibid., col. 1060A–C; of Dupont des Loges, ibid., col. 986B–C; of Maret, ibid., cols. 1018C–1019A; and of Mathieu, ibid., col. 939A. Others used a simple formula in their last testaments to reaffirm their intention to die in communion with the faith of the Roman Catholic Church.

16. Mansi 53:990D–991A; Joseph Foulon, "Instruction pastorale sur la providence de Dieu et son action dans les évènements actuels," in *Oeuvres pastorales,* 1:110.

tory in itself before any publication by the bishop of the diocese; and, consequently, the doctrines which it contains must be publicly taught."[17] Where Hugonin explains the decree's formal authority as pontifical, others see it instead as based on the validity of the council or on its expression of the faith of at least the great majority of bishops and the pope. Aubert comments on the curious way that the minority bishops were now bound to accept the decision of the council, even if it might have followed an illegal procedure—bound by precisely that gallican tradition that had fueled their opposition:

By virtue of the gallican principle itself, a definition promulgated by the pope and ratified by the episcopate as a whole should have been considered as infallible. Even if the procedure followed by the Council had been illegal, as some thought, it had to be recognized at least that the affirmation of pontifical infallibility had been ratified at Rome itself by a significant proportion of the episcopate and that, by adding to this subsequent individual adherences, moral unanimity was rapidly approaching.[18]

Maret probably found himself in the position of the isolated bishop whom he had described before the council: if one bishop in disagreement with the teaching of the others becomes more and more isolated in his position, he would eventually be obligated to submit to the teaching of the great body of bishops in agreement with the pope. And commenting on Nicea, he had written that, after the decision was made, "no doubt is allowed, no resistance tolerated. One must submit or cease to be a Catholic.[19] Although to David, Maret comments, "In my opinion, up until now this ecumenicity does not exist," his position is probably better reflected in this more balanced reflection he made after the close of the council: "The general question of ecumenicity especially of the fourth session is doubtful for us. Strong reasons argue against it; but on the other hand, the agreement of the Pope with the large majority made up of so many enlightened, pious prelates devoted to the Church, this agreement, I say, allows no settlement in an absolute fashion of this

17. "La réponse à ces questions n'est pas douteuse. Une Bulle pontificale et dogmatique est obligatoire par elle-même avant toute publication de l'Evêque du diocèse; et, par conséquent, les doctrines qu'elle contient doivent être publiquement enseignées" (Flavien Hugonin, "Lettre de Monseigneur à MM. les Curés [16 November 1870],"*La semaine religieuse du diocèse de Bayeux et Lisieux* 6 [27 November 1870]:760; also in Mansi 53:1038B–1039A).

18. Aubert, *Pie IX*, p. 361.

19. Maret, *Du concile général et de la paix religieuse*, 2:288, 1:163. Again, summariz-

question of ecumenicity." Yet he also commented, "It is only too evident that prejudice has dominated this assembly. One can say that the Vatican Council has been nothing but an acclamation under the guise of deliberation." So he tries to avoid the question of the ecumenicity of the council and concentrates on other reasons for its formal authority: "What has been the motive? What have been the meaning and the extent of the minority's submission? It can be stated that the greater number simply wished to make an act of obedience to the Sovereign Pontiff, without pronouncing on the ecumenicity of the 4th session." Mathieu writes to Friedrich von Schwarzenberg that the French minority will not challenge the validity of the council's decision lest scandal be aroused: "The French bishops of the minority will not go so far as to protest subsequently to either the Pope or the Council regarding the decisions of July 18. They accept without reserve what has been done and would not wish to begin, concerning the ecumenicity of the Council, any discussion which might bring about greater difficulties or more tragic scandals." Mathieu had earlier expressed his conviction that the minority would be bound by *Pastor aeternus* for the good of the order of the church: "I see no difficulty regarding submission among the bishops at our meeting. As for the manifestation of our feelings, it is impossible to do it either at the insistence of the newspapers or even because of the anxiety of some members of the clergy. To yield in this way would be to aggravate by our action an evil which is already too great, the overthrow of order and the destruction of authority." He writes to Schwarzenberg in the fall of 1870, "I did not retract anything of what I did conscientiously, but . . . I submitted to a definition that was made with the limits and in the proper terms."[20]

Place also appeals to the formal authority of the decree and to the peace of the church:

---

ing the binding authority of councils after their decision is reached, Maret says, "One must submit to the Church or cease to be a member of it" (ibid., p. 339).

20. Henri Maret to Augustin David, 10 October 1870, quoted in Hasler, *Pius IX*, 2:478, n. 24; Henri Maret, Personal Notes, quoted in ibid., n. 26; ibid., 1:81, n. 46, 2:493, n. 9; Jacques Mathieu to Friedrich von Schwarzenberg, cardinal of Prague, 21 September 1870, quoted in Granderath, *Histoire du concile du Vatican*, 3, 2:246–47; Mathieu to Henri Icard, 26 July 1870, quoted in Gadille, *La pensée et l'action politiques des évêques français*, 1:112; Mathieu to Friedrich von Schwarzenberg, 14 September 1870, quoted in Hasler, *Pius IX*, 2:492, n. 4.

Since the two decrees which have been issued and which are vested with the confirmation of the Holy Father are known, the peace of the church and the duty imposed to preserve the sacred unity whose value must be still better appreciated today, in the midst of the struggles which stain with blood human society, this peace and this duty demand that these constitutions be received by all the children of the Church, with deference, respect and submission, and I am convinced that nobody will fail in this duty.[21]

In a discussion of conscience, Place explains that the dignity and freedom of a person's conscience are not diminished by legitimate subjection to superiors: "a child . . . to his father and mother, a subject to the laws of his country, a parishioner to his pastor, a Catholic to the infallible oracle of truth." He gives an indication of his own sense of such submission when he compares a believer's acceptance of pontifical teaching with a child's submission to his parents and when he revels in the consolation brought by following one's conscience.[22]

Ramadié would rather die, he writes, than separate himself "from the unshakable rock on which rests the holy Church, the faith of Peter. . . . The Apostolic See separated from which salvation is impossible."[23] To his diocese, he writes, "Your submission like our own to the decrees of the Holy See is without reservation; we all proclaim aloud with St. Ambrose that *where Peter is, there is the Church.*" He notes that all of the bishops submitted to the teachings of the council as soon as they were confirmed by the high authority of the pope: "Thanks be to God for having given to the world, once again, the admirable sight of the always victorious unity of the Christian faith." Because of its principle of authority, the church is preserved from division. When a dogmatic definition is pronounced by the head of the church, all minds and wills submit lovingly, obeying Christ, because "to listen to the Church is to listen to God himself."[24]

21. Mansi 53:1036A–B.

22. "un enfant . . . à son père et à sa mère, un sujet aux tribunaux de son pays, un paroissien à son pasteur, un catholique à l'oracle infaillible de la vérité" (Charles Place, "Sur la conscience," *La semaine liturgique de Marseille* 17 [Supplément to 3 March 1878]:402). A biographer also writes in admiration of Darboy that he submitted like a child to the church's judgment (Guillermin, *Vie de Darboy*, p. xi).

23. Mansi 53:1033D.

24. "Votre soumission comme la nôtre aux décrets du Saint Siège est sans réserve; tous nous reconnaissons hautement avec Saint Ambroise que *là où est Pierre, là est l'Eglise*" (Etienne Ramadié, Letter to diocese publishing decrees of First Vatican

Meignan emphasizes the formal authority of the council in which, despite the long discussion, the Holy Spirit had spoken. He urges members of his diocese to prepare their hearts and minds to accept the teaching of the church with faith and submission and to understand the decrees better. "The Council has spoken; all must submit to its decisions in word, in mind and in heart."[25] Meignan accepts the formal authority of the council when he submits to its "already accomplished acts" and "all its future decisions." Thomas notes the difference of obligation for bishops before and after a council: "Free to proclaim and to defend their opinion even against the most respected majority, throughout all the debates, the bishops are obliged when the decree is accepted and is sanctioned by the pope to submit to it with as much docility as the humblest of the faithful."[26] Dupanloup and all other minority bishops submitted in this fashion, Thomas explains in a defense of the bishop of Orléans.

A good number of the French minority bishops explained their response to the formal authority of *Pastor aeternus* with the term *obedience*. David provides an example in his acceptance of the decree: "Never, not even for the briefest moment, did I conceive of being able to oppose a conciliar decree, from the instant of its confirmation by the Holy See and proclaimed in the traditional manner. . . . The first word that my priests heard from my lips on my return from the Vatican Council was this: As I am, in my diocese, the first in rank, so I wish also to be the first in obedience." The church never makes a doctrine the object of *de fide* definition, David explains, without first examining it fully. Each bishop, as witness and judge of the faith, freely speaks all that he finds in his conscience. From this rigorous examination results "a certainty superior to all human certainties."[27] But even then, the divine element has not yet intervened: "After all

Council, 6 February 1874, *Semaine religieuse du diocèse de Perpignan* 6 [1874]:75). "Que Dieu soit mille fois béni d'avoir donné au monde, une fois de plus, l'admirable spectacle de l'unité toujours victorieuse de la foi chrétienne" (ibid.). "écouter l'Eglise, c'est écouter Dieu lui-même" (ibid., p. 76).

25. "Le Concile a parlé; tous doivent se soumettre à ses décisions, de bouche, d'esprit et de coeur" (Guillaume Meignan, Speech at return from council, quoted in *La semaine champenoise* 5 [30 July 1870]:217).

26. Guillaume Meignan to Pius IX, 11 October 1870, quoted in Boissonnot, *Le Cardinal Meignan*, p. 307; Léon Thomas to François Lagrange, 15 April 1884, in Lagrange, *Vie de Dupanloup*, p. v.

27. Augustin David to Pius IX, 25 October 1870, quoted in Palanque, *Catholiques*

the reasons have been heard, all the testimonies recorded, after the council has deliberated with maturity and liberty, then the Church, through the mouth of its leader, pronounces and defines. At that moment every other voice must be silent; the Holy Spirit is present, according to the promise of Jesus Christ; the Church teaches: the world bows and believes: God has spoken."[28]

Some other French minority bishops evaluated the formal authority of the council so highly that they too thought in terms of obedience to its decisions. Bravard debates the issue no more but accepts the decree with docility: "Today, now that everything is over and judgment pronounced, I am silent, and, in the peaceful contemplation of my Catholic faith, I adhere with docility to the decisions made by the Council, asking God to use them for his glory and for the good of religion."[29] Darboy tells an acquaintance: "We know that the voice of the Church is the voice of God, that its decrees, dictated by the divine Spirit, are infallible, and, as obedient sons, as soon as it has spoken, all we have to do is to obey it and to carry out its teachings with all our strength in our words and in our actions."[30] Rivet recommends that his priests be obedient to God and the church, and he wishes to set a personal example of docility for them in his acceptance of the decisions of the council:

To obey in all things the sovereign law of God and the no less obligatory laws of the holy Church; to cling in mind and heart to the teachings of this authority which cannot err since our Lord Jesus Christ himself has promised

---

libéraux et gallicans en France, p. 178; "une certitude supérieure à toutes les certitudes humaines" (David, Circular Letter to Diocese, 26 May 1870, p. 342).

28. "Après que toutes les raisons ont été entendues, tous les témoignages recueillis, après que le Concile a délibéré en toute maturité et liberté, alors l'Eglise, par l'organe de son Chef, prononce et définit. En ce moment, toute autre voix que la sienne doit se taire: l'Esprit-Saint est présent, selon la promesse de Jésus-Christ; l'Eglise enseigne; le monde s'incline et croit: Dieu a parlé" (David, Circular Letter to Diocese, 26 May 1870, p. 342).

29. "Aujourd'hui que tout est terminé, que le jugement est prononcé, je me tais, et, dans le recueillement de ma foi catholique, j'adhère avec docilité aux décisions conciliairement prises, demandant à Dieu qu'il en retire sa gloire et le bien de la religion" (Jean Bravard, Circular Letter to Diocesan Clergy, 23 August 1870, quoted in *Revue catholique [Semaine religieuse] du diocèse de Coutances et Avranches* 3 [28 July 1870]:709; also in Mansi 53:1028D).

30. Georges Darboy in conversation with Kathleen O'Meara after the council; the quotation was written down from memory the day after their meeting, so it is a paraphrase only, though the writer believes that she has captured the sense and spirit of

to be with it until the end of time; although we are a judge and a legislator in this holy Church, it is a sacred and at the same time a very sweet duty to give you an example of the most absolute filial docility especially with regard to the decisions of the Council.

A sincere Catholic never contests "a solemn decision of the church assembled in an ecumenical council." The authority of these high assemblies has never been put in doubt, as the history of the church attests. In this case, Rivet continues, the formal authority of *Pastor aeternus* is clear: "Now, our very dear brothers, on this much disputed question on the infallibility of the Roman pontiff in the exercise of his supreme magisterium, the Church, gathered in the Vatican ecumenical Council, has made a pronouncement in such a way that doubt is no longer possible in this matter and that the minds most opposed to it have only to bow their heads and to submit."[31]

Years later, Foulon would say that love produces obedience, and obedience proves love. "Let us love the Church, let us love the Pope! It is no longer possible to make a distinction between these two loves." More than ever, he writes, faith requires total commitment. It is no longer possible to pick and choose among the pope's decisions, to maintain a prudent silence when in disagreement through individual free thought, to reject certain prerogatives of the pope which are out of season. "No, no, this faith without obedience and this respect without humility could never enter the mind of a true Christian," he exclaims, and continues:

Christians, our very dear brothers, be more and more persuaded, then, that the Church must be listened to in all things, for who does not listen to the Church does not obey God; know that truth is one and indivisible and that one must not attempt impossible compromises by allowing oneself to be dominated by private opinions; be certain that one must remain attached by all the strength of one's mind, by all the love of one's heart to the sacred Apostolic See and to the infallible authority of the universal doctor, the common father of both pastors and faithful; there alone is salvation.[32]

the archbishop (Kathleen O'Meara [Grace Ramsay], *Monseigneur Darboy: Souvenirs personnels*, trans. [Paris: Amyot, 1872], pp. 30–31).

31. François Rivet, "Lettre circulaire au clergé (22 August 1870)," quoted in Chevallier, *Rivet*, pp. 189–90.

32. Joseph Foulon, "Lettre pastorale prescrivant des prières à l'occasion de la mort de notre saint père le Pape Pie IX et pour l'élection de son successeur," in *Oeuvres pastorales*, 2:195; Joseph Foulon, "Instruction pastorale sur l'opposition à l'Eglise," in *Oeuvres pastorales*, pp. 96–97.

This emphasis on undivided obedience to the church—once it has reached a decision—seems to have been shared by many of Foulon's fellow bishops in the minority.

A few bishops distinguished between their obligation as judges during a council and their obligation as believers after its close. Callot, for example, writes, "The often painful duty of discussing and of judging has given place to the easier and the sweeter duty of accepting and submitting." After the decision of 18 July 1870, writes Ramadié, "from the day of this session, the Christian in me has taken the place of judge; the judge could be mistaken, the Christian is sure of being in the truth by being obedient." After the publication of the pontifical bulls, Hugonin writes, the pope no longer asks for "a personal judgment but an act of obedience." He continues, "We could not refuse it without repudiating the legitimate authority with which it is invested; submission is therefore obligatory. This second act is much easier than the first; it removes all responsibility.[33]

Ginoulhiac also distinguishes between his two roles. He first reminds the pope that his own actions at the council were not intended to oppose the interests of the Vatican, although many received the false impression that they were. They fail to realize that council members assume, as it were, two roles, "one, of judges; the other, of simple faithful." And thus, he continues, "If, as judges, they have to grant or deny approval according to the dictates of their own conscience, when some decree of the council is approved by the supreme pontiff, as faithful they are duty-bound to embrace it entirely and defend it."[34]

But in a conversation shortly before the council ended, Ginoulhiac uses the distinction in another way. When asked what the minority would do if they failed to achieve their desired revision, Ginoulhiac replies:

We are judges of the faith and Christians. If we cannot subscribe to the definition as judges, we will submit as Christians when the Holy Father has approved the constitution. But naturally those who will be forced to say *non placet* at the public session will lack vigor in defending, as Christians, a definition whose terms they could not approve as judges. His Eminence has

33. Mansi 53:1045C, 1033D; Flavien Hugonin, "Lettre de Monseigneur à MM. les curés (16 November 1870)," p. 760; also in Mansi 53:1038D.

34. Mansi 53:952C.

most opportunely brought to mind, as applicable to these circumstances, the teaching of Pius VI declaring that one must carefully assure that any decree on the faith will be accepted before promulgating it.[35]

Did French minority bishops have inner hesitations about the ecumenicity of the First Vatican Council which they did not express? The following comments about Place in a letter soon after the council's end suggest that he, at least, had more questions than he expressed:

Until now he does not admit that the Vatican meeting is a council nor that the dogma is a dogma, but he does not wish, either, to say the contrary because, he says, the value of unity is so great that it demands many sacrifices; he thinks that the future alone will reveal God's judgments; if, a hundred years from now, when all the passions have died down, the Church recognizes the Vatican Council and teaches the dogma, it is because both are matters of faith; if, on the contrary, the opposite happens, it will be God who will take upon himself to make known the truth.[36]

But most of the French minority bishops seem to have accepted the council's ecumenicity, believing that the council represented at least the teaching of the pope and the great majority of bishops. Some may have harbored doubts that the council had been a truly ecumenical council; they may have concluded simply that the teaching had enough authority to merit an act of obedience from them.

35. "Nous sommes Juges de la foi et chrétiens. Si nous ne pouvons pas souscrire à la définition comme juges, nous nous soumettrons comme Chrétiens, lorsque le S. Père aura approuvé la Constitution. Mais que naturellement ceux que l'on aura forcés à dire *non placet* à la session publique manqueront de vigueur pour défendre, comme chrétiens, une définition dont ils n'auront pas pu approuver les termes, en leur qualité de Juges. Son Grandeur a rappelé fort à propos, comme applicable à la circonstance, l'enseignement de Pie VI déclarant qu'avant de porter un décret sur la foi, il faut s'assurer soigneusement s'il sera reçu" (quoted in Colet, "Copie des procès-verbaux rédigés par Mgr Colet des séances tenues par les évêques de la minorité," fol. 70).

36. Madame Marie de Forbin d'Oppède to Lady Charlotte Blennerhassett, 26 December 1870, quoted in Hasler, *Pius IX*, 2:473, n. 31. These correspondents give me the chance to note the role women played in the discussions surrounding the council. Several women, most of them wives of diplomats or interested laymen, played hostess to evening *salon* gatherings for the bishops and others attached to the council, which were the occasion for discussion about the issues of the council. One biographer writes: "The lobbies of the House of Commons are not half, not a tenth part, so favourable for the work of persuasion and of canvassing as were the crowded *salons* presided over, not merely by the fair partizans on either side, but by neutral ladies. Votes changed sides with an ease and rapidity which at home would be the envy of

The most unusual example of the acceptance of *Pastor aeternus* for its formal authority is provided by the testament of de Las Cases. He does not know, he writes, whether a funeral oration will be pronounced at his death; but if one is to be preached, he does not want his conciliar position to be misrepresented. In fact, he claims, he really did oppose the schema during the council, and his opposition was not based simply on its inopportuneness but on the conviction that it was mistaken. This view was corrected, however, as soon as the vote was taken:

> Raised as I had been in anti-infallibilist doctrines, during the Council I imposed, not without sorrow, silence on my heart which suffered at not being in agreement on this point with his Holiness Pius IX, to let my conscience speak: it imposed on me the rigorous duty of defending what I then believed to be the truth. As long as the Council had not spoken I remained firm in my conviction; on the morrow of the definition God gave me the grace to be able to say in all truth, in the depth and the calm of my faith: "Today, I believe in infallibility as much as I disbelieved in it yesterday."

De Las Cases hopes that no one will say of him that he was "opposed only to the *opportuneness*," as seems to be said of many of his fellows in the minority. Without doubt, he continues, this view of the minority position, which the minority themselves would never have accepted, is being put forth in good faith by those who wish to serve the cause of infallibility. But de Las Cases objects to this interpretation of his fellows, and for two reasons: first, it is not true; and second, it fails to present the grandeur of the act of faith which the minority made in response to the formal authority of *Pastor aeternus:*

---

our whips and wire-pullers" (Edmund Purcell, *Life of Cardinal Manning, Archbishop of Westminster*, 2 vols. [London: Macmillan, 1896], 2:430, quoted in French by Palanque, *Catholiques libéraux et gallicans en France*, p. 161). Mourret mentions the influence which some of the more forceful women exerted on the opinions of the bishops (*Le concile du Vatican*, pp. 91–94). In addition, several of these women were involved before and after the council in extensive correspondence about conciliar issues, both with each other (see, for example, Roger Aubert and Jean-Rémy Palanque, "Lettres de Lady Blennerhassett à la Marquise de Forbin d'Oppède au lendemain du concile du Vatican," *Revue d'histoire ecclésiastique* 58 [1963]:82–135) and with bishops and other men interested in the council (see, for example, Jean-Rémy Palanque, "Le cercle de Madame de Forbin et le premier concile du Vatican [Documents inédits]," *Revue d'histoire de l'église de France* 48 [1962]:54–79). Some of the bishops did not believe that women had much to contribute to theology; Darboy called them derisively "petticoat theologians [les théologiennes en jupon]" (O'Meara, *Monseigneur Darboy*, p. 31). But I, of course, cannot agree with such an evaluation.

In my opinion, one was in danger of not being absolutely historically exact, since those who have died, whose conduct is being explained, were no longer there to give their own explanations; and one was adding nothing to that incomparable triumph of the Catholic faith after the Vatican Council, which the minority bishops left, without exception, docilely submissive to the definition, after having loyally, courageously, respectfully opposed it as long as it had not become an article of faith, as long as their conscience urged them on to the duty of defending what they believed to be the true doctrine of the Church.

De Las Cases hopes to combine his desire for accuracy with a new profession of faith in favor of infallibility.[37]

The understanding of the formal authority of *Pastor aeternus* which de Las Cases expresses here can serve as a summary of the views held by most of the French minority bishops on the decree's formal authority. They generally believed that the council had spoken infallibly and that their obligation after its close was simply to accept its decisions. This acceptance was envisioned as obedience by some and seems often to have been described as a sacrifice of personal conviction to the judgment of the church as a whole.

Conclusion

Both before and after its sessions, the French minority bishops attributed formal authority to the First Vatican Council. Because of this authority, they argued for the acceptance of *Pastor aeternus*. Whether authoritative because proclaimed by the pope, written by a council, or simply the evident expression of the faith of the great body of the church as represented by most of the bishops and the pope, *Pastor aeternus* was accepted because of its formal authority.

This case for the formal authority of *Pastor aeternus* seems surprisingly simple after the complex and nuanced arguments put forth against the schema during the council sessions. The French minority seem to have forgotten or abandoned some of their best arguments. Although they earlier raised some good questions about the validity of the council's procedures, now they proceed to abandon those questions. Whereas they often noted the necessity of clarity in formulation, now they accept the decree with all of its ambiguities. Where earlier they defended the freedom to hold a variety of opin-

37. Mansi 53:1042C–1043A.

ions on the relationship between pope and bishops, now they believe that freedom to be ended.

Strangest of all is the way that the French minority bishops discount the significance of their own opposition. When they leave the council before voting on 18 July, the minority explain that they do not want to break the unanimity of the vote. Though this action can be understood in part as the desire to avoid scandalizing the faithful, it also seems that the minority failed to take seriously enough their own substantial numbers (when combined with the minority bishops from other countries). Clear on the principle that infallible teaching must express the faith of the entire church, they failed, as it were, to count themselves among the church whose faith the council was called to express. This failure is well symbolized by the distinction that a few drew between obligation during and after a council: judgment, even for a bishop, ended immediately after the council's vote, and then only submission was left.

The use of the word *obedience* to express this obligation of submission after a council further underlines the simplicity of the French minority's thought on the formal authority of the decree. Their descriptions of obedience paint a picture that includes the sacrifice of personal conviction, the end of doubts and discussion, the kind of sudden transformation described by de Las Cases which allowed him to say, the day after the definition, "Today I believe in infallibility as much as I disbelieved in it yesterday."[38] Congar defines reception as that process by which one group truly makes its own as a rule the thought or decision of another, and he notes, "There is, in reception, something very different from what the Scholastics mean by obedience. . . . It implies a particular contribution of consent—perhaps even of judgment."[39] It seems that in their case for the formal authority of *Pastor aeternus,* the French minority bishops substituted a simple idea of obedience for full reception.[40]

38. Ibid., col. 1042D.
39. Yves Congar, "La 'réception' comme réalité ecclésiologique," *Revue des sciences philosophiques et théologiques* 56 (1972):370.
40. The actual understanding of obedience held by many of the French minority might also be criticized for what Waldemar Molinski says is a common fault in Catholic discussions of obedience, its representation "one-sidedly as the abandonment of self-will" (*Sacramentum Mundi,* s.v. "Obedience," by Waldemar Molinski). In addition, the French minority often seem to have opposed obedience to conscience, which is also inaccurate.

And why were they led to such a simple set of arguments, after all of their earlier sophistication? For the very same reason that had led them to oppose the schema in the first place, the French minority bishops now accepted *Pastor aeternus:* they believed that infallibility has an ecclesial character. They felt bound by the church and by a conciliar decision or a papal teaching that expressed the faith of the church. They had battled the schema because it seemed to lack a recognition of this conviction. And now, caught in their own trap, they felt they could do nothing else than accept the logic of their own earlier arguments.

8

On Material Authority

An Acceptable Interpretation of
Pastor aeternus *Is Possible*

———◆•▶———

"The minority has triumphed in its defeat," writes Maret after the council.[1] The theologian from the Sorbonne could make this claim because he had come to believe that the minority, after all, had succeeded in preventing the proclamation of an ultramontanist decree. Gradually, with careful explanations, other minority bishops came to agree that the content of *Pastor aeternus* could be interpreted in a way acceptable to their understanding. Such interpretations allowed them to argue for the material authority of the decree.

In the last chapter, we saw that a systematic framework stood behind the thought of the French minority bishops in their arguments for acceptance of *Pastor aeternus,* expressed by responses to the following questions: (1) Does the formal authority of *Pastor aeternus* require its reception? (2) Does the material authority of *Pastor aeternus* require its reception? In this chapter we will examine the affirmative answers of some French minority bishops to the second question.

Their affirmative answers were guarded. Rather than finding *Pastor aeternus* compelling, they found it acceptable when interpreted in certain ways. The French minority bishops struggled to find such interpretations, and for the most part their struggle was given impetus by their a priori assumption of the decree's formal authority. Since

1. Henri Maret, in personal notes written to himself, cited by Bazin, *Vie de Maret,* 3:218.

Pastor aeternus is binding on our faith, they reasoned, its content must be capable of yielding acceptable interpretations. They agreed with Meignan that infallible decisions demand not only external obedience but also obedience of the mind, "in order that this faith may not be blind, irrational," and so they developed interpretations that would allow them to make a reasonable assent to *Pastor aeternus*.[2]

The French Minority in Defense of Themselves

Before examining the interpretations which French minority bishops gave to *Pastor aeternus*, we must listen to their defense of their own opposition to the schema. Despite the criticisms of others, the French minority remained convinced that their opposition had been made in good faith.

Having reread his memoirs of the council and the minutes of the French minority meetings, Colet says that he has drawn "a kind of satisfaction," since they recalled for him many forgotten details, and "my conscience confirms me in the truth of what I have written." Reading over the minutes, "after so many events which justified the apprehensions of several of us, I had to admire more, perhaps, than I had in the course of the debates, the moderation, loyalty, good faith and above all the respect from which our meeting never deviated."[3] It was "uneasiness of conscience" that prevented him from attending the session for the final vote on 18 July.[4]

Unless he has proof, warns Hugonin, no one should harbor doubts that the bishops failed or betrayed their consciences. The bishops at the council were obligated to give their personal judgment on the proposed decrees "according to their sincere conviction." Bravard does not discuss his actions at the council, except to assure his diocese that all was done for love of the church and the pope. His acts and words, he says, "have been governed solely by my

2. Mansi 53:1032D.
3. "une sorte de satisfaction"; "ma conscience me confirme la vérité de mon récit"; "après tant d'événements qui ont justifié les appréhensions de plusieurs d'entre nous, m'a fait admirer plus que je ne l'avais fait peut être dans le cours des débats, la modération, la loyauté, la bonne foi et surtout le respect dont notre réunion ne s'est jamais départie" Charles Colet to Joseph Foulon, 12 December 1871, 4AI,2,1°, Archives de l'Archevêché de Paris).
4. Mansi 53:1018B.

conscience, whose deep and enlightened convictions may not be censured by anyone on earth, any more than anyone has the right to question the integrity of the judge of one of our supreme courts, even if his opinion is contrary to that of several others." Darboy also emphasizes the purity of the minority's intentions: "Nobody was more convinced of it than the Council fathers who had not the same point of view at all." He denies that "any personal concern" influenced his thought or acts at the council. In his last testament, Place writes, "I wish to die as I have lived, a devoted and submissive child of the holy, Catholic, apostolic and Roman Church. . . . I had no other desire than to serve it in all my activities at the Vatican Council."[5]

One senses the annoyance that many French minority bishops felt during and after the council when their good faith was questioned. Some ultramontanists even saw the course of the Franco-Prussian War or the deaths of minority members relatively soon after the council as divine punishment for their conciliar behavior.[6] Such an interpretation may have annoyed the minority less than did pressures from the Vatican, which commenced a policy of refusing routine dispensations and favors for a diocese in which a bishop had not yet declared his acceptance of conciliar decrees.[7] Colet writes darkly to Foulon on this bureaucratic centralization that interfered with episcopal rights: "If we had been able to make any preparations or to foresee how things would go, we would have been able to render great service to the Church by attacking Italianism instead of defending gallicanism.[8]

The atmosphere of criticism in which the minority found themselves after the council seems to have lasted many years. In 1884, six years after the death of Dupanloup, his fellow minority bishops still

5. Flavien Hugonin, "Lettre de Monseigneur à MM. les curés (16 November 1870)," p. 760, also in Mansi 53:1038C; Bravard, Circular Letter to Diocesan Clergy, 23 August 1870, p. 709, also in Mansi 53:1028C; Georges Darboy, Address to Clergy (25 July 1870), quoted in Palanque, *Catholiques libéraux et gallicans en France*, p. 182; Georges Darboy to Abbé Surat, archdeacon of Paris, 20 April 1870, *Collectio Lacensis* 7:1407B; Place, *Pieux souvenir*, pp. xxxii–xxxiii.

6. Palanque, *Catholiques libéraux et gallicans en France*, p. 177, n. 3; see also Bazin, *Vie de Maret*, 3:224, 183, n. 34.

7. Aubert, *Pie IX*, p. 363; note the postconciliar treatment of Maret by the Vatican, below.

8. "Si nous avions pu nous préparer, ou prévoir la manière dont les choses marcheraient, nous aurions pu rendre un grand service à l'Eglise en attaquant l'Italianisme au

find it necessary to defend the memory of his position at the council. People criticize Dupanloup for having expressed his opinion before the council, writes Thomas, but they ignore the provocation he received from the press and the publication of quite different views by other bishops. Dupanloup expressed his opinion that the doctrine was inopportune, not untrue, and at the council he sacrificed his popularity for his duty by expressing the same opinion. Thomas wonders what can be wrong with such behavior: "To blame him because of it would be to claim that the bishops convened to a council to discuss the affairs of the Church haven't the right to state clearly their opinion and that their sole duty is to vote the adoption of the decrees proposed to them. But all Catholic tradition and reason itself protest against such an assertion. Indeed, if this were so, what good would it be to have councils?" And Ramadié writes fiercely of "the deep and profound piety that inspired" all of Dupanloup's works, which were written for the public good.[9] But even these words of praise brought Ramadié much criticism.

In these ways, the French minority bishops continued to defend their conciliar behavior, explaining that their position had been taken out of love for the church.

Postconciliar Silence

One of the simplest ways by which the French minority dealt with *Pastor aeternus* after the council was silence. After their adhesions,

---

lieu de défendre le Gallicanisme" (Colet to Foulon, 12 December 1871, 4AI,2,1°, Archives de l'Archevêché de Paris). He continues: "Clerical Italianism means that Italy wishes to rule the Church, wishing that the sovereign pontiff and the cardinals named to the congregations be only Italians. It favors political Italianism which desires Rome as the capital of a universal republic. I have a fine thesis on this subject but I will likely never have the opportunity of developing it in a council [L'Italianisme clérial [*sic*] consiste en ce que l'Italie veut gouverner l'Eglise, ne voulant que le Souverain Pontife et les cardinaux proposés aux congrégations soient Italiens. Il favorise l'Italianisme politique qui veut Rome pour capitale d'une République universelle. J'ai une belle thèse là-dessus mais je n'aurai vraisemblablement jamais l'occasion de la développer en concile]" (ibid.). See also the comments of de Montclos on this letter of Colet, in *Lavigerie, le Saint-Siège et l'église*, p. 472.

9. Thomas to Lagrange, 15 April 1884, in Lagrange, *Vie de Dupanloup*, pp. iv–v; Etienne Ramadié, Article on Dupanloup in *Le correspondant*, 25 May 1879, quoted in Palanque, *Catholiques libéraux et gallicans en France*, p. 143; Etienne Ramadié, Circular Letter, October 1878, cited by Palanque, *Catholiques libéraux et gallicans en France*, p. 143.

they refrained from public comment, "calmly awaiting the carrying out of the designs of providence," as Maret's biographer explains.[10] Since the decree was given force within each diocese simply by its status as a conciliar decree promulgated by the pope, individual bishops were not obligated by canon law of the time to publish the decree within their dioceses. Although many ultramontanist journals nevertheless made publication of *Pastor aeternus* within each diocese a kind of orthodoxy test, many minority bishops waited a long time before they published the decree. Before he did so in 1872, Dupanloup inquired about how many other bishops had published *Pastor aeternus*.[11] Others, such as David and Bravard, never promulgated it locally at all. The successor of Bravard, Abel Germain, later promulgated the decree in an atmosphere of exaggerated personal devotion toward the pope, as though to make reparation for the dead bishop's lapse.[12]

Many bishops blamed their silence or delay in publication on the war or the demands of pastoral responsibilities; Darboy writes, "It is hardly a question of the Council any longer at this particular time; France is in the grip of problems which relegate to a second place sacristans and their Byzantine discussions." But Foulon promulgates the council's decrees, despite the troubled times, because "truth depends neither on peace nor war."[13]

The silence of the minority on the First Vatican Council is only too evident when one seeks major interpretations, speeches, or pastoral letters on the subject. Although some were written, and I will examine them in the next sections, the absence of a large quantity of commentary on the subject begins to make its own kind of silent point. We can get some indication of the minority's silence from the complaints of their enemies. One journalist complains long after the council's close that Dupanloup never publicly explicated the decree so as to retract the views expressed in his preconciliar brochures,

10. Bazin, *Vie de Maret*, 3:224.

11. Gadille, *La pensée et l'action politiques des évêques français*, 1:110–12. See ibid., p. 114, for a chronological chart of the publication of *Pastor aeternus* within the dioceses of minority bishops.

12. Abel Germain, *Proclamation solennelle des décrets du concile oecuménique du Vatican* (Coutances: E. Salettes Fils, 1876); Gadille, *La pensée et l'action politiques des évêques français*, 1:111.

13. Georges Darboy to Louis Isoard, future bishop of Annecy, 1 September 1870, quoted in Aubert, *Pie IX*, p. 361; Foulon, "Instruction pastorale sur la providence de Dieu et son action dans les évènements actuels," p. 110.

which remain on sale even after the council.[14] Another complains, "But the accompaniment of a precise and clear teaching was always lacking regarding a doctrine which he had mixed up so much and so covered with shadows."[15] A third writer criticizes the dearth of preaching on *Pastor aeternus* in Dupanloup's diocese after the council: "Officially everything is in order. But there is always a kind of agreement among everyone not to talk about the Council. There is never a question of it either in the acts emanating from authority or in the instructions addressed to the faithful. Yet mention is made of it in the new program of lectures and studies. The few preachers who have struck this chord have not been complimented; naturally a deep reserve has been all that came of it."[16]

What is the meaning of this reception of silence that the French minority gave to *Pastor aeternus*? Perhaps the words of Ginoulhiac provide the most realistic answer: "If we cannot subscribe to the definition as judges, we will submit as Christians when the Holy Father has approved the constitution. But naturally those who will be forced to say *non placet* at the public session will lack vigor in defending, as Christians, a definition whose terms they could not approve as judges."[17]

Use of Papal Titles

Despite their relative silence on *Pastor aeternus* after its publication, the French minority bishops nevertheless made at least some

14. Fèvre, *Le centenaire*, pp. 105–6.

15. Maynard, *Dupanloup et Lagrange*, p. 286.

16. Pelletier, *Mgr Dupanloup*, pp. 102–3. A strange episode manifests further the atmosphere with which the minority had to deal after the council. A member of a religious community, Mère Sainte Agnès, had begun correspondence with Dupanloup about spiritual matters in 1865 with the approval of two spiritual directors. In 1870 she writes to him in Rome that Christ has spoken to her in a way that suggested a desire for the definition of papal infallibility at the council. Palanque surmises that Dupanloup found this to be the machinations of the nun's Jesuit and Capuchin directors. After the council, Mère Sainte Agnès writes to Dupanloup of receiving more words from Christ, who now is waiting upon Dupanloup for a solemn act of adhesion to the council. On 24 November 1870, Dupanloup answers her letters, commenting that he sees no sign of the Spirit of God in her reported experiences. He expresses surprise that her superiors allow her to write him such letters: "I ask God to dispel your illusions" (François Pon, *Une page de surnaturel au concile du Vatican: La Mère Sainte-Agnès et Mgr Dupanloup* [Paris: Victor Retaux, 1905]; see also Palanque, *Catholiques libéraux et gallicans en France*, p. 106, n. 4, p. 162, n. 129, p. 181).

17. "Si nous ne pouvons pas souscrire à la définition comme juges, nous nous

aeternus was sometimes referred to, if only in passing. Although many of the passages containing such titles or addresses are isolated references to the teaching of *Pastor aeternus,* some are found in longer passages of interpretation, which I will examine more closely in later sections. But all of these titles or phrases indicate the way in which papal infallibility was portrayed.

Comparing the pope to the church, Foulon writes that both, though troubled, remain invincible. The infallibility of the pope is like the pyramids, indestructible despite changes around them. Citing 2 Tim. 2:9, Colet says that no worldly power can fetter the "infallible word" of the "common father." Thomas refers to the Roman church with the traditional "Mother . . . who received, along with the blood of the holy apostles Peter and Paul, the fullness of doctrine." He continues, "I cling with all my strength to your Apostolic See, for whoever remains with you gathers [in the harvest] and whoever does not gather scatters."[18]

Guilbert notes that the church must teach revealed truth, making it more precise "by its infallible magisterium" when useful. Meignan refers to "pontifical infallibility," and Bravard to the pope's "infallible authority." Ginoulhiac and Ramadié also mention the infallible authority of the pope, and Foulon writes that the church speaks "by the infallible voice of the vicar of Jesus Christ." The church itself, he explains, is "the infallible mouthpiece of truth," and the pope is its infallible oracle.[19]

Guilbert submits the edition of his book written after the council reference to it. The titles or brief descriptive phrases they use in addressing or referring to the pope reveal that the teaching of *Pastor*

---

soumettrons comme chrétiens, lorsque le S. Père aura approuvé la Constitution. Mais que naturellement ceux que l'on aura forcés à dire *non placet* à la session publique, manqueront de vigeur pour défendre, comme chrétiens, une définition dont ils n'auront pas pu approuver les termes, en leur qualité de Juges" (quoted in Colet, "Copie des procès-verbaux rédigés par Mgr Colet des séances tenues par les évêques de la minorité," fol. 70).

18. Joseph Foulon, "Lettre pastorale sur le péril des fausses doctrines et sur les remèdes qu'il convient de leur opposer," in *Oeuvres pastorales,* 1:291; Foulon, "Instruction pastorale sur la providence de Dieu et son action dans les événements actuels," p. 109; "infaillible parole . . . Père commun" (Charles Colet, "A l'occasion de son entrée dans son diocèse," *La semaine religieuse de la ville et du diocèse de Tours* 9 (30 January 1875):680, 684; Thomas quoted by Tapie, *Oraison funèbre de Thomas,* p. 16.

19. Guilbert, *La crise religieuse et la pacification,* p. 17; Guillaume Meignan, "Mém-

to "the infallible guardian of truth," and Hugonin writes at the start of his postconciliar book: "We will take every care to avoid anything that could upset susceptibilities which we respect; for we are docile children of the Church; we believe what it believes, we condemn what it condemns, and we submit all our writings to the judgment of its infallible head." The pope is "the incorruptible guardian" of the church, says Hugonin. He acts as the infallible doctor of truth and the prince of peace, says Thomas. For Meignan he is the "infallible interpreter"; for Guilbert he gives an "infallible word." Maret writes in his 1884 book, "But having no other rule of faith than the divine, infallible authority of the Church, of her supreme head, we submit this book entirely to the judgment of the pastor of pastors, of the bishop of bishops, of the vicar of our Lord Jesus Christ."[20]

Place uses the term *infallible* several times to refer to the pope or his work. Pius IX, he claims, confirmed his brothers "with an infallible authority"; he was "the infallible oracle of the truth." Truth comes from the "infallible lips of the common father of the faithful" or it is in the heart of ordained ministers of the church.[21] Place calls Rome the "center from which truth sends its light through the world," the fertile and unalterable source of the river of doctrine. In Rome is Peter, living in the person of his successor, who holds the

oire sur l'état présent de l'église et sur les préoccupations des esprits en France," quoted in Boissonnot, *Le Cardinal Meignan*, p. 345; "autorité infaillible" (Jean Bravard, Pastoral Letter for Lent on Love of the Church, *Revue catholique (Semaine religieuse) du diocèse de Coutances et Avranches* 7 [12 February 1874]:327); Jacques Ginoulhiac, Pastoral Letter for the Twenty-Fifth Anniversary of Pius IX, quoted in Cotton, *Oraison funèbre de Ginoulhiac*, p. 44; Etienne Ramadié, Pastoral Letter for Lent 1871, *Semaine religieuse du diocèse de Perpignan* 3 (25 February 1871):136; Foulon, "Instruction pastorale sur la providence de Dieu et son action dans les événements actuels," pp. 81, 107; Joseph Foulon, "Instruction pastorale sur l'oraison dominicale," in *Oeuvres pastorales*, 1:366.

20. Aimé Guilbert to Pius IX, 1875, in *La divine synthèse, ou l'exposé au double point*, 2d ed., 1:i–ii; Flavien Hugonin, *Philosophie du droit social* (Paris: E. Plon, Nourrit et Cie, 1885), p. viii; "le gardien incorruptible" (Flavien Hugonin, Pastoral Letter on *Etsi multa luctuosa*, *Semaine religieuse du diocèse de Bayeux et Lisieux* 10 [8 March 1874]:159; Thomas, *Deuxième congrès des catholiques de Normandie*, p. 7; Guillaume Meignan to Leo XIII, 24 June 1885, quoted by Boissonnot, *Le Cardinal Meignan*, p. 357; Mansi 53:1047B; Henri Maret, *La vérité catholique et la paix religieuse* (Paris: Dentu, 1884), quoted in Bazin, *Vie de Maret*, 3:462.

21. "l'oracle infaillible de la vérité" (Place, "Sur la conscience," p. 402; "lèvres infaillibles du Père commun des fidèles" (Charles Place, "Sur la nécessité et les moyens d'étudier la vie chrétienne," *La semaine liturgique de Marseille* 13 [Lent 1874]:208).

keys to heaven and earth, "in whose hands the torch of the faith will never go out or grow dim." Ramadié compares Pius IX to Christ, "stripped of his seamless robe and of his royal vesture." Never has a man spoken like the pope; he rules by love, says Ramadié. The papacy will never be silenced or overcome.[22]

The use of these titles and phrases for the pope shows some reference to the teaching of *Pastor aeternus* by the French minority bishops after the council. Some found it easy, perhaps, simply to insert such expressions into their pastoral letters and sermons without further elaboration of their meaning. Such an approach would have allowed this group to show their formal acceptance of *Pastor aeternus* without involving themselves in lengthy explanations or defenses of a decision they had opposed.

But some did offer arguments for the material authority of the decree—the arguments which follow.

Hindsight

One reason the French minority bishops offered for the acceptance of *Pastor aeternus* grew out of the wisdom of hindsight. Some found that their preconciliar fears about the bad consequences of a definition of papal infallibility were not realized.

In France, *Pastor aeternus* caused almost no immediate defections from the Roman Catholic Church among the laity, even those who were educated.[23] Such defections had been one of the frequently expressed fears of those bishops who argued that the schema was untimely. Despite his fears that a definition would cause schism, Foulon writes in 1878, the church in fact remains very united. Meignan's biographer writes that the proclamation of infallibility did not

22. Charles Place, "Il faut aimer Rome et le pape" (1880), in *Pieux souvenir*, pp. 199, 204; "dépouillé de sa robe sans couture et des vêtements de sa royauté" (Étienne Ramadié, Letter Publishing Decrees of the First Vatican Council, *Semaine religieuse du diocèse de Perpignan* 6 [1874]:76–77).

23. Although *Pastor aeternus* caused few immediate defections, I cannot assert the same about its long-range effects. It is arguable that part of the present crisis in French Catholicism stems from the passage of *Pastor aeternus*, if only because of its untimeliness, as argued by many of the French minority. See Palanque, *Catholiques libéraux et gallicans en France*, pp. 183–89, for a discussion of the few notable clerical or lay defections from the church in France that were the direct result of *Pastor aeternus*. In its absence of defections, France contrasted strikingly with Germany, where the Old Catholic schism affected a large number of believers.

produce the bad results Meignan had feared. After the pope's temporal power was removed, Meignan realized "how providential had
been the work of the Council in concentrating the spiritual authority
in the hands of the pope." Meignan himself writes of the profound
effect produced by Darboy's death at the hands of the Commune and
by the other difficulties the French church had been forced to endure:

Do you imagine, Sir, that, in the work of defending the Catholic Church
assaulted on all sides today by lodges and by governments, I am cutting myself off from the regular army, and above all from its leaders, my venerable
and beloved colleagues? . . . None of us are gallicans: there are no longer any
of them among us since Archbishop Darboy, that liberal-minded man, betrayed to the council by the minister who killed the Empire, dragged into
prison in the name of profaned liberty, fell under the bullets of the federate
troops.

Reminding his reader of the injustices the government inflicted on
the church, Meignan continues, "Gallicans! To cure them of their
weakness, the war that you are waging is a marvelous remedy for
them: it is you who have furnished the indestructible cement which
binds the clergy to the bishops, the bishops to each other and to the
pope."[24] And despite the minority's complaints that the schema contained unclear wording and would be easily misunderstood, Ramadié observes in promulgating the decrees that they are "full of light,"
so clear that they render "all commentary unnecessary."[25]

But not every minority bishop found all of his previous fears un-
warranted after the council. Guilbert cites "exaggerations which
either ignorance or bad faith would wish to impute to us in order to
throw odium or ridicule on this dogma," and he seems to have several "exaggerations" in mind.[26] Meignan also writes, in 1881, of the misunderstandings to which the papacy has been subject: "One of the
greatest of the present evils consists, finally, in the false idea that lay
people have of the *Syllabus* and of pontifical infallibility through a

24. Foulon, "Lettre pastorale prescrivant des prières à l'occasion de la mort de
notre saint père le Pape Pie IX et pour l'élection de son successeur," 2:189; Boissonnot,
Le Cardinal Meignan, p. 308; Guillaume Meignan to Francisque Sarcey, journalist,
spring 1880, quoted in ibid., pp. 361–62, n. 1.

25. "pleins de lumière . . . tout commentaire inutile" (Etienne Ramadié, Letter
Publishing Decrees of the First Vatican Council, *Semaine religieuse du diocèse de Perpignan* 6 [1874]:75).

26. Mansi 53:1047D.

lack of clear and precise explanations." Hugonin goes further, commenting darkly to a visitor that "the facts have clearly realized all the fears expressed by them (the members of the former minority) that, moreover, nothing was done, that the questions will be discussed again in another Council, on the death of the Pope."[27]

Thus, for some French minority bishops, the failure of their fears about a definition of papal infallibility to be realized in calamitous events provided some argument for reception of *Pastor aeternus*. Since the dreaded widespread schism or misunderstanding did not occur, reception of the decree seemed more acceptable to them. Other minority bishops, however, found some of their fears confirmed.

Papal Infallibility Located within the Context of Ecclesial Infallibility

Several French minority bishops argued for the material authority of *Pastor aeternus* by finding an interpretation of it which was acceptable to them. Rather than adopting the increasingly widespread ultramontanist interpretation, which would come to dominate the manuals,[28] these bishops adopted instead an understanding of *Pastor aeternus* that gave strict attention to the wording of the decree and located papal infallibility within the context of ecclesial infallibility.

The struggle of other minority groups and of moderate proponents of the schema also to interpret *Pastor aeternus* after the council aided the French minority bishops in their own quest for an acceptable interpretation. The pastoral letter from the German bishops' meeting at Fulda in the fall of 1870 reaffirmed the formal authority of the council.[29] And some minority fears were assuaged when the strict interpretation of Joseph Fessler, council secretary, was approved by Pius IX and thus considered an official interpretation.[30] The strict in-

27. Meignan, "Mémoire sur l'état présent de l'église et sur les préoccupations des esprits en France," p. 345; Fénessac on Hugonin to Pierre Chesnelong, senator, July 1875, quoted in Gadille, *La pensée et l'action politiques des évêques français*, p. 116.

28. *Sacramentum Mundi*, s.v. "Infallibility," by Heinrich Fries and Johann Finsterhölzl.

29. *Collectio Lacensis* 7:1733B–1735C.

30. Aubert, *Pie IX*, pp. 363–64; Joseph Fessler, *Die wahre und die falsche Unfehlbarkeit der Päpste: Zur Abwehr gegen Dr. Schulte*, 3d ed. (Vienna: Sartori, 1871).

terpretation by the Swiss bishops received similar approval.[31] The letter of Karl Hefele, a leader of the German minority and bishop of
Rottenburg, in which he accepted *Pastor aeternus* while giving it a
moderate interpretation, also encouraged the French minority in
their interpretive effort.[32] Colet asks Foulon if he knows about
Hefele's letter, praised by the nuncio of Munich and thus given a
certain authority. He finds it "the way to reassure the conscience of
several of the faithful."[33] The French minority were also instructed by
the eventual acceptance of the decree by Alphonse Gratry, the
French theologian who had publicly opposed the definition of papal
infallibility. Gratry finally became convinced that the decree had not,
after all, fulfilled his fears.[34] All of these interpretations emphasized a
careful reading of *Pastor aeternus* and rejected as exaggerations the
ultramontanist explanations. They gave support to the French
minority bishops' search for a way to interpret *Pastor aeternus*.

As we saw in the last section, though some French minority
bishops found the decree clear, several others believed that explanations were needed to correct misunderstanding of it. Meignan writes
that authorized publications on the meaning of *Pastor aeternus*
would help to correct "the false idea that lay people have of the *Syllabus* and of pontifical infallibility through a lack of clear and precise
explanations." This false idea grants to the pope a political and spiritual tyranny which he does not have. Such misunderstanding arises
frequently, according to Meignan, but it can be rectified by published explanations: "Some good books on this subject have already
been published by illustrious German bishops and they have already
done much to calm things down." Guilbert also refers to the dangers
of misunderstanding papal infallibility. A Catholic is obligated to
accept the conciliar definition, he writes, "while at the same time
avoiding exaggerations which ignorance and bad faith try to impute
to him in order to throw odium and ridicule on this dogma." And

31. An excerpt from the Swiss bishops' pastoral letter on *Pastor aeternus* was added
by a later editor to Fessler's book and is available in *The True and the False Infallibility
of the Popes: A Controversial Reply to Dr. Schulte*, trans. Ambrose St. John, 3d ed. (New
York: Catholic Publication Society, 1875), pp. 76–77.

32. Mansi 53:1058B–1059D.

33. "le moyen de rassurer la conscience en plusieurs fidèles" (Charles Colet to
Joseph Foulon, 11 November 1871, 4AI,2,1°, Archives de l'Archevêché de Paris).

34. Palanque, *Catholiques libéraux et gallicans en France*, pp. 186–87; see also the
similar view of Eugène Bernard, p. 185.

again he writes, "But let us beware of exaggerations."[35] Hugonin and
Colet both try to make clear that *Pastor aeternus* does not menace
civil government.[36]

Some French minority bishops emphasized that papal infallibility
operates only when the pope speaks as head of the church. Guilbert
sees infallibility as a kind of special divine assistance, given to the
church as a guarantee against error in the definition of doctrine. This
privilege was promised by Christ to the bishops united to their head,
Guilbert explains, and he continues: "It was also, in particular, to Peter and to his legitimate successors, that this assistance was promised,
when the savior prayed for him that his faith might not fail, and he
charged him to confirm his brothers; and again, when he gave into
his keeping the whole flock with the mission to feed the lambs and
the sheep." Guilbert cites the Swiss bishops' pastoral letter to show
that the decree limits in a very precise manner the field of the exercise
of the pope's infallibility. He points out that it is identical with that
of the teaching church:

He is infallible only and exclusively when, in his role as supreme teacher, he
makes, with regard to faith and morals, a decision which must be accepted
and considered obligatory by all the faithful. His infallibility is then that of
the teaching Church itself. His infallibility has no other scope and is essentially identical to that of the teaching Church; for the pope is never nor cannot ever be separated from the episcopate, no more than the head can be
separated from the members of a living body.

When the pope pronounces on a point of faith and morals, using, "as
head of the Church," his supreme doctrinal authority, "it is the infallible mouth of the Church which pronounces, it is the Church itself which proclaims the truth or condemns error."[37]

The infallibility of the pope is the same infallibility with which
Christ wanted his church provided when it defined matters of faith
or morals, writes Foulon in 1880[38] Meignan also emphasizes that *Pastor aeternus* does not give the pope the right to teach new doctrine,

35. Meignan, "Mémoire sur l'état présent de l'église et sur les préoccupations des
esprits en France," pp. 345, 347; Guilbert, *La divine synthèse, ou l'exposé au double point*,
2d ed., 2:273; Mansi 53:1047D.

36. Gadille, *La pensée et l'action politiques des évêques français*, 1:116.

37. Guilbert, *La divine synthèse, ou l'exposé au double point*, 2d ed., 2:272–74.

38. Foulon, "Instruction pastorale sur la providence de Dieu et son action dans les
événements actuels," p. 109.

something other than what the church has always believed. Papal infallibility "is not at all what the detractors of the Vatican Council
wished us to believe in their calumnious invectives," he explains.
"There are no new dogmas at all in the Church; there are only new
definitions." Furthermore, papal prerogatives are not personal to the
man but attached to the office. Neither is doctrinal infallibility im-
peccability, nor temporal in its subject matter. "The privilege of Peter . . . lies in the infallibility of the solemn decision, *ex cathedra*,
made by the judge in questions concerning faith and morals; it is restricted within the limits of revelation." The emphasis on conditions
of papal infallibility manifests Meignan's stress on the pope's ecclesial
role in teaching. While the pope is the court of final appeal in matters
of faith,[39] he speaks infallibly only "when he teaches *ex cathedra*, as
head of the Church, the living head." The pope does not create new
doctrines; rather "he will draw from the treasure of revealed matters
what is to be defined as of faith, he will show forth what is."[40]

The emphasis on the church as the context of papal infallibility is
also shown in an interesting way in a postconciliar interpretation of
Matt. 16:18 by Ramadié, who cites Cyprian's use of that text to show
that the church is founded on the bishops.[41] The ecclesial emphasis is
also evident in David, who explains that the pope is endowed with
"that infallibility with which the divine redeemer wished to arm his
Church in order to define what is doctrine in the matters of faith and
morals."[42] He notes that the pope defines *ex cathedra* when he speaks
"in his quality of pastor and of teacher," declaring a truth that belongs to the deposit of faith.[43] We can get some idea of Mathieu's
ecclesial emphasis from the views of a critic, who complains about
Mathieu's presentation of papal infallibility. Mathieu had emphasized that the decree emerged from the church's faith, whereas his
critic would have preferred more emphasis on the power of the pope

39. Mansi 53:1032C–D.

40. Meignan, Speech at return from council, p. 217.

41. Etienne Ramadié, "A l'occasion de sa visite pastorale pour l'année 1871,"
Semaine religieuse du diocèse de Perpignan 3 (30 April 1871):277–84. But Colet sees this
text as the basis for papal claims in *Sur l'église* (Tours: A. Mame, 1881), p. 4.

42. "cette infaillibilité dont le divin Rédempteur a voulu armer son Eglise pour
définir la doctrine de la foi et des moeurs" (Augustin David, "A l'occasion du XXVᵉ
anniversaire de Pie IX," *La semaine religieuse du diocèse de Saint-Brieuc et Tréguier* 4 [9
June 1871]:365).

43. David, *Oraison funèbre de Pie IX*, p. 18.

to define his own infallibility. Foulon sees in the definition of papal infallibility the principle for solving all heresies or religious difficulties.[44] His interpretation sees the purpose of papal infallibility as the service of truth in the church.

Dupanloup also places papal infallibility within a consideration of ecclesial infallibility in his guide for seminary training. The topic arises within a consideration of the question, "To explain the nature of the infallibility of the Church.—To tell how the divine assistance it implies differs from revelation and inspiration." The outlined answer begins by portraying revealed truths as the objective extension of the church's infallibility. It considers the types of pronouncements in which the church teaches infallibly and then moves into a consideration of the exercise of the church's infallibility. Here the outline locates papal infallibility, as well as other forms of the active exercise of the church's infallibility by the body of bishops and the nature of the "passive infallibility" it attributes to nonepiscopal believers:

1. To announce, explain, confirm by Scripture and tradition the decree of the Vatican Council defining pontifical infallibility;

2. How does the episcopal body, whether dispersed throughout the world or assembled in council, share in the privilege of infallibility?

3. What is passive infallibility? How does it differ from active infallibility? Is passive infallibility necessarily found by virtue of the promises of Christ, in the taught Church [l'Eglise enseignée]?

This location of papal infallibility within the context of ecclesial infallibility is also reflected somewhat in the guide's discussion of church government, which it explains was given by Christ to Peter and to the other apostles under Peter. To the church Christ promised indefectibility and perpetuity. The right to rule and teach the church, given directly by Christ, is found in plenitude in Peter and his successors.[45]

In his interpretation of *Pastor aeternus*, Dupanloup focuses more directly on the role of the successors of Peter, but understands this role as a building up of the unity of the church. Dupanloup begins

44. Bergier, *Supplément à la vie du Cardinal Mathieu*, p. 237; Joseph Foulon, "Lettre circulaire à l'occasion de la nouvelle édition des programmes d'examen des jeunes prêtres," in *Oeuvres pastorales*, 2:344.

45. *Programmes pour les études ecclésiastiques*, pp. 41, 42, 44, 32, 36–37.

his interpretation with a discussion of the promises of Christ, finding in Matt. 16:13–19 the basis for the conciliar decree. He cites other Petrine texts and continues with an interpretation of them:

> There it is, then, this august authority presiding over everything in the Church! There it is, this infallibility of the pontifical magisterium, in virtue of which Peter's successor cannot fall into error when he is defining *ex cathedra*, as pastor and teacher of all Christians, something that must be believed by everyone; there it is, this great teaching authority which in the holy catholic Church creates the bond between minds, the unity and strength of belief. If Christ gave teaching authority to the whole apostolic body for the perpetual spread of truth . . . he willed to give it in an elevated and special way to the head of the apostles for the unchangeable preservation of unity.

Christ wanted the bishops united, not only in heart but also in mind and word in the infallible teaching of truth. This unity of the episcopate, which serves the unity of all of the faithful, is safeguarded by means of Christ's establishment of the chair of Peter, Dupanloup explains, citing the opening lines of *Pastor aeternus*. To serve the unity of the church, Christ wanted the pope first in all things. Citing an older tribute of his own to Pius IX, Dupanloup ends by asserting his devotion in proclaiming the papal prerogatives.[46] His interpretation of papal infallibility places it in an ecclesial context by emphasizing that the papal authority in teaching serves the unity of the church.

But Dupanloup did not intend his interpretation to be understood at all as an agreement with the council's majority. When someone said to him in 1871, "However, Your Excellency, you were in fundamental agreement with your opponents," Dupanloup replied, "In fundamental agreement! Don't say that, we never were."[47]

Some French minority bishops found an acceptable interpretation of *Pastor aeternus* by firmly locating it within the context of ecclesial infallibility. First, in discussing any exercise of infallibility, whether by the pope or the bishops, they always emphasized that such an exercise of infallibility took place within the context of the church and articulated the faith already held by the whole church. In addition, by underlining the limits placed on papal infallibility in *Pastor aeternus*, they were able to show parallels between a pope and a council in

46. Félix Dupanloup, "Lettre pastorale portant publication des constitutions dogmatiques *Dei filius* et *Pastor aeternus* promulguées au concile du Vatican," in *Nouvelles oeuvres choisies*, 7 vols. (Paris: E. Plon et Cie, 1873–74), 7:294, 296-98, 301.

47. Palanque, *Catholiques libéraux et gallicans en France*, p. 59.

the exercise of infallibility, each of whom under certain conditions was seen to give words to the unchanging faith held by the whole church. Guilbert's explanation summarizes this approach. As Guilbert expressed it, they understood that the pope's infallibility "is then that of the teaching Church itself. His infallibility has no other scope and is essentially identical to that of the teaching Church"; its exercise is "the infallible mouth of the Church which pronounces, it is the Church itself which proclaims the truth or condemns error."[48]

Denials of Opposition and Claims of Victory

Two other arguments for the material authority of *Pastor aeternus* made by the French minority were closely related to each other. The first was the denial by some that they had ever really opposed the schema even during the council; they simply had questioned its opportuneness. The second was the claim by others that the council after all had not defined what they had opposed, namely the separate, personal, absolute infallibility of the pope, and that hence their opposition to its work could cease.

We can see how easily these two arguments could be merged or become confused with each other by listeners and even by the bishops themselves. When a minority bishop says, for example, that he never opposed the doctrine itself but merely found it inopportune, which argument is he really making? At first it seems that he makes the first—denial of any real opposition to the schema even during the council. But is that the "doctrine" to which he refers? Or is he rather making the second argument, claiming that after all he can accept the decree because his opposition at the council was directed against a version of the doctrine that never passed, not against the doctrine as actually found in *Pastor aeternus*?

The closeness of these two arguments may have provided a graceful loophole for the French minority after the council. They could explain their opposition as based merely on the doctrine's inopportuneness, while allowing themselves the satisfaction of knowing that their opposition at the council had succeeded after all in preventing the proclamation of separate, personal, absolute papal infallibility. It also provided a simple explanation for the minority's conciliar be-

48. Guilbert, *La divine synthèse, ou l'exposé au double point*, 2d ed., 2:274.

havior to later biographers and funeral orators, who frequently made the ambiguous and perhaps even untrue claim that their subject had never really opposed the doctrine, merely its opportuneness.[49] Because of the closeness of these two arguments, I examine them together here.

Colet writes that he had always considered the doctrine of papal infallibility theologically certain. "In raising it to the dignity of a Catholic dogma, the holy Vatican Council, as far as we are concerned, has only given the added merit of an act of faith to what was formerly an object of our faith." His funeral orator notes the haste with which Colet moved to change his diocesan catechism so that it conformed to the conciliar decree.[50] Dupanloup believed the doctrine of papal infallibility to be inopportune, not wrong, says Thomas in what he intends as a defense of the deceased bishop. Dupanloup himself had claimed the same position. In his letter of adhesion to Pius IX, Dupanloup writes, "I feel no confusion in this regard; I have written and spoken only against the opportuneness of the definition; as far as the doctrine is concerned, I have always professed it, not only in my heart but in public writings on which the Holy Father has seen fit to congratulate me by the most affectionate briefs; and I adhere to it again without difficulty."[51]

Pastor aeternus "decides nothing," Darboy comments according to one report. "I wasn't opposed to it as a theologian, for it is not false, but as a man, because it is inept."[52] A friend of Darboy suggests that the archbishop contrasted public acceptance with the internal judgment of conscience:

Since you belong to the army, he told me, you evidently cannot set yourself up in revolt against your leaders, nor attack the pope who is stronger than you. You must, therefore, exteriorly and in your official acts, submit to this infallibility and this Council. As far as your conscience is concerned you have enough intelligence, learning and honesty to know your own opinion. Whatever they say or do, *their dogma will never be anything but* INEPT and

49. It was against this representation of the minority that de Las Cases protests in his testament above, chapter 7 at note 37.

50. Quoted in Freppel, *Oraison funèbre de Colet*, p. 21. But see Colet's comments reported above, chapter 6 at notes 26–28.

51. Thomas to Lagrange, 15 April 1884, in Lagrange, *Vie de Dupanloup*, p. v; Mansi 53:990C–D.

52. Darboy, quoted by Hyacinthe Loyson, in Palanque, *Catholiques libéraux et gallicans en France*, p. 182.

their council a council of SACRISTANS. Therefore, live in peace; continue to work, at the same time shepherding your strength, and do your duty *without worrying about them.* Good-bye for now.

But in his common presentation of his position after the council, Darboy maintained that his opposition had been directed only against the opportuneness of proclaiming the doctrine, not against the doctrine itself. "It wasn't so much the decree itself as the opportuneness of it," he writes to Maret. "Everybody knows it and *as for me,* I said it out before the whole Council."[53] Having given no one any reason to doubt his feelings, he argues, it is superfluous to declare his adhesion. But he eventually writes to Pius IX, adhering "purely and simply" to *Pastor aeternus.* Darboy reminds the pope of the 16 July 1870 note from minority bishops, in which "we expressed the hope of achieving unanimity of the votes, if they adopted two or three corrections which did not affect the matter of the decree, but which softened the formula. It was especially the question of opportuneness which most concerned us, in mind as well as in heart, and the fear, alas! of seeing governments losing interest in the affairs of the papacy. I know indeed that men are not strong, they have just demonstrated this once again, and that God does not need them; however, he does make use of them sometimes. In any case, it is over."[54] After the council, Darboy reminisced about his opposition to the schema. Having gone to Rome to investigate the definition of a dogma that had always existed, "some of my colleagues and I found that this definition was incomplete, and as I was called upon to give my opinion I did so without fear or reticence." The definition was conceived in the following way: "The pope is infallible, when inspired by God, he settles a question of theology or of morality." Darboy wanted the council to inject the phrase, "and supported by the means of inspiration recognized in the church." This proposal was rejected; "they objected that it was clearly evident to every Catholic

53. Eugène Michaud, quoted in Hasler, *Pius IX,* 2:494, n. 16. See the rest of this footnote for Hasler's discussion of Darboy's stance toward the decree's content. Hasler's conclusion—that Darboy believed the decree to be false—relies too heavily on the partisan testimony of the journalist Jean Wallon and the conjectures of the Marquise de Forbin d'Oppède about Darboy's failure to promote the doctrine within his diocese. I think that I have captured a better sense of Darboy because I draw on both the reports of others and the archbishop's own public and private statements.

54. Mansi 53:965A–B.

and so well-taught and understood by all generations since St. Peter that its insertion would only be a vain repetition and a useless concession to the casuistic and indocile spirit of the age. The Holy Father inclined toward this opinion, the Council adopted it, we all, I was the first, accepted its decision and the discussion was closed."[55] Darboy presents his opposition, then, as a struggle to clarify the formula of the definition, rather than a fight against the doctrine itself.

Several French minority bishops emphasized that the teaching of *Pastor aeternus* had simply clarified an existing truth; it had not added a new doctrine to the faith. Meignan says that the pope simply manifested truth in defining, rather than creating new dogmas. "What is new is that this truth is given greater clarity; what is new is the promulgation of an ancient truth." The council had not discussed the truth of papal infallibility but the conditions "which would avert all misunderstanding."[56] Guilbert also maintains that the church sometimes clarifies contested issues, but "these truths formed part of Catholic teaching before the formal decision of the church."[57] And Rivet explains, "By declaring, by teaching the doctrinal infallibility of the Roman pontiff, the holy Vatican Council, therefore, only rendered more evident and more certain this prerogative of the vicar of Christ: a divine prerogative which henceforth no sincere Catholic could question."[58]

Thomas believed that the decree had succeeded in breaking through the debates of the schools. He notes that "these terms of gallican and of ultramontane, already old-fashioned for half a century, definitely died out at the Vatican Council."[59]

Maret struggled within himself to decide whether he could honestly adhere to *Pastor aeternus*. He believed that the decree was not clear in itself and therefore that some interpretation of its meaning was necessary: "The feeling behind the adherence of the bishops was

55. O'Meara, *Monseigneur Darboy*, pp. 29–30; on O'Meara's reliability, see chapter 7, note 30.
56. Meignan, Speech at return from council, pp. 216–17.
57. Guilbert, *La divine synthèse, ou l'exposé au double point*, 2d ed., 1:214.
58. "En déclarant, en enseignant l'infaillibilité doctrinale du Pontife Romain, le saint Concile du Vatican n'a donc fait que rendre plus évidente et plus certaine cette prérogative du Vicaire du Jésus-Christ: divine prérogative que désormais nul catholique sincère ne saurait contester" (François Rivet, "Lettre circulaire au clergé [22 August 1870]," pp. 189–90).
59. Thomas, *Deuxième congrès des catholiques de Normandie*, p. 15.

to obey the Pope. All right; and the Pope wishes us to obey the natural sense of the decree. Yes. But what is this natural sense? Is it perfectly clear? No, since we are arguing about it. The Council could, therefore, make it clear by completing it."[60] Maret, then, is concerned to interpret the decree. "One can conscientiously and sincerely accept the decree of 18 July, if this decree does not include the doctrine of *absolute, separate, personal* pontifical infallibility," he writes. One can show that the decree always assumes "the agreement of the Church" to *ex cathedra* decisions. Maret continues: "Taken as a whole and in the purport of its terms, the decree of 18 July could be interpreted in such a manner as to allow the minority to adhere to it without any reserve contrary to episcopal sincerity and dignity. In this way God willed to reward the generous and untiring efforts of a minority which sacrificed everything to be obedient to its conscience and to serve the true interests of the Church." In short, Maret believes, the school that wanted to change the church's constitution by defining the separate, personal, absolute infallibility of the pope did not succeed in its aim. "God did not allow it. The minority has triumphed in its defeat." Infallibility as defined by the council, he explains, is thus not separate, personal, or absolute: "It is not absolute, since one supposes conditions; it is not separate, since agreement and consent are implied; it is not personal, since it is not the result of only one person's study and everything does not depend on the pontifical will alone."[61] He writes to David, "I think that I have shown *what is* really *found* in the decree; and it is fortunate that what is found there is truly *what ought to be found.*"[62]

In other personal notes, Maret writes, "I adhere to the decree *purely* and *simply,* because I can give *only one meaning* to it, a meaning which preserves the true character of the constitution of the Church." The aim of the extreme ultramontanist school had been to make the pope entirely independent of the episcopate. But "this end was not attained by the decree, God willed it otherwise." He continues with an analysis of what the decree did accomplish:

60. Henri Maret, Personal Notes, quoted in Hasler, *Pius IX*, 2:493, n. 9.

61. Henri Maret in personal notes written to himself, quoted in Bazin, *Vie de Maret*, 3:218.

62. Henri Maret to Augustin David, 10 October 1870, quoted in Hasler, *Pius IX*, 2:479, n. 29.

A result has been obtained; it is that the infallibility of the pope has not its source in the episcopate but it is equally certain that the assistance and the preceding or concomitant assent of the episcopate is an essential *condition* of this infallibility. Another result has been obtained: that the pope is infallible in judgments *ex cathedra*; but the conditions surrounding these judgments are outlined. They are sufficient authority for our whole doctrine of the necessity of the assistance of the episcopate for all judgments *ex cathedra*, not as the cause but as a condition of pontifical infallibility.[63]

In another place, he writes, "The consent of the Church which seems to be left out here can be only the subsequent consent, which is not necessary, when there is a preceding and concomitant consent."[64]

The accord of bishops is seen as an essential condition for the pope's exercise of infallibility, even if it is not the cause or source of that exercise. With this understanding, Maret felt that he could agree with *Pastor aeternus*, and he sent his adhesion to the pope on 15 October 1870. He began plans to revise his book, *Du concile général et de la paix religieuse,* in light of the teaching of the First Vatican Council and to publish its third volume.

But Rome was not satisfied, and Maret heard that his book would be examined for doctrinal error. In a letter of 28 November 1870, Pius IX urged him to repudiate what he had written, but Maret replied on 29 January 1871 that his book did not basically contradict *Pastor aeternus.* It affirmed pontifical infallibility, he argues, *"in the meaning in which it has just been defined. . . .* I am questioning only one school of thought and not pontifical infallibility itself." He suggests that he be permitted to write a *Mémoire* showing that his book only contested a school of thought and that the teaching he gave on papal infallibility does not contradict the conciliar teachings "but basically conforms to them."[65]

Maret also appeals to Rome on procedural grounds. He notes that his book had expressed views once held by those in communion with Rome. If these views now are condemned, the views of those great thinkers of the past would also have to be condemned, even though those thinkers would have submitted to decisions of the church contrary to their own views if those decisions had been made during

63. Maret in personal notes to himself, quoted in Bazin, *Vie de Maret*, 3:219.
64. Maret, Personal Notes, quoted in Hasler, *Pius IX*, 2:479, n. 30.
65. Mansi 53:1023B–C.

their lifetime. In addition, his book tried to reconcile the views of the French tradition with those of Roman theologians. His book had not prevented him from taking a seat at the council, where his views had been freely expressed and shared by other bishops as well. His position is the same as that of other minority bishops, who wrote and voted according to their consciences. He appeals for justice on the basis of the free discussion that should characterize a council: "Are not all these acts covered by the inviolability proper to the character and the functions of a judge, in a solemn assembly opened by your Holiness himself? Does justice allow a judge to be punished for fulfilling what he considered a duty before God and in the eyes of the Church?" Are not controversies protected in the church until a final decision is made, he asks.[66]

Rome did not insist on its point further but asked Ginoulhiac to obtain a public retraction from Maret.[67] Maret withdrew his book from sale, and on 31 October 1871 rejected "whatever in his book and his *Défense* is opposed to the definition of the Council."[68] When his Faculty of Theology at the Sorbonne reopened in the fall of 1871, its first act was to record the assent of its members to the decrees of the council and especially to *Pastor aeternus*. In his last testament, Maret writes: "In order to conform to the intentions of the sovereign pontiff, I withdrew this book from circulation and I disclaimed and still disclaim what, in this book, as in my other writings, might be contrary to the Catholic faith, to the teaching of the Church and of the Holy See, to the definitions of the Vatican Council."[69]

In denying that they had opposed papal infallibility itself, and in claiming that the decree had after all not proclaimed the separate, personal, absolute infallibility of the pope, the French minority found their most convincing arguments for the material authority of *Pastor aeternus*. With this way of understanding the decree, they were able to find interpretations acceptable to their own thinking and thus were able gradually to justify to themselves the acceptance of a decision they had vigorously opposed. Aubert believes that the minority were correct in seeing that their concerns had after all been

66. Ibid., cols. 1019C, 1021C, 1019D–1020A, 1020C–1021A, 1022B.

67. Palanque, *Catholiques libéraux et gallicans en France*, p. 180.

68. Quoted in Bazin, *Vie de Maret*, 3:249. The preliminary letter of retraction is found in Mansi 53:1025C–1026D.

69. Bazin, *Vie de Maret*, 3:462.

served by the decree. He notes that although it occasioned increased pontifical intervention in local dioceses and supported centralized government, yet the decree clarified the exercise of infallibility by specifying conditions under which it operated and thereby eliminated many false ideas that had been widespread. After all, he argues, the decree satisfied the concerns of most of the minority bishops and thus made it possible for them to adhere to it soon after the council's end: "The nuances introduced into the definition appeared to them, on examination, to bring together the essence of their concerns and to avoid the exaggerated thesis of the neo-ultramontanes against which they had risen up." The decree passed on 18 July 1870 was "decidedly more nuanced than the primitive text and gave fundamental satisfaction to the legitimate demands of the great majority of the bishops." It is this, he argues, which explains the acceptance of *Pastor aeternus* even by the minority once they were "away from the heat of the battle."[70]

Writing before the council, Armand de Melun predicts that the council would realize neither ultramontanist hopes nor gallican fears but instead would surround papal infallibility with precautions and formalities. The result, he envisions, would be a pope who can err like everyone else except in a small, carefully defined area, thus leaving each with his freedom for judgment on the pope's acts. Thus in strengthening the pope in this one small area, the council would weaken him in all the others. Perhaps God would inspire such a decision, he thinks, "not to strengthen the position of his representative, but rather to put an end to that sort of glorification with which one is tempted to surround the sovereign pontiff, a glorification explained by the attacks by the enemies of the Church, but which seems to have overstepped the bounds a little."[71] In their response to the council after its close, the French minority seem to have agreed with this prediction.

Conclusion

The French minority bishops developed an interpretation of *Pastor aeternus* that allowed them to accept not only its formal authority

---

70. Aubert, *Pie IX*, p. 361; Aubert, "Concernant le tiers parti," p. 255.
71. Armand de Melun to unnamed correspondent, 8 September 1868, quoted in Palanque, *Catholiques libéraux et gallicans en France*, p. 190.

but its material authority as well. While they continued to defend the motives that led to their opposition to the schema, they nevertheless sometimes referred at least in passing to the pope's infallibility. Though many said little about the schema's content, others developed three lines of interpretation that allowed them to find *Pastor aeternus* acceptable in content. The three approaches, we saw, were: first, an emphasis on the ecclesial context of papal infallibility; second, a denial of opposition to anything but the opportuneness of the definition; and third, an assertion that after all the schema had not declared the separate, personal, absolute infallibility of the pope.

What can be said about these approaches? They seem to be in harmony with Darboy's remark that *Pastor aeternus* "decides nothing." That is, each emphasizes that the pope's infallibility operates, as it always has, to express the faith of the whole church. That the pope should at times exercise this infallibility they regard simply as a clarification of a belief always implicit in the church's faith. As Guilbert points out, the infallibility of the pope "is, then, that of the teaching Church itself."[72] Such an ecclesial interpretation excludes the extremes of the ultramontanist separate, personal, absolute papal infallibility, and to this "moderate" interpretation Maret could truly say that he had never been opposed.

After the council, some French minority bishops acted as though their arguments against the schema had been heard and implemented. They chose to interpret *Pastor aeternus* in a way that reaffirmed the view that they themselves had always held of papal infallibility. Their interpretations show their conviction that the ultramontanist view had not prevailed in the decree. As though they believed that a view as wrong as that of their opponents could not succeed, they explained the decree in light of their certainty that it had not succeeded. As Maret said, "God did not allow it. The minority has triumphed in its defeat."[73]

---

72. Darboy, quoted by Hyacinthe Loyson, in Palanque, *Catholiques libéraux et gallicans en France*, p. 182; Guilbert, *La divine synthèse, ou l'exposé au double point*, 2d ed., 2:274.

73. Maret in personal notes written to himself, quoted in Bazin, *Vie de Maret*, 3:218.

PART IV

The French Minority Bishops and the Ecclesial Character of Infallibility

9

The Central Emphasis

The Ecclesial Character of Infallibility

————◂●▸————

Over a century has passed since the French minority bishops developed argument after argument against the definition of papal infallibility at the First Vatican Council, only to find themselves faced with the need to find new arguments for accepting *Pastor aeternus*. Since that time, the questions and issues they raised in their struggle have changed and multiplied, and another council has been held by the Roman Catholic Church. The times and distance make it possible for us in a fresh, critical way to remember, interpret, and evaluate the French minority's position, and it is to this critical remembering, interpreting, and evaluating that this final chapter is devoted.

In the first section, I will recall the arguments of the French minority before, during, and after the council. Second, I will show that these arguments flowed from these bishops' conviction that infallibility has an ecclesial character. Finally, I will evaluate these arguments with their underlying conviction to determine their weaknesses and strengths in the context of present theological discussion.

Summarizing the Arguments of the French Minority Bishops

With common friendships and a common seminary training in the moderate gallican tradition behind them, the French minority bishops from liberal and gallican circles joined together to fight a common fear that the council would define the separate, personal, absolute infallibility of the pope. They brought with them to the council several shared theological presuppositions which formed a backdrop for their conciliar and postconciliar arguments.

Most believed that the church should adapt somewhat to modern governments and the modern spirit, though they did support the temporal sovereignty of the pope. Critical of journalists and others who undermined their episcopal rights, they emphasized the authority of the bishops to judge doctrine in council and to govern authoritatively within their dioceses. Their understanding of the ecumenical council especially emphasized the importance of the bishops, who represented the whole church and received divine assistance to teach correctly through the conciliar process of detailed study and lengthy deliberations in an atmosphere of freedom. Councils were infallible, then, because they represented the faith of the infallible church to which Christ had promised to be present always. The French minority bishops emphasized the immutability of dogma, and they tended to see their role as one of conserving an unchanging body of beliefs. They approached the First Vatican Council with high hopes, but gradually these hopes turned to the unifying fear that the council would define the separate, personal, absolute infallibility of the pope.

Against such a definition, the French minority bishops made three cases, which can be understood as flowing from a response of *no* to one, two, or three of the following questions: (1) Is the proposed teaching true? If yes, (2) Is the proposed teaching definable? If yes, (3) Should the proposed teaching be defined? A response of *no* to the last question led some French minority bishops to argue against the timeliness of a definition. Others, answering *no* to the second question as well, made a case against the definability of papal infallibility. A few answered the first question negatively as well by making a case against the truth of the schema on papal infallibility. While this threefold distinction behind their thought was usually not recognized by the bishops, a few made its presence explicit in their thought. Each case consisted of many arguments.

The first case held that the teaching on papal infallibility—as the French minority understood the proposed schema's presentation of that teaching—should not be defined. A definition should not be made unless believers are ready to receive it as expressing their faith, some argued. But many Catholics would not agree with a definition of papal infallibility, and so its proclamation would wound the church's unity. A decision that cannot be made unanimously or with sufficient time for deliberation, others said, would be unlikely to win reception. A council should never rush into any definition, and it should allow freedom of opinion on all matters except those absolutely requiring definition.

Other arguments in this first case against the timeliness of the definition of papal infallibility noted that a definition would impede reunion with Protestant, Anglican, and Orthodox Christians, or that it would alienate unbelievers and all imbued with the modern spirit. Some feared that a definition would arouse hostility from civil governments, and many believed that it would seem arrogant or be misunderstood.

The French minority bishops made a second case against the definability of the dogma as it was proposed in the schema. Sometimes they argued that papal infallibility could not be defined because of defects in the actual schema and other times that papal infallibility could never be defined in any schema. Noting the defects in the schema, some argued that a definition was impossible because it was not needed—since definitions can be made only when they are necessary. The schema fails to discuss ecclesial infallibility before it introduces papal infallibility, complained some bishops; its formulation is unclear and uses misleading arguments. Others complained about the haste and other irregularities surrounding the council's procedures or the lack of the clear unanimity of the whole church, which is required for defining.

Among those arguing that papal infallibility could never be defined, some said that it was incapable of clear formulation. Others believed that Scripture and tradition did not teach papal infallibility as clearly as necessary to establish the certitude required for a *de fide* definition. Many felt that papal infallibility was merely the opinion of one theological school and hence could never be defined as a dogma binding on the whole church.

In their third case, a few French minority bishops argued that the teaching of papal infallibility as they understood the schema to propose it—that is, separate, personal, absolute papal infallibility—was false. Some believed that it conflicted with the tradition of theological reflection in the church, which was silent on papal infallibility or even emphasized another view, such as the infallibility of councils. Many, such as Maret, complained that the teaching did not do justice to the authority of bishops, whose accord with the pope was necessary for an infallible definition. Finally, a few stressed that the exercise of infallibility was founded in the *consensus ecclesiae*. If the pope could infallibly define the faith, he did so on the condition that his definition really expressed the faith of the whole church. These bishops thought the doctrine of papal infallibility isolated the pope from the church as though cutting a head off from its body.

The French minority lost their struggle against the definition, and they absented themselves from the council when faced with *Pastor aeternus*. All, however, eventually accepted the decree. They made two cases in its favor, one from the formal authority of the decree and another from its material authority.

In their case from formal authority, the French minority bishops found ample arguments in their preconciliar stance, when they had noted the binding authority of ecumenical councils. Many had pledged their acceptance of the upcoming council's decisions in advance. After the council, the French minority argued simply that they were bound to accept *Pastor aeternus* because it had been passed by an ecumenical council, or promulgated by the pope, or represented the faith of the great majority of bishops and pope together. Some explained their response in terms of obedience, and others distinguished between their role as bishops—to judge—and their role as Christians—to obey. Many described their position as a sacrifice of personal conviction to the judgment of the church as a whole.

The case from the material authority of *Pastor aeternus* was accompanied by defenses of the minority's good faith at the council. Many French minority bishops said little about the decree after the council's end or implemented its teaching only by making scattered references to papal infallibility. But some sought interpretations of the decree that they could accept. Arguments were easier to find than some had anticipated, since a number of the calamities feared had not materialized. Some bishops argued that the decree could best be understood within a context of ecclesial infallibility; the pope simply at times could be seen to exercise that infallibility which they had always known the church to possess and which the bishops as a whole could also exercise. Others argued that they had never really opposed the dogma of papal infallibility but only its timeliness. Some argued that, after all, the schema had not ratified the ultramontanist vision of a separate, personal, absolute papal infallibility and so their opposition to the work of the council could end.

Interpreting the Arguments of the
French Minority Bishops

Why did the French minority bishops argue both that the proposed schema at the First Vatican Council should be rejected and that *Pastor aeternus* should be accepted? I have indicated that the answer to this question lies in the fundamental understanding of infallibility held by these bishops. This understanding emphasized that infallibility had an ecclesial character. Other bishops at the council would not have disagreed with this opinion, but it was not the organizing principle in their arguments. But the French minority bishops were so convinced of the ecclesial character of infallibility that they made it the central concept in their conciliar and postconciliar thought, such that all of their arguments were shaped by it. As for Martin Luther and the *sola fide*, so for the French minority bishops and the ecclesial character of infallibility: in each case, a concept assumed such centrality that, even when not made explicit, it determined the choice and arrangement of all other concepts and arguments.

To say that the French minority believed infallibility possessed an ecclesial character is in some sense to be redundant. Infallibility is a gift of divine assistance to the church, and in that sense by definition it has an ecclesial character—on this majority and minority bishops would have agreed. But precisely because they made the ecclesial character of infallibility their central organizing principle, the French minority bishops were able to go further in drawing out its implications. For them, *ecclesial* implied *communal*, that is, it meant that infallibility was a gift of assistance given to the communion that is the church. Because infallibility was ecclesial, it was necessarily communal; and from this the French minority drew specific implications for its purpose, subject, and exercise.

With this understanding, we can make sense of the puzzling, seemingly contradictory positions of the French minority, who first argued against and then in favor of the council's work. How can these positions be reconciled? Only if they both are understood to be products of the deeper conviction regarding infallibility's ecclesial character can this dilemma be resolved. To show how this deeper conviction shapes all of the French minority's arguments, I will show the way in which all their arguments—both those against the schema and those in favor of *Pastor aeternus*—flow from this deeper conviction of infallibility's ecclesial character. In so doing, I am giving a theological rather than a historical or psychological explanation for the otherwise puzzling arguments made for and against the council's work.

The French minority drew three conclusions from the ecclesial character of infallibility. First, they concluded that the purpose of infallibility was the good of the church. Second, they believed that the church was the subject of infallibility.[1] Third, they concluded that the exercise of infallibility was judged on the basis of evidence. These three corollary convictions—on the purpose, subject, and exercise of infallibility—will be examined in turn.

Infallibility's Purpose as the Good of the Church

Because infallibility had an ecclesial character, its purpose was the good of the church, the French minority believed. That is, they could make no sense of any plans or claims to define infallibility if doing so did not serve the good of the entire communion. This conviction underlay many of the arguments against the schema's timeliness, as well as some arguments in favor of both material and formal authority of the decree after the council.

Before the council, for example, the French minority argued that the schema was incapable of eliciting the unanimous agreement necessary for its effective promulgation in the church. They did not believe that the bare proclamation of a truth was adequate to serve the ecclesial purpose of infallibility if the truth would go unrecognized. To them, such proclamation seemed like the throwing of seed on stony ground.

The desire for a fertile seedbed and the conviction that infallibility failed in its very purpose if exercised in the absence of such a seedbed are evident in other arguments against timeliness. When Callot and Darboy point out that definitions should be made only when necessary and plead for freedom of opinion whenever possible, they also reflect the conviction that infallibility's purpose is the good of the

---

1. Of course, the French minority bishops do not mean this in a way that would set it in contradiction to the exposition by Gasser on *Pastor aeternus* shortly before its passage, in which he explained that God alone is infallible (Mansi 52:1214A). The French minority bishops are thinking rather of the created subject which is given divine assistance and hence possessed of infallibility.

church, not merely its instruction. When Dupanloup argues that the council should not alienate the Protestants, Anglicans, and Orthodox, when he begs his fellow bishops not to add burdens to the backs of those weak in faith or to widen the abyss between the church and modern unbelievers—in these arguments he also shows his conviction that infallibility must serve the good of the church. This emphasis emerges as well in the concern about the likelihood of misunderstanding to which the schema would be subject: such misunderstanding would lead to hostility from civil governments, to attacks from unbelievers, and to confusion and doubt on the part of Catholics. How would such results serve the ecclesial purpose of infallible defining, the French minority wondered?

Because they thought that infallibility's ecclesial character should be manifested by its service of the good of the church, the French minority bishops showed the same concern even after the council when they urged the acceptance of *Pastor aeternus*. That is, their emphasis on infallibility's purpose was more fundamental than arguments either for or against a definition of papal infallibility; rather, these arguments were shaped by the more fundamental concern. We can see this most clearly in their quick acceptance of *Pastor aeternus* without further debate because, as Mathieu explains, they thought that further debate would cause scandal and disorder in the church. Similarly, a few bishops even urged the material authority of the decree when they saw that their worst fears about its consequences did not materialize. What they had feared was a stony seedbed seemed to possess unexpected depths of receptive soil. When they recognized that *Pastor aeternus* after all had not resulted in the mass alienation of the modern world, intellectuals, or civil governments from the church, a few minority bishops concluded that the decree, to their surprise, had not failed to serve the church's good.

The Church as the Subject of Infallibility

Since infallibility had an ecclesial character, the French minority bishops believed it should serve the church's good, and the arguments I have been examining show this preoccupation. But these bishops also concluded from the ecclesial character of infallibility that the church is the subject of infallibility. This emphasis appears again and again as an underlying reason for both arguments against

the definition and those in favor of *Pastor aeternus*. At times the
bishops note it directly, as when they complain that ecclesial infallibility should be treated before any discussion of papal infallibility, or
when they note that the schema omits an adequate presentation of
the bishops' role as successors of the apostles. Callot criticizes the
wording of the schema because it suggests that infallibility resides
exclusively with the pope, and Darboy finds the schema unclear
about the need of the bishops' common consent for deciding definitions of the faith.

At other times, the emphasis on the church as subject of infallibility leads the bishops to stress the need for accord of pope and
bishops in any *de fide* definition or the ecclesial base that founds any
such definition. Again and again, they remind their hearers of the
need for a *consensus ecclesiae* before any definition of papal infallibility
can be made. But because such a *consensus* is lacking, they argue, the
council is bound not to arrive at such a definition. Some of the
French minority, such as Callot and Meignan, note that many parts
of the church of their day do not hold a belief in papal infallibility.
Others, such as Dupanloup, David, and Ginoulhiac, draw attention
to the doctrine's absence in the history of theological reflection.
Accusations that the schema separates the pope from the church or
that it erects a teaching of one school into a dogma also underline the
truth that the church is the subject of infallibility.

Gradually the French minority bishops came to believe that *Pastor
aeternus* retained, at least minimally, the truth that the church is the
subject of infallibility. Because they came to believe this, the French
minority bishops felt able to accept the decree. Maret is most clear
about this requirement for his acceptance, noting that the decree had
not after all declared the pope's separate, personal, absolute infallibility; God had not permitted such a disaster. Although the council did
not find the source of papal infallibility in the episcopate, Maret
writes, it did conclude that the antecedent or concomitant accord of
the episcopate was a necessary condition of the exercise of infallibility. Only because he finds the council affirming the need for accord
between pope and bishops can Maret accept its decree.

Other bishops argue in favor of acceptance of *Pastor aeternus* for
related reasons. Some interpret the council's work in accord with
their earlier view of what it should do, understanding papal infallibility as simply the expression of ecclesial infallibility. The pope's infal-

libility is that of the teaching church, writes Guilbert; when he pronounces infallibly, the church itself speaks through its infallible
mouth. Meignan reminds his hearers that the pope cannot teach new
doctrines. And some applied their belief in ecclesial infallibility in
another way after the council. Since Christ ensures that the church is
protected from error in its conciliar pronouncements, they reason,
he has assisted the First Vatican Council in its decree on papal infallibility. Again, however, this somewhat circular argument demonstrates the extent to which French minority bishops were concerned
to safeguard the idea that the church is subject of infallibility. When
they became convinced that the vast majority of the bishops accepted
Pastor aeternus, they felt compelled by their own logic to accept it as
well.

The Exercise of Infallibility as Judged on the Basis of Evidence

If these arguments made before, during, and after the council
placed the emphasis on the church as the proper subject of infallibility, other arguments focused on the exercise of infallibility. The
French minority believed that a judgment on whether or not infallibility could be, or had been, exercised was made on the basis of evidence grasped as sufficient. If certain signs manifested themselves
within the communion of the church, the French minority took
them as the evidence that a proposed teaching could be defined, or
that a particular definition had indeed been infallibly taught. As
Robinson Crusoe reasoned from the fresh footprint that he was not
alone, so, the French minority bishops believed, one ought to reason
from evidence to the possibility or the fact of infallibility's exercise.

In their thought on evidence, the French minority concerned
themselves with two different problems. One involved a first task of
judging whether a proposed teaching could be defined, that is, could
be taught infallibly. The second involved a later task of judging
whether a definition already made had been infallibly taught, that is,
whether a defined teaching was truly an exercise of infallibility.

The first concern with evidence focused on the judgment of
whether or not a proposed teaching could be defined. The French
minority bishops believed that certitude—indeed, certitude that was
more than human, David insisted—was necessary before a *de fide*

definition could be made. In discussing the means of achieving such certitude, they emphasized the *consensus ecclesiae* as evidence sufficient to ground certitude. Finding unanimity throughout the churches or among themselves on a doctrinal teaching seemed to them sufficient evidence that the teaching was held with more than human certitude. Again, they regarded the affirmations of the teaching in Scripture or in the tradition of the church as clear evidence that a council could teach it infallibly because these clearly pointed to the faith of the whole church. Their conviction that such evidence was absent made the French minority unwilling to vote for the proposed definition.

The second kind of judgment concerned itself with whether a definition actually made was indeed an exercise of infallibility. The search for evidence sufficient for making this judgment itself shows the French minority's ecclesial emphasis in their understanding of infallibility, since they insist on the need for criteria available to the church to judge a papal or episcopal act.

There were many examples of focus on this second kind of judgment in the French minority's thought. For instance, sometimes they seek evidence within the council itself as to whether infallibility is being exercised. Conciliar procedures served as one form of evidence which they felt could ground this judgment. Lack of freedom to discuss thoroughly the issues facing the council, poor acoustics, erroneous use of scriptural or historical texts, the absence of unanimity: all of these problems seemed to be evidence that the council was failing to define infallibly.

Again, their search for evidence sufficient for judging that a definition represented a *de fide* teaching showed itself in their remarks on the conditions to which papal infallibility would be subject. Dupanloup insists that any definition of papal infallibility would have to specify the conditions for its exercise, but he raises doubts from history and theological debate that such conditions could ever be specified adequately. Complaints that the formulation is unclear or open to misunderstanding seem also to arise out of concern for the issue of conditions because they focus on the failure either to specify conditions or to meet the particular condition of clarity in formulation.

After the council, the French minority were faced with making this second kind of judgment for themselves about whether *Pastor aeternus* had been infallibly taught. Again, they focused on evidence as the means by which to reach a judgment, this time in arguments for the acceptance of the decree. Many explained that a conciliar pronouncement, especially combined with its acceptance by a large majority of the church's bishops and its proclamation by the pope, was for them sufficient evidence to judge with certitude that the decree was infallibly taught. Some even explained that their judgment no longer was appropriate: only obedience was demanded in the face of such an unmistakable sign of certitude by the church. Others said that the council had not after all overlooked the kind of evidence required for infallible defining—the *consensus ecclesiae,* agreement with the Scriptures and tradition, accord of pope and bishops. Some even implied that they could find the council unanimous in its decision, since they had removed their own discordant voices.

Concluding Remarks on Interpreting the Arguments of the French Minority Bishops

I have been seeking an interpretation by which to understand the puzzling behavior of the French minority bishops during and after the council, and such an interpretation has emerged in the unifying concern they brought to all their arguments. This unifying concern focused on the ecclesial character of infallibility, and I distinguished within this concern three corollary conclusions: the purpose of infallibility as the good of the church, the church as the subject of infallibility, and the exercise of infallibility as judged on the basis of evidence. Because they judged these aspects of their concern for the ecclesial character of infallibility to have been ignored, the French minority opposed the schema during the council. Because they were able to satisfy themselves that this concern had, after all, not been essentially transgressed by *Pastor aeternus,* they accepted the decree.

The French minority bishops, then, opposed the definition of papal infallibility because they believed that it did not show clearly the ecclesial character of infallibility. When the council passed *Pastor aeternus,* however, these bishops—although not happy that a definition had been made—were yet able to accept it in good conscience when they satisfied themselves that after all it did in fact retain at least minimally the idea of infallibility's ecclesial character. When we grasp this point, we can perhaps lay to rest the tendency to misunderstand the position of the French minority which has plagued discussion of their thought ever since the council ended. I said in the preface that many interpreters of the minority oversimplify their ideas or present them as merely inopportunists. Mourret, for example, finds that almost all of the French minority "accepted the dogma of the infallible authority of the pope, but did not consider it opportune to define it, at least immediately." He is concerned that certain of Darboy's arguments against the opportuneness of the doctrine appeared to attack the doctrine itself, and he suggests that Dupanloup sided with the minority simply because of his hatred for Veuillot. Forty years later, Palanque notes that, though Maret faced real doctrinal questions over the definition of papal infallibility, neither Darboy nor Dupanloup had contested anything other than the opportuneness of the definition. And recently August Hasler argues that many minority bishops were not inopportunists but had substantive arguments against the definition. But he understands their acceptance as submission and their interpretation as evasion.[2]

All of these views, including that of Hasler, suffer from the same weakness: they all seem to assume that the doctrine itself is transparently clear and that the positions of the minority can be easily classified as simply for or against it.[3] Thus they find it necessary to downplay either the French minority's genuine opposition to the definition during the council or their genuine acceptance of the decree after the council. Such a perspective distorts the French minority's position.

But the discernment of the complexity of that position and of its organization around the central concern for infallibility's ecclesial character allow us four insights.

First, we can appreciate more fully how the French minority—as part of the council's minority—contributed to the actual shaping of

2. Mourret, *Le concile du Vatican*, pp. 159, 288–89, 301;Palanque, *Catholiques libéraux et gallicans en France*, pp. 180–81; Hasler, *Pius IX*, 2:447–51, 401, 474–84.

3. Roger Aubert escapes this simplified understanding of the French minority by making distinctions among the different positions they held. Although most agreed "on the basis" of the decree and hence adhered without difficulty, he writes, others had maintained "their gallican conviction" up to the council's end. They doubted that "the pontifical prerogatives went as far as the Council claimed." But when no major episcopal reaction against the council developed, they were bound by their own principles to see in this acceptance the quasi-unanimity of the teaching church and hence to accept the decree on that authority (Roger Aubert, "L'ecclésiologie au concile du Vatican," in D. O. Rousseau, ed., *Le concile et les conciles* [Paris and Chevetogne: Editions du Cerf and Editions de Chevetogne, 1960], p. 272). Again, he notes that more

the decree. Because of their reservations, the text was modified to eliminate some of their fears, allowing them to find the decree at least acceptable.

But, second, the reception of the definition by the French minority was possible only within the context of their new arguments about the decree's authority. For some, this was simply an appeal to its formal authority. But others could offer their reception only after they had developed an interpretive framework showing that the decree did not really negate the ecclesial character of infallibility.

That such an interpretive framework should have been deemed necessary for the reception of *Pastor aeternus* ought not to surprise us in view of what we have already seen of the French minority's conviction of infallibility's ecclesial character. The interpretive framework developed by some French minority bishops highlights the complex quality of the teaching actually proclaimed by the council. Jean-Pierre Torrell cautions against oversimplifying the doctrine taught by the council. "If we simply say: the pope is infallible," he notes, "we are claiming to say in four words what the Council expressed in ten lines of exceptional density. That cannot be done without risk."[4] In their interpretive framework after the council the French minority show a similar care to bring out the nuances of the teaching. Convinced as much after the council as before it that infallibility had an ecclesial character, they felt bound to show that they accepted *Pastor aeternus* only because the decree had preserved this insight to their—albeit grudging—satisfaction.

But, third, their interpretive framework also helps us to understand more fully the way in which interpretation of any conciliar teaching is a part of its reception by the church. "In effect, those who wish to defend—or to discard—a univocal view of infallibility have failed to appreciate the reception of a conciliar definition as an ecclesial hermeneutical process," points out John Ford. "A spectrum of interpretations was legitimated" by participants at the First Vatican

---

among the French minority than among the German minority accepted papal infallibility "basically," but some hesitated to accept as a revealed truth "the personal infallibility of the sovereign pontiff independently of a ratification by the episcopate" (Aubert, *Vatican I*, p. 115).

4. Jean-Pierre Torrell, "L'infaillibilité pontificale est-elle un privilège 'personnel'? Une controverse au premier concile du Vatican," *Revue des sciences philosophiques et théologiques* 45 (1961):245.

Council, he notes, especially by the minority bishops. "In effect their submission implies a further broadening of the spectrum of acceptable interpretations of infallibility."[5] This is that "particular contribution of consent—perhaps even of judgment" involved in the process by which an ecclesial body makes its own the thought or decision of another, "recognizing . . . in the matter promulgated, a rule suitable to its life," which Congar believes necessary to reception.[6]

Karl Rahner notes the inevitable use of theologumena whenever a dogma of the faith is explained. Furthermore, he continues, "Anyone who makes statements involving faith does not need to, and in fact cannot, adequately distinguish by reflection in them the dogmatic proposition from the theologumenon. Otherwise he could completely eliminate the theologumenon." Revelation, he explains, always makes use of the system of concepts and tools available to the hearer at a given time.[7] Thus some interpretation was necessary for every group of bishops at the First Vatican Council, not only for the French minority, to assimilate the dogmatic teaching of *Pastor aeternus*.[8]

But, fourth, when I say that the French minority bishops did not evade the decree just because they interpreted it, I am suggesting more for their interpretation than simply its legitimacy within a range of possible interpretations. With the distance of more than a hundred years, the theologumena used by the French minority seem increasingly to express more adequately than did those of their opponents the enduring dogmatic truth which the council attempted to state. The interpretive work of the French minority then seems not only legitimate but prophetic.[9]

Evaluating the Arguments of the French Minority Bishops

How can we draw on the arguments of the French minority bishops before and after the council to deepen our understanding of

---

5. John T. Ford, "Infallibility: A Review of Recent Studies," *Theological Studies* 40 (1979):301, 289, 298.

6. Congar, "La 'réception'," p. 370.

7. *Sacramentum Mundi*, s.v. "Theologumenon," by Karl Rahner.

8. See, for example, Cwiekowski's discussion of the range of responses to *Pastor aeternus* among English bishops in *English Bishops*, pp. 276–314.

9. Congar, "Bulletin d'ecclésiologie," p. 288.

papal infallibility? Where do their arguments need correction in light of later insights? I will approach the evaluation of the French minority following the division I used in the last section: first, arguments based on the purpose of infallibility as the good of the church; second, arguments based on the view of the church as subject of infallibility; and third, arguments based on infallibility's exercise as judged on the basis of evidence.

Infallibility's Purpose as the Good of the Church

The French minority were correct in holding that infallibility's purpose is the good of the church, and their arguments on timeliness generally were made to underline this conviction. Looking back on these arguments, we can see often that their insights were only too accurate.

The French minority had a good sense for the role of dogmatic statements in symbolizing and effecting the unity of the church, a role that is increasingly emphasized as well in contemporary discussion of the function of dogmatic statements.[10] For them, a dogmatic statement that was unnecessary and divisive seemed a contradiction in terms. The widespread respect for the authority of the pope seemed to make a definition of papal infallibility superfluous, while its specification as a dogma of the faith seemed to strain without cause the fragile bonds that held many Catholics to the church.

If their grasp of the unifying function of dogma was accurate, how accurate were their fears about the bad effects the dogma would have? Aubert and Gadille concur in emphasizing how large in the minds of the French minority loomed their fear that civil governments would interpret a definition as interference in the temporal sphere.[11] But they found that these fears did not materialize after the council, at least not in the way that they had anticipated. With the help of such contributions as the German bishops' pastoral statement

---

10. See, for example, Walter Kasper, "The Relationship between Gospel and Dogma: An Historical Approach," in Edward Schillebeeckx, ed., *Man as Man and Believer,* Concilium, vol. 21 (New York: Paulist Press, 1967), pp. 153–67; Karl Rahner, "What Is a Dogmatic Statement?" in *Theological Investigations,* 20 vols. (Baltimore: Helicon Press, 1966), 5:42–66; Edward Schillebeeckx, "The Creed and Theology," in *Revelation and Theology,* 2 vols. (New York: Sheed and Ward, 1967), 1:203–17.

11. Aubert, *Vatican I,* pp. 118–20; Gadille, *La pensée et l'action politiques des évêques français,* 1:116.

of 1872 and John Henry Newman's "Letter to the Duke of Norfolk" in response to William Gladstone, the limits of the pope's infallibility were shown to have made impossible his infallible interference in the affairs of state.[12] Although the picture of a pope who held control over the votes of Catholic citizens still troubled some countries, an increasingly secular world more often showed indifference or merely polite appreciation toward papal teaching. As Ramadié had feared, the definition of papal infallibility, ironically, led many to diminish the authority they actually attributed to the pope's teachings.[13]

When the French minority bishops argued that a definition of papal infallibility would impede efforts toward the reunion of the different Christian communions, they were more accurate than in their political presentiments. Orthodox, Anglican, and Protestant churches believed that the definition by the First Vatican Council presented a nearly insurmountable obstacle to reunion.

Even within the present atmosphere of ecumenical progress, Christians outside of the Roman Catholic communion find difficulty with papal infallibility as it was formulated at the First Vatican Council. The Lutheran–Roman Catholic Dialogue in the United States explores the possibility that Lutherans need perhaps no longer regard the Roman Catholic doctrine of papal infallibility "as anti-Christian and therefore as a barrier to the unity of the churches," and it concludes on a hopeful note. Yet it was forced to begin by reminding the two churches, "The promulgation of papal infallibility in 1870 appeared to Lutherans as the deepening of an already serious disagreement."[14] In their own reflections on the dialogue with Roman Catholics, the Lutherans rejoice that they now "often find it dif-

---

12. The German bishops' statement is in Hans Küng, *The Council, Reform and Reunion* (New York: Sheed and Ward, 1961). pp. 194–99; John Henry Newman, "Letter to the Duke of Norfolk," in Newman and William Gladstone, *Newman and Gladstone: The Vatican Decrees*, ed. Alvan S. Ryan (Notre Dame: University of Notre Dame Press, 1962) pp. 73–203.

13. See also three paragraphs that John Henry Newman did not include in his "Letter to the Duke of Norfolk" in which he expresses his fear that "the actual tendency of the definition . . . will be to create in educated Catholics a habit of scepticism or secret infidelity as regards all dogmatic truth" (quoted in Cwiekowski, *English Bishops*, p. 311).

14. Lutheran–Roman Catholic Dialogue (U.S.), "Teaching Authority and Infallibility in the Church: Common Statement," in Paul Empie, T. Austin Murphy, and Joseph Burgess, eds., *Teaching Authority and Infallibility in the Church*, Lutherans and Catholics in Dialogue 6 (Minneapolis: Augsburg Publishing House, 1980), no. 3.

ficult to pinpoint exactly where or how we differ from each other on the question of infallibility."[15] Yet they start by reminding their readers:

> Ever since its definition in 1870, the dogma of papal infallibility has been widely seen as both theologically and emotionally the most divisive of all the issues separating the Roman Catholic communion from the churches of the Reformation. . . . Antipapal polemics have remained a major part of the Lutheran stance. The First Vatican Council seemed to confirm all former suspicions. Its definition of infallibility was seen by many as the final step in the direction of papal absolutism, widening the gap between Roman and Reformation churches and making the break irreparable.[16]

In its statement "Authority in the Church I," the Anglican–Roman Catholic International Commission similarly draws attention to the difficulties the 1870 definition created for Anglicans. Although they appreciate the conditions laid down by the First Vatican Council for its exercise, the authors comment, "Anglicans find grave difficulty in the affirmation that the pope can be infallible in his teaching." In addition, they write, "The claim that the pope possesses universal immediate jurisdiction, the limits of which are not clearly specified, is a source of anxiety to Anglicans who fear that the way is thus open to its illegitimate or uncontrolled use." The writers of "Authority in the Church I" acknowledge the "very rigorous conditions laid down at the First Vatican Council" for "the doctrine of infallibility" as well as the fact that "the First Vatican Council intended that papal primacy should be exercised only to maintain and never to erode the structures of the local churches."[17]

I believe that in their statement "Authority in the Church II," the commission members provide a theological framework within which disagreements over infallibility between Anglicans and Roman Catholics can be overcome. But even at the end of that statement, they observe that *infallibility* "is a term applicable unconditionally only to God, and that to use it of a human being, even in highly restricted circumstances, can produce many misunderstandings."

15. Lutheran–Roman Catholic Dialogue (U.S.), "Teaching Authority and Infallibility in the Church: Lutheran Reflections," in ibid., no. 16.

16. Ibid., nos. 4–5.

17. Anglican–Roman Catholic International Commission, "Authority in the Church I," *The Final Report* (London: Catholic Truth Society and Society for the Promotion of Christian Knowledge, 1982), no. 24c–d.

They also note sadly that "the ascription to the bishop of Rome of infallibility under certain conditions has tended to lend exaggerated importance to all his statements."[18] My point is simply to demonstrate that the First Vatican Council posed for those outside of the Roman Catholic communion a further serious obstacle to reunion, precisely as the French minority bishops had predicted.

Why were those bishops able to foresee so clearly the difficulties a definition of papal infallibility would raise for those not in communion with Rome? Probably their contact with French Protestants gave them both information and a sense of the actual effects that such a definition would have, as well as a pastoral concern for the reunion of the church. They could tell that the definition of papal infallibility would postpone the day of that reunion.

Similarly, it was probably again their contact with French society, awash with new ideas from the Enlightenment, the French Revolution, and modern science, that gave them a sensitivity to the difficulties the definition would pose for modern minds. Here again, the group showed prophetic insight.

Bernard Lonergan dates the beginning of the shift in theology's context at 1680: "Then it was that Herbert Butterfield placed the origins of modern science, then that Paul Hazard placed the beginning of the Enlightenment, then that Yves Congar placed the beginning of dogmatic theology." He adds ironically, "When modern science began, when the Enlightenment began, then the theologians began to reassure one another about their certainties."[19] This process of reassurance can be seen in some way to peak in the concern to clarify the pope's role in the teaching office of the church in the middle of the nineteenth century at the First Vatican Council. But by then, despite their concern for reassurance, theologians were increasingly living in what Dietrich Bonhoeffer named "a world . . . come of age," its vision emerging from what Lonergan has called a "classicist world-view" into "historical-mindedness."[20]

18. Anglican–Roman Catholic International Commission, "Authority in the Church II," *The Final Report*, no. 32.
19. Bernard Lonergan, "Theology in Its New Context," *A Second Collection* (Philadelphia: Westminster Press, 1974), p. 55.
20. Dietrich Bonhoeffer to Eberhard Bethge, 8 June 1944, in Dietrich Bonhoeffer, *Letters and Papers from Prison*, ed. Eberhard Bethge (New York: Macmillan, 1967), p. 168; Bernard Lonergan, "The Transition from a Classicist World-View to Historical-Mindedness," in *A Second Collection*, pp. 1–2.

The French minority shared the theologians' concern for reassurance, but they also had some awareness of the movement I have been describing. Some had tried their hand at a modern apologetic—Dupanloup in catechetics, Meignan in scriptural exegesis, Ginoulhiac in dogmatic theology, Maret in church-state relations. Others as well, if they were not instructors, yet knew enough about the implications of the turmoil of their times to sense that a definition of papal infallibility was not in touch with them. I do not mean that they approved, or even could have spoken, of the shift to historical-mindedness. But I do mean that if they themselves were not making the shift, they at least vaguely sensed that many were making it.

Their knowledge of the modern mentality may also have contributed to their wise advice against the passage of formulations that could easily be misunderstood. Dupanloup had warned: "Doubtless here theologians will be able to distinguish the nuances and the fine points and to show that this is not exactly a definition, but how will the multitude of those who are not theologians discern that the pope who is fallible even as pope in such and such an act is no longer fallible in this or that other act? . . . In the eyes of the public, that will still be infallibility." This misunderstanding began soon after the council. Meignan complains of "the false idea that lay people have of the *Syllabus* and of pontifical infallibility through a lack of clear and precise explanations." Writing on the abuse to which the definition of 1870 has been subjected, Thils comments: "Certain pastors have tirelessly continued to defend and to exalt the papacy. The Catholic faithful, when they were in the grip of a doctrinal difficulty, turned then to the pope as toward the possessor of a charism which assures omniscience. . . . For many, the pope is the infallible teacher—if not in theory, at least in fact—in any statement of some importance." Congar also notes the tendency to attribute infallibility to the ordinary magisterium of the pope, as well as "a real inflation of the category of infallibility." And the Lutheran–Roman Catholic statement on infallibility comments sadly, "Often for the popular mind, and also in theological manuals, it [the dogma] was thought to imply that all papal utterances are somehow enhanced by infallibility."[21] The French minority bishops foresaw this confusion, and now their hesitation seems like prudence.

21. Dupanloup, *Observations sur la controverse*, p. 41; Meignan, "Mémoires sur l'état

To manifest the credibility of the council, the French minority often urged that its proceedings be unhurried and that its decision be unanimous. These insights were ignored by their contemporaries after the council. Yet they cause us a century later, after witnessing the unhurried pace and moral unanimity of the Second Vatican Council, to wonder about the reliability of the First Vatican Council. It is not reassuring to examine the oddly circular reasoning of some French minority bishops after the council, when they decided to leave rather than vote *non placet* and thereby destroy the council's appearance of unanimity. Their concern for the order and peace of the church led them to construct an ex post facto unanimity. This reasoning did not equal in insight their earlier insistence on the value of unanimity. That earlier insistence remains their more valuable contribution to us on the importance of unanimity for the credibility and proclamation of conciliar teaching.

In their arguments based on the purpose of infallibility as the good of the church, the French minority often seem prophetic now in the accuracy with which they read the signs of the times.

The Church as the Subject of Infallibility

The French minority bishops often manifested their conviction that the church is the subject of infallibility. In arguments before the decree was promulgated, this issue emerges repeatedly in the discussions of the definability and of the truth of the teaching. After the council, in both material and formal arguments, the bishops continue to manifest this conviction.

These bishops had a good sense of the way dogmatic definitions "carry with them and express the consent of the whole community."[22] This sense led them to insist on careful scholarship when the texts from Scripture and the history of the church were examined. They understood these texts to express the mind of the church in

---

présent de l'église et sur les préoccupations des esprits en France," p. 345; Thils, *L'infaillibilité pontificale,* p. 254; Yves Congar, "Infaillibilité et indéfectibilité," *Revue des sciences philosophiques et théologiques* 54 (1970):607–8; U.S. Lutheran–Roman Catholic Dialogue, "Teaching Authority and Infallibility in the Church: Common Statement," no. 2.

22. From a *relatio* of *Lumen gentium,* quoted in Harry McSorley, "Some Forgotten Truths about the Petrine Ministry," *Journal of Ecumenical Studies* 11 (1974):234.

earlier ages, and this mind seemed to bind them as much as the present church's mind. In their insistence on this, the French minority frequently showed a rich sense of the church in time, with all of its diversity of insights. Their understanding that dogmas defined infallibly express the faith of the whole church was another reason that they emphasized the need for unanimity among conciliar members and the need for the *consensus ecclesiae*. It led them as well to remind their hearers that a council never advocates the views of only one school of theologians. Because of their sense that the entire church was the subject of infallibility, they also pointed out weaknesses which we recognize today even in the final formulation of the definition. It is many of these weaknesses that led to the misunderstandings mentioned in the last section. Clarification of the formulation constituted one of the major tasks for Roman Catholic theologians as they sought to explain the teachings of the council after its close.[23] After noting the widespread misunderstandings of papal infallibility, Thils gives some hint of his work's purpose when he notes, "Before declaring that infallibility is nonsense, one must find out what it is exactly and to what it pertains."[24]

If the French minority bishops were correct in grasping the need to take into account these factors—the witness of Scripture and theological tradition, the need for unanimity, and the need to avoid endorsing the views of a single theological school or formulating an unclear dogmatic definition—they nonetheless failed to grasp what a subsequent, more historically conscious Catholic theology came to call the development of dogma. Aubert writes: "In spite of judicious and often very learned remarks regarding the limits of pontifical infallibility and about the participation of the bishops in the infallible magisterium of the Church, the minority remained most of the time in a perspective of 'theological fixedness,' incapable of giving a role to the development of dogma."[25] The French minority bishops often

---

23. The attempts at explanation are too numerous to list; it is the constant task of Roman Catholic commentaries on this subject. See, for example, Newman, "Letter to the Duke of Norfolk"; Fessler, *The True and the False Infallibility of Popes*; and, more recently, Thils, *L'infaillibilité pontificale*; Dejaifve, *Pape et évêques au premier concile du Vatican*; Georges Dejaifve, *"Ex sese, non autem ex consensu ecclesiae," Eastern Churches Quarterly* 14 (1962):360–78; McSorley, "Some Forgotten Truths," pp. 232–34; Jean-Marie Tillard, "The Horizon of the 'Primacy' of the Bishop of Rome," *One in Christ* 12 (1976):5–33.

24. Thils, *L'infaillibilité pontificale*, p. 255.   25. Aubert, *Vatican I*, p. 223.

conceived the Catholic faith as a body of truths, which had been given as a deposit to the church at the start of its life. If theologians disagreed among themselves about some teaching, that in itself showed that the teaching could not be a part of the body of truths known always, everywhere, and by everyone.

We should not underestimate how radically this "archaizing theological mentality"[26] affected the thought of these bishops. Although on one level, they sought to be faithful to the demands of history, we must conclude that they had barely begun to perceive the full ramifications of the questions posed by the historicity of understanding. Maret made the unchanging constitution of the church the whole basis for his argument against the definition. Ginoulhiac maintained that, of the two kinds of revealed truths, practical and speculative, those practical truths necessary for Christian life are never doubted by believers. Such certitude is the necessary evidence for their definition. Even Meignan—one of the few biblical scholars of his day who really grasped the implications of modern critical exegesis—still used his understanding of critical exegesis primarily within this vision of a fixed body of truths. The Scriptures must be correctly interpreted, he argued, according to their meaning at the time of composition, not in the terms of later imposed meanings. He concluded from this, however, that papal infallibility could not be found in the Scriptures with the certitude that the schema argued. In short, although the French minority bishops were painfully conscious of history and variation within theology, they opted in favor of the unchanging and immutable to describe those truths necessary for saving faith. An elaboration of a theory of development of dogma would fall to other thinkers.

That the church itself is the subject of infallibility so impressed itself upon the French minority bishops that they made the witness of those voting in favor of *Pastor aeternus* a cause of their own final acceptance of the decree. Although there is a certain logic in this argument, it does not stand as an example of careful thinking. Its main faults lie in the substitution of obedience for a true theory of reception and in the French minority's failure to take seriously the significance of their own numbers when combined with the rest of the minority. As a whole, the minority made up not a negligible

26. Ibid., p. 116.

proportion of the council members, and their opposition to *Pastor aeternus* was significant for judging whether the council had achieved the unanimity the French minority saw as so important. But the French minority seemed to overlook their own significance. A more creditable act, if not theory, of reception can be found elsewhere, in their arguments on the material authority of the decree.

The conviction that the church is the subject of infallibility served also as the strong hermeneutical principle that allowed the French minority bishops to interpret the conciliar decree in a way that they could find acceptable. Although even Dechamps, ultramontanist archbishop from Malines, had assured the minority bishops that papal infallibility was not separate, personal, or absolute,[27] the French minority bishops remained unconvinced. Only after they examined the decree and reflected further after the council were they able to be at peace that the decree could be read in such a way that it did not imply the separate, personal, absolute infallibility of the pope. Instead, they argued, the pope, under certain conditions, can speak with that infallibility which is first given to the church. His infallibility is not other than that of the church. The French minority bishops' opposition to the schema was based on their fear that a separate, personal, absolute papal infallibility would be proclaimed. Their ability to say that, after all, the council had not done this can aid us in our interpretation of *Pastor aeternus* today. To read into the decree an ultramontanist interpretation does not give enough credit to the judgment of these bishops, who were able to stay in full communion with the Roman Catholic Church without changing their basic convictions. If we take seriously their reception of *Pastor aeternus,* we should read it with the help of their eyes.

In fact, it is their interpretation of the decree that seems clearly to have come to dominate today's understanding of *Pastor aeternus.* The Second Vatican Council reaffirms the ancient foundation of the French minority's presupposition when it emphasizes, "The body of the faithful as a whole, anointed as they are by the Holy One (cf. John 2:20, 27), cannot err in matters of belief."[28] In interpreting *Pastor aeternus,* many French minority bishops insisted on basing their discussion on just this ancient foundation, which affirms the reliability of the faith of the entire church. They then placed discussion of

27. Dejaifve, *Pape et évêques,* p. 95.
28. *Lumen gentium* 12, in Abbott, ed., *Documents of Vatican II,* p. 29.

the infallibility of the teaching office of the church, whether bishops or pope, within this context. While today we would emphasize a more active role for the laity than the French minority bishops did, the pattern at least of their interpretation is still widely followed. Edward Schillebeeckx can serve as an example in his discussion of papal infallibility. He begins by pointing first to this passage from the Second Vatican Council and only then explains papal infallibility in its light: "The Roman Catholic Church goes on to speak of the 'infallibility of office,' the subject of which is, on the one hand, the world episcopate in unity with the Pope and, on the other, the Pope in communion with the world's bishops and the universal faith of all Christians."[29]

In their interpretations of *Pastor aeternus,* today's theologians have also recovered from the ancient church a more lively sense of the representative quality of the bishop, who as corporate person testifies to the faith of his local church in council. Heinrich Fries and Johann Finsterhölzl explain:

Though the Councils have been considered as representations of the Church since Tertullian . . . this way of understanding the infallibility of the papal office was slow to find acceptance. The main reason for this is to be sought in the preludes to Vatican I, in the ambiguities of its texts and a one-sided exposition of its doctrines. . . . When the Pope teaches infallibly . . . he speaks as an organ of the Church, which is represented, concentrated and manifested in him.[30]

But it was just such an emphasis on the representative character of the bishops in council that many French minority bishops retained throughout their discussions during the council. Some extended this idea of a representative or corporate person to their interpretation of papal infallibility in *Pastor aeternus* after the council's close.

In fact, Avery Dulles comments that because of the work of the "moderates" at the First Vatican Council, the definition of papal infallibility "commits one to very little":

Minimalistically, or even strictly, interpreted, it is hardly more than an emphatic assertion that the pope's primacy, as defined in the first three chap-

29. Edward Schillebeeckx, "Infallibility of the Church's Office," in Schillebeeckx and Bas van Iersel, eds., *Truth and Certainty,* Concilium, vol. 83 (New York: Herder and Herder, 1973), p. 89.
30. *Sacramentum Mundi,* s.v. "Infallibility," by Heinrich Fries and Johann Finsterhölzl.

ters of *Pastor aeternus,* extends also to his teaching power. He is not only the first pastor but also the first teacher in the Church. In view of his special responsibility for the unity of the whole Church in the faith of the apostles, it is antecedently credible that in him the infallibility of the whole Church may come to expression.[31]

The French minority bishops were strong in their thinking on the role of the episcopate in the exercise of infallibility. They emphasized that the bishops were truly judges of the faith and thus that the accord of bishops with the pope was necessary to proclaim a dogmatic definition. In their frequent emphasis on the bishops' role, the French minority bishops should not be understood primarily to be reinforcing their own authority. Rather, they reflect in this emphasis an understanding of the church as communion. It is to the apostles as a group, they often remind their hearers, and not only to Peter, that Christ entrusted his commission to teach. Only this group, then, was the adequate judge of teaching, and for the French minority bishops that judging was a significant task. Some bishops seemed to see bishops as the unique carriers of the capacity to make this judgment for the entire church. Others emphasized more the role of bishops as representatives of their local churches. All, however, conceived infallibility as exercised by the church as subject, and for them it seemed self-evident that this meant a group.

A good number of the minority bishops at the council, according to Aubert, were basically satisfied with the decree, but they had hoped to see the obligation of papal teaching to rely on the tradition of the entire church stated more explicitly.[32] In fact, the schema was modified to meet many of the fears the minority bishops expressed about the reduction of episcopal authority. While noting these modifications, we can nevertheless share Dejaifve's regret that "the constitution *Pastor aeternus* was not more explicit concerning the collegial magisterium of the teaching Church."[33]

The Second Vatican Council made progress in correcting this omission in a more balanced picture of the church's infallibility by emphasizing that the entire body of the faithful does not err in mat-

31. Avery Dulles, "Papal Authority in Roman Catholicism," in Peter J. McCord, ed., *A Pope for all Christians?* (New York: Paulist Press, 1976), p. 64.

32. Aubert, "L'ecclésiologie au concile du Vatican," p. 270.

33. Dejaifve, in *Pape et évêques,* traces many modifications of the final decree made in response to minority fears about reducing episcopal authority. For the quotation see p. 136.

ters of faith and by making explicit the collegiality of the body of bishops in their role as teachers and judges of the faith. These theological developments would have pleased the French minority bishops. Yet I wonder if they would not have urged the Second Vatican Council to go further in underlining the communal nature of the teaching office in the church. By this I do not mean that the French minority envisioned an active teaching role for the laity. Some of them still use the phrase "teaching church" to refer to the episcopate. But even this understanding often included the sense of the representative role of the bishop, testifying to the faith of his local church in council with other bishops who testified in like manner about their own local churches. At the core of the French minority bishops' emphasis on episcopal authority lies an ecclesiology of communion, rather than one of pyramidal structure. Rather than understanding the pope as basis for the church's unity and truth, the French minority believed instead that he expressed that unity and truth, serving as "a ministry of communion, unity and expression of the common faith."[34] I think it was this ecclesiology of communion, with its corresponding view of the papacy, that led them to fear so deeply a separate, personal, absolute papal infallibility. It was also this ecclesiology of communion that lay behind, without necessitating, the gallicanism that Butler, among others, believes was definitively "ruled out" at the council.[35]

Today we can see easily that the Second Vatican Council points us toward an ecclesiology of communion, which needs now to be further developed. The French minority bishops give us some sense of what such an ecclesiology would look like. Does not this also suggest that even their moderate gallicanism might well be an opinion to be reconsidered so as to retrieve sound elements from it that may be of positive value for a contemporary ecclesiology of communion? If the French minority's concern about the rights of bishops was a theoretical concern, it was for many also a very practical worry. The minority as a whole, writes Aubert, feared the tendency "in practice to annihilate the episcopate."[36] They feared, as Dupanloup expressed it,

34. The phrase is used by Congar in discussing this distinction in ecclesiologies made by Klaus Schatz about the German minority bishops. Congar is reviewing the book of Schatz, *Kirchenbild und Päpstliche Unfehlbarkeit*, in his "Bulletin d'ecclésiologie," p. 287; see also Jean-Marie Tillard, "The Church of God Is a Communion," *One in Christ* 17 (1981):117–31.

35. Butler, *Vatican Council*, 1:24.   36. Aubert, *Vatican I*, p. 117.

that the definition of papal infallibility would reduce their role as judges to that of mere echoes. This concern extended into the discussion of both papal primacy and papal infallibility. The minority, notes Wilfrid Dewan, were not satisfied by simple assurances that the jurisdiction of the pope would not interfere with their own jurisdiction; they were concerned to clarify how, in the concrete, these two jurisdictions would work together in their dioceses.[37] Darboy, the incisive leader of the French minority, had behind him the bitter experience of Rome's heavy-handed intervention in his diocesan affairs. He and the bishops he led knew the practical dangers to episcopal authority that could flow from an overemphasis on the papacy, what Colet darkly called "Italianism" in a letter to Foulon after the council. And in fact, Aubert writes, the council's failure to specify limitations on papal primacy has encouraged undue interventions by pope and curia into the life of the church.[38]

Do we not have much to learn from the practical insights of the French minority bishops about the concrete undermining of bishops' authority? How often in ecumenical discussion have the fears expressed grown largely out of the centralized exercise of the papal primacy and teaching office! As the Anglican–Roman Catholic International Commission's statement on authority succinctly expresses it, "Although primacy and conciliarity are complementary elements of *episcope* it has often happened that one has been emphasized at the expense of the other, even to the point of serious imbalance."[39] If we must work on formulating a new ecclesiology of communion, we also have a long way to go until it is implemented.

The Exercise of Infallibility as Judged on the Basis of Evidence

The French minority bishops believed that the ecclesial character of infallibility implied the need to judge whether infallibility had been, or was being, exercised. They believed that certain signs would provide the evidence sufficient for such judgments.

37. Wilfrid Dewan, " 'Potestas vere episcopalis' au premier concile du Vatican," in Yves Congar and B. D. Dupuy, eds., *L'épiscopat et l'église universelle* (Paris: Editions du Cerf, 1962), p. 671.
38. Aubert, "L'ecclésiologie au concile du Vatican," pp. 283–84.
39. Anglican–Roman Catholic International Commission, "Authority in the

One sign to which they frequently refer is the free and lengthy discussion required at a truly ecumenical council. They note this point not in reference to papal infallibility but in agonized reflection on the proceedings of the council at which they found themselves called to exercise their role as judges. The French minority complained that they were not truly free. This view appears in several forms: in complaints about the council rule, in references to the moral pressure under which they felt themselves placed, in concern about the undue haste with which they felt the council was proceeding in a matter of such importance, even in the concern about the poor acoustical facilities of the meeting hall. What can we say about this charge against the council?

In past discussions of the minority, commentators have tended to dismiss their complaint that the council was not free. Mourret cites the journal of Icard: "The Vatican Council incontestably had enough liberty to give value to its acts. There was freedom of speech and a moral freedom in voting." Noting that all deliberative assemblies always exert some moral pressure on their members, Icard notes that the Holy Spirit uses even human passions to accomplish his intentions for a council. Butler concludes at the end of his chapter on the liberty of the council: "When all has been weighed up, the fact stands out that there was no real interference with freedom of speech, or thoroughness of discussion, or independence of voting; and so the oecumenicity of the Vatican Council cannot properly be called in question on the score of defect of liberty." Dejaifve, in a slightly more cautious confirmation of this view, writes: "In spite of these restrictions, in spite even of the pressure from without and within the assembly,—inevitable when men meet to decide upon a common action, even when they are 'men of God, gathered together in the Holy Spirit' . . .—it is scarcely arguable that the fathers did not enjoy, at the Vatican Council, the freedom essential to every deliberative assembly." In support of his position, Dejaifve cites the witness of Ollivier and of the published record of the conciliar speeches. The mere existence of a minority as well as a majority and the freedom to articulate different views, he argues, show that the council was free. More recently, Aubert holds the same position in his book on the council. He notes the general freedom of expression, assembly, and voting which the minority enjoyed, even though he reports as well the pressure of the French press and the interventions and attitude of Pius IX, which he regards as regrettable. He agrees with Icard that the council, if lacking full and perfect liberty, yet had enough liberty of expression and voting that its acts were valid. Finally, in his book on the minority, Hasler has taken the opposite stand, arguing with the Old Catholics that the council was not free. Even the debate during the council, he argues, shows no real discussion of the doctrine to be defined.[40]

The question of the liberty of the council is too large to resolve here, although Aubert's reflections seem, of those cited, the most judicious. But I offer two observations about the liberty which the French minority said they lacked. First, in their concern for conciliar liberty, they again anticipate the insights and procedures of the Second Vatican Council, which encouraged an atmosphere of open discussion and lengthy and careful preparation of conciliar decrees. Second, the subjective impression of the minority present at the council should be understood to be an important part of the evidence in arriving at an answer to the question of whether the council was truly free. Surely it is a puzzling oversight to ignore the repeated complaints of these bishops that they feared for the liberty of the council. In juridical or moral questions, we would not hesitate to include the subjective state of the person as important for our considerations of his freedom. Yet at times the complaints of the minority bishops seem to be ignored or dismissed in favor of some more "observable" criteria such as their right to speak or their freedom of assembly. Surely the perception by many of these bishops that the council lacked adequate liberty suggests at least that their own response to it afterward involved a significant crisis of conscience. When combined with their pleas for unanimity, does not this question about the council's liberty raise for us some serious questions about the council's validity?[41]

40. Mourret, *Le concile du Vatican*, pp. 148–49; Butler, *Vatican Council*, 2:208; Dejaifve, *Pape et évêques*, pp. 22–23; Aubert, *Vatican I*, pp. 244–46; Hasler, *Pius IX*, 1:170–77, 327–31.

41. There are, of course, also reasons to question the council's ecumenicity such as its exclusion from voting of the Orthodox and of those other Christian communions which Vatican II suggested were part of the Church of Christ; see Luis M. Bermejo, "The Venice Statement and Vatican I," *Bijdragen* 39 (1978):244–69; Yves Congar,

Because the French minority bishops believed that infallibility was exercised ecclesially, they sought other evidence on whose basis Christians could judge the presence of that clarity and certitude required for definitions of the faith. With this intention, they frequently note that Scripture and the history of theology and of the church fail to provide the clear and unanimous support necessary. We have seen that this concern with the witness from the past shows in part the French minority's conviction that the church is subject of infallibility, but such witness also functioned for them as a criterion of certitude.

Hasler notes the importance of critical reflection on the theological and historical reasoning of the minority.[42] Such critical reflection shows both strengths and weaknesses. On one hand, they used scriptural and historical materials with a somewhat static and mechanical method. Even those who acknowledge the possibility of a development in the church's understanding, such as Ginoulhiac and Meignan, do not envision such a development in a matter so basic to the faith. At times they seem to treat Scripture and tradition as though they were containers of clear propositions; unless all of these propositions were in unambiguous agreement with each other, no definition could be considered. In addition, of course, they rarely applied methods of historical criticism to texts they examined.

On the other hand, their almost mechanical commitment to thoroughness gave them a good overall sense of Scripture and the history of the tradition. They often stress the importance of scriptural texts, such as those on the authority of the apostles, which the schema has one-sidedly ignored. Meignan criticizes the schema for its distorted interpretation of the scriptural texts, and he argues that papal infallibility cannot be proven from the New Testament at all. Other bishops criticize distortions they find in the use of texts from earlier thinkers, or they point out the inconsistency of enforcing faith in a teaching denied implicitly or explicitly by former theologians or

---

"1274–1974: Structures ecclésiales et conciles dans les relations entre Orient et Occident," *Revue des sciences philosophiques et théologiques* 58 (1974):355–90; Francis Dvornik, "Which Councils Are Ecumenical?" *Journal of Ecumenical Studies* 3(1966):314–28; Richard McBrien in John Kirvan, ed., *The Infallibility Debate* (New York: Paulist Press, 1971), pp. 49–51; Harry McSorley in ibid., p. 93, n. 105; McSorley, "Some Forgotten Truths," pp. 234–35.

42. Hasler, *Pius IX*, 1:7.

saints. Their commitment to thoroughness, in short, at least forces them to deal with a wider range of material than they found the majority willing to face. Especially instructive to us is the insistence of the French minority on fidelity to history. For them, theological assertions must always take historical events into account. The example many gave was the case of Honorius,[43] but several gave other examples and Dupanloup made a list of events from history which he thought a definition of papal infallibility would contradict. Their desire for thoroughness, their drive for certitude, and their static notion of the church's understanding of the faith all combine to give the French minority bishops a keen sense, not of historical method, but at least of attention to history as a locus for theologizing. Ford suggests that the debates at the council might be understood as disagreements about the correct relationship between historical critique and theological inquiry or, again, as a methodological conflict between historical and systematic approaches to theology.[44] In this debate, the position of the French minority bishops gives a surprising foretaste of the modernist crisis to come. And their carefulness, as represented in the warning of de Las Cases, can still instruct us: "To deny historical facts or destroy them with the most trifling hypotheses, to shun the words of the most ancient and renowned fathers or else to interpret them in a new way, as we often see done, to introduce new prerogatives as though they were very old, while in the most certain documents of history the ancient church was utterly unaware of them— what else would this be but to take up the side of the skeptics themselves?"[45]

The rest of the French minority's search for sufficient evidence by which to judge the exercise of infallibility might be summed up in their last effort to include the phrase "relying on the testimony of the churches" in the text. In this eleventh-hour effort, we see their arguments on the importance of formulating the conditions under which a pope would exercise infallibility, the need for consensus of the

---

43. Thils writes, "It is easily understood that the opponents of infallibility found in this fact [the condemnations of Honorius] a weighty argument: if one insists on the minimal conditions demanded for a dogmatic definition by certain enthusiasts of infallibility, the condemnations of Honorius acquire considerable authority" (*L'infaillibilité pontificale*, p. 40).

44. Ford, "Infallibility," pp. 286, 300.   45. Mansi 52:342B–C.

church as evidence of its exercise, and the importance of the accord of bishops. We have seen how these arguments emphasize the church as the subject of infallibility, but here we also see in them an understanding of the church's consensus as evidence that infallibility could be, or had been, exercised. But the council, fearing gallicanism, introduced the phrase "and not from the consent [*consensus*] of the Church."[46]

Aubert has noted the unfortunate wording of this phrase, which seems to isolate the pope from the church and thereby confirm precisely the fears of the minority bishops about a separate, personal, absolute papal infallibility.[47] The theological commission at the Second Vatican Council recognized the same danger.[48] It is not hard to see why the French minority felt they could not in conscience vote for such a formulation.

Today we recognize that this formulation wished to exclude only an understanding of infallibility's exercise that would juridically bind the pope to seek a vote from the bishops. Aubert explains that "the Vatican Council had no intention of denying that the pope, the voice of tradition, should always remain in close contact with the *mind* [*sensus*] *of the Church* in order to exercise his infallible magisterium." Thils, in another explanation, points out that the council presupposed that the pope's teaching be in doctrinal accord (*consensio*) with revelation, but not necessarily by an act of assent (*consensus*). "If the Fathers of Vatican I did not insist on this point," he explains, "it is because the distinction between *consensus* (act of assent) and *consensio* (real agreement concerning the doctrine) was not clearly formulated from the beginning." He adds, "The anti-gallicanism of the majority was unfortunate in this regard." Dejaifve explains that the council recognized the moral necessity for the consent of the church in the exercise of conciliar or papal infallibility, but it feared to make consent a juridical condition.[49]

If we recognize that the formulation does not exclude, but indeed presupposes, the pope's agreement with the faith of the entire church, we can yet regret that the depth of the minority's insight on

46. Aubert, *Vatican I*, p. 235.
47. Ibid.; see also Aubert, "L'ecclésiologie au concile du Vatican," p. 281.
48. Their remarks were drawn to my attention by McSorley, "Some Forgotten Truths," p. 219; see his discussion of the phrase, pp. 232–34.
49. Aubert, *Vatican I*, p. 235; Thils, *L'infaillibilité pontificale*, p. 250; Dejaifve, *Pape et évêques*, p. 130.

infallibility's exercise was lost. I suggest that this insight lay in the epistemology of the French minority bishops.

I have suggested that behind the arguments on the church as subject lay an ecclesiology of communion. In a similar way, behind the arguments on the ecclesial exercise of infallibility lay an epistemology that was perhaps slightly less inadequate than that of the majority. I think that the search for evidence by the French minority manifests an implicit, groping acknowledgment that human knowing—even the knowing of what is part of the deposit of faith—involves a judgment of the human mind.

Thils notes the majority's belief that the pope, if he defined, would, because of the promises of Christ, be faithful to revelation. The others, "arguing from the fact that divine assistance is not a revelation," demanded human "efforts" to safeguard the truth of his definitions.[50]

How does human reason aided by God's assistance determine whether a teaching should be defined? How does it learn whether a definition, already made, was in fact an exercise of infallibility? These were key questions for the French minority, and to them the majority seemed at times not even to have wrestled with the problems the questions posed. The French minority answered these questions with the search for sufficient evidence. Inherent in this idea of evidence is the realization, as Lonergan has explained it, that human knowing is more than merely seeing.[51] If knowing is like seeing, then knowing whether a teaching is part of the deposit of faith could be learned simply by taking a look. But if knowing involves a more complex set of operations, if it is fundamentally not intuitive but discursive, culminating in judgment that is based upon grasping evidence as sufficient, then the church can know that a teaching could be, or had been, defined only through grasping that the teaching has satisfied certain conditions.

This is not a juridical insight, but rather an understanding of the difference between something merely hypothesized and something actually known. The very question that the French minority felt

50. Thils, *L'infaillibilité pontificale*, p. 198.
51. For a brief account of Lonergan's explanation of human knowing, see the first chapter of his *Method in Theology* (New York: Herder and Herder, 1972). For a longer account, see his *Insight: A Study of Human Understanding* (New York: Philosophical Library, 1957).

bound to ask and answer—Is the proposed teaching definable?—
shows the discursive model of human knowing with which they
were operating. The long lists of criteria whose fulfillment would
serve as sufficient evidence of infallibility's exercise similarly show, in
an obscure way, the French minority's recognition that knowledge,
even divinely assisted knowledge, finally must include the step of
judgment, a step which ipso facto involves the grasp of evidence as
sufficient. The French minority did not say that such grasp of evidence as sufficient makes a proposed teaching true. Rather, they said
that the grasp of evidence as sufficient is the means by which the
church, subject of infallibility, comes to know that a proposed
teaching could be defined, or that a definition has been correctly
made.[52] That is, they saw that human knowing does not create the
order of being, but they also grasped dimly that the order of being
can be known by humans only through the discursive operations of
the human mind.

I am not saying that the French minority knew in detail the episte-
mological principles which transcendental realists have recognized
and which Lonergan has explicated with special clarity. Rather, I am
saying that their insistence on evidence which the church must grasp
as sufficient manifests an accurate, if not expressly articulated, understanding of cognition.

This understanding of cognition is closely tied to their emphasis
on infallibility's ecclesial character. Because they took knowing to include judgment, they maintained the possibility of error in judgment. They saw that even popes had made such errors, and they concluded that God's assistance to his church made use of the human
mind in a self-correcting communal setting, where one's error in
judgment could be corrected by another. They did not think human
knowing was like a vision—it was not inspiration, insisted Ginoulhiac—but rather the result of laborious effort. It was this knowing
that God assisted as he had promised, not by eliminating it and re-
placing it with a vision but rather by being present to the human
minds of a self-correcting community, where one's error in judgment
could be corrected by another, and only the common teaching of a
doctrine by the whole church was adequate evidence that the church

52. See Werner Küppers, "Reception, Prolegomena to a Systematic Study," in
World Council of Churches, *Councils and the Ecumenical Movement,* World Council of
Churches Studies 5 (Geneva: World Council of Churches, 1966), pp. 442–65.

was speaking by the Holy Spirit. Thus their cognitional theory, though grasped but dimly, goes hand in hand with their emphasis on the ecclesial character of infallibility.

It seems that the French minority took the teaching of the First Vatican Council after its close to represent such a consensus—for them the promulgation of *Pastor aeternus* by a pope or a council served as evidence sufficient for their own judgment to accept the doctrine. We can see that they were not entirely consistent with the depth of their earlier epistemology. But that earlier thought is so strong that in it we can still find tools with which to judge even this later, weaker reasoning.

Conclusion

In their strengths and their weaknesses, the French minority bishops have much to teach us. We should avoid their static understanding of the development of dogma and their collapse of reception into obedience. But we might well make our own their lively sense of the modern spirit, their concern for reunion among Christians, their ecclesial emphasis in interpreting *Pastor aeternus,* their strong emphasis on the authority of the bishop, their belief in free and careful investigation, their commitment to history, their prudent insistence on evidence by which the actual or potential exercise of infallibility could be judged. Their thought yields a rich theological crop if we will take time to harvest it.

In addition to these particular theological insights, however, the French minority also teach us something about the breadth of the church. On many issues, these bishops had very different views from those held by the majority at the council. Yet they still found a place in the Roman Catholic Church, and they even contributed to the development of the Second Vatican Council's thought in a way they could not have foreseen.

Perhaps this fact illustrates quite simply that central conviction of the French minority bishops: it is to the whole church that God's assistance has been promised. Theologians whose views are ignored or rejected during their lives might yet be shown to have contributed to the church's teaching of the truth. The breadth of the church extends backward and forward through time, and outward to include even those whom we call "minorities." The French minority bishops would be glad that we remember this breadth.

Appendix

Texts of the Proposed Schema and of Pastor aeternus*

First Dogmatic Constitution on the
Church of Christ
Proposed for the
Consideration of the Most
Reverend Fathers
(9 May 1870)

First Dogmatic Constitution
on the
Church of Christ
[*Pastor aeternus*]
(18 July 1870)

Pius, bishop, servant of the servants of God, with the approval of the sacred Council, for everlasting memory of the matter. The eternal shepherd and bishop of our souls, in order to perpetuate the salutary work of his redemption until the consummation of the world, determined to establish the holy Church, in which, as in the house of the living God,[1] all the faithful might be held together by the bond of one sole faith and one sole charity. Therefore, for this reason, before he was glorified, he prayed to the Father that those who believe in

[1]Cf. 1 Tim. 3:15.

Pius, bishop, servant of the servants of God, with the approval of the sacred Council for everlasting memory of the matter. The eternal shepherd and bishop of our souls, in order to perpetuate the salutary work of redemption, determined to establish the holy Church, in which, as in the house of the living God, all the faithful might be held together by the bond of one faith and one charity. For this reason, before he was glorified, he prayed to the Father not for the apostles only, but for those also who would believe in him through their word, that all might be one, even as the Son himself and the Father are

*Translations are mine, done in close collaboration with Richard Toporoski. The proposed schema with its footnotes is in Mansi 52:4B–7D; *Pastor aeternus* with its footnotes is in Mansi 52:1330B–1334D. In translating these texts, I have been guided, though not determined, by the translations of *Pastor aeternus* in Broderick, trans., *Documents of Vatican I*, pp. 53–63, and in Josef Neuner and Heinrich Roos, trans. Latin into German, *The Teaching of the Catholic Church*, ed. Karl Rahner, trans. into English by Geoffrey Stevens (Staten Island, N. Y.: Alba House, 1967), pp. 220–29. At many places, however, I differ from their translations. I have taken the liberty of setting the canons from the proposed schema within their related chapters, rather than at the end of the schema as printed in Mansi, to allow easier comparison with *Pastor aeternus*. The footnotes are translated just as they appear in Mansi, excluding only Mansi's guidance on their location.

him might all be one, even as the Son himself and the Father are one.[2] Therefore, the most wise architect,[3] for the purpose of preserving this unity of faith and communion in his Church continuously, established in blessed Peter the apostle the perpetual principle and visible foundation of this twofold unity. Upon the strength of this foundation an eternal temple was to be erected; and in the firmness of this faith the Church should raise its height to heaven.[4] And because the gates of hell are arising on all sides with daily increasing hatred against this divinely established foundation, we judge it necessary for the protection, safety, and increase of the Catholic flock committed to us, with the approval of the sacred Council, to set forth for all the faithful to believe and to hold, according to the ancient and constant faith of the universal Church, the teaching about the institution, the perpetuity, and the nature of the sacred apostolic primacy, on which depends the strength and welfare of the whole Church, and to proscribe with a merited judgment of condemnation the contrary errors and those which are so destructive to the Lord's flock.

[2] Cf. John 17:1, 21 + .
[3] Cf. 1 Cor. 3:10.
[4] St. Leo the Great, Sermon 4 (in some editions 3) on the day of his consecration.

one. Therefore just as he sent the apostles whom he had chosen for himself from the world as he himself had been sent by the Father: so he willed there to be shepherds and teachers in his Church until the consummation of the world. But, in order that the episcopate itself might be one and undivided, and through priests closely united to one another the whole multitude of believers might be preserved in unity of faith and communion, he set blessed Peter over the other apostles and established in him the perpetual principle and visible foundation of this twofold unity. Upon the strength of this foundation an eternal temple was to be erected; and in the firmness of this faith the Church should raise its height to heaven.[1] And because, to overthrow the Church, if this were possible, the gates of hell are arising on all sides with daily increasing hatred against its divinely established foundation, we judge it necessary for the protection, safety, and increase of the Catholic flock, with the approval of the sacred Council, to set forth for all the faithful to believe and to hold, according to the ancient and constant faith of the universal Church, the teaching about the institution, the perpetuity, and the nature of the sacred apostolic primacy on which rests the strength and solidity of the whole Church, and to proscribe and condemn the contrary errors so destructive to the Lord's flock.

[1] St. Leo the Great, Sermon 4 (in some editions 3) on the day of his consecration.

Chapter 1: The Institution of the Apostolic Primacy in Blessed Peter.
We teach and declare, therefore, that by Christ the Lord, according to the testimony of the Gospel, primacy of jurisdiction over the whole Church of God was immediately and directly promised and bestowed on blessed Peter the apostle. For it was to Peter alone that Christ, the Son of the living God, said: And I say to you, you are Peter, and on this rock I will build my Church, and the gates of hell shall not prevail against it. And I will give you the keys of the kingdom of heaven; and whatever you shall bind on earth shall be bound also in heaven, and whatever you shall loose on earth shall be loosed also in heaven.[5] And it was upon Simon Peter alone that Jesus, after his resurrection, bestowed the jurisdiction of supreme shepherd and ruler over his entire fold, saying: Feed my lambs, feed my sheep.[6] Openly opposed to this clear teaching of the sacred Scriptures, as it has always been understood by the Catholic Church, are the damnable opinions of those who, overturning the form of government instituted by Christ the Lord in his Church, deny that Peter alone, before all the apostles, whether separately as individuals or all together, was endowed by Christ with true and proper primacy of jurisdiction; or who assert that the same primacy was not granted immediately and directly to blessed Peter himself, but to

[5]Matt. 16:18-19.
[6]John 21:15-17

Chapter 1: The Institution of the Apostolic Primacy in Blessed Peter.
We teach and declare, therefore, according to the testimony of the Gospel, that primacy of jurisdiction over the whole Church of God was immediately and directly promised and bestowed on blessed Peter the apostle by Christ the Lord. For it was to Simon alone, to whom he had long before said, "You shall be called Cephas,"[2] that the Lord—after Simon had uttered his confession, saying, "You are the Christ, the Son of the living God"—addressed these solemn words: "Blessed are you, Simon Bar-Jona, for flesh and blood did not reveal this to you, but my Father who is in heaven. And I say to you, you are Peter, and on this rock I will build my Church, and the gates of hell shall not prevail against it. And I will give you the keys of the kingdom of heaven; and whatever you shall bind on earth shall be bound also in heaven, and whatever you shall loose on earth shall be loosed also in heaven."[3] And it was upon Simon Peter alone that Jesus, after his resurrection, bestowed the jurisdiction of supreme shepherd and ruler over his entire fold, saying, "Feed my lambs; feed my sheep."[4] Openly opposed to this clear teaching of the sacred Scriptures, as it has always been understood by the Catholic Church, are the vicious opinions of those who, overturning the form of government instituted by

[2]John 1:42.
[3]Matt. 16:16-19.
[4]John 21:15-17.

the Church, and through the
Church to Peter as its minister.

Christ the Lord in his Church,
deny that Peter alone before the
other apostles, whether separately
as individuals or all together, was
endowed by Christ with true and
proper primacy of jurisdiction; or
who assert that the same primacy
was not granted immediately and
directly to blessed Peter himself,
but to the Church, and through
the Church to Peter as its
minister.

Canon 1. If anyone shall say that
blessed Peter the apostle was not
constituted by Christ the Lord as
the chief of all the apostles and as
the visible head of the entire
Church Militant; or that the same
Peter received directly and immediately from the same our
Lord Jesus Christ only a primacy
of honor, but not of true and
proper jurisdiction, let him be
anathema.

[*Canon.*] If anyone, therefore,
shall say that blessed Peter the
apostle was not constituted by
Christ the Lord as the chief of all
the apostles and as the visible
head of the whole Church Militant; or that the same Peter received directly and immediately
from the same our Lord Jesus
Christ only a primacy of honor,
but not of true and proper jurisdiction, let him be anathema.

*Chapter 2: The Perpetuity of the
Primacy of Blessed Peter in the Roman Pontiff.* That which the chief
of the shepherds and great
shepherd of the sheep, the Lord
Christ Jesus, instituted in the
blessed apostle Peter[7] for the constant welfare and unceasing good
of the Church, must, by the will
of the same founder, remain continually in the Church which,
founded on a rock, will stand
firm until the end of the world.
For no one doubts, in fact it has
been known in all ages, that the
holy and most blessed Peter,
chief and head of the apostles,

*Chapter 2: The Perpetuity of the
Primacy of Blessed Peter in the Roman Pontiff.* That which the chief
of the shepherds and great
shepherd of the sheep, the Lord
Christ Jesus, instituted in the
blessed apostle Peter for the constant welfare and unceasing good
of the Church, must, by the will
of the same founder, remain continually in the Church which,
founded on a rock, will stand
firm until the end of the world.
Certainly no one doubts, in fact
it has been known in all ages,
that that holy and most blessed
Peter, chief and head of the apostles, pillar of the faith, and
foundation of the Catholic

[7]I Pet. 5:4; Heb. 13:20.

pillar of the faith, and foundation of the Catholic Church, who received the keys of the kingdom from our Lord Jesus Christ, savior and redeemer of the human race, lives, presides over, and exercises judgment even until now and always in his successors, the bishops of the holy Roman See, which was founded by him and consecrated with his blood.[8] In consequence, whoever succeeds Peter in this chair acquires, according to the institution of Christ himself, the primacy of Peter over the whole Church. The disposition of truth remains, therefore, and blessed Peter, persevering in the strength of rock which he received, has not abandoned the government of the Church undertaken by him.[9]

Church, received the keys of the kingdom from our Lord Jesus Christ, savior and redeemer of the human race, and lives, presides, and exercises judgment even until now and always in his successors, the bishops of the holy Roman See, which was founded by him and consecrated with his blood.[5] Therefore, whoever succeeds Peter in this chair acquires, according to the institution of Christ himself, the primacy of Peter over the whole Church. The disposition of truth remains, therefore, and blessed Peter, persevering in the strength of rock which he received, has not abandoned the government of the Church undertaken by him.[6] For this reason, it has always been necessary that every church, that is, the faithful everywhere, agree with the Roman Church on account of its more powerful authority, so that in this See, from which the rights of blessed communion flow to all, they may, as members joined to the head, grow together into one united body.[7]

Canon 2. If anyone shall say that it is not by the institution of Christ the Lord himself that blessed Peter should have perpetual successors in the primacy over the whole Church; or that the

[*Canon.*] If anyone, therefore, shall say that it is not by the institution of Christ the Lord himself or by divine right that blessed Peter should have perpetual successors in the primacy over the whole Church; or that the

[8]Cf. Labbus, *Collectio conciliorum,* 3:1154. Council of Ephesus, chapter 3. Speech of Philip, legate of the Apostolic See; collection of Saint Peter Chrysologus, Letter to Eutyches the priest.
[9]St. Leo the Great, Sermon 3 (in some editions 2), chapter 3.

[5]Cf. Council of Ephesus, chapter 3.
[6]St. Leo the Great, Sermon 3 (in some editions 2), chapter 3.
[7]St. Irenaeus, *Adversus haereses,* Book 3, chapter 3; and the Council of Aquileia (381), St. Ambrose in the midst of the bishops, Letter 11.

Roman pontiff is not by divine right the successor of blessed Peter in the same primacy, let him be anathema.

Roman pontiff is not the successor of blessed Peter in the same primacy, let him be anathema.

Chapter 3: The Power and Nature of the Primacy of the Roman Pontiff. Hence, adhering first to the decree of our predecessors, the Roman pontiffs, and then to the clear and explicit definitions of previous general councils, we reaffirm the profession of faith of the Ecumenical Council of Florence. According to that profession, all Christ's faithful must believe that the holy Apostolic See and the Roman pontiff possess the primacy over the whole world; and that the Roman pontiff himself is the successor of blessed Peter the chief of the apostles and the true vicar of Christ, and that he is head of the whole Church and father and teacher of all Christians; and that to him in blessed Peter was delivered by our Lord Jesus Christ full power of feeding, ruling, and governing the universal Church; as is contained also in the acts of the ecumenical councils and in the sacred canons.

Accordingly, we teach and declare that this power, which is properly the power of episcopal jurisdiction, is ordinary and immediate; and that, in regard to it, the shepherds and faithful—both individually and collectively—of particular churches of whatever rite and dignity, are bound by the duty of hierarchical subordination and true obedience, not only in matters pertaining to faith and morals, but also in

Chapter 3: The Power and Nature of the Primacy of the Roman Pontiff. Therefore, relying on the plain testimony of the sacred writings, and adhering to the clear and explicit decrees both of our predecessors, the Roman pontiffs, and of the general councils, we reaffirm the definition of the ecumenical Council of Florence. According to that definition, all of Christ's faithful must believe that the holy Apostolic See and the Roman pontiff possess primacy over the whole world; and that the Roman pontiff himself is the successor of blessed Peter the chief of the apostles and the true vicar of Christ, and that he is head of the whole Church and father and teacher of all Christians; and that to him in blessed Peter was delivered by our Lord Jesus Christ full power of feeding, ruling, and governing the universal Church; as is contained also in the acts of the ecumenical councils and in the sacred canons.

Accordingly, we teach and declare that by the disposition of the Lord, the Roman Church possesses preeminence of ordinary power over all other churches, and that this power of jurisdiction of the Roman pontiff, which is truly episcopal, is immediate; and that, in regard to it, the shepherds and faithful—both individually and collectively—of whatever rite and dignity, those pertaining to the discipline and government of the Church spread through the whole world; so that by maintaining with the Roman pontiff both unity of communion and unity in the profession of the same faith, the Church of Christ may be one flock under one supreme shepherd.

This is the doctrine of Catholic truth, from which no one can deviate without danger to faith and salvation. Now so far is this power of the supreme pontiff from being opposed to that ordinary and immediate power of episcopal jurisdiction by which the individual shepherds of particular churches feed and rule the individual flocks assigned to them that the power of these shepherds is asserted, strengthened, and defended by the supreme and universal shepherd, as St. Gregory the Great says: My honor is the honor of the universal Church. My honor is the solid strength of my brothers. I am truly honored when the honor due to every single one is not denied.[10]

Moreover, it follows from that supreme power of jurisdiction of the Roman pontiff that the right to communicate freely with the shepherds and flocks of the whole Church in the exercise of this his office is necessary to this pontiff so that they can be taught and directed by him in the way of salvation. We condemn and reject, therefore, the opinions of those who say that this communication of the supreme head

are bound by the duty of hierarchical subordination and true obedience, not only in matters pertaining to faith and morals, but also in those pertaining to the discipline and government of the Church spread through the whole world; so that by maintaining with the Roman pontiff both unity of communion and unity in the profession of the same faith, the Church of Christ may be one flock under one supreme shepherd. This is the doctrine of Catholic truth, from which no one can deviate without danger to faith and salvation.

Now so far is this power of the supreme pontiff from obstructing that ordinary and immediate power of episcopal jurisdiction by which the bishops—who, appointed by the Holy Spirit, have succeeded to the place of the apostles—feed and rule as true shepherds the individual flocks assigned to them that the power of these shepherds is asserted, strengthened, and defended by the supreme and universal shepherd, according to the words of St. Gregory the Great: "My honor is the honor of the universal Church. My honor is the solid strength of my brothers. I am truly honored when the honor due to every single one is not denied."[8]

Moreover, it follows from that supreme power of the Roman pontiff to govern the whole Church that he has the right to communicate freely with the shepherds and flocks of the whole

[10]St. Gregory the Great to Eulogius of Alexandria, Letter 30.

[8]Letter to Eulogius of Alexandria, book 8, Letter 30.

with shepherds and flocks can be impeded licitly; or who render this communication subject to the secular power so as to contend that decisions by the Apostolic See or on its authority for the government of the Church do not have force and effect unless confirmed by the assent of the secular power.

And since, by the divine right of apostolic primacy, the Roman pontiff presides over the whole Church, we also teach and declare that he is the supreme judge of the faithful,[11] and that in all cases subject to ecclesiastical examination recourse can be had to his judgment;[12] but that a judgment of the Apostolic See, than whose authority there is no greater, must be revised by no one, nor may anyone judge its judgment.[13] They wander from the straight path of truth, therefore, who affirm that it is permissible to appeal from judgments of Roman pontiffs to an ecumenical council as to an authority superior to the Roman pontiff.

[11]Pope Pius VI, Brief *Super soliditate* (28 Nov. 1786).
[12]Ecumenical Council of Lyons II.
[13]Letter of Nicolas I to Emperor Michael.

Church in the exercise of this his office so that they can be taught and directed by him in the way of salvation. We condemn and reject, therefore, the opinions of those who say that this communication of the supreme head with shepherds and flocks can be impeded licitly; or who render this communication subject to the secular power so as to contend that decisions by the Apostolic See or on its authority for the government of the Church do not have force and effect unless confirmed by the assent of the secular power.

And since, by the divine right of apostolic primacy, the Roman pontiff presides over the whole Church, we also teach and declare that he is the supreme judge of the faithful,[9] and that in all cases subject to ecclesiastical examination recourse can be had to his judgment;[10] but that a judgment of the Apostolic See, than whose authority there is not greater, must be revised by no one, nor may anyone judge its judgment.[11] They wander from the straight path of truth, therefore, who affirm that it is permissible to appeal from judgments of Roman pontiffs to an ecumenical council as to an authority superior to the Roman pontiff.

[9]Pope Pius VI, Brief *Super soliditate* (28 Nov. 1786).
[10]Ecumenical Council of Lyons II.
[11]Letter of Nicolas I to Emperor Michael.

Canon 3. If anyone shall say that the Roman pontiff has merely the function of inspection or direction, but not full and supreme power of jurisdiction over the whole Church, not only in matters pertaining to faith and morals, but also in matters pertaining to the discipline and government of the Church spread throughout the whole world; or that this power of his is not ordinary and immediate, whether over the churches all together and individually, or over the shepherds and the faithful all together and individually, let him be anathema.

[*Canon.*] If, then, anyone shall say that the Roman pontiff has merely the office of inspection or direction, but not full and supreme power of jurisdiction over the whole Church, not only in matters pertaining to faith and morals, but also in matters pertaining to the discipline and government of the Church spread throughout the whole world; or that he has only the more important part, but not the whole fullness of this supreme power; or that this power of his is not ordinary and immediate, whether over the churches all together and individually, or over the shepherds and the faithful all together and individually, let him be anathema.

Chapter 4: The Infallibility of the Roman Pontiff. Furthermore, this Holy See has always maintained, the constant practice of the Church confirms, and the ecumenical councils themselves have handed down that supreme teaching power is also included in the supreme power of apostolic jurisdiction that the Roman pontiff, as successor of Peter the chief of the apostles, possesses over the whole Church. And so, following the solemn professions of faith especially of those general councils in which the East came together with the West into a unity of faith and love, with the Fourth Council of Constantinople we believe: The first salvation is to keep the rule of right faith, and to deviate in no way from those things established by the fathers. And because the inten-

Chapter 4. The Infallible Magisterium of the Roman Pontiff. Furthermore, this Holy See has always maintained, the constant practice of the Church confirms, and the ecumenical councils themselves—especially those councils in which the East came together with the West into a unity of faith and love—have declared that supreme teaching power is also included in the apostolic primacy itself which the Roman pontiff, as successor of Peter the chief of the apostles, possesses over the whole Church. For the fathers of the Fourth Council of Constantinople, following in the footsteps of their predecessors, gave forth this solemn profession: The first salvation is to keep the rule of right faith. And because the intention of our Lord Jesus Christ

tion of our Lord Jesus Christ when he said, You are Peter, and upon this rock I will build my Church cannot be overlooked,[14] what was said is proved by the results; because in the Apostolic See the Catholic religion has always been preserved unstained, and its teaching has been honored as holy. And Christ's faithful are obliged to follow this Apostolic See in all things, so that they may merit to be in one communion with the same See, in which resides complete and true the solidity of the Christian religion.[15] And with the Second Council of Lyons we profess: The Holy Roman Church possesses over the whole Catholic Church supreme and full primacy and preeminence, which it truly and humbly acknowledges that it has received, along with plenitude of power, from the Lord himself in blessed Peter the chief or head of the apostles, whose successor is the Roman pontiff. And just as the Roman Church is duty bound beyond all others to defend the truth of the faith, so also must any questions that arise concerning faith be defined by its judgment.[16] And with the Council of Florence we repeat: The Roman pontiff is the true vicar of Christ, and head of the whole

[14]Matt. 16:18.
[15]From the formula of Pope St. Hormisdas, just as it was proposed by Hadrian II to the fathers of the eighth ecumenical Council, Constantinople IV, and subscribed to by them.
[16]From the profession of faith put out by the Greeks in the ecumenical Council Lyons II.

when he said,[12] "You are Peter, and upon this rock I will build my Church" cannot be overlooked, what was said is proved by the results; because in the Apostolic See the Catholic religion has always been preserved unstained, and its teaching has been honored as holy. Desiring, therefore, not to be in the least degree separated from the faith and doctrine of this See, we hope that we may merit to be in the one communion which the Apostolic See preaches, in which resides complete and true the solidity of the Christian religion.[13] With the approval indeed of the Second Council of Lyons, the Greeks professed: The holy Roman Church possesses over the whole Catholic Church supreme and full primacy and preeminence, which it truly and humbly acknowledges that it has received, along with plenitude of power, from the Lord himself in blessed Peter the chief or head of the apostles, whose successor is the Roman pontiff. And just as the Roman Church is duty bound beyond all others to defend the truth of the faith, so also must any questions that arise concerning faith be defined by its judgment. Finally, the Council of Florence defined: The Roman pontiff is the true vicar of Christ, and head of the whole Church and father and teacher of all

[12]Matt. 16:18.
[13]From the formula of Pope St. Hormisdas, just as it was proposed by Hadrian II to the fathers of the eighth ecumenical Council, Constantinople IV, and subscribed to by them.

Church and father and teacher of all Christians; and to him in blessed Peter was delivered by our Lord Jesus Christ full power of feeding, ruling, and governing the universal Church.[17] Hence, with the approval of the sacred Council, we teach and declare as a dogma of faith that the Roman pontiff, to whom in the person of blessed Peter it was said, in addition to other things, by our Lord Jesus Christ himself: I have prayed for you, that your faith may not fail; and do you, when you are converted, strengthen your brothers,[18] is, by virtue of the divine assistance promised to him, unable to err when, exercising the office of supreme teacher of all Christians, in accordance with his own apostolic authority he defines what in matters of faith and morals must be held by the whole Church as a matter of faith or rejected by it as contrary to faith; and that decrees or judgments of this kind, irreformable of themselves, must be received and held with the full submission of faith by every Christian as soon as they become known to him. But, because infallibility is the same whether in the Roman pontiff as head of the Church or in the whole Church teaching in union with its head, we define in addition that this infallibility also extends to one and the same object.

[17]Cf. John 21:15-17.
[18]Luke 22:32.

Christians; and to him in blessed Peter was delivered by our Lord Jesus Christ full power of feeding, ruling, and governing the universal Church.

To satisfy this pastoral duty, our predecessors have always made untiring efforts that Christ's saving doctrine might be propagated among all the peoples of the earth, and with equal care watched that it might be preserved genuine and pure where it had been received. Therefore, the bishops of the whole world, now singly, now assembled in synods, following the long-standing custom of the churches and the form of the ancient rule, reported to this Apostolic See those dangers especially which arose in matters of faith, so that the harm to faith might be repaired there most particularly where faith cannot suffer failure.[14] Moreover, the Roman pontiffs, as the condition of the times and the circumstances recommended, sometimes convoking ecumenical councils or seeking out the mind of the Church spread throughout the world, sometimes through particular synods, sometimes using other helps which divine providence supplied, defined as to be held those things which with the help of God they had recognized as consonant with sacred Scripture and apostolic traditions. For the Holy Spirit was not promised to the successors of Peter that by his revelation they might make known new doctrine, but that by his assistance they might consci-

[14]Cf. St. Bernard, Letter 190.

entiously keep and faithfully expound the revelation or deposit of faith delivered through the apostles. And indeed it has been their apostolic doctrine that all the venerable fathers have embraced, and the holy orthodox doctors have venerated and followed, knowing most fully that this See of holy Peter remains always untouched by any error according to the divine promise of the Lord our savior made to the chief of his disciples: "I have prayed for you, that your faith may not fail; and do you, when you are converted, strengthen your brothers."[15]

This charism, therefore, of truth and faith that never fails was divinely conferred upon Peter and his successors in this chair so that they might carry out their high duty for the salvation of all; so that the whole flock of Christ, turned away by means of them from the poisonous food of error, might be nourished by the food of heavenly doctrine; so that, with the occasion of schism being removed, the whole Church might be preserved in unity and, relying on its foundation, might stand firm against the gates of hell.

But since in this present age, in which the salutary efficacy of the apostolic office is especially needed, not a few are found who disparage its authority, we judge it entirely necessary to assert solemnly the prerogative which the only-begotten son of God deigned to join to the highest pastoral office.

[15]Luke 22:32.

Therefore, faithfully adhering to the tradition understood from the beginning of the Christian faith, we, for the glory of God our savior, the exaltation of the Catholic religion, and the salvation of Christian peoples, with the approval of the sacred Council, teach and define that it is a dogma divinely revealed: that the Roman pontiff when he speaks *ex cathedra*, that is, when in discharge of the office of shepherd and teacher of all Christians, in accordance with his supreme apostolic authority he defines a doctrine regarding faith or morals to be held by the whole Church, by the divine assistance promised him in blessed Peter, is possessed of that infallibility with which the divine redeemer willed that his Church should be endowed in defining doctrine regarding faith or morals; and that therefore such definitions of the Roman pontiff are irreformable of themselves, and not from the consent [*consensus*] of the Church.

[*Canon 4.*] If anyone, God forbid, shall presume to contradict this our definition, let him know that he has fallen away from the truth of the Catholic faith and from the unity of the Church.

[*Canon.*] Now if anyone, God forbid, shall presume to contradict this our definition, let him be anathema.

Bibliography

Unpublished Sources

Archives Nationales, Paris

AB XIX 522: Dupanloup papers on religious affairs
AB XIX 524: French minority bishops' correspondence
AB XIX 526: Correspondence to Dupanloup

F^{19} 1.933: Papers on the First Vatican Council
F^{19} 1.939: Preconciliar teachings on infallibility in France by diocese
F^{19} 1.940: Papers on the First Vatican Council
F^{19} 2.448: Darboy, Dupanloup, and Mathieu dossier
F^{19} 2.500: Hugonin dossier
F^{19} 2.531: Papers on the First Vatican Council
F^{19} 2.537: Dupont des Loges dossier
F^{19} 2.551: Callot dossier
F^{19} 2.553: Dupanloup dossier
F^{19} 2.575: David dossier
F^{19} 2.588: Colet dossier
F^{19} 2.506: Guilbert dossier
F^{19} 6.177: De Las Cases dossier

Archives de l'Archevêché de Paris

4AI,1: Correspondence on the First Vatican Council
4AI,2,1^0: On Colet's "Souvenirs du concile du Vatican" and "Copie des procès-verbaux rédigés par Mgr Colet des séances tenues par les évêques de la minorité"
4AI,2,2^0: Charles Colet. "Souvenirs du concile du Vatican"
4AI,2,3^0: Charles Colet. "Copie des procès-verbaux rédigés par Mgr Colet des séances tenues par les évêques de la minorité"
4AI,3: Press clippings on the First Vatican Council

1DVII, 1: Correspondence by Darboy (1862–71)
1DVII, 4: Darboy at the First Vatican Council, dossier

4BI, 2: Dupanloup dossier
4BI, 7: Dupanloup dossier

271

Published Sources

Abbott, Walter M., ed. *The Documents of Vatican II*. New York: Guild Press, 1966.

Acton, John. *Lord Acton and His Circle*. Edited by Francis Gasquet. London: Burns and Oates, 1906.

Anglican–Roman Catholic International Commission. "Authority in the Church I," "Authority in the Church: Elucidation," and "Authority in the Church II." In *The Final Report*, pp. 47–98. London: Catholic Truth Society and Society for the Promotion of Christian Knowledge, 1982.

Aubert, Roger. "Documents concernant le tiers parti au concile du Vatican." In *Abhandlungen über Theologie und Kirche*, pp. 241–59. Festschrift für Karl Adam. Düsseldorf: Patmos-Verlag, 1952.

———. "L'ecclésiologie au concile du Vatican." In *Le concile et les conciles*, edited by D.O. Rousseau, pp.245–84. Paris and Chevetogne: Editions du Cerf and Editions de Chevetogne, 1960.

———. "La géographie ecclésiologique au XIXᶜ siècle." In Maurice Nédoncelle et al., *L'ecclésiologie au XIXᵉ siècle*, pp. 11–55. Paris: Editions du Cerf, 1960.

———. "Mgr Dupanloup et le Syllabus," *Revue d'histoire ecclésiastique* 51 (1956):79–142, 471–512, 837–915.

———. "Monseigneur Dupanloup au début du concile du Vatican." In *Miscellanea Historiae Ecclesiasticae*, pp. 96–116. Congrès de Stockholm, 1960. Louvain: Publications Universitaires de Louvain, 1961.

———. "Motivations théologiques et extra-théologiques des partisans et des adversaires de la définition dogmatique de l'infaillibilité du pape à Vatican I." In *L'infaillibilité: Son aspect philosophique et théologique*, edited by Enrico Castelli, pp.91–111. Aubier: Editions Montaigne, 1970.

———. *Le pontificat de Pie IX (1846–1878)*. Augustin Fliche and Victor Martin Series Histoire de l'église depuis les origines jusqu'à nos jours, no. 21. Paris: Bloud et Gay, 1952.

———. *Vatican I*. Paris: Editions de l'Orante, 1964.

Aubert, Roger, and Palanque, Jean-Rémy. "Lettres de Lady Blennerhassett à la Marquise de Forbin d'Oppède au lendemain du concile du Vatican." *Revue d'histoire ecclésiastique* 58 (1963):82–135.

Aubert, Roger, et al. *Concilium Vaticanum I: Concordance, index, listes de fréquence, tables comparatives*. Louvain: Publications du Centre de Traitement Electronique des Documents de l'Université Catholique de Louvain, 1977.

Audinet, J. "L'enseignement *De Ecclesia* à St-Sulpice sous le Premier Empire, et les débuts du gallicanisme modéré." In Maurice Nédoncelle et al., eds., *L'ecclésiologie au XIXᵉ siècle*, pp. 115–39. Paris: Editions du Cerf, 1960.

Bailly, Louis. *Theologia dogmatica et moralis*. 9 vols. Dijon, 1789.

———. *Tractatus de Ecclesia*. Dijon, 1771.

Bertrand, Auguste Constant. *Réponse à l'oraison funèbre de M. Colet, archevêque de Tours*. Tours: E. Arrault et Cie, 1884.

Bazin, Georges. *Faculté de Théologie de Paris: Ouverture des cours.* Paris: Jules Delalain, 1864.

———. *Vie de Mgr Maret, évêque de Sura, archevêque de Lépante, primicier de l'insigne chapitre de Saint-Denys, doyen et professeur de la Faculté de Théologie en Sorbonne.* 3 vols. Paris: Berche et Tralin, 1891.

Bécel, Jean Marie. *Oraison funèbre de Mgr David, évêque de Saint-Brieuc et Tréguier.* Vannes: Galles, 1882.

Bergier, Jean François. *Supplément à la vie du Cardinal Mathieu, en son vivant archevêque de Besançon.* Besançon: J. Bonvalot, 1883.

Bermejo, Luis M. "The Venice Statement and Vatican I." *Bijdragen* 39 (1978):244–69.

Besson, L. F. *Vie de son éminence Mgr le Cardinal Mathieu, archevêque de Besançon.* 2 vols. Paris: Bray et Retaux, 1882.

Betti, Umberto. *La costituzione dommatica "Pastor Aeternus" del concilio Vaticano I.* Rome: Pontificio Ateneo "Antonianum," 1961.

Bevenot, Maurice. "Thesis and Hypothesis." *Theological Studies* 15 (1954):440–46.

Bishop, Maria Catherine, ed. *A Memoir of Mrs. Augustus Craven* (Pauline de la Ferronnays). 2 vols. London: Richard Bentley & Son, 1894.

Boissonnot, Henri. *Le Cardinal Meignan.* Paris: Victor Lecoffre, 1899.

Bonhoeffer, Dietrich. *Letters and Papers from Prison.* Edited by Eberhard Bethge. New York: Macmillan, 1967.

Bonnefoy, F. J. E. *Oraison funèbre de son éminence le Cardinal Thomas, archevêque de Rouen.* La Rochelle: Rochelaise, 1894.

Bouvier, Jean Baptiste. *Institutiones theologicae ad usum seminariorum.* 6 vols. Mans, 1834.

Bravard, Jean. "De son prochain départ pour le saint concile du Vatican." *Revue catholique (Semaine religieuse) du diocèse de Coutances et Avranches* 3 (2 December 1869):147–50.

———. *Distribution des prix au petit-séminaire et collège diocésain de Valognes.* Valognes: G. Martin, 1854.

———. Letter to abbé Croulebois (5 January 1870). *Revue catholique (Semaine religieuse) du diocèse de Coutances et Avranches* 3 (13 January 1870):242–43.

———. Letter to abbé Croulebois (13 March 1870). *Revue catholique (Semaine religieuse) du diocèse de Coutances et Avranches* 3 (24 March 1870):404–8; (31 March 1870):423–25.

———. Letter to abbé Febvrier (8 December 1869). *Revue catholique (Semaine religieuse) du diocèse de Coutances et Avranches* 3 (16 December 1869):181–87.

———. "Lettre pastorale et mandement de Monseigneur l'évêque de Coutances et d'Avranches, au clergé et aux fidèles de son diocèse, pour le carême de 1870." *Revue catholique (Semaine religieuse) du diocèse de Coutances et Avranches* 3 (3 March 1870):354–59; (10 March 1870):371–74.

———. Pastoral Letter for Lent on Love of the Church. *Revue catholique (Semaine religieuse) du diocèse de Coutances et Avranches* 7 (12 February 1874):323–28.

———. Pastoral Letter on the Council. *Revue catholique (Semaine religieuse) du diocèse de Coutances et Avranches* 2 (17 June 1869):602–5.

———. *Société des antiquaires de Normandie: Discours prononcé par Mgr Bravard*. Coutances: Daireaux, 1872.

Broderick, John F., trans. *Documents of Vatican I, 1869–1870*. Collegeville, Minn.: Liturgical Press, 1971.

Bulletin religieux du diocèse de La Rochelle et Saintes 5 (1869)–6 (1870).

Burke, Eugene. "The General Council in the Teaching of the Church." In *The General Council*, edited by William J. McDonald, pp. 1–22. Washington, D.C.: Catholic University of America Press, 1962.

Butler, Cuthbert. *The Vatican Council: The Story Told from Inside in Bishop Ullathorne's Letters*. 2 vols. London: Longmans, Green and Co., 1930.

Cabrières, F. M. A. *Eloge funèbre de sa grandeur Mgr Etienne Emile Ramadié, archevêque d'Albi*. Montpellier: J. Martel Ainé, 1884.

Callot, Irénée. *A l'occasion de son entrée dans son diocèse*. Lyon: J. B. Pélagaud, 1867.

"Captivité et mort de Mgr Darboy." *Le correspondant* 75 (25 May 1878):577–613; (10 June 1878): 761–88.

Catta, M. *Dom Guéranger et le premier concile du Vatican*. Cenomani: J. Bouvet, 1962.

Chevallier, Gustave. *Mgr Rivet, évêque de Dijon*. Dijon: L'Union Typographique, 1902.

"Chronique diocésaine." *La chronique religieuse de Dijon et du diocèse* 5 (20 November 1869):1032–33.

La chronique religieuse de Dijon et du diocèse 5 (1869)–8 (1872).

Colet, Charles. "A l'occasion de son entrée dans son diocèse." *La semaine religieuse de la ville et du diocèse de Tours* 9 (30 January 1875):680–88.

———. "Lettre circulaire prescrivant des prières à l'occasion des élections." *La semaine religieuse de la ville et du diocèse de Tours* 10 (12 February 1876):705–8.

———. "Pour la publication de l'encyclique de Notre Père le Pape à l'occasion du jubilé de l'année sainte 1875." *Le semaine religieuse de la ville et du diocèse de Tours* 9 (13 February 1875):731–37.

———. "Sur le courage chrétien." *La semaine religieuse de la ville et du diocèse de Tours* 10 (26 February 1876):37–47.

———. "Sur les luttes de la vie chrétienne." *La semaine religieuse de la ville et du diocèse de Tours* 9 (13 February 1875):715–21.

Collectio Lacensis: Acta et decreta sacrorum conciliorum recentiorum. Vol. 7. Freiburg im Breisgau: Herder, 1890.

Congar, Yves. "Bulletin d'ecclésiologie." *Revue des sciences philosophiques et théologiques* 60 (1976):281–308.

———. "Infaillibilité et indéfectibilité." *Revue des sciences philosophiques et théologiques* 54 (1970):607–8.

———. "La 'réception' comme réalité ecclésiologique." *Revue des sciences philosophiques et théologiques* 56 (1972):369–403.

———. "Remarks on the Council as an Assembly and on the Church's Fundamentally Conciliar Nature." In *Report from Rome II: On the Second Session of the Vatican Council*, pp.173–97. Translated by Lancelot Sheppard. London: Geoffrey Chapman, 1964.

————. "1274–1974: Structures ecclésiales et conciles dans les relations entre Orient et Occident." *Revue des sciences philosophiques et théologiques* 58 (1974):355–90.

Congar, Yves, and Dupuy, B. D., eds. *L'épiscopat et l'église universelle*. Paris: Editions du Cerf, 1962.

Conzemius, Viktor. "Die Minorität auf dem Ersten Vatikanischen Konzil: Vorhut des Zweiten Vatikanums." *Theologie und Philosophie* 45 (1970): 409–34.

Cotton, Charles. *Oraison funèbre de Mgr Jacques Marie Achille Ginoulhiac, archevêque de Lyon et de Vienne, primat des Gaules*. Lyon: P. N. Josserand, 1876.

Cwiekowski, Frederick J. *The English Bishops and the First Vatican Council*. Louvain: Publications Universitaires de Louvain, 1971.

Darboy, Georges. "Des conciles récemment tenus en France." *Le correspondant* 27 (25 November 1850):193–218.

————. "Des leçons théologiques du P. Perrone." *Le correspondant* 20 (25 November 1847):521–39.

————. "Les deux puissances au moyen age." *Le correspondant* 33 (25 November 1853):161–97.

————. "Le journal de Mgr Darboy au concile du Vatican (1869–1870)." Edited by André Duval and Yves Congar. *Revue des sciences philosophiques et théologiques* 54 (1970):417–52.

————. *Lettre à M. l'abbé Combalot en réponse à ses deux lettres à Mgr l'archevêque de Paris*. Paris: Sagnier et Bray, 1851.

————. *Lettre pastorale de Mgr l'archevêque de Paris sur la divinité de Jésus-Christ et mandement pour la carême de l'année 1864*. Paris: Adrien le Clere et Cie, 1864.

————. *Mandements, lettres pastorales, etc.* Paris: Leclere, 1863–71.

————. *Nouvelle lettre à M. l'abbé Combalot en réponse à sa nouvelle attaque contre NN. SS. de Paris et d'Orléans*. Paris: Sagnier et Bray, 1851.

————. *Oeuvres pastorales*. 2 vols. Paris: Adrien le Clere, 1876.

David, Augustin. "A l'occasion du XXVᵉ anniversaire de Pie IX." *La semaine religieuse du diocèse de Saint-Brieuc et Tréguier* 4 (9 June 1871):365–66; (16 June 1871):381–83.

————. *Allocution de Mgr l'évêque de Saint-Brieuc et Tréguier à l'ouverture du Congrès de l'Association Bretonne*. Saint-Brieuc: L. Prud'homme, 1880.

————. Circular Letter on Public Prayers for the French Army. *La semaine religieuse du diocèse de Saint-Brieuc et Tréguier* 3 (6 August 1870):442–46.

————. Circular Letter to Diocese (6 January 1870). *La semaine religieuse du diocèse de Saint-Brieuc et Tréguier* 3 (29 January 1870):121–24.

————. Circular Letter to Diocese (26 May 1870). *La semaine religieuse du diocèse de Saint-Brieuc et Tréguier* 3 (4 June 1870):341–44.

————. *Le combat d'Auvours*. Saint-Brieuc: L. Prud'homme, 1874.

————. "La Foi consolatrice [incomplete]." *La semaine religieuse du diocèse de Saint-Brieuc et Tréguier* 2 (6 March 1869):181–84; (13 March 1869):193–96.

————. Letter on Confidential Letter of 17 June 1870. *La semaine religieuse du diocèse de Saint-Brieuc et Tréguier* 3 (25 June 1870):37.

————. *Note de Mgr l'évêque de Saint-Brieuc sur la fermeture du petit séminaire de Dinan.* Saint-Brieuc: L. Prud'homme, 1881.

————. *Oraison funèbre de Pie IX.* Saint-Brieuc: L. Prud'homme, 1878.

————. "Oraison funèbres." In F. L. C., *Les enfants de Saint-Brieuc morts pour la patrie en 1870–71.* Saint-Brieuc: Francisque Guyon, 1882.

————. Pastoral Letter for Lent on Church and State [incomplete]. *La semaine religieuse du diocèse de Saint-Brieuc et Tréguier* 5 (15 March 1872):205–7.

————. Pastoral Letter on Cult of St. Joseph. *La semaine religieuse du diocèse de Saint-Brieuc et Tréguier* 4 (3 March 1871):197–200; (10 March 1871):211–14.

————. "Sur la cinquantaine de S.S. Pie IX." *La semaine religieuse du diocèse de Saint-Brieuc et Tréguier* 2 (3 April 1869):229–31.

————. "Sur la nécessité de s'unir par la charité." *La semaine religieuse du diocèse de Saint-Brieuc et Tréguier* 7 (6 March 1874):193–97; (20 March 1874):218–22.

————. "Sur la situation présente." *La semaine religieuse du diocèse de Saint-Brieuc et Tréguier* 3 (7 October 1870):557–60.

————. "La Veille du Départ." *La semaine religieuse du diocèse de Saint-Brieuc et Tréguier* 3 (20 November 1869):5–7.

Debidour, Antonin. *L'église catholique et l'état sous la Troisième République (1870-1906).* 2 vols. Paris: Félix Alcan, 1906.

————. *Histoire des rapports de l'église et de l'état en France de 1789 à 1870.* Paris: Félix Alcan, 1898.

Dejaifve, Georges. "Ex sese, non autem ex consensu ecclesiae," *Eastern Churches Quarterly* 14 (1962):360–78.

————. *Pape et évêques au premier concile du Vatican.* Brussels: Desclée de Brouwer, 1961.

Denzinger, Henry, and Schönmetzer, Adolf, eds. *Enchiridion symbolorum: Definitionum et declarationum de rebus fidei et morum.* 32d ed. Freiburg im Breisgau: Herder, 1963.

Dictionnaire de la Bible. S.v. "Meignan, Guillaume René," by Octave Rey.

Dictionnaire de théologie catholique. S.v. "Bailly, Louis," by É. Dublanchy.

————. S.v. "Conciles," by J. Forget.

————. S.v. "Darboy, Georges," by A. Largent.

————. S.v. "Déclaration de 1682," by C. Constantin.

————. S.v. "Dupanloup, Félix Antoine Philibert," by A. Largent.

————. S.v. "Gallicanisme," by M. Dubruel.

————. S.v. "Ginoulhiac, Jacques Marie Achille," by E. Mangenot.

————. S.v. "Hugonin, Flavien Abel Antoine," by É. Mangenot.

————. S.v. "Libéralisme catholique," by C. Constantin.

————. S.v. "Maret, Henri Louis Charles," by E. Amann.

———. S.v. "Vatican (Concile du)," by J. Brugerette and E. Amann.

———. *Lettres choisies*. Edited by François Lagrange. 2 vols. Paris: Jules Gervais, 1888.

Dictionnaire d'histoire et de géographie ecclésiastiques. S.v. "Bravard (Jean Pierre)," by Paul Calendini.

———. S.v. "Darboy (Georges)," by François Guédon.

———. S.v. "David (Augustin)," by Roger Aubert.

———. S.v. "Dupanloup (Félix Antoine Philibert)," by Roger Aubert.

———. S.v. "Foulon (Joseph)," by Jacques Gadille.

Dizionario Ecclesiastico. S.v. "Mathieu, Adriano Giacomo Maria," by Luigi Berra.

Douhaire, P. "Le concile." *Le correspondant* 80 (10 October 1869):5–46.

Dubourg, Auguste R. M. *Oraison funèbre de Mgr Augustin David, prononcée à l'occasion de l'inauguration solennelle de son tombeau dans la cathédrale de Saint-Brieuc*. Saint-Brieuc: René Prud'homme, 1891.

Dulles, Avery. "Papal Authority in Roman Catholicism." In *A Pope for All Christians?* edited by Peter J. McCord, pp. 48–70. New York: Paulist Press, 1976.

Dupanloup, Félix. *L'athéisme et le péril social*. Paris: Charles Douniol, 1866.

———. *Avertissement adressé par Mgr l'évêque d'Orléans à M. L. Veuillot rédacteur en chef du journal "l'Univers."* Orléans: Ernest Colas, 1869.

———. *Le catéchisme chrétien: Suivi d'un sommaire de toute la doctrine du symbole par Bossuet*. Orléans: Blanchard, 1865.

———. *La convention du 15 septembre et l'encyclique du 8 décembre*. Paris: Charles Douniol, 1865.

———. *Défense de la liberté de l'église*. 2 vols. Paris: Régis Ruffet et Cie, 1861.

———. *De la pacification religieuse*. Paris: J. Lecoffre, 1845.

———. *Discours de Mgr l'évêque d'Orléans prononcé à l'Assemblée Nationale sur l'indépendance nécessaire du Saint-Siège et le calomnies répandues dans ces derniers temps contre le clergé*. Paris: Charles Douniol, 1871.

———. *Exposition des principales vérités de la foi catholique tirée des ouvrages de Fénelon*. Tours: Alfred Mame et Fils, 1870. 2d ed. 1875.

———. *Histoire de Notre-S. Jésus-Christ*. Paris: H. Plon, 1870.

———. Introductory Letter to Alcide Hyacinthe du Bois de Beauchesne, *Louis XVIII, sa vie, son agonie, sa mort*, 2 vols. Paris: H. Plon, 1871.

———. *Journal intime de Monseigneur Dupanloup*. Edited by L. Branchereau. Paris: P. Tequi, 1902.

———. *La journée du chrétien par Bossuet, ou manuel de piété recueilli des oeuvres de Bossuet*. Paris: Denaix, 1838.

———. "Lettre." In abbé de Torquat, *Conciles d'Orléans*. Orléans: Ernest Colas, 1864.

———. *Lettre à M. le Vᵗᵉ de la Guéronnière en réponse à sa brochure "La France, Rome et l'Italie."* Paris: Charles Douniol, 1861.

———. *Lettre de M. l'évêque d'Orléans au clergé et aux fidèles de son diocèse à l'occasion des fêtes de Rome et pour leur annoncer le futur concile oecuménique*. Paris: Charles Douniol, 1867.

———. *Lettre de Mgr l'évêque d'Orléans au clergé et aux fidèles de son diocèse avant son départ pour Rome.* Paris: Charles Douniol, 1869.

———. *Lettre sur le futur concile oecuménique.* Paris: Charles Douniol, 1868.

———. *Mgr Dupanloup devant le Saint-Siège.* Edited by H. L. Chapon. Orléans: H. Herluison, 1880.

———. *Mgr Dupanloup: Lettres de direction sur la vie chrétienne.* Edited by H. L. Chapon. Paris: P. Lethielleux, 1905.

———. *The Ministry of Catechising.* London: Griffith Farrar, 1899.

———. *The Ministry of Preaching.* London: Griffith Farrar, 1891.

———. *Nouvelles oeuvres choisies.* 7 vols. Paris: E. Plon et Cie, 1873–74.

———. *Observations sur la controverse soulevée relativement à la définition de l'infaillibilité au prochain concile.* Paris: Charles Douniol, 1869.

———. *Oeuvres choisies.* 4 vols. Paris: Régis Ruffet et Cie, 1862.

———. *Oeuvres pastorales.* 7 vols. Paris: E. Plon et Cie, 1873–74.

———. *Où allons-nous?* Paris: Charles Douniol, 1876.

———. *Réponse de Mgr l'évêque d'Orléans à Mgr Manning archevêque de Westminster.* Paris: Charles Douniol, 1869.

———. *La souveraineté pontificale selon le droit catholique et le droit européen.* 2d ed. Paris: Lecoffre, 1860.

———. "Speech at the Catholic Congress of Malines." *Catholic World* 6 (1868):587–94.

———. *A Study of Freemasonry.* London: Burns & Oates, 1875.

———, ed. *Etude de la religion proposée aux jeunes filles d'après un exposé de la doctrine chrétienne.* Le Mans: Beauvais, 1868.

Dupont des Loges, Paul. *Oeuvres choisies.* Edited by L. Willeumier. Paris: Charles Poussielgue, 1901.

Durand, M. R. "Communication de M. R. Durand—Mgr David, évêque de Saint-Brieuc (1862–82) et le concile du Vatican." *Bulletin de la Société d'Histoire Moderne,* ser. 3, 5 (23 April 1911):43–47.

———. "Mgr Darboy et le Saint-Siège." *Bulletin de la Société d'Histoire Moderne,* ser. 2, 7 (December 1907):6–8; (January 1908):9–11.

Dutoit, Henri Edouard. *Dupanloup.* Paris: Desclée de Brouwer et Cie, 1933.

Dvornik, Francis. *The Ecumenical Councils.* New York: Hawthorn Books, 1961.

———. "Which Councils Are Ecumenical?" *Journal of Ecumenical Studies* 3 (1966):314–28.

Enciclopedia Cattolica. S.v. "Ginoulhiac, Jacques Marie Achille," by Niccolò Del Re.

———. S.v. "Place, Charles Philippe," by Silvio Furlani.

Faguet, Emile. *Mgr Dupanloup: Un grand évêque.* Paris: Hachette et Cie, 1914.

Falloux du Coudray, Alfred Pierre Frédéric de. *L'évêque d'Orléans.* 3d ed. Paris: Didier et Cie, 1879.

"Félix Dupanloup, Bishop of Orléans." *Catholic World* 28 (1879):538–48.

Fessler, Joseph. *Die wahre und die falsche Unfehlbarkeit der Päpste: Zur Abwehr gegen Dr. Schulte.* 3d ed. Vienna: Sartori, 1871.

Fèvre, Justin. *Le centenaire de Mgr Dupanloup.* Paris: A. Savaète, 1903.

Ford, John. "Infallibility: A Review of Recent Studies." *Theological Studies* 40 (1979):273–305.

Foulon, Joseph. *Allocution de Mgr Foulon à la réunion annuelle d'Institut Catholique à Paris, le 19 novembre 1884.* Besançon: Paul Jacquin, 1885.

————. *Histoire de la vie et des oeuvres de Mgr Darboy, archevêque de Paris.* Paris: Poussielgue Frères, 1889.

————. *La justice allemande et l'évêque de Nancy: Lettre pastorale de Mgr Foulon à l'occasion du couronnement solennel de la statue de la Sainte Vierge vénérée dans le sanctuaire de N.-D. de Sion.* Paris: Bureaux de la Semaine Religieuse, 1874.

————. *Oeuvres pastorales de Monseigneur Foulon.* Edited by François Jules Demange. 2 vols. Nancy: Société Nancéienne de Propagande, 1882.

Foulon, Joseph; Place, Charles; et al. *Exposé de la situation faite à l'église en France et déclaration des éminentissimes cardinaux.* Besançon: H. Bossanne, 1892.

Freppel, Charles Emile. *Oraison funèbre de Mgr Colet, archevêque de Tours.* Angers: Germain et G. Grassin, 1884.

Gadille, Jacques. "L'épiscopat français au premier concile du Vatican." *Revue d'histoire de l'église de France* 56 (1970):327–46.

————. *La pensée et l'action politiques des évêques français au début de la IIIᵉ République, 1870/1883.* 2 vols. Paris: Hachette, 1967.

Garnier, Charles. *Mgr Hugonin, évêque de Bayeux et Lisieux, sa mort et ses obsèques.* Bayeux: Octave Payon, 1898.

Gautherot, Gustave. *L'échange des otages: Thiers et Mgr Darboy.* Paris: Plone-Nourrit & Cie, 1910.

Germain, Abel. *Proclamation solennelle des décrets du concile oecuménique du Vatican.* Coutances: E. Salettes Fils, 1876.

Gimpl, Caroline Ann. *The "Correspondant" and the Founding of the French Third Republic.* Washington, D.C.: Catholic University of America Press, 1959.

Ginoulhiac, Jacques. *Le concile oecuménique.* Paris: C. Douniol, 1869.

————. *Les épîtres pastorales, ou réflexions dogmatiques et morales sur les épîtres de saint Paul à Timothée et à Tite.* Paris: Victor Palmé, 1866.

————. *Histoire du dogme catholique pendant les trois premiers siècles de l'église et jusqu'au concile de Nicée.* 2 vols. Paris: Auguste Durand, 1852. 2d ed. 3 vols. 1866.

————. *Lettre de Mgr l'évêque de Grenoble à l'un de ses vicaires généraux, sur la "Vie de Jésus," par M.E. Renan.* Grenoble: Baratier frères et fils, 1863.

————. *Oraison funèbre de Monseigneur Marie Nicolas Fournier, évêque de Montpellier.* Montpellier: Auguste Seguin, 1835.

————. *Les origines du christianisme.* 2 vols. Paris: A. Durand et Pedone Lauriel, 1878.

————. *Le sermon sur la montagne, avec des réflexions dogmatiques et morales.* Lyon: P. N. Josserand, 1872.

Granderath, Theodor. *Histoire du concile du Vatican depuis sa première annonce jusqu'à sa prorogation d'après les documents authentiques.* 3 vols. Brussels: Librairie Albert Dewit, 1907–14.

Guéranger, Prosper. *De la monarchie pontificale.* Paris: Victor Palmé, 1870.

————. *Défense de l'église romaine contre les accusations du R. P. Gratry.* Paris: Victor Palmé, 1870.

Guérin, Paul. *Concile oecuménique du Vatican: Son histoire, ses décisions en latin et en français, avec tous les documents relatifs à ses délibérations.* 3d ed. Bar-le-Duc: Bertrand, 1877.

Guilbert, Aimé. *Abolition du Concordat et séparation de l'église et de l'état.* Bordeaux: Duverdier et Cie, 1885.

————. *A l'occasion de sa translation à l'archevêché de Bordeaux.* Amiens: Delattre-Lenoel, 1883.

————. *A l'occasion de son cardinalat.* Bordeaux: Duverdier et Cie, 1889.

————. *La crise religieuse et la pacification.* Amiens: Delattre-Lenoel, 1880.

————. *La démocratie et son avenir social et religieux.* 2d ed. Bordeaux: Feret et Fils, 1886.

————. *Des devoirs du prêtre touchant la politique et une leçon de catéchisme sur les élections.* Gap: J. C. Richaud, 1876.

————. *Discours prononcé à la distribution des prix du petit-séminaire et collège diocésain de Valognes.* Valognes: G. Martin, 1865.

————. *La divine synthèse, ou l'exposé au double point de vue apologétique et pratique de la religion révélée.* 2d ed. 3 vols. Gap: J. C. Richaud, 1875.

————. *La divine synthèse ou l'exposé dans leur enchaînement logique des preuves de la religion révélée.* Valognes: G. Martin, 1864.

————. *La divine synthèse ou l'exposé rationnel au double point de vue apologétique et pratique de la religion révélée suivie de monde et Dieu.* 3d ed. 2 vols. Bordeaux: Feret et Fils, 1889.

————. *L'église et la république: A MM. les sénateurs, les députés et les électeurs.* Gap: J. C. Richaud, 1879.

————. *Lettre de Mgr l'évêque de Gap à un sénateur sur la crise religieuse présente.* Gap: J. C. Richaud, 1879.

————. *Lettre pastorale et mandement de Mgr l'évêque d'Amiens à l'occasion de sa prise de possession.* Amiens: Delattre-Lenoel, 1879.

————. *Lettre pastorale et mandement de Mgr l'évêque de Gap à l'occasion de son entrée dans le diocèse.* Gap: Delaplace, 1867.

————. *Monde et Dieu ou le fini l'infini* [sic] *et leurs rapports.* Gap: J. C. Richaud, 1879.

————. *Portant publication de la lettre encyclique de N.S.P. le Pape Léon XIII du 28 décembre 1878.* N.p., n.d.

————. *Portant publication des lettres apostoliques de S.S. le Pape Léon XIII annonçant un jubilé universel à l'occasion de son exaltation au trône pontifical.* Gap: J. C. Richaud, 1879.

————. *Sur l'avenir social du catholicisme.* Amiens: Delattre-Lenoel, 1881.

————. *Sur le recrutement du clergé de France, à MM. les sénateurs, les députés et les électeurs.* Amiens: Delattre-Lenoel, 1881.

————. *Sur le salut.* Amiens: Delattre-Lenoel, 1880.

————. *Sur les dangers de la mauvaise presse.* Amiens: Delattre-Lenoel, 1882.

————. *Sur les droits de Dieu.* Amiens: Delattre-Lenoel, 1881.

Guillermin, Joseph-Abel. *Vie de Mgr Darboy, archevêque de Paris.* Paris: Bloud et Barral, 1888.

Hasler, August. *Pius IX. (1846–1878), Päpstliche Unfehlbarkeit und 1. Vatikanisches Konzil.* 2 vols. Stuttgart: Anton Hiersemann, 1977.

Hefele, Charles Joseph. *Histoire des conciles d'après les documents originaux.* 11 vols. Paris: Letouzey et Ané, 1907–52.

Hennesey, James. *The First Council of the Vatican: The American Experience.* New York: Herder and Herder, 1963.

Houtin, Albert. *La question biblique chez les catholiques de France au XIXeme siècle.* Paris: Alphonse Picard et Fils, 1902.

Houtin, Albert, and Couchoud, P. L. *Du sacerdoce au mariage: Gratry et Loyson (1870–72).* Paris: Editions Rieder, 1927.

Houtin, Albert, and Sartiaux, Félix. *Alfred Loisy: Sa vie, son oeuvre.* Bibliography and bio-bibliographical index by Emile Poulat. Paris: Editions du Centre National de la Recherche Scientifique, 1960.

Hughes, Philip. *The Church in Crisis.* Garden City, N. Y.: Doubleday, 1960.

Hugonin, Flavien. *Circulaire de l'abbé F. Hugonin, directeur de l'Ecole des Carmes aux évêques de France pour leur faire connaître la nouvelle organisation de l'Ecole et solliciter leur appui.* Saint-Cloud: Mme Veuve Belin, 1862.

————. *Dieu, est-il inconnaissable?* Paris: Roger, 1895.

————. *Discours de Mgr l'évêque de Bayeux et Lisieux dans sa cathédrale le dimanche 8 janvier 1888 à l'occasion de la solennité du jubilé sacerdotal de Léon XIII.* Bayeux: Octave Payan, 1888.

————. *Discours de S.G. Mgr l'évêque de Bayeux et Lisieux au Congrès des Associations Ouvrières Catholiques à Caen.* Bayeux: Octave Payan, 1886.

————. *Discours d'ouverture. Société des Antiquaires de Normandie.* Caen: F. Le Blanc-Hardel, 1869.

————. *Du droit ancien et du droit nouveau.* Paris: Victor Palmé, 1887.

————. *Etudes philosophiques.* Paris: Victor Lecoffre, 1894.

————. *Etudes philosophiques: Ontologie, ou étude des lois de la pensée.* 2 vols. Paris: Eugène Belin, 1856–57.

————. *Lettre de Mgr l'évêque de Bayeux à un habitant de Caen à l'occasion de l'expulsion des Frères de l'Ecole Saint-Pierre.* Bayeux: Octave Payan, 1880.

————. *Lettre de Mgr l'évêque de Bayeux et Lisieux aux membres des Comités de l'Enseignement Catholique Libre.* Bayeux: Octave Payan, 1882.

————. *Lettre de Mgr l'évêque de Bayeux et Lisieux sur l'enseignement de la philosophie aux professeurs de nos établissements diocésains.* Bayeux: Octave Payan, 1893.

————. *Lettre de S.G. Mgr l'évêque de Bayeux et Lisieux au Comité Catholique des Oeuvres Ouvrières de Caen.* Bayeux: Octave Payan, 1886.

————. *Notice sur l'enseignement du catéchisme dans le diocèse de Bayeux et Lisieux depuis le XVIe siècle jusqu'à nos jours.* Bayeux: Octave Payan, 1890.

————. *Philosophie du droit social.* Paris: E. Plon, Nourrit et Cie, 1885.

Hyenne, S.-Et. *Le monument élevé à S.E. le Cardinal Mathieu, archevêque de Besançon, est-il bien à sa place?* Besançon: M. Ordinaire, 1882.

Icard, Henri. *Traditions de la compagnie des prêtres de Saint-Sulpice pour la direction des grands séminaires.* Paris: Victor Lecoffre, 1886.

Jedin, Hubert. *Ecumenical Councils of the Catholic Church.* New York: Herder and Herder, 1960.

————. *Strukturprobleme der Ökumenischen Konzilien.* Cologne: Westdeutscher Verlag, 1963.

Justice, A. *Mgr Guilbert et le parti catholique.* Paris: P. Lethielleux, 1898.

Kasper, Walter. *Die Lehre von der Tradition in der Römischen Schule.* Freiburg: Herder, 1962.

————. "The Relationship between Gospel and Dogma: An Historical Approach." In Edward Schillebeeckx, ed., *Man as Man and Believer,* pp. 153–67. Concilium, vol. 21. New York: Paulist Press, 1967.

Keller, Albert. *La fin du gallicanisme et Mgr Maret, son dernier représentant.* Alençon: Veuve Félix Guy, 1900.

Kirvan, John, ed. *The Infallibility Debate.* New York: Paulist Press, 1971.

Klein, Félix. *L'évêque de Metz, vie de Mgr Dupont des Loges, 1804–1886.* Paris: Charles Poussielgue, 1899.

Küng, Hans. *The Council, Reform and Reunion.* New York: Sheed and Ward, 1961.

Lacombe, H. de. "Le Cardinal Meignan." *Le correspondant* 146 (25 January 1896):386–89.

————. "Mgr Dupanloup." *Le correspondant* 85 (10 October 1880):1–74.

Lagrange, François. *Life of Monseigneur Dupanloup.* Translated and abridged by Mary Elizabeth Herbert. London: Chapman and Hall, 1885.

————. *Vie de Mgr Dupanloup, évêque d'Orléans.* 3 vols. Paris: Poussielgue frères, 1883–84.

Las Cases, Félix de. *A l'occasion de son entrée dans son diocèse.* Angers: Lainé frères, 1867.

————. *Lettre de Mgr de Las Cases, évêque de Constantine et d'Hippone au R.P. Ratisbonne, directeur général de l'Archiconfrérie des Mères Chrétiennes.* Nice: Charles Cauvin, 1869.

Lavedan, L. "Mgr Dupanloup." *Le Correspondant* 77 (25 October 1878):1137–47.

Lease, Gary. Review of *Der Konziliarismus als Problem des neueren katholischen Theologie,* by Hans Schneider. *Journal of Ecumenical Studies* 15 (1978):747.

Ledrain, E. "Portraits et souvenirs, 1869–1870." *Revue bleue* 4th ser., 17 (29 March 1902):385–88; (5 April 1902):417–21.

Lelong, Etienne. *Oraison funèbre de Monseigneur Frédéric-Gabriel–Marie–François de Marguerye, ancien évêque de Saint-Flour, d'Autun, Chalon et Mâcon, chanoine du premier ordre du chapitre de Saint-Denis.* Autun: Michel Dejussieu, 1876.

Lenaway, Mary Albert. *Principles of Education according to Bishop Dupanloup.* Washington, D.C.: Catholic University of America Press, 1942.

Lesur, Emile, and Bournand, François. *S.E. le Cardinal Foulon, archevêque de Lyon et de Vienne, primat des Gaules: Sa vie et ses oeuvres.* Paris: Delhomme et Briguet, 1893.

Loisy, Alfred. *Mémoires pour servir à l'histoire religieuse de notre temps*. 3 vols. Paris: Emile Nourry, 1930–31.

Lonergan, Bernard J. F. *Insight: A Study of Human Understanding*. New York: Philosophical Library, 1957.

———. *Method in Theology*. New York: Herder and Herder, 1972.

———. "Theology in Its New Context." In *A Second Collection*, pp. 55–67. Philadelphia: Westminster Press, 1974.

Lutheran–Roman Catholic Dialogue (U.S.). "Teaching Authority and Infallibility in the Church." In *Teaching Authority and Infallibility in the Church*, edited by Paul Empie, T. Austin Murphy, and Joseph Burgess, pp. 11–68. Lutherans and Catholics in Dialogue 6. Minneapolis: Augsburg Publishing House, 1980.

McAvoy, Thomas. *The Americanist Heresy in Roman Catholicism, 1895–1900*. Notre Dame: University of Notre Dame Press, 1963.

McSorley, Harry. Review of *Pius IX. (1846–1878), Päpstliche Unfehlbarkeit und I. Vatikanisches Konzil*, by August Hasler. *Journal of Ecumenical Studies* 16 (1979):320–23.

———. "Some Forgotten Truths about the Petrine Ministry." *Journal of Ecumenical Studies* 11 (1974):208–36.

Mansi, Joannes Dominicus. *Sacrorum conciliorum nova et amplissima collectio*. Vols. 50–53. Graz: Akademische Druck u. Verlagsanstalt, 1961.

Marcilhacy, Christianne. *Le diocèse d'Orléans sous l'épiscopat de Mgr Dupanloup, 1849–1878*. Paris: Plon, 1962.

Maret, Henri. *Du concile général et de la paix religieuse*. 2 vols. Paris: Henri Plon, 1869.

———. *Le pape et les évêques: Défense du livre sur le concile générale et la paix religieuse*. Paris: Henri Plon, 1869.

———. *La verité catholique et la paix religieuse*. Paris: Dentu, 1884.

Marguerye, Frédéric de. "Lettre pastorale pour l'établissement d'une association diocésaine en faveur de l'oeuvre des séminaires et des écoles." In *Collection intégrale et universelle des orateurs sacrés* 84:669–704. Edited by Jacques Migne. 2d ser., vols. 68–99. Paris: Petit-Montrouge, 1856–66.

———. "Marie a été conçue sans péché." In *Collection intégrale et universelle des orateurs sacrés* 84:704–19. Edited by Jacques Migne. 2d ser., vols. 68–99. Paris: Petit-Montrouge, 1856–66.

———. "Oraison funèbre de Monseigneur le Cardinal de Rohan-Chabot (27 mars 1833)." In *Collection intégrale et universelle des orateurs sacrés* 84:751–68. Edited by Jacques Migne. 2d ser., vols. 68–99. Paris: Petit-Montrouge, 1856–66.

Margull, Hans Jochen, ed. *The Councils of the Church*. Philadelphia: Fortress Press, 1966.

Martimort, Aimé Georges. *Le gallicanisme*. Paris: Presses Universitaires de France, 1973.

———. *Le gallicanisme de Bossuet*. Paris: Les Editions du Cerf, 1953.

Mathieu, [Jacques-Marie-Adrien-] Césaire. *Discours prononcés par S. Em. Mgr le Cardinal Mathieu dans la discussion de l'adresse du Sénat à sa majesté l'Empereur*. Paris: Charles Douniol, 1861.

————. *Un mot du Cardinal Mathieu, sur la brochure: "Pape et Empereur," de M. Cayla.* Paris: Adrien le Clere, 1860.

————. *Le pouvoir temporel des papes justifié par l'histoire: Etude sur l'origine, l'exercise et l'influence de la souveraineté pontificale.* Paris: Adrien le Clere, 1863.

————. *Sénat: Discours prononcé par S. Em. le Cardinal Mathieu, sénateur, dans la discussion de l'adresse.* Paris: Charles Lahure, 1865.

Maurain, Jean. *La politique ecclésiastique du Second Empire de 1852 à 1869.* Paris: F. Alcan, 1930.

Maynard, Michel Ulysse. *Mgr Dupanloup et M. Lagrange son historien.* Paris: Société Générale de Librairie Catholique, 1884.

Meignan, Guillaume. *La crise protestante en Angleterre et en France.* Paris: Charles Douniol, 1864.

————. *Une crise religieuse en Angleterre.* Paris: Charles Douniol, 1861.

————. *David, roi, psalmiste, prophète, avec une introduction sur la nouvelle critique.* Paris: Victor Lecoffre, 1889.

————. *De l'irréligion systématique.* Paris: Jules Gervais, 1886.

————. "Du prochain concile oecuménique." *La semaine champenoise* 3 (13 February 1869):658–64.

————. *Etude sur les causes de l'impiété.* Besançon: J. Bonvalot, 1862.

————. *Les évangiles et la critique au XIXᵉ siècle.* Paris: Victor Palmé, 1870.

————. "Lettre circulaire et mandement (16 June 1870)." *La semaine champenoise* 5 (2 July 1870):154.

————. "Lettre circulaire et mandement (28 July 1870)." *La semaine champenoise* 5 (5 August 1870):226–27.

————. "Lettre circulaire et mandement de Mgr l'évêque de Châlons, à l'occasion de son départ pour le concile oecuménique du Vatican." *La semaine champenoise* 4 (4 November 1869):451–56.

————. *Le monde et l'homme primitif selon la Bible.* Paris: Victor Palmé, 1869.

————. *Pastoral Letter for Lent 1870. La semaine champenoise* 4 (26 February 1870):690–97.

Menna, Nicola. *Vescovi italiani anti-infallibilisti al concilio Vaticano.* Napoli: A. Intravaja, 1958.

"Mgr Dupanloup et le Saint-Siège." *Le correspondant* 153 (November 1888):153.

"Monseigneur Darboy et le Saint-Siège: Documents inédits." *Revue d'histoire et de la littérature religieuses* 12 (1907):240–81.

Montclos, Xavier de. *Lavigerie, le Saint-Siège et l'église de l'avènement de Pie IX à l'avènement de Léon XIII (1846–1878).* Paris: Editions E. de Boccard, 1965.

Mourret, Fernand. *Le concile du Vatican d'après des documents inédits.* Paris: Bloud et Gay, 1919.

Murray, John Courtney. *We Hold These Truths: Catholic Reflections on the American Proposition.* New York: Sheed and Ward, 1960.

Nédoncelle, M., et al. *L'ecclésiologie au XIX siècle.* Paris: Les Editions du Cerf, 1960.

Neuner, Josef, and Roos, Heinrich, trans. *The Teaching of the Catholic*

Church. Edited by Karl Rahner. Translated into English by Geoffrey Stevens. Staten Island, N.Y.: Alba House, 1967.

New Catholic Encyclopedia. S.v. "Conciliarism. (Theological Aspect)," by Ladislas Orsy.

————. S.v. "Councils, General (Ecumenical), Theology of," by Ladislas Orsy.

Newman, John Henry, and Gladstone, William. *Newman and Gladstone: The Vatican Decrees*. Edited by Alvan S. Ryan. Notre Dame: University of Notre Dame Press, 1962.

"Nouvelles du diocèse." *Semaine religieuse du diocèse de Perpignan* 1 (27 November 1869):796–98.

"Nouvelles et faits religieux du diocèse." *Revue catholique (Semaine religieuse) du diocèse de Coutances et Avranches* 3 (14 April 1870):451–55.

Ollivier, Emile. *L'église et l'état au concile du Vatican*. 3d ed. 2 vols. Paris: Garnier Frères, 1879.

O'Meara, Kathleen [Ramsay, Grace]. *Monseigneur Darboy: Souvenirs personnels*. Translated. Paris: Amyot, 1872.

Pagès, Pierre Michel. *Mgr Dupanloup: Sa vie, ses écrits, sa doctrine*. Paris: Delhomme et Briguet, 1895.

Palanque, Jean-Rémy. *Catholiques libéraux et gallicans en France: Face au concile du Vatican, 1867-1870*. Aix-en-Provence: Editions Ophrys, 1962.

————. "Le cercle de Madame de Forbin et le premier concile du Vatican (Documents inédits)." *Revue d'histoire de l'église de France* 48 (1962):54–79.

Pelletier, Victor. *Mgr Dupanloup: Episode de l'histoire contemporaine, 1845–1875*. Paris: Haton, 1876.

Perraud, Adolphe. *Oraison funèbre de Mgr François Victor Rivet, évêque de Dijon*. Autun: Dejussieu Père et Fils, 1884.

Perrone, Giovanni. *Praelectiones theologicae*. 9 vols. Rome, 1835–42.

Place, Charles. "A l'occasion de son prochain départ pour le concile oecuménique." *La semaine liturgique de Marseille* 8 (21 November 1869):832–39.

————. "Approbation." In *Manuel de piété*. By Rev. Frère Cyprien. 5th ed. Lafoye: Vannes, 1927.

————. "Lettre." In *Synodus Diocesana Massiliensis*. Marseille: P. Chauffard, 1877.

————. *Lettre circulaire de Mgr l'archevêque de Rennes au clergé de son diocèse*. Rennes: H. Vatar, 1879.

————. "Lettre circulaire sur la mort de notre très-saint père le Pape Pie IX." *La semaine liturgique de Marseille* 17 (1878):266–69.

————. *Lettre de l'archevêque de Rennes à M. le Président de la République*. Rennes: H. Vatar, 1880.

————. "Lettre de S.E. le Cardinal Place." In l'abbé Tapie, *Notes et souvenirs sur l'abbé Petit*. Paris: La Semaine Religieuse, 1889.

————. *Note du Cardinal Place au sujet des attaques dirigées contre lui par l'auteur du "Testament d'un antisémite."* Rennes: H. Vatar, 1891.

————. Pastoral Letter for Lent on Modern Errors. *La semaine liturgique de Marseille* 12 (Lent 1873):210–19.

———. *Pieux souvenir de son éminence le Cardinal Place*. Paris: Victor Lecoffre, 1895.

———. "Pour la publication de l'indulgence plénière, en forme de jubilé." *La semaine liturgique de Marseille* 8 (4 July 1869):501–6.

———. "Sur la conscience." *La semaine liturgique de Marseille* 17 (Supplement to 3 March 1878):396–407.

———. "Sur la nécessité et les moyens d'étudier la vie chrétienne." *La semaine liturgique de Marseille* 13 (Lent 1874):201–11.

———. "Sur le courage chrétien." *La semaine liturgique de Marseille* 15 (5 March 1876):234–42.

———. "Sur le prochain concile oecuménique." *La semaine liturgique de Marseille* 8 (14 February 1869):181–88.

Pon, François. *Une page de surnaturel au concile du Vatican: La Mère Sainte-Agnès et Mgr Dupanloup*. Paris: Victor Retaux, 1905.

Poulat, Emile. *"Les semaines religieuses": Approche sociohistorique et bibliographique des bulletins diocésains français*. Lyon: Centre d'histoire du catholicisme, 1973.

Poupard, Paul. *Correspondance inédite entre Mgr Antonio Garibaldi internonce à Paris et Mgr Césaire Mathieu archevêque de Besançon*. Rome: Presses de l'Université Grégorienne, 1961.

Pressensé, Edward de. *Le concile du Vatican: Son histoire et ses conséquences politiques et religieuses*. Paris: Sandoz et Fischbacher, 1872.

———. "Mgr Dupanloup, son historien et ses adversaires." *La revue bleue* 34 (1884):582–87.

Programmes pour les études ecclésiastiques et conseils aux jeunes prêtres sur l'étude des différentes branches de la science sacrée: Rédigés conformément aux ordonnances de Mgr Dupanloup, évêque d'Orléans, pour l'usage de son clergé. Orléans: Ernest Colas, 1875.

Rahner, Karl. "What Is a Dogmatic Statement?" In *Theological Investigations*, 5:42–66. 20 vols. Baltimore: Helicon Press, 1966.

Ramadié, Etienne. "A l'occasion de sa visite pastorale pour l'année 1871." *Semaine religieuse du diocèse de Perpignan* 3 (30 April 1871):277–84.

———. Letter to Diocese Publishing Decrees of the First Vatican Council. *Semaine religieuse du diocèse de Perpignan* 6 (12 February 1874):74–78.

———. "Oraison funèbre de Monseigneur le Cardinal de Rohan-Chabot." In *Collection intégrale et universelle des orateurs sacrés* 84:764–74. Edited by Jacques Migne. 2d ser., vols. 68–99. Paris: Petit-Montrouge, 1856–66.

———. Pastoral Letter for Lent 1870. *Semaine religieuse du diocèse de Perpignan* 2 (26 February 1870):134–39.

———. Pastoral Letter for Lent 1871. *Semaine religieuse du diocèse de Perpignan* 3 (18 February 1871):117–21; (25 February 1871):134–39; (4 March 1871):152–57; (11 March 1871):168–73.

———. Preface to *Les derniers jours de Mgr Dupanloup*. Paris: V. Goupy et Jourdan, 1879.

———. *Quelques caractères de la société chrétienne et mandement pour le carême de l'an de grâce 1868*. Perpignan: Charles Latrobe, 1868.

———. "Sur quelques erreurs des temps modernes." *Semaine religieuse du diocèse de Perpignan* 1 (1869):84–90.

Revue catholique (Semaine religieuse) du diocèse de Coutances et Avranches 2 (1869)–4 (1871).

Rivet, François. Sermon for Lent on the Divinity of Christianity. In *Collection intégrale et universelle des orateurs sacrés* 84:34–48. Edited by Jacques Migne. 2d ser., vols. 68–99. Paris: Petit-Montrouge, 1856–66.

———. "Sur l'église." In *Collection intégrale et universelle des orateurs sacrés,* 84:100–118. Edited by Jacques Migne. 2d ser., vols. 68–99. Paris: Petit-Montrouge, 1856–66.

———. "Sur l'orgueil." In *Collection intégrale et universelle des orateurs sacrés,* 84:88–99. Edited by Jacques Migne. 2d ser., vols. 68–99. Paris: Petit-Montrouge, 1856–66.

Rondet, Henri. *Vatican I.* Paris: P. Lethielleux, 1962.

Rousseau, D. O., ed. *Le concile et les conciles.* Paris and Chevetogne: Editions du Cerf and Editions de Chevetogne, 1960.

———. *L'infaillibilité de l'église: Journées oecuméniques de Chevetogne.* Namurci: Editions de Chevetogne, 1962.

Roux, Hébert. *Le concile et le dialogue oecuménique.* Paris: Editions du Seuil, 1964.

Sacramentum Mundi. S.v. "Council," by Hans Küng.

———. "Infallibility," by Heinrich Fries and Johann Finsterhölzl.

———. "Obedience," by Waldemar Molinski.

———. "Theologumenon," by Karl Rahner.

Salomon, Michel. *Mgr Dupanloup.* Paris: P. J. Béduchaud, 1904.

Schatz, Klaus. *Kirchenbild und päpstliche Unfehlbarkeit bei den Deutschsprachigen Minoritätsbischöfen auf dem I. Vatikanum.* Rome: Università Gregoriana Editrice, 1975.

Schillebeeckx, Edward. "The Creed and Theology." In *Revelation and Theology* 1:203–17. 2 vols. New York: Sheed and Ward, 1967.

———. "Infallibility of the Church's Office." In *Truth and Certainty,* pp. 77–94. Edited by Edward Schillebeeckx and Bas van Iersel. Concilium, vol. 83. New York: Herder and Herder, 1973.

Semaine catholique de Lyon 3 (1869–70).

La semaine champenoise: Revue religieuse et littéraire du diocèse de Châlons-sur-Marne 3 (1869)–5 (1870).

Semaine religieuse de Coutances et Avranches 5 (1872)–7 (1874).

La semaine liturgique de Marseille 8 (July 1869)–17 (1878).

La semaine religieuse de la ville et du diocèse de Tours 9 (1874)–10 (1876).

La semaine religieuse du diocèse de Bayeux et Lisieux 5 (1869)–10 (1874).

La semaine religieuse du diocèse de Grenoble (1869–70).

Semaine religieuse du diocèse de Nice 2 (1873–74).

Semaine religieuse du diocèse de Perpignan 1 (1869)–6 (1874).

La semaine religieuse du diocèse de Saint-Brieuc et Tréguier 2 (1868)–10 (1876).

La semaine religieuse, historique et littéraire de la Lorraine [later: *Semaine religieuse du diocèse de Nancy et de Toul*] 6 (1868)–8 (1871).

Skydsgaard, Kristen E., ed. *The Papal Council and the Gospel*. Minneapolis: Augsburg House, 1961.

Sola, Jean. *Discours prononcé à la distribution des prix du lycée impérial de Nice*. Nice: Canis, 1863.

————. *Discours prononcé à la distribution des prix du lycée de Nice*. Nice: Caisson et Mignon, 1873.

Stearns, Peter. *Priest and Revolutionary: Lamennais and the Dilemma of French Catholicism*. New York: Harper & Row, 1967.

Tapie, Jean Romain. *Oraison funèbre de son éminence le Cardinal Thomas, archevêque de Rouen*. La Rochelle: Noel Texier, 1894.

Théologie de Toulouse. 6 vols. Toulouse, 1828.

Thils, Gustave. *L'infaillibilité pontificale: Source—conditions—limites*. Gembloux: J. Duculot, 1968.

————. *Primauté pontificale et prérogatives épiscopales*. Louvain: E. Warny, 1961.

Thomas, Léon. *Deuxième Congrès des catholiques de Normandie: Discours de S.G. Mgr l'archevêque de Rouen*. Rouen: Mégard et Cie, 1885.

————. *Discours prononcée dans la cathédrale de Poitiers à la clôture du 5ᵉ Concile de la Province de Bordeaux*. La Rochelle: Drouineau, 1868.

————. *Discours sur Jeanne d'Arc*. Rouen: Cacniard, 1892.

————. *Lettre de Mgr l'évêque de La Rochelle et Saintes à son éminence le Cardinal-archevêque de Bordeaux*. La Rochelle: P. Dubois et L. Mehaignery, 1880.

————. "Lettre de S.G. Mgr l'archevêque de Rouen à son clergé relative aux conférences ecclésiastiques. In *Programme d'études pour les conférences ecclésiastiques*. Rouen: E. Cagniard, 1887.

————. "Lettre pastorale à l'occasion de son départ pour le concile oecuménique." *Bulletin religieux du diocèse de La Rochelle et Saintes* 6 (13 November 1869):229–36; (20 November 1869):241–48.

————. *Messe solennelle célébrée le 14 février 1889 pour les soldats morts au service de la France: Allocution de S.G. Mgr l'archevêque*. Rouen: Espérance Cagniard, 1889.

————. *Oeuvres choisies*. 3 vols. Rouen: Cagmaru, 1891.

————. "La paix de l'âme chrétienne." *Bulletin religieux du diocèse de La Rochelle et Saintes* 5 (6 February 1869):373–77; (13 February 1869):385–89.

————. "Sur le catéchisme." *Bulletin religieux du diocèse de La Rochelle et Saintes* 5 (23 January 1869):349–56.

Thysmans, R. "Le gallicanisme de Mgr Maret et l'influence de Bossuet." *Revue d'histoire ecclésiastique* 52 (1957):401–65.

Tillard, Jean-Marie. "The Horizon of the 'Primacy' of the Bishop of Rome." *One in Christ* 12 (1976):5–33.

————. "The Roman Catholic Church: Growing Towards Unity." *One in Christ* 14 (1978):217–30.

Torrell, Jean-Pierre. "L'infaillibilité pontificale est-elle privilège personnel? Une controverse au premier concile du Vatican." *Revue des sciences philosophiques et théologiques* 45 (1961):229–45.

———. *La théologie de l'épiscopat au premier concile du Vatican.* Paris: Les Editions du Cerf, 1961.

Touchet, Stanislaus. *Mgr Hugonin, évêque de Bayeux et Lisieux: Sa vie, sa mort et ses funérailles.* Bayeux: S. A. Duvant, 1898.

Vallin, Pierre. "Pour l'histoire du concile du Vatican I: La démarche de la minorité auprès de Pie IX, le 15 juillet 1870." *Revue d'histoire ecclésiastique* 60 (1965):844–48.

La vérité sur Mgr Darboy: Etude précédée d'une lettre à S.E. le Cardinal Foulon. Gien: Paul Pigelet, 1889.

Vineau, Charles de. *Bishop Dupanloup's Philosophy of Education.* Washington, D.C.: Catholic Education Press, 1930.

Vitelleschi, Marchese [Leto, Pomponio]. *The Vatican Council: Eight Months at Rome during the Vatican Council, Impressions of a Contemporary.* London: John Murray, 1876.

Watkin, E. I. *The Church in Council.* London: Darton, Longman & Todd, 1960.

World Council of Churches. *Councils and the Ecumenical Movement.* World Council of Churches Studies 5. Geneva: World Council of Churches, 1968.

Index of Persons

Aubert, Roger, xivn, xvn, xvii,
xviin, xviii, xx, 7n, 18n, 19n, 20n,
21n, 22n, 23n, 24n, 25n, 26n, 28,
28n, 31, 31n, 32, 33, 33n, 42, 42n,
43n, 45n, 47n, 69n, 70n, 72n, 77n,
105, 105n, 106, 107n, 112n, 127n,
130n, 153n, 156n, 182, 182n, 190n,
196n, 198n, 204n, 216, 217n,
232–33n, 235, 235n, 241, 241n,
242n, 245, 246, 246n, 247, 247n,
249, 249n, 252, 252n

Bailly, Louis, 19, 19n, 21
Bouix, Marcel, 80, 159
Bossuet, Jacques, 12, 18, 20, 21, 43,
44, 52n, 60n, 107, 119, 128, 147,
156n, 162n
Bravard, Jean-Pierre (bishop of
Coutances and Avranches), 7, 24n,
29, 29n, 46, 46n, 55, 55n, 57, 57n,
58, 58n, 61n, 63, 94, 100, 101, 101n,
127, 137, 137n, 138, 138n, 175,
175n, 176, 176n, 177, 186, 186n,
192, 196n, 198, 200, 201n
Butler, Cuthbert, xviin, 7n, 37n, 69n,
70n, 76n, 77n, 110n, 246, 246n, 249

Callot, Jean-Baptiste-Irénée (bishop of
Oran), 8, 23, 81, 93, 94, 96, 98, 99,
115, 119, 121, 125, 126, 132, 226,
228
Colet, Charles-Théodore (bishop of
Luçon), 8, 23, 23n, 24n, 26, 26n, 29,
29n, 33n, 34n, 37, 38n, 47, 49, 50n,
55, 55n, 64, 69, 69n, 71, 75, 76, 77,
77n, 80, 80n, 82, 82n, 83, 83n, 91,
91n, 94, 94n, 105, 106, 106n, 119,
120, 120n, 126, 126n, 127, 128, 129,
129n, 130, 130n, 132, 132n, 133,
151, 151n, 152, 152n, 153, 153n,
154, 155, 155n, 164, 171, 181, 189n,
195, 195n, 196, 197n, 200, 200n,
205, 205n, 206, 207n, 211, 211n, 247
Congar, Yves, xvii, xviin, xx, xxii,
170, 170n, 192n, 234, 234n, 238,
240n, 246n, 247n, 249n
de Cuttoli, Pierre-Paul (bishop of

Ajaccio in Corsica), 8, 18, 22, 23,
24n

Darboy, Georges (archbishop of Paris),
xxn, 8, 11, 13, 19, 19n, 20n, 22,
22n, 23, 24n, 26, 28, 32, 32n, 33,
33n, 34, 35, 36, 36n, 37, 38, 39n,
43, 44n, 45, 45n, 48, 48n, 49n, 50,
50n, 51, 51n, 52, 52n, 56, 56n, 57,
57n, 61, 62n, 64, 64n, 65, 66n, 74,
74n, 77, 77n, 82, 83, 95, 96, 97, 98,
104, 104n, 107, 110, 110n, 113, 115,
121, 123, 127, 129, 130, 130n, 131,
135, 139, 142n, 154, 154n, 159,
159n, 171, 178n, 184n, 186, 186n,
190n, 193, 196, 196n, 198n, 203,
211, 211n, 212, 212n, 213, 218,
218n, 226, 228, 232
David, Augustin (bishop of Saint-
Brieuc), 8, 20n, 23, 29, 30, 33, 39,
44, 44n, 45, 45n, 46, 46n, 48, 49, 53n,
61, 61n, 78, 78n, 80, 80n, 81, 83,
120, 125n, 126n, 127n, 132, 139,
139n, 146, 155, 156, 156n, 157,
158, 158n, 171, 178, 178n, 182,
183n, 185, 185n, 186n, 198, 207,
207n, 214, 214n, 228, 229
Dechamps, Victor (archbishop of
Malines), 8in, 84n, 92, 92n, 93,
109n, 118n, 122, 122n, 131n, 132n,
136n, 137n, 150, 150n, 243
Dejaivfve, Georges, xvn, xvii, xviin,
241n, 243n, 245n, 248, 252
Devoucoux, Jean (bishop of Evreux),
7, 175, 175n
von Döllinger, Ignaz, 27
Dupanloup, Félix-Antoine-Philibert
(bishop of Orléans), 5, 9, 10, 11, 14,
17n, 23, 23n, 24, 24n, 26, 26n, 27,
27n, 31, 31n, 32, 33, 34, 35, 35n,
38, 38n, 39, 39n, 41, 42, 42n, 43,
43n, 45, 45n, 47, 47n, 48, 49n, 50n,
52, 52n, 53n, 54, 54n, 55, 55n, 56n,
57, 57n, 58, 58n, 60, 60n, 64, 64n,
65, 65n, 66, 66n, 68, 71, 72, 72n,
73, 73n, 74, 76n, 78, 78n, 79n, 80,
81n, 83, 84, 84n, 91, 92, 92n, 94,

Index of Topics

"And not from the consent of the Church," xiv, xv, 6, 171, 251–55, 269. *See also* First Vatican Council: events

Anglicans, 101–104. *See also* Unity of the church: and overcoming Christian divisions

Apostles, 49, 55, 57, 58, 112, 123, 131, 133, 134, 143–44, 147, 155, 158, 166, 169, 228, 245, 250

Arguments (against proposed schema) on definability: binding quality of Scripture and tradition, 91, 120–22, 223, 228, 230, 240, 250; clarity and certitude, 135–39, 185, 223, 229–30, 241, 247–55; difficulties with definition's formulation, 122–28, 223, 228, 241; freedom in theologically disputed questions, 119–20, 223, 228, 230, 241; necessity a requirement for definition, 117–19, 223, 230, 235; need for consensus of the church, 132–35, 223, 230, 240, 245, 250, 251–55; procedural irregularities, 128–32, 223, 230, 248

Arguments (against proposed schema) on timeliness: freedom in theological opinion and unanimity in definitions of faith, 97–100, 223, 226, 235; haste and public opinion, 100–101, 223, 240, 248; hostility from civil governments, 110–12, 223, 235; humility, 115, 223; modern spirit, 106–10, 223, 235, 238; open to misunderstanding, 112–15, 223, 227, 230, 239; reunion of separated Christians, 101–6, 223, 227, 236–38; unity of belief and the good of the church, 93–97, 222–23, 235

Arguments (against proposed schema) on truth: accord of pope and bishops, 154–63, 223–24, 228, 230, 240, 245, 251–55; authority of bishops undermined, 152–54, 223, 228, 240,

245, 251–55; consensus of the church, 163–70, 224, 228, 230, 240–41, 250, 251–55; opposition from tradition, 91, 143–52, 223, 228, 230, 240, 250

Arguments (for *Pastor aeternus*) on formal authority: postconciliar views on formal authority, 181–91, 224, 231, 242–43; preconciliar views on formal authority, 176–81, 224

Arguments (for *Pastor aeternus*) on material authority: denials of opposition and claims of victory, 210–17, 224, 228, 231, 243; hindsight, 202–4, 224, 227, 235–36; papal infallibility located within context of ecclesial infallibility, 204–10, 224, 228–29, 231, 243; postconciliar silence, 197–99, 224; use of papal titles, 199–202, 224

Arguments, framework of the, 89–93, 117, 124, 142, 175–76, 190–91, 194, 210–11, 222, 224

Bishops: authority of, 24–25, 48, 53, 54, 69, 80, 81, 114–15, 123, 125–26, 139, 152–54, 228, 246–47; as judges, 46, 48, 50, 55–56, 64, 114–15, 139, 147, 149, 154, 155, 160, 164, 166, 167, 179, 185, 186, 188, 199, 216, 222, 224, 245; as witnesses (or representatives), 49, 64, 66, 115, 121, 139, 164, 167–68, 185, 244–45, 246–47. *See also* Infallibility in the consensus of the church; Infallibility in the consensus of pope and bishops

Church-State relations, 10, 11, 13, 37–43, 69–70, 73–74, 109, 110–12, 223. *See also* Government of France

Dei Filius, 3

294